A WORLD OF CHANCE

Although financial markets often try to distance themselves from gambling, the two have far more in common than is usually thought. When there were no financial institutions such as banks, people disposed of expensive items and governments raised money quickly through lotteries. Gambling tables fulfilled the roles that venture capital and banking do today. Gamblers created clearinghouses and sustained liquidity. When gamblers created prices in futures markets, they were redefined as speculators. Today they are hedge fund managers or bankers. Although the names have changed, the actions undertaken by these parties have essentially stayed the same. This book discusses chance, risk, gambling, insurance, and speculation to illuminate where societies stood, where society is today, and where we may be heading.

Reuven Brenner holds the Repap Chair in the Desautels Faculty of Management at McGill University in Montreal, Canada, and is a partner at Match Strategic Partners. The author of seven other books, including *Gambling and Speculation* (Cambridge University Press, 1990, with Gabrielle A. Brenner) and *Rivalry: In Business, Science, among Nations* (Cambridge University Press, 1987), he examines what makes societies and firms leapfrog over others or fall behind them. The *Wall Street Journal, Financial Times, New York Times, Boston Globe, Times* of London, *Asia Times*, and *Smart Money* have reviewed his books. He has worked with financial institutions throughout North America, and with companies such as Bell Canada and Knowledge Universe. Brenner has also been a frequent commentator in leading media around the world. *Forbes Global*'s columnists have put two of Brenner's titles on their list of recommended books for all time and profiled him in a cover story titled "Leapfrogging." Brenner has served on the board of several companies, received a Fulbright fellowship and the Killam Award, and is a Fellow of the Royal Society of Canada.

Gabrielle A. Brenner is associate professor of economics at the École des Hautes Études Commerciales in Montreal, Canada. She holds a Ph.D. in economics from the University of Chicago and has written about entrepreneurship and antitrust. She previously worked at Lexecon and has served as a consultant to the World Bank, the United Nations Industrial Development Organization, and the Canadian International Development Agency.

Aaron Brown is risk manager for AQR Capital Management in Greenwich, Connecticut. He holds degrees in applied mathematics from Harvard University and finance from the University of Chicago. He has worked as a trader, portfolio manager, head of mortgage security, and risk manager for such Wall Street firms as Morgan Stanley and Citigroup; taught finance at Fordham and Yeshiva universities; and ran a public mutual fund. Brown is the author of *The Poker Face of Wall Street.*

By Reuven Brenner:

History – The Human Gamble (1983)

Betting on Ideas: Wars, Invention, Inflation (1985)

Rivalry (Cambridge University Press, 1987)

Gambling and Speculation (Cambridge University Press, 1990), with Gabrielle A. Brenner

Educating Economists (1992), with David Colander

Labyrinths of Prosperity (1994)

The Force of Finance (2002; Canadian edition title: *The Financial Century*)

A World of Chance

Betting on Religion, Games, Wall Street

REUVEN BRENNER
McGill University

GABRIELLE A. BRENNER
École des Hautes Études Commercials

AARON BROWN
AQR Capital Management

CAMBRIDGE
UNIVERSITY PRESS

CAMBRIDGE UNIVERSITY PRESS
Cambridge, New York, Melbourne, Madrid, Cape Town, Singapore, São Paulo, Delhi

Cambridge University Press
32 Avenue of the Americas, New York, NY 10013-2473, USA

www.cambridge.org
Information on this title: www.cambridge.org/9780521711579

First published 2008

Printed in the United States of America

A catalog record for this publication is available from the British Library.

Library of Congress Cataloging in Publication Data
Brenner, Reuven.
A world of chance : betting on religion, games, Wall Street / Reuven Brenner,
Gabrielle A. Brenner, Aaron Brown.
p.   cm.
Includes bibliographical references and index.
ISBN 978-0-521-88466-2 (hardback) – ISBN 978-0-521-71157-9 (pbk.)
1. Risk.   2. Competition.   3. Decision making.   4. Wealth.   5. Social history.   6. Gambling.
7. Chance.   I. Brenner, Gabrielle A.   II. Brown, Aaron, 1956–   III. Title.
HB615.B733   2008
306.4′82–dc22   2007052044

ISBN   978-0-521-88466-2 hardback
ISBN   978-0-521-71157-9 paperback

Dedicated to John Dobson
Passionate about freedom, about the country,
philanthropic,
a friend

Contents

Preface

Which explains the unusual origins and approach of this book.

The next best thing to a guaranteed good future – if such a guarantee exists – is a chance to it.

How some societies created far more chances for their members than did others is the story that we tell in this book from an unusual, though to us logical, angle. That angle involves looking at the question through the prism of games of chance, of futures and of financial markets, and of the ways people have acted when facing a variety of risks and then deciding to leap into the unknown. It turns out that gamblers and risk-takers brought to life businesses and institutions that allowed the rest of society to have more options. It also turns out that though financial markets often tried to distance themselves from gambling, the two have far more in common than is usually thought. And there is nothing wrong with that.

When there were no financial institutions – as we view them today – such as banks, lotteries were the ways in which both relatively expensive items were disposed of and governments raised money quickly. Gambling tables often fulfilled roles similar to venture capital and banking today. Gamblers created the clearinghouses and also sustained liquidity. When they bet on price distributions, however, they were suddenly redefined as speculators. Today they are called hedge fund managers or bankers. Closer inspection reveals that though the words changed, the actions these parties undertook stayed the same.

At all times people have taken into account risk and uncertainty. Observers often have stated that people overestimate their chances of winning when gambling, that randomness fools them, that they are inconsistent in the ways they make their decisions when facing risks. We do not find that to be the case. Yes, people make mistakes, and, at times, many commit the same mistake, following conventional wisdom. We find that it is such conventional wisdom that fools them, leading them to believe that there is far less randomness than there actually is.

The vast majority of people have been betting with their heads and not over them. Neither randomness nor uncertainty have really fooled them. Rather, societies created institutions that stood for the belief that there is no randomness or mistakes to start with. Everything had to have a cause. At the dawn of history, when tribes were small and isolated, this even made sense. When people live in isolated, small communities, there can be no markets, no specialization, no pricing, and no formal insurance. There is no such thing as the law of large numbers in such societies. But people must decide. Beliefs and institutions bestow legitimacy on decisions, suggesting that things are "under control."

When populations grow and people move, they leap into the unknown and take chances by noticing emerging patterns – or what they think are patterns. This is when conflicts with those blinded by the past start and when debates about risk, chance, and gambling become more illuminating. Milan Kundera once observed that stupidity was not ignorance, but the nonthought of received ideas. This observation applies all too well to discussion surrounding gambling, speculation, and financial markets from antiquity to the present day.

Some societies end up sticking longer with the old beliefs and institutions, and others allow people to challenge their luck. Some societies stick with the principle of "everything is prohibited unless explicitly allowed," which fits an immobile world, whereas others move to the principle of "everything is allowed unless explicitly prohibited."

Unsurprisingly, it is the latter society that creates more options, more ways for its people to take chances. True, allowing such experimentation creates not only more trials but also more errors. But in order to move into the future, especially as each society adjusts to its increasing numbers and greater mobility, there is no other way. To do so, it must give scope to gambling and to speculation. Gamblers' and speculators' bets allow the pricing of what people want. It also turns out that there is a form of governance that draws on similar principles of trial and error (i.e., referenda and initiatives) wherein people can vote on what they want. In 75 percent of the cases in the United States, voters decided on the legalization of gambling through this process.

By examining what gamblers, risk-takers, and people financing them actually achieved, we get a better understanding not only of how to deal with risks, uncertainty, and ways to either price or otherwise deal with rare events but also of how societies leapfrogged one over the other. At the same time, we can also see how competitors spread false accusations against gambling and risk-taking – and why religious institutions and governments were often among these competitors. False languages covered these accusations, which shaped laws and regulations affecting a variety of companies associated with the risk business for decades and centuries, at times in unpredictable ways. The act passed on October 13, 2006, in Washington (the UIGEA, or Unlawful Internet Gambling Enforcement Act), prohibiting financial institutions from transfering payments to online gambling companies, is just the latest example.

John Gay's epitaph on his monument in Westminster Abbey is "Life is a jest, and all things show it; I thought so once, and now I know it." A mocking phrase? Perhaps. But we find that in societies that turned out to be successful, people acted as if life was a game, where they both played the game and, occasionally, changed the rules of the game by designing new institutions. We also find that a good way to understand why some societies thrived and others fell behind is by examining a variety of facts and sequences of events from this gambling angle. We find too that successful societies are those that became more tolerant toward risk-taking and betting, and that brought to life businesses and institutions allowing for "possibilities and probabilities to become the very guides to life" (to quote Bishop Butler).

As this observation is one of the conclusions of this book, it turns out that Gay's witticism is far more than that. Life *is* a jest. But to win this leapfrogging game among both people and societies, one should better learn how and when to take risks and how and when to leap into the unknown.

Our initial interest when writing a first book on this topic, twenty years ago (and parts of it even earlier), was neither gamblers, casinos, lotteries, and future markets nor philosophizing about chance and religion, and laws and regulation surrounding the gambling and futures business. We were just interested in solving a mathematical puzzle linked to gambling and insurance that economists and mathematicians have been struggling with for decades. It is the way that we refuted conventional approaches that led us both to articulate a unique view of human nature (summarized in the appendixes in this book) wherein one cannot distinguish between chance and necessity, and to examine in greater depth topics covered in this book and elsewhere.

Acknowledgments

Many people now take a partisan rather than an impartial view of issues covered in this book. We are in the fortunate position that the first book we wrote about them was set in the early 1980s (*Gambling and Speculation: A Theory, a History, and a Future of Some Human Decisions*, Cambridge University Press, 1990), before politics distorted the discussion.

In 1990 both Cambridge University Press and Princeton University Press wanted to publish the book. Some of the reviewers at the time renounced their customary anonymity and signed their reviews – among them was William McNeill, the great historian, to whom we are grateful for many insights. At the time we also received feedback from people in many fields and occupations. Among the many who commented, occasionally at great length on either the manuscript or, later, the 1990 book, were Milton Friedman; Gary Becker; Alan Blinder, the previous vice chairman of the Federal Reserve; Anna Schwartz; T. W. Schultz; Anatol Rapoport; William Eadington; Eugene Martin Christiansen; John Hey; David Hochfelder; Mark Perlman; and Jonathan Hughes. Irving Ebert and Stephen Shipman were among those who commented on this book. I expressed my gratitude to them all then, and I express my gratitude again here, to the anonymous reviewers too.

I single out Aaron Brown (the coauthor of Chapter 5) for special thanks, not only for the collaboration, but also for his comments on the entire book. The book would not have taken the shape it took without his meticulous feedback and his earlier writings on topics covered in this book.

Special thanks are also due to Claude Montmarquette, my former colleague at the Department of Economics of the Université de Montréal, for his contribution to the statistical examinations in the book.

We also want to thank the interlibrary loan staff at HEC Montréal for their help in finding rare documents and Sylvie Buffa and Lucie Boudreault for their faultless typing.

Last, but not least, we want to thank our editors for their patience and meticulous work.

ONE

From Religion to Risk Management: What to Do When Facing Uncertainty?

Reuven Brenner and Gabrielle A. Brenner

Which shows how societies dealt with uncertainty and risk when their population was small and immobile, and when it grew; why traditions and customs can be wisdom, but often become wrong when circumstances change.

Thomas Jefferson called the lottery a "wonderful thing: It lays taxation only on the willing." In one sense, Jefferson's statement is erroneous. After all, taxing tobacco and pornography implies that the tax is imposed only on those willing to smoke or to watch. Yet these actions do not necessarily turn indulging in either act into a wonderful thing.

Jefferson's statement may be linked to Britain's tax on tea, which, when imposed on the unwilling American settlers, resulted in the tea being thrown into Boston's harbor – certainly a way to avoid paying taxes. One can only speculate on the future of colonies if Britain, instead of imposing tax on tea, had decided to raise revenues by selling lotteries on the North American continent.

In another sense, though, Jefferson was right: governments would be better off taxing and regulating an activity that many people want to pursue, even if it is not perhaps perceived as particularly virtuous, rather than outlawing it. Yet where are the Jeffersons when one needs them?

On October 13, 2006, the president of the United States signed a bill – the Unlawful Internet Gambling Enforcement Act (UIGEA) passed by Congress – to make it illegal for financial institutions to transfer payments to online gambling companies, whose services millions of American citizens were buying. A close examination of the sequence of events suggests that politicians did not learn much from past experience with prohibitions, did not know the subject they were voting on, or were manipulated by a wide range of interests – protecting the states' tax base among them. These interests had a strong stake in weakening the online gambling companies, inventing accusations against gambling and disguising such views behind "moral" arguments. True, the roots of some of these arguments can be traced

1

to antiquity. But a closer look reveals that, though one can understand why political and religious leaders as well as private interests condemned gambling then, those reasons have gone with the wind by now. Or they should have, because there is no evidence to back them.

For centuries, opposition to gambling has been linked to deeply held beliefs that allowing probability, risk, and chance to play visible, significant roles in society, and letting industries develop around them, would have serious detrimental consequences. These beliefs all have roots in times, thousands of years ago, when they made sense. When populations are small and immobile, the law of large numbers does not operate – by definition. Not surprisingly, only in 1837 did Siméon-Denis Poisson, a French statistician, coin the phrase "law of large numbers." And the mathematical study of risk began only in 1654, with Pierre de Fermat and Blaise Pascal. There cannot be much specialization, there cannot be many markets, and there cannot be many visible prices when a population is small, sparsely distributed, and ~~inly im~~mobile.

~~rance~~ people had against fire, illness, floods, or other misfortunes in such circumstances were family, tribe, religion, and all enforcing implicit insurance based on such ties. Religion sustained the perception that decisions in the face of what we would today call incalculable risks are under control, and rulers of the tribes and the priesthood managed them properly. This proper management was done by priests with exclusive rights to throw dice, bones, or other devices and who taught, at the same time, that a higher authority controlled the outcome of the throw. It may seem to us like gambling – but it wasn't. The dice, the bones, and the Urim and Thummim were tools used in rationalizing decisions, much as sophisticated geometry was in the hands of astrologers later, or, more recently, as trivial algebra and erroneous statistics have been in the hands of Keynesians and macroeconomists.

As the population and its mobility grew, traditional institutions and beliefs have weakened, there has been more specialization, more activities have been priced, and new institutions and beliefs have spread to deal with risks and to mitigate the effects of leaps into the unknown, legitimizing other ways of making decisions. But ancient artifacts stayed, words stayed – though they lost their original meaning. What happened, though, is that ancient beliefs, institutions, and rituals, whose origins became lost in the mist of time, became associated with notions of eternal virtue and eternal codes of moral behavior rather than with particular times and places. After all, in many societies around the world charging interest is still taboo, as a result of misunderstood and misinterpreted biblical texts written thousands of years ago.[1]

Still, recall that whereas the last five "dont's" of the Ten Commandments (don't kill, don't steal, don't bear false witness, don't covet, and don't commit adultery) are sound advice for the ages, "don't gamble" is not on the list. As it turns out, with excellent reasons.

Origins of Lasting Prejudice

The origin of the word "lot" is the Teutonic root *hleut*, the pebble that priests or judges cast to decide disputes and divisions of property.[2] This is also the source of the Italian word *lotteria*, and the French *loterie*, which eventually came to mean "a game of chance." To this day, however, in both Dutch and English, the word "lot" has broader meanings: it refers not only to lottery tickets but also to human destiny. These two current uses of the same word are not accidental. Devices used today in games of chance were originally used exclusively during religious rituals when authorities made important decisions.

Proverbs 16:33 expresses most clearly the idea that the divine will is reflected in the fall of lots: "The lot is cast into the lap, but the whole disposing thereof is of the Lord." This legitimizes their use, and eliminates the link to chance. Perusal of the Bible reveals that the priesthood regularly cast lots to discover God's will on issues such as the election of a king (1 Sam. 10:20–1), the scapegoat for the atonement ritual (Lev. 16:8–10), and the identification of parties guilty of sacrilege (Josh. 7:10–26). Lots – Urim and Thummim[3] – were also used when the high priesthood had to select important dates or Saul to be the King of Israel (1 Sam. 10), for example. The drawing of lots in this case only confirmed the intuition of Samuel, who had already anointed Saul (even if we may be left wondering what would have happened if the draw suggested another option).

Lots were used to choose members of important groups: the inhabitants of Jerusalem after the exile to Babylon (Neh. 11:1), and the soldiers in the first attack against the rebel tribe of Benjamin (Judg. 20:9–11).[4] The drawing of lots in such ceremonies was called *goral* – which means both "little ball" and "fate." Casting lots was used to divide land and other forms of wealth or duties. In Numbers 26:52–6, for example, one finds: "The Lord said to Moses ... the land shall be divided by lots; according to the name of the tribes of their father they shall inherit. Their inheritance shall be divided according to lot" (a custom also found in Mesopotamia). Eleazar, Ithamar, and their sons, the heirs of Aaron the high priest, divided the priestly duties by lots (1 Chron. 24).[5]

Note that the drawing of lots for such purposes was called *payis* – which means "to pacify." With good reason: the lot falls independent of he said–she said, and was perceived as either solving or preventing mighty quarrels. Actually, the situation involved more he said–he said, taking into account both the frequent reference to the use of lots in allocating the priests' duties and to the Talmud's frequent reference to the quarrelsome temperaments of the priests.[6] There were a number of ideas underlying such use of lots, ideas that reappear in the work of mathematicians and statisticians during the sixteenth century. One idea was that the use of lots in disputes was the proper way to allocate duties and reward among contenders because the outcome did not depend on whether a person had higher or lower status.

Practices similar to those mentioned in the Bible were found among "primitive tribes," where bones, sticks, arrows, and lots were shuffled and thrown – exclusively by the tribal seer, who then disclosed the message for the future, a message revealed by the supernatural spirit who controlled the throw. Native American Indians, for example, believed that their gods were the originators of their gambling games with colored stones and that the gods determined the outcome.[7]

Pre-Islamic Arabia practiced the casting of lots to determine guilt. In the case of Yunus (Jonah), the Quran refers to the biblical use of lots (*sahama*) to discern the blame for the wrath of heaven. In the midst of a storm, his fellow sailors threw Jonah, on whom the lot fell, into the sea.[8] Apparently, lot casting was used in legal proceedings too, in cases such as manumission, divorce, and the allocation of inheritance.

Greek mythology describes similar practices. The gods cast lots to divide the universe among them. Zeus got the sky; Poseidon, the seas; and Hades, the loser, the underworld.[9] In the *Iliad*, Hector puts lots in a helmet and casts them to decide who will strike the first blow in the duel between Paris and Menelaus.[10] The root of the Greek word *dike*, meaning "justice," is another word that meant "to cast" or "to throw," a relationship also found in Hebrew (*thorah, yoreh*).[11] On Greek coins, the figure of Dike, the goddess of justice, sometimes blends with the figure of Nemesis (vengeance) and with that of Tyche, the goddess of fortune.[12] And, as among the ancient Hebrews and in latter-day Islam, in ancient Greece lots were drawn to divide an inheritance and to select some magistrates,[13] a custom Rome also practiced.[14] In the Mahabharata, the world itself is conceived as a game of dice that Shiva plays with his queen, and the main action of the book concerns King Yudhistira's game of dice with Kauravas, and an entire chapter describes the creation of the "dicing-hall-sabha."[15] Still, all these have absolutely nothing to do with risk or gambling, but with ways of making decisions when facing what today we call uncertainty.

Even in the sixteenth century, borough officers in England were still occasionally chosen by lot. In 1583 the Chapter of Wells Cathedral apportioned patronage in this manner. In 1653 a London congregation proposed that a new Parliament should be selected from nominees chosen by each religious congregation "by lot after solemn prayer."

Who among condemned men should die was also a decision made by casting lots, the lucky ticket saying "Life Given by God." A court decision in 1665 allowed juries to cast lots to resolve their differences as an alternative to retrial when the juries could not reach a decision. Although by the eighteenth century it had become a serious offense for juries to reach their decision in this way, John Wesley still used lots to determine the Lord's will, arguing that they could be used in exceptional cases when long prayer and debate did not help bring about a decision. He said, however, that the matter was not settled by "chance," for "the whole disposal thereof is of the Lord."[16]

Volatile Beliefs

From time to time, and more as the eighteenth century approached, observers started disputing the view that supernatural powers controlled the throw of the dice. They interpreted the prohibition on people's use of the dice as a way to sustain perceptions that the priesthood knew something that ordinary people did not. "Our priests are not what simple folks suppose; their learning is but our credulity," wrote Voltaire. In fact, one finds such reactions in earlier times too. Each time that a belief and institutions associated with it weakened, people's betting instinct and a stronger belief in chance surfaced. These interludes lasted until some observers invented new beliefs, condemning betting and belief in chance, and succeeded to enforce them.

In ancient Greece, the worship of fortune and of fate started when the belief in the Olympian religion collapsed.[17] Pliny (23–79 CE) made these observations:

Throughout the whole world, at every place and hour, by every voice, Fortune alone is invoked and her name is spoken; she is the one dependent, the one cuplrit, the one thought in men's minds, the one object of praise, the one cause. She is worshipped with insults, counted as fickle and often as blind, wandering, inconsistent, elusive, changeful, and friend of the unworthy... We are so much at the mercy of chance that Chance is our God.[18]

Later, as Rome was weakening (with its population in rapid decline), some writers noted – inaccurately, confusing cause and effect – that "it was the poisonous notion of chance [that] was weakening the fibre of the Roman."[19] They contrasted the widespread belief in luck and worship of the goddess Fortuna with the fact that the word "fortune" cannot be found in the New Testament – which was emerging as a new source of authority for managing human affairs. As Perkins (1958) summarizes the debate:

> It would appear that the life envisaged by the New Testament writers had no place for gambling or for the acknowledgement of luck. As the years passed, the Christians were influenced to some extent by the prevailing Roman customs, for we find Tertullian writing in the second century: "If you say you are a Christian when you are a dice player, you say what you are not, for you are a partner with the world." (p. 8)

The early church fathers and councils clearly condemned gambling among all Christians. Canon law forbade games of chance; two of the oldest church laws threatened excommunication of both clergy and laity found gambling.[20]

During medieval times (which came about after a rapid and significant drop in the Roman empire's population), the distinction between magic and religion, and between providence and chance, was blurred. In spite of condemnations of gambling, the medieval church did not deny that people were able to manipulate God's grace for earthly purposes. Aquinas, Boethius, and Dante all had stressed that the notion of divine providence did not exclude the operation of chance and luck. It was during the sixteenth and seventeenth centuries when the power of the church was declining further and new beliefs established themselves that the attacks on chance became once again a central theme in public debates.[21]

From Religion to Risk, from Lots to Betting

When people do not know how to solve some problems, when they do not know how to calculate risks – which is often the case today – yet they must decide on a course of action, they have to "manage" that risk. But how do we manage when facing such uncertainty, when there are no probability distributions to guide us but we must still claim legitimacy for the decision and have the authority to act?

Throughout history, people invented a maze of institutions to answer this question and ways to bestow legitimacy on such decisions, although there was nothing we would call scientific to underlie them. Institutions and traditions created perceptions as if there were no uncertainty or the uncertainty were mitigated, and those in decision-making positions knew what they were talking about and doing, backed, occasionally by what contemporaries claimed was scientific. Does anyone know today the magnitude of error in the models that some hedge funds might be using?

We know that when populations were small, isolated, most risks could not even be assessed. This does not imply that people did not design prudent strategies or that they acted blindly – even if with the passage of time we consider decisions they made imprudent, capricious, and blind.[22] We consider the outcome of casting lots, throwing dice, a matter of chance. But if a society believes that spiritual power controls the outcome, that the priesthood has the exclusive right to throw these devices and the priesthood is held in esteem, then decisions based on such throws can be, and have been, perceived as legitimate ways of making decisions. No smallest element of chance would have been perceived when leaders and priests made decisions based on throwing lots – just as the word of rating agencies, Moody's and Standard and Poor's, until recently had been taken at face value. The reality has always been that societies face uncertainty. The question they have to solve is the following: how do we legitimize decisions to act?

If relying on lots sounds "primitive," consider how later generations, including ours, have been making decisions in the face of uncertainty (i.e., situations when we do not know the probability distribution). In ancient Greece people flocked to oracles to resolve their doubts and to seek guidance in private and public affairs. No decision on engaging in war, on signing a treaty, or on enacting a law was made without oracular approval. Were decisions based on oracles' forecasts any better than those based on the throw of the dice or of lots?

Later, for centuries, monarchs and governments relied on religion and astrology to make decisions. For more than a century, rulers perceived astrology as an exact science, and books, presenting extremely complex geometrical calculations linking decisions to the position of stars, claimed legitimacy for their forecasts.[23] The mathematical complexity, like sacred languages of religions in earlier times, sustained exclusivity for a while.[24]

In England, from the time of Elizabeth to that of William and Mary, the status of judicial astrology was well established. In the time of Charles I, the most learned and most noble did not hesitate to consult astrologers openly. In every town and village, astrologers – just like priests in earlier times – were busy casting dates for prosperous journeys and for setting up enterprises, whether shops or the marching of the army; rulers kept their own councils of astrological advisers.[25]

Jump a few centuries ahead and consider what happens today: governments consult economists in every municipality, county, state, country, or, on global matters, the International Monetary Fund. Yet what passed for science for a few decades – going by the name "macroeconomics" – has been discarded, or at least is in the process of imploding. Just like astrology, macro-economics wore the masks of science – models, numbers, complex equations, predictions, claims of forecasting, "professors" of macroeconomics, journals and books published by academic presses, and expanding national and international bureaus gathering statistics created and sustained legitimacy for a while. John Maynard Keynes and his followers were widely celebrated – some were awarded Nobel Prizes. Yet macroeconomics, as astrology or views about controlling the outcome of throwing lots, had no foundation.[26] It seemed solid, but at a closer look it melted into thin air: what the majority believed in was actually false.

Macroeconomics was based on a new language, which Keynes invented and which his mediocre followers (to whom Keynes referred to as "fools"[27]) developed to esoteric depth. Most readers today would be struck by just how ridiculous the content of macroeconomic articles and books affecting policies has been. Keynes and his followers claimed that government bureaucracies, collaborating with central banks and independent of institutions in a country, could create eternal prosperity by solving a few equations with a few unknowns, and that central banks could print money with abandon without risking inflation. The models also assumed that whereas entrepreneurs, businesspeople, and ordinary people suffer random bouts of pessimism and optimism – subject to atavist animal spirits – politicians and government bureaucracies were immune to such primitive emotions. It is true that a minority stood up to these especially silly premises of the Keynesian school (the deceased Milton Friedman being the most prominent), where it did not matter if a country was centralized, dictatorial or not. But reasoning is never enough to defeat false views, in particular when those views rationalize increasing power in the hands of governments and rulers.

It took decades and bad inflationary experience for the Keynesian school of managing risk to be gradually discarded. Being leapfrogged and risking default are the mothers of invention; people fight over paradigms and language.[28] For a few decades, though, academics, heavily subsidized by governments, legitimized views by drawing on the Keynesian jargon. They suggested that it was a science able to guide fiscal and monetary policies to manage incalculable risk, and to shape policy debates. Keynesians saw risks as generated by the aforementioned unpredictable animal spirits – random, irrational, unprovoked, unreliable sentiments. However, Keynesians assumed, as noted previously, that these spirits strike only the hoi polloi, businesspeople in particular, but not – hold your breath – government bureaucracies and central bankers. The latter, Keynesians said, know how to mitigate the commoners' randomly fluctuating emotions. The fact that people's actions could be a *reaction* to politicians' animal spirits – short-term political interests of gaining and enforcing powers – was simply assumed away.

Governments had every incentive to subsidize spreading the Keynesian view, because it taught that bureaucrats and politicians were in a better position than businesspeople and the investing public to make decisions – a claim the lot-casting priesthood and astrologers made during earlier times. If rulers then had incentives to subsidize the priesthood and astrologers to gain legitimacy for their decisions, so did governments in our times when they subsidized macroeconomists. One difference between earlier and more recent times is that, in a world of small numbers and lack of specialization, religion and the throw of the dice offered legitimacy, but today many still believe that academic affiliation does. Academia and think tanks are identified – mistakenly – as institutions engaged in detached scientific inquiry. Although, by now, much academic study only wears the masks of science, and its legitimacy has been eroding rapidly – as happened to many facets of religion and astrology in the past.[29]

But what, then, will replace macroeconomics today? What will be the new institutions that legitimize making decisions when one faces incalculable risks? And what happens during the transition? Surprising as it may seem, the sequence of events and the debates surrounding gambling offer insights into answers to these questions, because gambling has been tightly linked with the development of financial markets, as Chapters 4, 5, and 6 will show.

During periods of transition from one way of legitimizing decisions to another, people fight about language, laws, regulations, and the viability of businesses and institutions. They do so because perceptions of risk and uncertainty, and institutions to mitigate them, suddenly change. The old institutions try to protect rituals, language, and power, and the new ones try to show that the older ways of dealing with risk were wrongheaded. Yet, even as the new ways of looking at the world spread, the older views, prejudices, and institutions do not disappear. Occasionally they are still powerful enough to bring about harmful laws and regulations. This is often where debates about gambling, risk-taking, and laws and regulations come into the picture.

The answer to the question of what will replace the older ways of making big decisions in the face of incalculable risks today has been unfolding before our eyes for the past decades, even if the link to risk-taking, gambling, and financial issues has not always been made explicit.

Financial markets, with the necessary political and legal institutions surrounding them, are emerging, giving legitimacy to decisions in the

face of incalculable risks, replacing both spheres of decisions that government bureaucrats occupied in the more recent past and rulers' drawing
on astrologers', priests', and oracles' decisions before. Societies recognize
that risk-taking makes them natural resources, and gamblers are needed to
achieve that. This substitution does not happen richer than smoothly; it
happens through trial and error, as in every endeavor. As a brief first example, consider how the junk-bond market, whose legitimacy was questioned
by associating it with gambling and Ponzi schemes, transformed into the
high-yield-bond market within a span of fifteen years, with few questioning today its benefits. As the next chapters show, gambling often acted as
a banking institution and was equally misunderstood. Also, both clearinghouses and investment banks have their origins in gambling establishments.
In fact, many other institutions that are part of established financial markets
today have their origins in gambling and were often misunderstood. Also,
closer examination reveals that occasional surges in people's willingness
to gamble have been due to governments' and central banks' grave mistakes. These mistakes suddenly raised questions and brought about debates
that eventually helped correct misperceptions about risk, pricing, and
gambling.

Yet one may now ask, How do we know that theories and institutions
legitimizing the use of financial and betting markets to make decisions would
turn out to be any different from fads like astrology, macroeconomics, or
the throw of the dice? Maybe we are also suffering from professional and
linguistic deformations? The answer to the last question is no, and, once
again, the analyses and history surrounding all facets of gambling, broader
and narrower, show why.

There is a significant difference between the use of information drawn
from liquid, democratized financial markets to make big, tough decisions
and the ways in which our ancestors, and most countries to this day, still
are making decisions. The difference is simple. Decisions based on throwing
lots, on astrology, on macroeconomics, have been made exclusively by rulers,
relying on either central authority, or on priests, astrologers, or macroeconomists. In contrast, decisions based on information derived from deep
financial markets rely on the outcomes of millions of people's opinions –
many gamblers and risk-takers among them, who put up money to back their
opinions and who come from all spheres of life. Such decisions offer better guidance for actions than do their alternatives. Deep, liquid, financial –
speculative – markets turn out to be the best institutions for aggregating
information. But to have such markets and achieve this goal, capital must
be *dispersed* and there must be institutions in place to hold all parties to a
transaction accountable (a path that is not quite smooth today because of

regulatory obstacles, such as the mere presence of the two rating agencies, which, combined with other regulatory requirements on banks and insurance companies but not on other financial institutions, weaken accountability and bring about the type of mortgage debacle that the United States faces today).[30]

Can a million people occasionally go wrong and suffer from herd instinct? The answer is yes – as the performance in financial markets of Warren Buffet and a few other extremely successful contrarians suggests, and as a few entrepreneurs in other activities, whether business, sciences, or the arts, suggest too. The contrarians in financial markets – call them gamblers, speculators, investors, or, in Buffet's case, "oracle" – are entrepreneurs too, who have the skill of better understanding mispricing and the guts and credibility to access capital and then reallocate it.

But even if investors are occasionally wrong, such an observation could not justify objections to relying on liquid financial markets to make decisions about the allocation of capital in the face of incalculable risks. The question is this: When is a society more likely to prevent persistence in mistaken decisions? When a few select people who have little money at stake make decisions, or when risk-takers and gamblers put their money where their mouths are and make decisions?[31] The answer is simple: with their money at stake, people think harder and correct their mistakes more quickly. Their access to credit is limited. Central authorities, or those backed by them, face such constraints to a lesser degree. They have access to taxpayers' money, can sell national resources, or can borrow against both.

And correcting mistakes quickly is what makes societies richer – and happier. Gamblers and risk-takers, when held accountable, have been very much part of the sequence of events that helped societies leap into the unknown. True, they committed mistakes when doing so. But they also corrected those mistakes and others quickly. There is no science to making decisions in the face of uncertainty – incalculable risks, that is. There cannot be. But there are ways to manage such uncertainty: the best way is to rely on information drawn from the bets of millions of people who put up money to back their ideas and challenge their luck.

Some may bring up the much-publicized bankruptcy of Long-Term Capital Management (LTCM) as a counterexample. But that case, just as the present subprime mortgage sequence of events, strengthens rather than weakens the points made previously. If it were not for the maze of rating-linked regulations, it is unlikely that the mortgage debacle would have taken place. The banks, insurance companies, and other financial institutions would have invested more in their own credit analyses, reexamining even those securities that Moody's and Standard and Poor's rated as triple A.

As for LTCM, it was a hedge fund, with two Nobel Prize winners in economics on board, Myron Scholes and Robert Merton. Their presence implied that there were rigorous financial models to price, among others, Russian government bonds – even though postcommunist Russia could have hardly offered enough history or reliable institutions to properly estimate the probability distributions of devaluation and default.[32] And how can the belief that the mainly U.S. Treasury–backed International Monetary Fund would continue to bail out countries to sustain political stability be assessed? The resultant probability distributions would have nothing to do with scientific rigor. In fact, there is no way of knowing the extent to which the models LTCM used were wrong. Nevertheless, what is useful to recall about this episode is that it turned into a nonevent, in the sense that neither the United States nor the world financial markets were destabilized by LTCM's bankruptcy, and it is not clear to what extent even the intervention of the Federal Reserve was needed. After all, Warren Buffet even made an offer to buy LTCM in the midst of the upheaval and clean up the mess.

The same conclusion holds true for consequences of the technology bubble and other bubbles. Financial markets were sufficiently resilient to correct the impact of financial miscalculations and mispricing. Compared to the flagrant, long-lasting costs brought about by centralized decisions on allocating capital in most countries (killing tens of millions of people among them) – in Russia under communism, for example – the mistakes brought about by mispricing in financial markets are little more than a rounding error. How can one compare the costs of mistakes in financial markets with the ones communism or other dictatorships have imposed on the world?

An in-depth look at events linked to facets of gambling, of origins of prejudices toward risk and risk-takers, allows us to draw the previous conclusions. It also allows us to question prejudices that have accumulated over centuries about gamblers, for an impartial picture of this facet of human behavior and of the industry. We emphasize the word "impartial," because today politics has turned gambling into a partisan issue, and works written about the subject are categorized as being in favor of the industry or against it, as if any examination of facts and sequence of events surrounding the issue must have a political agenda. We wrote a book on the subject back in the late 1980s, parts of which are integrated here, much before gambling spread in the United States and around the world. Our interest then was to solve both a mathematical puzzle that had long preoccupied scientists (the solutions to which appear in Appendix 1), and to articulate our view of human nature, which is quite different from the conventional views then and now. To see if our views were in the ballpark, we had to confront wide-ranging evidence, some related to gambling and financial markets. The twenty years that have since passed brought about much evidence that only fails to contradict the twenty-year-old analyses – which is always the best way to prove impartiality. After all, we could not have been aware twenty years ago of the new evidence that would unfold.

Chance and Providence: Upstairs, Downstairs

Keith Thomas observed that if there was a common theme that ran through the debates of Protestant theologians during the sixteenth and seventeenth centuries, it was the denial of the very possibility of chance and accident.

In England, the debate about chance versus Providence was taking place while England's population doubled during the 120 years before the Civil War. The increase was accompanied by changes in every facet of English society: trade, agriculture, industry, education, social mobility, and, of course, urbanization and overseas settlement.[33] These centuries saw an unprecedented ferment of business, scientific, and intellectual activity. New textiles were imported from the East; consumption of sugar, tea, and coffee soared; innovations in agriculture such as growing root crops and clover, systematic crop rotation, and beneficial leases all spread during these centuries.[34] The period between 1540 and 1640 saw the growth of wealth, of landed classes and professions, and a massive shift in wealth away from the church and Crown and away from both the very rich and the poor toward the upper-middle and middle classes as, among others, real estate became more liquid. Much political turmoil characterized these centuries too.[35] How do people make sense of such turbulence? Which channels are legitimate ways to riches, and which ones are not? The answer that age gave was that anything linked to chance was not quite legitimate.

In his *Institutes of the Christian Religion* (1559), John Calvin wrote:

For what would you be more ready to attribute to chance, than when a limb broken off from a tree kills a passing traveler? But very different is the decision of the Lord . . . Who, likewise, does not leave lots to the blindness of fortune? Yet the Lord leaves them not, but claims the disposal of them himself . . . For although the poor and the rich are blended together in the world, yet, as their respective conditions are assigned to them by Divine appointment, he suggests that God, who enlightens all, is not blind, and thus exhorts the poor to patience.[36]

To make fortune into a goddess was a grave mistake, emphasized the Anglican Homilies, and "that which we call fortune," wrote the Elizabethan bishop Thomas Cooper, "is nothing but the hand of God, working by causes and for causes that we know not. Chance or fortune are gods devised by man and made by our ignorance of the true, almighty and everlasting God."[37] Every Christian had to know that life was not a lottery, but reflected the working out of God's purpose: the events of this world were not random, but ordered. Pierre de Joncourt, a French Protestant, published in 1713 the book *Quatre lettres sur les jeux du hazard*, in which he argued that because gambling constitutes a profane use of lots, all such games are blasphemous and should be forbidden.[38]

Lewis Bayly, in the influential devotional guide *The Practice of Piety* (1613), blamed fires on people's practice of making preparations for market day on the Sabbath. Sickness too was attributed to God's will, and it was argued that "health comes from God, not from doctors."[39] This view is not surprising, as governments and insurance companies started to use statistics about mortality and illness only toward the end of the eighteenth century in England. It took time – and population growth – for statisticians to discover regularities related to the law of large numbers, upon which insurance companies would later base their calculations and determine premiums. Thus, the teachings of most theologians and moralists until the latter part of the seventeenth century, drawing still on authorities rationalized in a world of a small and relatively immobile population, should not be surprising.

Gradually, a new angle appeared in the condemnation of beliefs in chance, namely, that the rich are rich not because of chance, but because they did something good. The new teaching said that the poor, about a third or half of the population at the time, should be patient in their poverty, blame themselves, not rebel, and accept their fate. Obviously, the new doctrine of people getting their just rewards made its greatest appeal to members of the rising groups: the merchants, the shopkeepers, and the aspiring artisans.[40] For the poor a doctrine teaching that they have only themselves, their idleness to blame, was unlikely to resonate.[41] For them it made more sense to believe that part of the outcome was due to luck, which induced them to gamble, among other things, as their sole avenue of hope (winnings even financed start-up ventures, as discussed in Chapter 5).[42]

"Since the World is but a kind of lottery, why should Gamesters be begrudged the drawing of the Prize? If . . . a Man has his estate by chance, why should not my chance take it away from him?" wrote James Collier in "An Essay upon Gaming" (in *A Dialogue between Gallimachus and Delomedes*, 1713).[43] Indeed, the poor gambled and also believed in magic, witchcraft, and methods of divination. They also drank, which at least temporarily anesthetized them to their adverse circumstances. It is not surprising that the new religions tried to discredit such beliefs and also gambling and drinking. We'll say more about these pastimes in the next chapter.

Islam too condemns gambling to this day, the ban being related to the tenet that blind fate is not the governing force of human destiny. Historians have observed that the assertion of purposeful divine control as against the belief of pre-Islamic Arabs in a capricious fate was the main theme of the divine revelation received by the Prophet.[44] Early Muslim theological thinking used gambling as a metaphor to illustrate the concern with free will against predestination. As Islam became more established, gambling became severely condemned, because the Prophet's vision was that people lived in a world with a definite purpose, from beginning to end completely determined by God, a purpose that did not permit anything left to chance.

In his book *Science of Conjecture* (2001), James Franklin remarks that in Islamic law the idea of contracts involving risk survived – but only for the purpose of prohibiting them. He adds that "the Prophet forbade games of chance and, according to authoritative traditions, also any contract that involved *gharar* – any risk, uncertainty or speculation." People could not sell future crops, or future fish – unless its catching was certain because the water was shallow and the water belonged to the vendor.

This new perception of the world gained currency in Muhammad's time, when Arabia Peninsula was divided among warring tribes, some nomadic and others settled in agricultural oases and towns. With their numbers growing, these tribes found themselves in an ideological and institutional vacuum because the traditional customs and beliefs that fit smaller groups were weakened. Within two decades all Arabia was united into a new religious-political community (there is no distinction between politics and religion in Islam to this day). Within twenty years following Muhammad's death, the army of this new "tribe" seized the richest provinces of the Byzantine empire and destroyed the Sassanian state.[45]

Conclusion

To summarize, until the seventeenth century, religious teachings regarding the use of lots as a direct appeal to divine providence when making decisions were widespread. The association with the heavens implied that casting lots, throwing dice, should be treated seriously, with proper ritual and respect, and used only in cases when men were incapable of making decisions based on precedent. The throw was sacred, and done by the priesthood. Casting lots was not perceived as having anything to do with gambling but with the right way of making decisions.

Most of the priesthood condemned the use of lots, dice, and gambling for money. The attitude is understandable: If the hoi polloi used the devices and discovered probability distribution, what would happen to the magic, the sacred, the ritual, and the priesthood's exclusivity in explaining and making decisions? And how could the priesthood then legitimize its role and sustain the stamp of decision-making authority?

Refusal to deal explicitly with uncertainty and risks rather than just gambling led to the reluctance to use probability to price life insurance until the 1830s. Although, by then, the mathematics of games of chance had been known for 250 years. But insurers still had to claim that life insurance was deterministic sharing rather than a bet that one would die. Insurers claimed that because everyone dies, life insurance was not a bet but an investment: whether they believed in such a statement sincerely, we do not know. (It's also irrelevant: they acted as if they did.) If this view sounds strange, consider that in our days Islamic bonds are not allowed to impute interest rates explicitly because of Quranic prohibitions, drawing on biblical prohibitions (wrongheaded too, or misunderstood).

The preceding views concerning the role of chance in human affairs and prejudice against gambling can be traced to our days. But rulers, judges, and priests were not the only groups threatened by people's expression of belief in chance and their willingness to gamble, take risks, and leap into the unknown. Over time, a large number of ever-changing groups used the ancient prejudices to lobby for the outlawing of gambling and risk-taking. Who were these groups, and what were the wide variety of false accusations they invented that have brought about more confusing laws, regulations, and debates about gambling and risk-taking to this day? We examine these questions in the next chapter.

TWO

Anything Wrong with Gambling as a Pastime?

Reuven Brenner and Gabrielle A. Brenner

Which shows how false ideas about risk, gambling, and pastimes gain currency.

Old ideas often get rehashed, dressed in new jargons, and pass for evidence. The previous chapter examined the origins of some such ideas, which to this day pass for people's moral beliefs, influencing debates about risk-taking in general and gambling in particular. This chapter discusses a wide range of innovative – and false – arguments still used today to condemn and outlaw people's entertainment choices in general, and their gambling, and occasionally their drinking, in particular. Many of these ideas may strike readers first as strange, as ideas belonging to distant pasts, ideas that should have long ago been discarded.

But it is impossible to reject the view that a variety of selfish, disguised interests, rather than sincere beliefs, have been behind ferocious attacks against gambling and other forms of entertainment. The accusers repeatedly achieved their goals of either eliminating the competition or myopically ensuring government bureaucracies of a tax base (though the alternatives would have been far better, as is discussed in later chapters).

On occasion, one can find paper trails, like those in the recent Jack Abramoff scandal in Washington, that trace in minute detail the spread of false ideas about gambling in political circles. Abramoff's manipulations to incite opposition to new gambling businesses so as protect existing ones by dusting off ancient prejudices would make a Machiavellian proud.

In 1999 Abramoff, a Washington lobbyist now in jail (OK, so Machiavellians may not be that proud), promised to access three thousand pastors, ninety thousand religious households, the Alabama Christian Coalition, the Alabama Family Alliance, and the Christian Family Association to defeat a bill in the Alabama State Legislature. This bill would have allowed casino-style games on dog-racing tracks, which would have competed with the Choctaw tribe's casino. The Choctaw paid the companies Abramoff has been associated with some $2 million in 1999 alone for activities linked to the dog-track bill, and to oppose an Alabama state lottery. Such manipulations of public opinion, appealing to deep-rooted prejudices, have a long history in people's entertainment options in general, and on gambling-related ones in particular.

When businesses fear competition, they use lobbyists, politicians, the priesthood, and pliable "intellectuals," be they academics at universities or at think tanks – all part of what one may call the jargon, perception-shaping business – to spread a variety of false, not to say strange, ideas. They do so to bring about legislation that protects the threatened enterprises and bureaucracies: some perhaps do so naively but sincerely. When bureaucracies want to sustain their position or expand and fear losing tax revenues, they undertake similar actions. One must cut through the veil of language, and find out whether there was any evidence to back the opinions. Often, it seems, people with the best intentions were fooled, and ideas lingered on for decades, centuries, and even millennia, shaping laws and regulations.[1]

People may declare that they are in favor of competition. In principle? Perhaps. But in practice, businesses as well as political and other institutions threatened by competition and by people's revealed preference of reallocating time from traditional pastimes used means fair and foul to slow down the competition. They did so either by outright legislation or by making access to capital markets of potential competitors more costly, if not prohibitive. Occasionally they went further, invoking patriotism and nationalism to achieve their goals. Recall Samuel Johnson's statement, "Patriotism is the last refuge of a scoundrel." So it was, a refuge sought after by opponents of gambling already back in the fourteenth century. Not much new under this sun.

What Did Gambling Have to Do with Military Readiness?

In the seventeenth century, English statutes on games of chance reflected two distinct attitudes. Before that, the law did not prohibit games, but rather some of their negative consequences, and decreased military preparedness was claimed to be a major one. Whether there was any truth behind that accusation is doubtful, because the military lobby made the accusation.

The lobby said that people preferred to play dice rather than spend money on bows and arrows and spend time mastering their use.[2] In response, in 1388 Richard II secured the passage of a statute requiring people to buy items necessary for the martial arts, and to stop spending money on "tennis, football, coits, dice, casting of stone kaileg, and other such importune games."[3]

A statute of Edward IV in 1477 forbade the use of houses to play games of chance. Apparently, members of the army that Edward IV had disbanded after returning from the expedition to France liked to play. A statute of Henry VIII in 1541 repeated the arguments found in the two earlier statutes. It condemned popular gaming because it was claimed to diminish military ability and to disrupt public order.[4] But this statute too was passed on petition of the bowyers, fletchers, stringers, and arrowhead makers, and was called the "act for maintenance of archery and debarring of unlawful games." The petition mentioned that people were inventing new games, such as "logating in the fields" and "slide thrift, otherwise called shove groat," and emphasized that these inventions might cause the loss of trade and archery to Scotland "and other places of the realm."[5] Today we call such petitions protectionism, and they are often passed under similarly far-fetched premises.[6]

Except for a brief reference to games of chance in the Case of Monopolies (1603), which noted that the common law did not prohibit the playing of games, no significant changes occurred in English gaming law until 1657. Legislation enacted during this year allowed any loser in a gaming transaction to sue for the recovery of twice the sum. The statute also declared that all gambling debts arising after June 24, 1647, were "utterly void and of no effect."

Although this particular legislation did not survive, its content foreshadowed subsequent civil law on gambling in England. As we show in subsequent chapters, looking at gambling as a financial institution sheds light both on this and on earlier statutes, including on the unusual requirement of not having to pay back gambling debts. These statutes, affecting the gambling businesses only, were passed in an attempt to prevent venues of social mobility that were deemed unacceptable. In simple words, they had to do with the view that people should neither lose their ranks nor become rich by chance, because that brings about a something-for-nothing frame of mind.

Of course, these views were never drawn to their logical conclusion and used to advocate taxing inheritance at 100 percent. After all, if one drew this argument to its logical conclusion, one would have to ask, What does inheritance have to do with merit? We are not saying the inheritance should be taxed away – it should not be. We only point out the inconsistency in the arguments of those who wanted – and still do – to prohibit gambling because it brings about a something-for-nothing mentality.

Before we show the facts and sequence of events that brought about such statutes and examine gambling in this chapter as a pastime rather than from a risk and uncertainty angle, let us look at policies toward people's choices of entertainment over the ages. Recent patterns in the sequence of events leading to the adoption of restrictive policies toward gambling, the 2006 UIGEA in particular, become then more easily recognizable.

Prohibitions on New Ways of Having Fun

The Puritans who settled in the area that is now Massachusetts condemned gambling because they opposed "idleness."[7] The Massachusetts Bay Colony in its first year of existence outlawed not only the possession of cards, dice, and gaming tables, even in private homes, but also dancing, singing, and all "unnecessary" walking on Sundays. The blue laws of Connecticut (1650) denounced game playing because it caused too much time to be spent "unfruitfully."[8] Only in 1737 did Massachusetts legislators amend the antigambling laws by noting that lawful games and exercises are innocent and moderate recreations.[9]

In fact, all the new leisure industries were attacked throughout the eighteenth, nineteenth, and twentieth centuries, in both the United States and England, shaping prejudices to this day. The eighteenth century saw intensified attacks on drinking, some sports, and other leisure activities too. The preoccupation with people's leisure was such that observers of the times thought that these pastime choices were one of the great problems England faced.

The concern was working-class leisure choices, which observers perceived as a threat to "ordered" society.[10] Observers claimed that the problem was crime and idleness – though evidence is lacking[11] – and gambling was linked to both and more. Authorities feared that the gathering of a great number of people, those who attended lottery drawings in particular, would provide the starting point for riots and revolutions.[12] Another issue was that the increasing variety of options of spending one's leisure time seemed to threaten traditional cultural homogeneity and undermine social harmony. What was hiding behind these concerns?

Lord Edward Bulwer-Lytton (1803–73), a popular English novelist and politician, coined such phrases as "the great unwashed," "pursuit of the almighty dollar," and "the pen is mightier than the sword," even if today his name is associated with bad writing. When commenting on the new laws England passed during the nineteenth century, his writing was clear and to the point. He wrote that "the very essence of our laws has been against the social meetings of the humble, which has been called idleness, and against the amusements of the poor, which have been stigmatised as disorder." Close examination reveals that he was right. Let us take a look at the emergence and disappearance of English prohibitions, and then at the changing attitudes in the United States. Some of the false arguments are still floating around today.

English Prohibitions on Poor People's Pastimes

Festivals and holidays characterized popular culture in the villages of the eighteenth century and earlier. They were linked with seasonal work of agricultural societies, when recreation and work were not always separate. Hunting and fishing for both profit and pleasure were typical. Storytelling accompanied the work of spinners and servants; one member of such groups of workers was appointed to read aloud to the others. Technology now substitutes for storytellers – such as iPods and visible multitasking – but behavior patterns stay the same.

Women gossiped over their sewing or at the communal water source, as now both women and men do around watercoolers. Festival days and fairs broke up the year, and the workweek was irregular. Rituals that we now view as brutal and excessive were common: sports using animals were popular, and during holidays excessive drinking, eating, and fighting were tolerated.[13] (Dogfights are still popular, as the indicted Atlanta Falcons quarterback Michael Vick's bankrolling of such operations in 2007 shows.) On such occasions, when playing games of chance in particular, the mingling among social ranks was tolerated, though who was at the top of the social pyramid was never in doubt, as the rights to start and stop games were assigned to them.[14]

Criticism of how poor people chose to spend their leisure was common. Medieval preachers denounced festive gatherings and sporting contests, because these diversions took place when people were supposed to go to church and be engaged in religious rituals. Regulations on gambling were imposed in the name of either diminishing riots and fighting or making rank distinctions, as gaming was permitted among the rich at all times but limited among the poor to the twelve days of Christmas. There were also concerns raised that the poor would default on their taxes if they lost too much in gambling.[15] As we will see in Chapter 5, when looking at gamblers' behavior in the United States, there may have been some truth to this: people often preferred to pay their gambling debts over their taxes – though, as we show, mistaken fiscal and monetary policies brought these attitudes about.

The rapidly increasing population and its mobility during the eighteenth and nineteenth centuries, which led to density in cities, also led to the breakdown of many traditional pastimes, attending church in particular.

Changing demographics also gave incentives to invent new pastimes, as work and recreation, which previously intermingled, now were separate.

The employers of the Industrial Revolution complained about irregular work patterns as a result of customary holidays and habits of drinking on the job. But by the eighteenth century it became customary to think of a "normal" work day as ten hours with two hours for meals. It was not an accident that much intellectual preoccupation of the eighteenth and nineteenth centuries involved defining what was normal and deviant behavior, and much of the rapidly developing science of statistics was devoted to this purpose.[16]

Although work became separate from recreation, those working in the new industries in the cities at the end of the eighteenth and the beginning of the nineteenth century did not have either much time or much space to enjoy traditional recreations. The number of traditional full-day holidays taken by clerks and workers had fallen significantly. Bank of England staff, for example, had enjoyed forty-two holidays in the eighteenth century. By 1830 that number was down to eighteen, and by 1834 only Christmas and Good Friday were allowed, to prevent interruption of business. The shift toward intense but less time-intensive pastimes becomes understandable.

Factories introduced a Saturday half holiday only from the mid-nineteenth century, and the number of public holidays was not increased until the passage of the Bank Holiday Act of 1871. The *Times* of August 6, 1872, praised the new legislation with these words: "Rational, sober, and modest amusements are more and more supplanting all others, and the riots which made some old-fashioned folks doubt whether Holidays could do people any good has become all but a thing of the past."[17] Before this conclusion was drawn, laws, regulations – many misguided, as later recognized – and voluntary organizations reshaped English people's pastimes.

The temperance movement was the most prominent among the voluntary organizations. This movement and others believed that encouragement and regulations were necessary to teach people self-discipline in a world in which ways of enforcing customary behaviors were breaking down:

The lower class of people are at this day so far degenerated from what they were in former times, as to become a matter of astonishment. . . . And if we take the judgement of strangers . . . we shall find them all agreed, in pronouncing the common people of our populous cities, to be the most abandoned, and licentious wretches on earth. Such brutality and insolence, such debauchery and extravagance, such idleness, such irreligion . . . and contempt of all rule and authority, human and divine, do not reign so triumphantly among the poor in any other country . . . And the reason for this . . . : Our people are *drunk with the cup of liberty!*[18]

Observers saw the breakdown as directly linked to the rising population and to the movement from villages to cities, and to the resultant breakdown in the effectiveness of family and traditional institutions in enforcing discipline. The perceived breakdown, combined with the new range of entertainment options to fit the new working hours, shed light on the unusual alarm with which many viewed new recreational choices, blood sports, gambling, and drinking prominent among them.

Opposition to cockfighting and bullbaiting reached a peak with a series of local acts against them. The rationale was that such pastimes were inconsistent with the greater control and order required at the workplace.[19] This campaign had its class undertones: whereas the violent and bloody activities of the poor were all under attack (cock, dog, and bear fighting), fox hunting was not – which remains "high-class" entertainment to these days. Throughout the eighteenth century laws protected the hunting rights of the rich. The gaming laws provided legal immunity to the landed hunter but imposed penalties of death or imprisonment on the poor who crossed the recreational divide. To shoot foxes was strictly forbidden (the hounds were responsible for the killing), and the farmers had to comply, even though foxes were taking their chickens and geese. In 1809 an article in the *Edinburgh Review* remarked:

A man of ten thousand a year may worry a fox as much as he pleases, may encourage the breed of a mischievous animal on purpose to worry it; and a poor labourer is carried before a magistrate for paying sixpence to see an exhibition of courage between a dog and a bear! Any cruelty may be practised to gorge the stomachs of the rich, none to enliven the holidays of the poor.[20]

Such restrictive legislation by then had a history in England. In 1671 an act had disqualified all except the landed classes from game hunting, and another act in 1692 further added that "inferior Tradesmen, Apprentices, and other dissolute Persons neglecting their trades and employments should not preserve to hunt, hawk, fish or fowl." A century later, in 1796, William Pitt, the prime minister, defended similar legislation, arguing that "too liberal an indulgence in this amusement [the competitive shooting of game], they [the poorer] might be diverted from more serious and useful occupation."[21]

In 1833 the *Quarterly Review* criticized such legislation on exactly such grounds and argued that horse racing should in fact be promoted, because thousands of the less fortunate could take part. But the act of 1740 to restrain the excessive increase in horse races was passed because "the great number of Horse Races for small Plates, Prizes or Sums of Money, have contributed very much to the encouragement of idleness, to the Impoverishment of many of the meaner sorts of subjects of this Kingdom." The act confined matches (as opposed to races) to two locations, New Market and Black Hambleton in Yorkshire, exclusive venues for the rich.[22]

Just as did laws regulating gambling and shooting, this law reflected the fear of the idleness of the poor if they won, and lack of confidence in the judgment of members of this class to choose their recreations. Some believed that the poor made such bad judgments when gambling, overestimating the chances of winning, that they should thus be prohibited from doing so. Closer examination, presented in later chapters, shows that this was not true: statistics about the chances of winning were widely disseminated even during the eighteenth and nineteenth centuries, and people were well aware of them.[23]

In England Thomas Macauley and James Mill (who wrote the often-reprinted *Essay on Government* for the fifth edition of the *Encyclopaedia Britannica*) had the most prominent debates about the topic of bad judgments. Macauley wrote that "it is the grossest ignorance of human nature to suppose that another man calculates the chances differently from us, merely because he does what, in his place, we should not do." Mill responded by saying that "strange" tastes may be corrected by education. There was no evidence then and there is none today to suggest that people overestimated their chances of winning. What happened then is what happens today: those with lesser opportunities bought more lotteries or played more games in which they could win large prizes.[24] But they bet with their head, and not over it, as the evidence presented in later chapters shows, allocating a small fraction of their wealth to the only chance of "making it." When all other venues for becoming rich are or become gradually closed, what financial instrument offers the only chance, small as it is, of living the good life?

If Not Cockfights, How About a Drink?

Another recreation under attack in various countries and at various times was drinking. Although people always drank, during the eighteenth and early nineteenth centuries drinking became widespread. Why? A kind of "perfect storm" brought such popularity about in the United States. Later other "storms" and strange coincidence led to the prohibition of alcohol in the United States.

Alcoholic beverages had few substitutes as thirst quenchers. In the countryside, safe drinking water became scarcer as the population grew.[25] Even with the increased investment in water companies after 1805, London's water was still unpurified, and London's hospitals gave alcoholic drinks to their patients, not just because they were painkillers, but also because they were safe. Milk was not only double the price of beer, but also dangerous to drink (it was not yet pasteurized, and its anonymity in urban areas facilitated adulteration). Tea became popular only after 1830, when the price fell sharply. But increased consumption of beer and other alcoholic beverages was also because the pub, where people drank, gambled, and watched "cruel" sports, became one of the central places around which men's social lives turned.[26] They had no other place to turn to.

Many historians documented the rise of the pub as the center of entertainment, drinking, and betting among the poor. On October 18, 1849, the *Morning Chronicle* announced that it would publish a series about the moral, intellectual, material, and physical condition of the poor throughout England for eighteen months, about the way they spent their leisure time in particular.[27]

One article refers to the effects on the family life of women working in factories from adolescence. Having less time to look after their families, they encouraged their husbands to spend more time outside the house, in pubs in particular. It was not just their wives' encouragement that led men there. Lack of light, heat, furniture, and space did not make the house into a comfortable home. As a commentator then put it:

One of the worst features . . . is the cheerlessness with which it invests the poor man's house. On returning from work, instead of finding his house in order, and a meal comfortably prepared for him, his wife accompanies him home, or perhaps arrives after him . . . The result is that . . . he goes to the nearest alehouse . . . A great deal is lost also through the unthrifty habits of his wife. Her experience at out-door labour has been acquired at the expense of an adequate knowledge of her in-door duties. She is an indifferent cook – a bad housewife in every respect.[28]

(Now one can speculate and blame the Industrial Revolution for the origins of the not-so-palatable traditional English food. A similar process may be taking place now, as more men and women work and have little time to learn how to cook or clean. Today, instead of pubs, people may go for Starbucks, takeout, or a microwavable dinner.)

Again, the difference between poor and rich people's outlooks is clear. The middle classes advocated domestic pleasures and valued privacy; moralists wrote that people should find both "within their own doors" rather than in "assemblies, gatherings and crowds."[29] What they failed to understand is that whereas the poor had houses, they could not be transformed into "homes" with the money they could be saving by avoiding gambling, drinking, or occasionally dressing up.

This is not so different from today either. Forgoing sitting in Paris's coffeehouses or Starbucks in New York and London would not speed up the purchase of an apartment in any of these cities. Winning a lottery, though – a ticket bought with a few bucks, or forgoing one tall latte a week – may. Meanwhile, sipping a $5 latte for half an hour is also better than going home to a $2,000 minuscule box that passes for an apartment in Manhattan and London, or to under-the-roof, rundown rooms in Paris. The latter are romantic only in illusions created on the Metropolitan Opera's large stage in performances of Puccini's *La Bohème*.

In 1858 a temperance reformer understood what many others in the movement did not: "Sociable pleasures were precious to working men for whom alternative recreations were scarce; to abandon drink was to abandon society itself, unless some alternative grouping were provided.[30] And Robert Malcolmson, a historian examining English recreational patterns, concluded that "dressing up and spending freely for a holiday were relatively accessible means of winning approval," whereas "many other channels through which status might... have been achieved, especially those which the middle class favored, were... blocked off... What seemed rational from the people's point of view was regarded by middle class observers as criminally extravagant and irresponsible."[31]

It was only in the second half of the nineteenth century that parks and playgrounds became widespread, that railways enabled excursions, and that bicycles, music halls, and organized sports became common.[32] It was then too that religious institutions started offering leisure alternatives. At first, finding themselves operating in a competitive leisure market, they attacked the competition. The priesthood condemned railways, bicycles, and music halls, perceiving them as a threat to morality. But as the secular world offered a greater variety of entertainment,[33] religious picnics ceased to satisfy, and the churches, trying to recruit and hold on to members, began to tolerate what they had previously condemned. By 1890 they had admitted outdoor games and dancing.[34] They made innovations in the chapels, which had better music by 1880, and organized bazaars, concerts and drama, sewing, and cricket and football clubs; at one point they tried to get a monopoly on bingo and gambling for charity purposes.

Secular Theories Condemning Gambling

Secular ideologies, with politicians' often-hidden agendas behind them, fueled attacks on the recreation choices of the poor too, gambling singled out once again.[35]

Although toward the end of the eighteenth century Adam Smith argued that no society can be "flourishing or happy, of which a greater part of the members are poor and miserable," many still believed in the mercantilist doctrine of the utility of poverty. From this angle, having a large low-wage economy was beneficial, for otherwise the country could not export. High wages were believed to threaten England's competitive position, because they were assumed to make workers lazy – as did windfalls from games of chance (though never from inheritance, as noted before). If one already had an established business, isn't this a very convenient theory to believe, or to pretend to believe in? What could be better than denying hungry, ambitious, poor people access to domestic credit, thereby diminishing threats of competition?

The established view was that poverty was the motivation both for making greater effort and for spending less on nonproductive activities, rather than giving people incentives and opportunities. Traditional doctrines saw with suspicion avenues for getting rich that did not require effort – such as setting up gambling establishments and playing. William Temple, in his *Reflections on Various Subjects Relating to Arts and Commerce* (1752), suggested that "to hold the lower Orders to Industry, and guard the Morals of the poor, on whom all Nations must rely for Increase and Defence, is the truest Patriotism."[36]

Never mind that the view of how the poor would have behaved if they had higher wages was never supported by evidence. Yes, the facts are that the poorer people, who had no access to credit and capital at the time, spent their relatively small discretionary incomes and occasional small windfalls on drink, gambling, occasionally dressing up, or on a glorious binge. But if they saved those small amounts, would that have changed anything in their life? Because they had no access to capital – not really.

Recall Alfred Doolittle's answer to Professor Henry Higgins, in *My Fair Lady*, when the latter wants to offer him a relatively large sum of money. He prefers the smaller amount, because that he would just spend on drinks with friends. Saving that amount could not have made a difference in his or anyone's standard of living anyway. A large sum, however, would turn him into a prudent, respectable man – meaning, among other things, settling down and marrying his mistress, but possibly losing contact with his fellows, still mired in poverty. Indeed, when Doolittle unexpectedly gets a large windfall, because of Professor Higgins's joke of recommending him as a "great moralist," that's what he does: he marries his mistress.

Historians such as McKibbin (1979) and Dixon (1980a) conclude that gambling made few demands on those who played, and it had no significant material consequences. Various commissions at the end of the nineteenth century could find no causal relationship between gambling and poverty, or between gambling and crime (other than that gambling was illegal, and those who played were criminals. This accusation, though, is similar to those made under communism against entrepreneurs, even ones who just sold homemade food. What the commissions found was that poverty led people to gamble and to drink.[37] However, expenditures on both did not represent a severe strain on their resources but were, in general, strictly controlled. Yet several influential authors treated gambling as the greater evil (viewing drinking as destroying people piecemeal, whereas gambling wrecked families in a single throw).[38] They saw gambling as a cause of drinking, and claimed that gambling could not be controlled in the way that drinking can be.[39]

Thus, gambling was linked with the debate over the proper nature of leisure, with secular economic models – and not just with either the Protestant outlook or the role of risk and chance in society. Poor people's involvement in new leisure industries was deemed illegitimate because leisure could be respectably enjoyed only when work was put first. As Seton Churchill's *Betting and Gambling* (1894) put it, working-class gambling had to be controlled because the "the law of labour . . . one of the most obvious of God's laws" was being disturbed by gambling.[40]

If There Are No Circuses for the Masses, How to Calm Them Down?

The attacks against gambling in the second half of the nineteenth century, which drew now more on "academic," secular theories, took place during an era frequently referred to in English history as the Great Depression. The rate of growth in industrial production dropped from 33 percent between 1860 and 1870, to 20.8 percent between 1870 and 1880, and 17 percent between 1880 and 1900. Britain's competitive performance in world markets was also disappointing, falling behind that of both the United States and Germany.[41]

The loss of industrial preeminence provoked a number of reactions, from the protectionist fair-trade movement of the 1880s to public discussions of what made Germany click and England fall behind.[42] One conclusion was that redistributive policies would lead to greater social harmony, diminishing the workers' discontent and increasing productivity. This was also a period when part of the propertied classes who were not moved by Charles Dickens's advocacy were looking at the European continent's frequent revolutionary outbursts and the rumblings at home. The riots of the unemployed in London in 1886 and 1887 were a vivid reminder, the *Times* noticing on February 9, 1886, that for a couple of hours, the West End was in the hands of the mob.[43]

One conclusion of the debate was that "Fair Trade, Commercial Consuls, Technical Colleges – good and necessary as they are – will not avail to stem the inroad of the German, unless our manufacturers and merchants brace themselves."[44] (Does all this sound familiar, especially for those who remember the U.S. debates on falling behind Japan during the 1980s, or who follow CNN's Lou Dobbs's weekly preaching about the United States falling behind just about everyone because of weak tariff protection?) But how to make the working class work harder, become more productive, and restore England to its previous glory?

Because gambling violated the law of labor, prohibiting gambling came to be perceived as a step in that direction. Magistrates testified before the 1901–2 committee on gambling that "if the betting craze goes unchecked, the sober youth of Germany will take the reins of the commercial world."[45] Academics lent the basis for such views. In 1906 Arthur Shadwell, in his *Industrial Efficiency: A Comparative Study of Industrial Life in England, Germany and America*, described the English working class as "the most indolent and degenerate section of 'a nation at play' ... Money that the workers should have 'invested' in British industry ... was instead being wasted in betting, and so, if there was unemployment, the workers had brought it on themselves."[46]

The British failed to pay attention at the time to the quite well-known pattern of declining entrepreneurial spirit in countries that lose their young and restless, who migrate to new shores with greater opportunities. They also failed to note the significant drop in birthrate and the longer life expectancy since 1860 as related to the slump and the structural changes that occurred.[47] Instead, the frequently repeated idea of gambling causing idleness passed as evidence, leading to the attacks that culminated in the 1906 Prohibitive Betting Act, which disallowed the use of a house, office, room, or other place for betting.[48]

But while gambling was prohibited, drinking was not.[49] The reason for the different legislative treatment might have been that the brewers had a strong political lobby, linked to well-connected agricultural and industrial interests as well as to financial and retail outlets. The alcohol industry was a well-established, major employer; sellers of drink were as numerous as those of food. In contrast, the owners of gambling businesses came from working-class backgrounds and had no political clout. The fact that all forms of gambling were forbidden except some linked to horse racing suggests the same pattern. Racing was a traditional pastime for the wealthy (think of Ascot), whereas other forms of betting were less so.[50]

How Did the United States Come to Prohibit Drinking?

Some patterns concerning drinking and opposition to it in the United States at the end of the nineteenth century are similar to those in England. In the

1830s few Americans had ever heard of beer. Rum and whiskey were the favorite beverages. However, by 1880 thousands of enterprising German immigrants had transformed American tastes, and beer had become the American national beverage.

Drinking alcoholic beverages became then – in the last two decades of the nineteenth century – even more of an issue in the United States than abortion or online gambling are now. The temperance movement spread and used lobbying tools that would put Jack Abramoff to shame. This episode in American history is worth noting, as there are parallels with the sequence of events that led to the UIGEA, which prohibits financial institutions from transfering money to online gambling companies.

As in England, saloons in the United States became the poor people's refuge. Breweries bought the real estate where the saloons opened. This was a time when breweries standardized production and, expanding rapidly, were looking for new places of distribution. They found such places in saloons, which proliferated. The temperance movement actually became politically successful when, under the name of the Anti-Saloon League, it targeted the saloons rather than drinking.[51]

The obstacle to lobbying attempts to get lawmakers to pass a constitutional amendment prohibiting the sale of alcoholic beverages were the beer barons, who had their clout too. They supported politicians, invested in newspapers, and used a grassroots organization, at the time called the National German-America Alliance, to spread the beer culture. With World War I and Congress's passing of the Trading with the Enemy Act in 1917, which allowed the United States to confiscate property of enemy nationals, this somewhat accidental association between the breweries and the league helped bring about their downfall and, inadvertently, Prohibition.

Once the 1917 act passed, the head of the Anti-Saloon League, Wayne Wheeler, wrote A. Mitchell Palmer, the government's custodian of alien property, that alien Germans controlled Anheuser-Busch and other Milwaukee companies. August Busch succeeded in preventing confiscation, though he had two sisters living in Germany, married to Germans, and his mother happened to be visiting Germany when the war started. He brought her back rapidly to the United States when Wheeler started his machinations.

But Wheeler won.[52] President Woodrow Wilson ordered all breweries to be closed in September 1918 – the declared objective being to save grain for the war effort. As Maureen Ogle notes, though, the war's end was by then in close sight – it ended two months later, on November 11. Nevertheless, Prohibition lasted until 1933. During this time some brewers produced soft drinks and "near" (nonalcoholic) beer. Others diversified – the real estate that once housed the saloons offering an unexpected financial cushion. Most brewers, though, went bust.

Prohibition brought about a wide range of problems, from the Mafia to widespread corruption, which is discussed in detail in Chapter 7, and imposed costs for decades.

The 1906 Act and Since: Familiar Patterns

It is not true that only the interests representing the upper classes, the race-course owners, and some racecourse bookmakers were behind the 1906 prohibitive English legislation. This "class law," as it was then called, which made it more difficult for the poor to bet but did not impose constraints on rich people's venues for betting, was passed with the support of the Labour Party too, not just the Tories.[53] Why?

The leaders of the Labour Party thought what religious leaders had thought in previous centuries: if the poor spent time drinking, gambling, and reading racing news, their instruction in moral behavior on the one hand, and in political activism and the benefits of socialism on the other hand, would be slowed down.

The labor leaders' opinion was possibly shaped by the fact that the demand for tips and racing news played a large part in the development of the popular press. Half of the evening papers started in the 1870s and 1880s had a close association with sports and gambling. To think that, if betting were prohibited, the working class would choose to read or listen to political treatises instead of reading the racing news seems unlikely. But the Labour Party's views were not as strange as they might seem to us now. Its members may even have believed in them sincerely (members of the Labour Party during the twentieth century believed in far stranger ideas, which brought the United Kingdom to its knees).

The Roman idea of the link between diminishing social unrest by giving circuses to the masses (even if not gambling) was gaining acceptance – though the idea was articulated differently. Already in 1833 people were arguing that "it was well known that healthy, happy men were not disposed to enter into conspiracies. Want of recreation generated incipient disease, and disease, discontent; which in turn led to attacks upon the Government."[54]

This is a superficial statement in the sense that a society where new enter-tainment options are offered is also a society where there is access to cap-ital and competition prevails in many spheres of life. Such opportunities give hope, and such hope has a calming effect, rather than merely provid-ing greater entertainment options. Correlation is not causation. Denying opportunities and ways to spend money, on entertainment options in particular, diminishes incentives and makes people, risk-takers in particular, restless – which does not mean that they would bet necessarily on Marx. They may as well have bet on other far-fetched ideas, or have migrated.

Believing as the Labour Party leaders did that restlessness due to prohibitions could be channeled into political energy, whereas "the displacement of political energy [leads] into apolitical and hence conservative leisure,"[55] seems quite a stretch. The evidence is, in fact, that prohibitions lead people either to continue to do the same things as they did before, only illegally, or to invent new pastimes. And although it is true that when all goes well and people prosper they pay less attention to politics, this is what politics should achieve – isn't it? Good times allow people to focus their energies on private, specialized pursuits. But Labour Party leaders seemed to believe genuinely that the 1906 legislation prohibiting gambling would serve their agenda for social reform.[56]

Such a line of thought was a facile, superficial variation on Otto von Bismarck's more profound insight a few decades before, when he passed social legislation, with whose impact we live to this day. He was the one who introduced both the age of retirement, at sixty-five, and social security. As he remarked in 1878, "if the worker had no more cause for complaint, then the roots of socialism would be chained off."[57] In contrast, the English Labour Party wanted people to continue to complain and divert their energies from gambling to demands against the rich, hoping that this would help their socialist causes.

The prohibition on working-class betting continued until 1960, when the Betting and Gambling Act legalized betting shops.[58] Today, among western countries, England has the most accommodating legislation toward all facets of gambling. People can bet on virtually anything, from the weather to political events – with winnings tax-free. And lottery bonds (or premium savings bonds, backed by the U.K. government, discussed in later chapters) are among the most prominent savings vehicles in the country, contradicting much superficial reasoning and academic treatises about gamblers being irresponsible spenders, or about gambling being inconsistent with prudent behavior.[59]

The Change in English Attitudes and Laws

By the 1960s poverty was not linked to either gambling or drinking, but to unemployment and lack of access to education and health services. Socialized education and socialized health care, rather than private education and health care, came to be seen as the solutions.

To finance government spending in these areas, suddenly the benefits of gambling – as a monopoly of the state – being a voluntary tax (a false notion, as is discussed in detail in coming chapters) were now rediscovered and acknowledged. It was also acknowledged that the prohibition of gambling was ineffective: people continued to gamble and the police were unable to enforce the law.[60] The 1978 Rothschild Commission summarized the findings.

When commenting on the 1906 act, the commission concluded that, indeed, the intention was to restrict off-course betting to the wealthier section of the population. But "in practice, [the law was] hopelessly ineffective. Bookmakers satisfied the wish of the ordinary British punter to stake a few shillings on a horse either by operating illegal betting offices or employing a runner to secure illegal cash bets in the street. Instead of suppressing betting among poorer people, the law produced resentment and attempts to corrupt the police, contempt for authority and a bookmaking trade operating outside the law, prey to protection rackets and gang violence."[61] In other words, when prohibited from gambling, the English poor did not flock to read socialist treatises, they gambled illegally instead.

Although England seemed to learn the lessons from prohibiting a pastime that people wanted to pursue, other countries did not. As we discuss later, when looking at U.S. regulatory history concerning gambling, the 2006 UIGEA, which prohibits financial institutions from transferring payments to online gambling companies, it is impossible to discard the possibility that something other than genuinely held beliefs were at stake. Not only does the act protect state and Native American monopolies on gambling, but also Congress, by passing the law, allowed states to put themselves in a strong negotiating position. They will be able, eventually, to extract more tax payments from online gambling companies once they approve them as taxed and regulated businesses, like all others.

It is also impossible to discard the possibility that, as in England, many companies – from Indian casinos to racetracks and (though not land-based casinos, as it turns out) state governments – had a strong interest in passing this law and weakening the online gambling companies. It would not be the first time in U.S. legislative history that such a sequence of events took place.

Law and Gambling in the New World

Antigambling legislation eventually became a feature of all U.S. states during the nineteenth century. The reason for its adoption differed from region to region. What settlers first found was a sparsely populated wilderness where a new "tribe" was to develop. But according to what vision should this new tribe be shaped?

Recall that the Puritans who settled in Massachusetts condemned gambling because they opposed idleness, and they outlawed the possession of cards and gaming tables as well as dancing, singing, and unnecessary walking on Sundays. The 1650 blue laws denounced gaming because it caused time to be wasted. The Great Migration (1630–40) and the rising merchant class (which gradually converted to the less restrictive Unitarian faith) led to the gradual transformation of the interpretation of criminal law from God's punishing of sin to the state's maintaining of public order.

The transition has been typical of all societies that shift from small to large numbers: when the population is small, there cannot be much specialization. And customs, traditions, enforce good behavior. When the population and its mobility increase, enforcing tradition and custom becomes difficult; beliefs that shape good behavior are weakened; people invent new institutions; and laws, police, and a wide variety of nongovernmental institutions enforce and teach what is good behavior.

In 1737 Massachusetts legislators amended the antigambling laws by noting: "All lawful games and exercises should not be otherwise used than as innocent and moderate recreations, and not as trades or callings, to gain a living or make unlawful advantage thereby."[62] Still, as late as 1748, a New Jersey act equated idleness and immorality with fraud and the corruption of youth. Thus, once again, one must be careful in interpreting references to gamblers as criminals. Their only *crime* may have been gambling.

By the twentieth century, some religious institutions came full circle, sponsoring bingo games – once a sin – and lobbying governments to give them exclusivity on the pastime. Reverend Francis Talbot, a Catholic priest, wrote, "I cannot grow frenzied with the puritanical precisionists who rate the bourgeois pastime of bingo as a major sin . . . Played under proper auspices . . . the worst harm that bingo causes is a sore throat. Church bingo parties are a healthy substitute for gossip teas, lovesick movies and liberal-minded lectures."[63]

By this time, though, new interests had emerged to attack the gambling industry. In the 1920s the New Jersey Chamber of Commerce opposed gambling on two grounds. First of all, retailers and established sources of entertainment such as movie theaters would lose business during the racing season. Also, it claimed, petty crimes would "increase enormously." Whereas the second complaint is understandable, closer examination reveals that it is linked with tourism rather than gambling: large, transitory crowds provide easy prey, and the criminals themselves can more easily disappear into the crowd. The first attack is to be expected and should be discounted: people may preach for competition in principle, but companies do not like it in practice. And new ways of spending one's leisure time are always a threat to traditional ways – as we see today with people's shift toward spending more time on the Internet and on wireless devices, and less time reading newspapers.

In many states, the first form of gambling to be decriminalized was bingo. The first step toward its legalization occurred in Massachusetts in 1931, with Rhode Island following in 1937. Pari-mutuel betting was next, and New Hampshire, Ohio, and Michigan legalized it in 1933.[64] We shall take a closer look at what happened during and after the Great Depression in later chapters, when we discuss government finance in particular.

Conclusion

The gambling industry, viewed as part of the entertainment business, is not different from any other industry. Entrepreneurs have built pubs, hotels, casinos, racecourses, and theaters. Others produce computers, slot machines, and video terminals; still others have invented a variety of games and offer them online. Other entertainment industries build concert halls, amusement parks, and theaters, and people write plays, music, and scripts. If fashion sells newspapers, magazines, and Web sites – so does betting news. The demand for tips and racing news played a large part in the development of the popular press in the United Kingdom. Newspapers that refused to publish such information on moral grounds folded.

Today people would be hesitant to mention gambling and opera – which some view as the pinnacle of high culture and a rarefied entertainment option – in the same breath. This was not always the case. The great Italian opera houses – from Naples's San Carlo to Milan's La Scala – were sustained by their gambling saloons. These were vast halls adjoining the theaters where faro tables and roulette (*rouge-et-noir*, as it was referred to then) were most popular. Gioacchino Rossini, the most famous and well-paid composer at the time, earned just two hundred ducats a month as musical director of San Carlo but one thousand ducats a month as his share from the house's tables.[65]

His famous impresario Domenico Barbaja, who owned the opera-casino entertainment complexes, commissioned operas and ballets – R&D, that is – from the gambling revenues.[66] A remnant of this arrangement survived in Monte Carlo, after Austrian authorities prohibited gambling at La Scala and the revolution in Naples closed down the tables there too. They did so fearing crowds would spark a revolution in the opera house, as it was one of the few places where people could then gather legally.[67] Aside from opera houses, people had no right to assemble in a crowd anywhere else. In Chapter 7 we will look at this relationship between gambling and cultural enterprises from other financial and fiscal perspectives.

Las Vegas has been recently reinventing this entertainment and financial combination. Although some would not lump Andrew Lloyd Webber, Cirque de Soleil, the Lipizzaner stallions from Vienna, and Celine Dion together with Rossini, they may still consider them a few steps up from the variety shows that have been popular in the past.[68] And Luciano Pavarotti did not hesitate to accept promotion from the New Jersey Casino Association or singing gigs in Atlantic City.

Briefly, as far as entertainment choices go, gambling should not be viewed differently from other entertainment options. As the sequences of events presented in this chapter have shown, the accusations against allocating time for gambling had no foundations. One question that arises is: Are there situations when societies allocate too many resources to gambling? As the evidence that unfolds in the next chapters suggests, there may be cases when we should look at gambling not as entertainment, but as a financial consideration. But this happens when governments rely too much on their monopoly powers to tax gambling; when governments commit grave monetary and fiscal mistakes, which induce people to gamble more; or when regulations prevent a large segment of the population from having access to capital.

After all, ask the following question: if people have no access to credit, what can they do with the small amounts of discretionary income that they accumulate? Even if they saved it, but could not borrow against future income to buy a car or an apartment, and enhance income potential, how could saving the small amounts change their lives? In contrast, taking on debt would discipline, motivate, and change people's spending habits (much as having kids, the biggest debt people take on does for the vast majority of people). Leveraging one's savings, which then comes together with commitment to regularly pay debt, is an incentive to make more efforts, to work harder, and to spend less on cockfights, pubs, and gambling. It is not surprising that, according to some historians, the invention of installment credit has been among the major financial innovations to bring about prosperity.[69]

But incentives to save and take on debt either to invest in an expansion of a business or to start a new one diminish significantly when regulations, taxes, inflation, and devaluation make it either impossible or far more costly to borrow. Why not, then, blow the little discretionary income on gambling, drinking, or dressing up? We shall present evidence and discuss the sequence of events on this point in the next chapters, also linking it to "tulipmania," which never really was the event most people seem to imagine.

It is only from this broader regulatory/fiscal/inflation/devaluation angle that one could say that, at times, too much investment flows to lotteries or casinos, or for that matter to drinks and, occasionally, to bets on extreme ideas. But in this case the source of the problem is not the people who must be cured from their vices. As it turns out, the source of the problem is governments and central banks, which gave preferential treatment to casinos and lotteries to sustain monopoly pricing (and tax revenues) and/or are pursuing mistaken fiscal and monetary policies.

If this is the case, the solutions for those who believe that today there are too many resources allocated to gambling are neither education of the public nor prohibition. One solution is to withdraw preferential treatment to segments of the gambling industry. Protecting the lottery business from competition and letting government bureaucracies manage this business brought about overreliance on this source of tax revenue. And by giving privileged status to casinos on Indian reservations, governments have, inadvertently though with the best of intentions perhaps, brought about a misallocation of resources, and they may not be doing a favor anymore to such groups (though initially the privileges might have helped).

If such changes were made, people would gamble either for fun or to become rich. Gambling in all its incarnations would become a normal activity like all others, not to be singled out for any special attention.

When Plenty smiles – alas! She smiles for a few –
And those who taste not, yet behold her store,
Are as the slaves that dig the golden ore –
The wealth around them makes them doubly poor.
George Crabbe

THREE

Are You Rich? Risk-Taking and Gambling, or the Leapfrogging Instinct

Reuven Brenner and Gabrielle A. Brenner

Which shows that some forms of gambling are entertainment and other forms offer the only chance for a good life for those who fall on hard times or reach the age of fifty and have not "made it."

Today most people gamble either for entertainment or for the chance to become rich. Entertainment is not only the obvious playing of cards among friends or gambling in Las Vegas or Macao, but also making small bets on a sports team, or on any idea that crosses one's mind. It is possible to do the latter legally in the United Kingdom, if one finds enough people interested in the idea – see Tradesports.com, for example. Such commitment or backing of ideas with a few dollars heightens people's enthusiasm and involvement, and also helps keeping scores. It turns even boring topics into fun ones, and adds excitement to predictable games in sports, because people have a stake in the outcome.

These are games that people also play everyday and everywhere, whether betting on their favorite sports team in university dormitories or on who in the office will violate a commitment to lose weight. How often do people respond to a statement with, "Do you want to bet?" Words are cheap, and if the other side does not want to bet, you know that he or she is not quite confident. Even a few bucks can make something more serious and fun than if there is absolutely nothing at stake. Such betting is for making everyday life – and conversations – a bit more interesting and serious, and for enjoying football games and races more intensely. The amounts spent on such bets are no different from paying a few bucks more on coffee in the morning or on T-shirts in a vacation place to bring memories back weeks, months, or years later.

But this is not the type of betting and risk-taking that this chapter or the rest of the book is about. The previous chapters dealt with religious and other objections to gambling, and showed why they have been misguided. They also showed why objections to gambling as entertainment had no foundations. So, what makes gambling so special, as to be singled out for so much debate, regulation, and taxation?

This chapter sets the basis for the rest of the book and shows that the best way to answer these questions is to view gambling as a financial option, a reflection of people's willingness to take risks, where gambling becomes part of the portfolio allocation – and far more. The rest of the book shows that, indeed, one can best understand companies and institutions that offer people the opportunity to gamble by looking at them as financial intermediaries – including governments in their present monopolistic roles as casino and lottery manager and operator. Once we look at gambling, lotteries, and futures markets from this angle, the controversies surrounding gambling become clearer too, and we can separate easily the reality about gambling from much of the political and other noise that has been created around it. Such an examination also reflects human nature and the sequence of events that gamblers and risk-takers have been involved in to shed light on historical events. This chapter deals with the simplest financial issues linked to gambling, whereas the next chapters deal with more complex and, for most readers, probably unexpected and surprising ones linked to futures markets and to gambling as a substitute for banking.

If people reach the age of fifty or fifty-five and have not "made it," what are their financial options to still live the good life? Except for allocating a few bucks to buy lottery tickets, it is hard to think of any other option. If people find themselves down on their luck and see no immediate opportunities to get rich, what can they do to sustain their hopes and dreams? Allocating a fraction of their portfolios on games with a chance to win a large prize is among the options. And when people are leapfrogged – that is, when some "Joneses" who were "below" them jump ahead – how can they catch up? They will tend to challenge their luck too for a while, taking risks that they might have contemplated before in business, financial markets, and other areas but did not follow up on with action.[1] These people occasionally buy lottery tickets too, participate in other games where they have the chance to win large prizes, futures markets among them (as shown in Chapter 4), and sometimes bet on venturing into new lines of business.

These behavior patterns are predictable – the gambling and risk-taking instinct of those leapfrogged (the same instinct that explains the taking of insurance by those who got ahead) is a basic one.[2] Suppressing it – as many societies have done by putting obstacles in the way of financing risk-taking – turns out to be the most effective away for societies to fall behind, sometimes into possible oblivion.

The risk-taking, leapfrogging instinct and ways to properly channel and finance it are at the core of understanding broader issues too, such as why some societies leapfrogged others.[3] This book focuses on exploring one facet of this behavior pattern as reflected in only some universes of chance, be those gamblers, businesspeople in this sector, legislators, competitors and, unavoidably, social scientists and historians writing about the subject, as the previous chapters already showed.

If You Are Not Rich, What Do You Do?

We shall mainly discuss here players in games like lotteries, where it is possible to win large prizes. Players of other games, be it cards among friends, bingo, online poker, or games at land-based casinos on a vacation in Las Vegas, Atlantic City, or Monte Carlo, or any of the peaceful French resorts in the Alps or the Atlantic coast, are a diverse group. They seek entertainment. Widows are disproportionately represented in bingo halls. Playing bingo for hours is a cheap way to spend time in the company of other widows. Well-to-do young males play poker and other games online, and some use the sites to learn the games and prepare themselves for visits to land-based casinos, where they do not want to lose face and arrive inexperienced. Such gambling has little or nothing to do with risk-taking or philosophizing about chance, but with entertainment.

Visits to any of the gambling meccas, large and small, where tourists spend hundreds, thousands, or tens of thousands of dollars, is not different in magnitude from spending on alternative pastimes. Going out for a night on the town in Manhattan, say, a Broadway show followed by dinner can easily run $500 for two, not counting hotel and travel, which is the same as leaving that amount one night at a casino table. And leaving $10,000 or more on the roulette table is comparable to renting a boat or a plane for a day to take a brief leave for an exotic destination. Viewed from an entertainment angle, gambling is not different from any other business in the entertainment sector, whether one looks at the consumer or at a business – never mind the accusations already discussed in the previous chapter. But once we say that gambling *is* a financial consideration, and that people allocate part of their portfolio to gamble, the issue becomes something different, sharper and clearer.[4]

There have been many attempts to understand gambling behavior, and we saw some in the previous chapters. But economists have looked at all games of chance as if they belonged to one category – whether the maximum prize was one dollar or a million. The prevailing view has been that gambling is a matter of taste. Those who like risks gamble, whereas those who do not like risks do not. Although this viewpoint has led to the development of numerous mathematical models of esoteric depth, it cannot shed the slightest light on any facts.[5]

Freud explained gambling differently. He once wrote that a gambler is a man who, because of a death wish toward his father – quite a taste – has developed guilt feelings. To punish himself he gambles with an unconscious wish to lose. This seems a rather strange theory (as there is no evidence that gamblers killed their fathers or tried to), but it should be noted that, to his credit, Freud ultimately discarded the theory in a letter to Theodor Reik.[6] Psychoanalysts have either related gambling to the Oedipus complex (another taste for which there is no evidence) or dealt mainly with the behavior of compulsive gamblers, a subject we touch on briefly later, as a tiny fraction of the population exhibits such behavior.[7]

In contrast to the economics and psychoanalytic literature, in which few attempts have been made to relate gambling to social conditions, the sociology literature has done just that.[8] Many authors have argued that when conventional avenues for social mobility are closed, people will find nonconventional ones, which may include crime and gambling. Whereas evidence exists to support this view, evidence also exists to contradict it. There have been numerous nonegalitarian societies where there was no social mobility and yet not much crime or gambling either.[9]

As we pointed out before, if one wants to understand facets of gambling and risk-taking, it is better to distinguish between two types of games. One type, where both stakes and prizes are small (relative to one's wealth), reflects the choice of a pastime. Both the poor and the rich gamble, though not necessarily on the same games. The poor play slot machines, whereas the rich either go to charity balls where the tax-deductible contribution includes participation in raffles or spend their vacations in Monte Carlo, where they can rent a yacht, go to the casino, or bet on horse racing. The losses incurred from such games can be compared to the price one pays for other types of entertainment, and they have less to do with people's willingness to take risks than with how they choose to entertain themselves.

Viewed as entertainment, the gambling industry is not different from any other. Gambling businesses build casinos, theaters, and hotels. They buy sophisticated computers and video terminals. They employ statisticians and artists. They invent new games and use new communication channels. There is no difference between going to a casino and choosing another pastime.

Other types of gambling do not take time to play and have nothing to do with leisure time. People put up money for the chance to win prizes large enough to become rich – though they know that the chances of winning are minuscule. But just as businesspeople make decisions based on possibilities other than the most probable result (after all, what is the chance of coming up with a successful drug approved by the Food and Drug Administration), so does the person buying a lottery ticket. People do not buy them because they are interested in the most probable result – which is losing the money invested in the price of the tickets. The facts, summarized subsequently and in the next chapters, leave no doubt that people gamble on some games for the chance, no matter how small, to become rich. Whereas entrepreneurs find financial backers and bet on ventures with the possibilities of high profits, though they are not very probable, other people buy lottery tickets for the possible, though not most probable, outcome. They finance themselves by giving up a few beers or spending on more fashionable clothes. Gambling on lotteries reflects that decision on the margins between giving up some consumption and allocating that money to the small chance of becoming rich. No other financial asset in one's portfolio has the features of the lottery.

When people are suddenly leapfrogged, they pin their hopes on undertaking risks they shunned before: some play games of chance and others venture into entrepreneurial or criminal acts.[10] An opposite reaction happens when people leapfrog their fellows: they gamble less, insure themselves instead, and avoid taking risks. To put it simply, too much wealth breeds a search for security, whereas some types of insecurity breed risk-taking, where people make more efforts and bet on new ideas in particular. When certain groups fall behind and others outdo their key referent groups, one would expect to find contradictory tendencies: some people start to gamble, gamble more, and take more risks, and others try to restore stability and advocate insurance. This is just a sketch (details can be found in Appendix 1), but we shall see later on how we can understand patterns in sequences of events by keeping in mind this leapfrogging feature of human nature.[11] First, however, let us examine in light of this sketch the narrow picture concerning predictions linked with gambling only:

- A chance to win the big prize is one of the main reasons for lottery-ticket buying, or playing other games with large prizes.
- Those who perceive fewer opportunities will plan to spend a greater fraction of their wealth on lotteries than will the relatively rich.

- People of all classes who have not previously gambled may decide to do so when they suddenly lose part of their wealth (e.g., when they are fired or fear the increased probability of unemployment, and so on).

By the phrase "those who perceive fewer opportunities," we do not mean only people who have lower income. A $15,000 income for a fifty-year-old is a different indicator of wealth from the same income for a twenty-year-old. The fifty-year-old realizes that there are no other ways of becoming significantly richer. Thus, one would expect that older people, rather than younger people, with the same measured income will gamble. Hope is like health insurance: the older you get, the more it costs. For a person with one child, a $15,000 income assures better chances than it does for a person with four children: on the same income, the greater is the number of children, the poorer is the family. Thus, we would expect that people with the same measured income who have more children would also spend a relatively greater fraction of their income on lottery tickets.

These statements already suggest why some studies on gambling may be misleading.[12] In them, information was gathered on the income of the buyer or of his or her household without looking at gamblers' age or family structure. Sometimes the information on income seemed sufficient only to reach the conclusion that lower-income groups tend to spend a higher fraction of their income on lotteries. At other times, the income of the gambling population seemed, at first sight, too high to support this claim. However, as is pointed out previously, income provides biased information about people's incentives to buy lottery tickets.

The facts we summarize in the next section draw from our 1990 book, titled *Gambling and Speculation*. We have not found any research since then that added insights to our findings as far as the previous predictions are concerned. Moreover, none of the elaborate statistical analyses conducted since then went through the double-checking of data that we did then – necessary in all fields of study, but on a matter as controversial as gambling is needed even more. As it turns out, data gathered by national bureaus of statistics about gambling were already unreliable then, before illegal sports betting (estimated at $93 billion in the United States now) or Internet gambling (estimated in the tens of billions of dollars) were in the picture (the detailed statistical analyses appear in Appendix 2).[13] Before we present features of our analyses, the next section presents and discusses other people's findings to see whether, indeed, games of chance with large prizes are best examined as a financial consideration that reflects people's portfolio allocations.

Facts

The Attraction of Big Prizes

If people want either to become rich or to restore their wealth after losing parts of it, games of chance with small prizes will not be of interest to them, but others with big prizes will. Indeed, most market researchers of lotteries in the United States found that "while people like to be winners, they also want to win 'a lot of money.' This is the universal dream, and apparently is the primary reason why people buy lottery tickets."[14]

A survey done by the New York State Lottery found that the typical ticket buyer was motivated by the hope of winning a big prize. Another, by the Massachusetts State Lottery Commission, found that the public overwhelmingly favored a single top prize of $100,000 over several prizes of $1,000.[15] (These numbers refer to the 1980s, when the dollar was stronger). A U.S. government report on gambling found that 77 percent of the people polled gambled to get rich. Landau, in his guide on how to create a successful lottery, concluded that experience shows that there must be a prize that will improve people's circumstances in a way they cannot achieve otherwise.[16] After examining lotteries in countries such as England, Colombia, Spain, Australia, Ghana, and West Germany, Rubner too reached the conclusions that "it is mainly the size of the top prize that determines their success, and the number of small prizes has been cut down to make way for bigger top prizes."[17] Both a report of the Royal Commission on gambling carried out in the United Kingdom in 1951 and a 1977 market research study by Loto-Québec reveal that the expectation of a large prize is the main reason people give for purchasing lottery tickets. So did a survey done in Cameroon and Senegal among lottery players.[18] Stumbling on a treasure is a universal dream.

Lotteries with many unequal prizes – some of which are very large – are not inventions of our times. This has been one of their characteristic features since the seventeenth century.[19] Although the spread between the largest and the smallest prizes has varied across countries and time, Sprowls speculated that these differences depended on the discrepancy between being poor and being rich in the particular country at the particular time.[20] For example, he found that the largest prizes in England in the late eighteenth and early nineteenth centuries were greater than in the United States in the same period, and he links this with the fact that discrepancies in wealth in England at that time were also greater. It may not be accidental that since 1980 first prizes in the United States have reached the level of tens of millions of dollars, and that several multistate lotteries since then have offered prizes in the hundreds of millions of dollars, though increased competition can shed light on this trend too.

In contrast, in the traditional bingo game the maximum prize is a few thousand dollars. However, as we have pointed out, participants (widows are disproportionate in this group) view bingo, which requires one's presence during the game, as a cheap pastime rather than as a means of getting rich. Already the 1976 U.S. government report *Gambling in America* stated that "middle-aged and elderly women, widows, and those earning under $5,000 a year are highly represented among the 'heavy' bingo players.... Bingo is viewed more in 'social' terms than other forms of gambling; most players play to have a good time" (p. 163).[21] Nothing has changed.

One question that can be raised is this: if it is true that large prizes make lotteries attractive, why do small prizes exist to start with? Sprowls found that these small "consolation prizes are essentially refunds which are an inducement to try again" in hopes of winning in the future.[22] Indeed, we found both that the smaller winnings are frequently rebet and that people often stop gambling on lotteries altogether when they win the larger prizes. More will be said on this point in a later section, when we discuss our findings, which are derived from a large database.[23]

The Poor and Those Falling Behind

Many surveys have found that poorer people spend a greater proportion of their income on lotteries. Rosen and Norton (1966), who examined the buying pattern in New Hampshire; Brinner and Clotfelter (1975), who did a study of Maryland; Lemelin (1977) and McLoughlin (1979), who did studies of Quebec and Ontario, respectively; Heavey (1978), who did one of Pennsylvania; Clotfelter and Cook (1989), who have done studies of California and Maryland; and Brenner, Lipeb, and Servet (1996), who did a survey in Cameroon and Senegal all reached this same conclusion.[24]

In their analysis of Maryland's lottery buyers, Clotfelter and Cook found a negative relationship between spending on lotteries and income and education, and discovered that African Americans spend more than whites. The difference between whites and African Americans was most striking for those belonging to the lowest income categories, suggesting that poor whites may believe they have more opportunities to get richer than believe poor African Americans. The 1976 report *Gambling in America* also showed that families whose yearly income was less than $5,000 were spending on average 0.3 percent of it on lotteries. Families in the $5,000–$10,000 income range were spending 0.23 percent of their income on them, whereas those in the $10,000–$15,000 range were spending only 0.13 percent.[25] These results were obtained without even making adjustments for age and family structure, adjustments that could have strengthened them, as we suggest later.

Examining the British evidence, Newman concludes that, with the single exception of casino gaming, a higher proportion of the mass of wage earners gamble on each of the various gambling activities, and so it "can be stated with confidence that gambling is predominantly a proletarian predilection."[26] Newman also found that single women are relatively less inclined to gamble than married ones: for every ten single female bettors there were fifteen married ones in similar age groups. Also, 30 percent of married men aged eighteen to thirty-four bet on horses, but only 20 percent of single men did in the same age group. Although Newman does not present evidence on the number of children, one can speculate that married people, whether women or men, are likely to have more children than the single ones. He also found that betting on football pools and playing bingo are forms of betting that are significantly more attractive to older than to younger people; only with casino gaming is the tendency reversed.[27]

But, as we noted before, there is no reason to put all gambling in one basket. For older people, casinos and other forms of betting are a way to spend a day in their retirement, as the following excerpt from a 1988 *New York Times* article so perfectly describes, and has absolutely nothing to do with gambling as a matter of allocating one's portfolio:

Most weekday bettors [who take the trips to Atlantic City, where they eat casino-subsidized lunch for $2.50] live on Social Security and pensions. But if they are exploited, encouraged to go in too deep, there's no sign of it. They say they never bet beyond their limit. One after another approvingly recites this refrain: Bet with your head; not over it. Win or lose, these visitors seem to know, and get, what they want: the day's outing to Atlantic City is a welcome way to break up the week. They sit on the boardwalk, dine on restaurant food (and especially prize those places where pickles are free) and most of all, they enjoy the thrill of slot machines that swallow endless nickels, quarters and dollar slugs. The casinos also know and get what they want. They clear about 18 cents on every dollar wagered. These old people are not nutty about gambling; they are not eager to see casinos come to New York. They enjoy the journey and the long dreamy day. If casinos came closer, the Atlantic City adventure would, like so much else in their lives, be over.[28]

A bit sad, perhaps. But it does not seem worthy of any condemnation.

Back to gambling as a financial option. Similar conclusions can be reached from examination of data on Swedes who bet on soccer games. Betting on sports is not different from a lottery, although it requires investing time not only in knowing the game but also in closely following information about team members.[29] It is not surprising that sports executives scrupulously follow rules of promptly disclosing information about injuries and other matters one would classify as inside information. Fans do not care if other fans get the information about a quarterback getting the flu, or being injured a few minutes ago. But for the more than 100 million Americans who wager an estimated $96 billion on sports (in 2006), it matters a lot.[30] With information thus made available to all, soccer pools and lotteries can be compared, especially when it is recalled that for pools the discrepancy between the price of participation and potential gains is as large as it is for lotteries.

It is worth elaborating on the findings Sam Walker summarized, which show just how close sports betting markets are to financial ones. In sports, as in financial markets, there are investment newsletters. For a while, Robert Stoll's suggestions in his letters on how to bet so as to "leave less than 1% chance of exhausting their bankrolls" worked better than others' recommendations. Walker quotes a professional gambler from Indiana, Elihu Feustel, who says that Stoll is "the only winning handicapper I know who makes his living selling this information." Stoll uses a complex mathematical model, which he adjusts with "100 situational angles" to forecast patterns, including psychological ones. As his models proved successful, since 2005, Stoll noticed that minutes after e-mailing his advice, the lines on the games shifted, as sports bookmakers adjusted the odds to make his recommendations less likely to pay off. In finance this is known as an efficient market, when investors quickly absorb information they deem relevant. Notice too that an entrepreneur with an unusual insight can correct mispricing, and make money for himself and his clients – for a while.

Nechama Tec compiled data on 812 gamblers (all men) between the ages of eighteen and fifty-five. They provided information on occupations and income but not on age or family structure.[31] Still, the classification by occupation shows that 60 percent of respondents with working-class-type occupations are regular bettors, compared with 45 percent of those with middle-class-type occupations and 40 percent with upper-class-type ones. When gambling is linked with income, Tec found that 38 percent of those who come from higher-income homes, 46 percent from middle-income homes, and 61 percent from lower-income homes play regularly. Tec also found that among those whose parents own a business, 43 percent gamble regularly, compared with 54 percent of those whose parents do not own a business. Layton and Worthington (1999), in their analysis of the socioeconomic determinants of gambling in Australia, found that recipients of aged and veterans' affairs payments are more likely to gamble at lotteries.

To get a clearer picture, we examined surveys of winners (of $1 million or more) in Michigan for the years 1973–80. There were forty-six such winners.

The survey included age at the time of winning, occupation, and, for some, the number of children and grandchildren. Another survey found that in New York there were eight such winners in 1977–78; for each, age and occupation were given. We compared the winners' sample characteristics with the total Michigan and New York populations as given in the 1970 census.[32]

The average age of the Michigan and New York winners was fifty-four, whereas the average age of the Michigan and New York populations over age sixteen was 27.9. Among the winners, 10 percent (seven to be precise) were younger than thirty-five, whereas 60 percent (thirty-four of the fifty-four) were older than fifty.[33] Further, the winners' average number of children was five (for the twenty-nine winners for whom this data were given), and the average number of grandchildren was six (these averages do not even include one winner who had seven children and thirty-two grandchildren). Occupations (when the winner was not retired) were all characteristic of the poor or lower middle class: the winners were janitors, factory workers, and so forth. The probability that such a sample is a random one for the population older than age sixteen is low.

Kaplan and Kruytbosh (1975) found similar evidence when they compared the age distribution of winners and the population at large in the states of New York and New Jersey. Persons older than age forty-one were overrepresented among winners (72 percent of the winner sample, only 52.9 percent of the New York population, and 78 percent versus 53.2 percent in New Jersey), whereas the age group of sixteen to thirty was underrepresented. All the evidence summarized thus strongly suggests that the lottery-playing population tends to be older and poorer and to have more children than the rest of the population.

Other evidence, often supplied by government-managed lotteries, however, seems at first sight to provide a different picture. For instance, in Quebec, 63 percent of the people whose annual income is between C$10,000 and C$15,000 are occasional or regular players. These incomes may be average for a young, childless couple, but they are low for an older one with four children. Thus it would be misleading to conclude from the information on income alone that in Canada, in contrast to in other countries, the middle class constitute the majority of lottery players, as Loto-Québec keeps insisting.

We took a closer look at education and age statistics in the data. The reason for looking at education is that it is positively correlated with income. If we find that the lottery-ticket-buying public is relatively less educated, we can conclude that relatively poorer and older people bought the lottery tickets in Canada too. This is indeed what we found. Of people polled, 58 percent had up to seven years of schooling, 53 percent had eight to twelve years, 42 percent had thirteen to fifteen years, and only 39 percent with more than sixteen years answered that they were regular or occasional buyers of Inter-Loto tickets. The trends were similar for all other lotteries as well.

At the same time, the group aged forty-five to fifty-four and those fifty-five and older represented the highest percentage of the lottery-ticket-buying public. Considered alone, this finding may have two explanations. Either these are the ages when people are at the peak of their earning power, or only when one attains these ages does one finally realize that the only way to procure a fortune is by winning the lottery. Considering the previous data, which show that people with less schooling bought more tickets, the second conclusion seems to be the valid one.

This conclusion is strengthened by evidence given in a detailed survey of 93 (out of 190) winners of a big prize of Loto Canada between the years 1974 and 1978.[34] The age group of fifteen to twenty-four represents 7.6 percent of the winners but 26.2 percent of the population, whereas the proportion of people aged forty-five and older is 46.6 percent in the sample versus 37.3 percent in the general population. These facts may explain why the average family income of the winners was $18,962, whereas the mean Canadian family income was $16,095.[35] Although at first sight these numbers do not seem to indicate a poorer population of lottery-ticket buyers, that impression is again erroneous because of the lack of adjustment for either age or the number of children.[36] The mean income of a family whose head belonged to the age group forty-five to fifty-four was C$21,237 (recall that about 50 percent of the winners were aged forty-five and older, and that the average family income of all winners was $18,962).[37]

Reversal of Fortune

But it is not worth pressing this point too much, because we expected two groups to invest in lotteries.

We expected not only the poorer and the elderly to spend a relatively greater fraction of their income (or more correctly, their wealth) on lottery tickets, but also others who suddenly realized that their opportunities significantly diminished owing to illness, accident, loss of job, or other misfortune.[38] The resultant decision to purchase lottery tickets, a reaction to a sudden loss and less security, will not be a regular, planned one, but rather a spontaneous one. This kind of reversal of fortune can happen to anybody, rich or poor, young or old, with or without schooling.

Once we put together the two categories of people – the poorer who plan and those suddenly falling on hard times who may decide to buy lottery tickets – it is possible to misinterpret the data and reach inaccurate conclusions. Just how misleading such aggregate data can be depends on the percentage of people who decide to buy spontaneously relative to the percentage of people who plan to buy tickets. We have found only one survey that raised this question:[39] it found that 50 percent of people buy them spontaneously and the rest plan to purchase them.[40] This evidence may suggest only that something less than 50 percent of the lottery-ticket buyers may be old and poor. The rest may be young or may have no children but were subjected to an unexpected, unfortunate event (losing a job, not getting the significant raise expected, and so forth).

We found only anecdotal evidence in various sources before we undertook our detailed statistical research summarized below. Devereux suggested in his massive study on gambling that "the well adjusted middle class salaried employee may lose his job for a variety of causes that lie partially or wholly beyond his control [and] gambling may appear as one of the by-products of this sequence."[41] Scodel (1964) labels gambling a safety valve for that fraction of the middle class that is afraid to lose their position or, in the case of upwardly mobile ethnic minorities, insecure about their social insurance as Americans. And a poll in Quebec (where unemployment had reached and all-time high of 15 percent in the early 1980s) revealed that people reported that the money they had previously spent on beer and wine they now reallocated and invested in lottery tickets.[42]

Qualitative evidence supports this view of reallocation of one's portfolio. Tec (1964) found that in Sweden gambling behavior was well correlated with a person's dissatisfaction at work, and Brunk (1981) concluded that in the United States dissatisfaction with current income was a strong reason for lottery-ticket buying. The already mentioned detailed survey of ninety-three winners of big prizes of Loto Canada between 1974 and 1978 asked the winners whether before they won their prizes they thought they could still advance in their careers. Of the sixty-eight winners who answered the question, 51.5 percent said no. Moreover, 41.6 percent answered that they expected their situation either to stay unchanged or to deteriorate. To the question "Would you choose the same job again?" 29 percent answered no, and 36 percent answered that they would not like their children to do the kind of work they were doing. Only 19 percent answered that they would.

These answers suggest two things. First, the winners come from both groups (the poor who planned to spend relatively large amounts on lotteries and those who suddenly became poorer and dissatisfied and decided to gamble). Second, the winners are relatively old: it is hard to believe that 51.5 percent of the working population consider themselves already at a dead point in their careers. (In the numerous works summarized by Campbell and Converse, the percentage of dissatisfied workers varied between 11 percent and 23 percent only).[43]

Further evidence suggesting a positive relationship between the propensity to gamble and being relatively poor and frustrated also comes from another direction. Numerous studies have found that French Canadians earned less than English Canadians did (although the difference narrowed in the 1970s).[44] Thus, one would expect that French Canadians would gamble relatively more and be disproportionately represented among the winners. Indeed, out of the ninety-three winners in the preceding sample, forty-five (or 48.9 percent) were Francophones, whereas in 1975 they represented only 25.6 percent of the population.

But one must be careful with the interpretation of these data. Of the winners, 67.8 percent were Catholics and 28.9 percent were Protestants. Yet in Canada in 1976, 47.3 percent of the population was Catholic and 43.4 percent Protestant. Thus, Catholics are overrepresented among the winners. Two interpretations can be given of this fact. First, the Catholic Church has tended to be less disapproving of gambling than the Protestant churches,[45] and one may thus expect that people belonging to the former will gamble more than those belonging to the latter. (Among the winners, 62.3 percent of the Catholics and 50 percent of the Protestants stated that their religion was either "very important" or "important" to them.)[46]

The second interpretation of the nonproportional participation according to religion is linked to the previous information on Francophones and non-Francophones. Because the overwhelming majority of Francophones are Roman Catholics and Francophones are disproportionately represented among the winners, one would expect that Catholics would be overrepresented in the sample. However, there are more Catholic winners in the sample (sixty-one) than there are Francophones (forty-five). Because in Canada Catholics have lower average incomes than other religious groups, one could predict that they tend to spend relatively more on lottery tickets and thus are disproportionately represented among the winners.[47] There are not enough data to be able to say which interpretation (the religious one or the one based on the Catholics' lower wealth) has greater predictive power.

This same survey reveals that two regions – the Maritime Provinces and Quebec – that had relatively lower incomes were overrepresented among the winners. Among the million-dollar single winners, 50 percent were residents of Quebec, whose proportion of the 1976 population was only 27 percent.

The Maritime Provinces were the residence of 40.5 percent of the winners whose residence was neither Quebec nor Ontario, whereas their population represented only 25.6 percent of the Canadian population outside Quebec and Ontario.[48]

Statistical Analysis: Correcting Its Pitfalls

Detailed data on lottery-buying patterns are available in Canada. We hoped that with their help we could carry out the best comparison between predictions and facts. A closer examination of the data reveals, however, that we were a bit too optimistic.

Detailed data are indeed available, but they turn out to be quite inaccurate, which has to do with the way people answer questions about gambling patterns and that nobody has bothered to double-check. With an appropriate, though unusual, statistical procedure, we did a reasonable correction and examination, which we explain subsequently, before getting to the findings.

Two samples were at our disposition. One is based on a study commissioned by Loto-Québec in 1980. A random sample of 2,015 Quebecers were interviewed on their spending patterns in several types of lotteries, on their socioeconomic characteristics, and on their attitudes toward lotteries and gambling in general. When analyzing this sample, we considered only spending on lotteries that had a relatively large prize (C$50,000 and up – these were the 1980s). We also had to eliminate some of the observations because of missing variables and were thus left with only 851 usable observations.

The second sample is based on a survey of expenditures of 10,937 Canadian families made by Statistics Canada in 1982, where one of the items on the list was spending on lotteries. Although this data set seemed at first sight impressive, we soon discovered that it has a number of problems. First, no distinction is made between expenditures on lotteries that offer a relatively large prize and ones that do not. But this is the least of the problems. We found that if one adds up the sums people said they spent on lotteries (using the appropriate statistical procedure), one comes up with C$47.3 million for the Atlantic Provinces, C$264 million for Quebec, C$308 million for Ontario, and C$137 million for western Canada.[49]

If people's answers were in the ballpark, added up, the total amount people declared they spent on lotteries should more or less equal the respective provincial lotteries' revenues (because each has a local monopoly). But they were off the mark by 35 percent in western Canada, 39.2 percent in Ontario,

40 percent in the Atlantic Provinces, and 49 percent in Quebec. Although some of the differences can be explained by the fact that foreigners too buy tickets, they contribute only 10 percent of the revenues.[50] Thus, there is a large unexplained discrepancy between what Canadians say they do and what they actually do, at least as concerns their gambling expenditures, which Statistics Canada did not notice.

The discrepancy may be explained in several ways. One explanation is that people simply do not remember well how much they spent during the year, because the sums they spend are relatively small. To compound the effect, older people gamble relatively more and may have less reliable memories. But this explanation is insufficient: it could as well produce overestimation as underestimation.

Another explanation might be that people do not think about including the small winnings that they rebet on lotteries as part of the income spent on them.[51] Depending on the lottery, 16 to 24 percent of revenues is redistributed in the form of prizes of less than C\$100 (between 11 and 17 percent is redistributed in the form of prizes of under C\$10). Suppose that one wins such a prize and decides to spend part or all of it on lotteries in addition to the planned weekly expenditure on lottery tickets. When asked about total expenditure at the end of the year, people answer approximately by multiplying the planned weekly amount by fifty-two and forgetting to declare the small winnings. In this case, underdeclaration by the relatively poor should result, because if the poor spend disproportionately, they are the ones who win, disproportionately, the small prizes.

Yet another explanation for the underdeclaration may be that people do not tell the truth about their spending on lotteries. Such spending is open to condemnation, and some spending is on betting that is illegal (as is the case with an estimated \$93 billion on sports betting in 2006 in the United States).[52] This would not be the first time that, for these or other reasons, people have not made accurate declarations about their expenditures on games of chance. McKibbin remarked that in 1895 Henry Higgs, a pioneer investigator of people's expenditure patterns, noted that his efforts to collect data gained ground very slowly, because "many people talk about it as being a stomach policy of the bourgeoisie, whereby the bad management of the working classes should be demonstrated."[53] Considering the condemnations of gambling, this should not come as a surprise.

Thus, although Higgs provided data on housing, food, and clothing, there were no data about "pleasures." Indeed, Higgs's American publisher commented that it was strange that he "made no reference to any allowance in . . . budgets for amusement expenditure. The budget of an American work-man of the same class would assuredly include a regular weekly outlay for amusement."[54] McKibbin adds that the budget of British workers would also include such an allowance, even if, for the reason mentioned previously, the category of amusement was not included in the statistical data.

The compilers of a family expenditure survey for the year 1964 report what Statistics Canada does not: when families are asked to detail personal expenditures, they understate the expenditure on items about which they feel guilty: tobacco, alcohol, and gambling.[55] Thus, it is useful to emphasize that one should not expect too much from the statistical results, no matter how sophisticated the method used, on controversial topics in particular, unless one corrects for such problems.[56]

Once we corrected for the biases (by introducing constraints from lottery revenues to reflect the correct amounts spent), both the Loto-Québec and the Statistics Canada data led to results that, on the whole, seem consistent with the picture drawn until now. There are no surprises: the poor, the older, and those who fall behind play more, and the upwardly mobile play less.[57] In brief, the results fail to reject the view that these people consider gambling on games with large prizes as part of their allocation of portfolio over their lifetime. Readers interested in the statistical methods we came up with to correct for inconsistencies between declared spending and total revenues of lotteries, a double check that, as far as we know, nobody else has done, will find them in the statistical appendix (Appendix 3) at the end of the book.

Are Gamblers Reckless or Criminals?

Arbiters of morals and some social scientists have had rather negative atti-tudes toward gamblers in general, not only lottery players, arguing that they overestimate their chances, are unstable, and destroy their family life, and so they recommend outlawing all forms of gambling. There is no evidence whatsoever to support any of these views.

First, the previously quoted British Royal Commission on gambling con-cluded that gamblers were as aware as nongamblers of the unprofitable nature of gambling, in the sense of most probable outcome, and did not overestimate the chances of winning. In fact, as is shown in later chapters, even in the eighteenth and nineteenth century, information about proba-bility distributions of winning prizes was widely disseminated, and buyers requested them.

Second, although no distinction has been made between gamblers playing only lotteries and those who play other games of chance, the following information is revealing. According to the U.S. government's report *Gambling in America*, the following leisure activities characterize gamblers: they watch somewhat less television than nongamblers, read more newspapers and magazines, and read about as many books. Gamblers devote more time to opera, lectures, museums, nightclubs, dancing, movies, theater, and active sports. They also socialize more with friends and relatives and participate more in community activities. The few things that they spend much less time on include home improvements, gardening, knitting, sewing, and, yes, going to church.[58] These do not seem to be mortal sins.

In their book *Gambling, Work and Leisure* (1976), Downes and his cowriters provide little evidence to support the view that the majority of gamblers spend their money recklessly, whether money laid out on stakes or money earned from winnings. The facts are that the vast majority budget their expenditures and most gamblers use any large winning thriftily and sensibly,[59] often spending it on home-centered items.[60] Devereux too noted that, in more stable working-class neighborhoods, gambling takes the form of disciplined petty gambling.[61]

In betting on horse races, small wins are rebet more often than large ones; rebetting is largely confined to regular bettors, although even among the latter group three times as many save their winnings or spend them on household goods as those who rebet them.[62]

A similar picture emerges from Newman's examination of British evidence. Two-thirds of adult Britons gamble regularly, some more and others less. Manual wage earners, as already noted, predominate, especially among those who play more frequently. But Newman concludes that their "self restraint, exercised in the interest of prolonged participation, reduces their proportionate losses, enabling them to recoup a larger proportion of their stakes," and adds that gamblers have greater budget awareness than nongamblers.[63] He also notes that these regular gamblers are tough minded; they emphasize virtues of self-interest, personal effort, and independence; and they are suspicious of strangers, of outsiders, and in particular of government bureaucracies, displaying a pronounced hostility toward the open-handedness of the welfare state.[64]

Swedish surveys paint similar pictures. Gamblers and nongamblers discharged their familial, occupational, and social duties in a similar fashion. Gambling did not interfere with attempts to advance through conventional channels of social mobility; rather, it seemed to provide an additional strategy that served this goal. When gamblers and nongamblers were compared, neither their intention to establish businesses nor their participation rates in training to improve their jobs differed. Nor was any relationship found between gambling and crime, marital instability, or the degree of participation in community activities. On the contrary, gamblers participated in adult education courses more than nongamblers (41 percent of gamblers versus 33 percent of nongamblers in the same age group).[65]

Igor Kusyszyn found five psychological studies done since 1928 comparing people who gambled with those who did not. The studies reached the same conclusion: the differences were insignificant. Kusyszyn did his own study (in collaboration with Roxana Rutter) in 1978, comparing thirty-five heavy gamblers, forty-two who gambled less, nineteen nongamblers, and twenty-four lottery players. They not only found heavy gamblers to be "as psychologically healthy as the non-gamblers" but also found that light gambling did not lead to more intense gambling (the light gamblers had been playing for fifteen years on average).[66] Thus, their conclusion was similar to that of Weinstein and Deitch: light gambling is not a stepping-stone to heavy gambling. The majority of lottery players persist in their habit of betting small amounts.[67]

The Royal Commission on gambling in the United Kingdom also found that "generally speaking, the average expenditure on gambling must be considerably less than the average expenditure on other indulgences such as alcoholic liquor or tobacco." "The great majority of those who take part in gambling do not spend money on it recklessly and without regard to the effect of their expenditure on the standard of living of themselves and their families." "We find no support for the belief that gambling, provided that it is kept within reasonable bounds, does serious harm either to the character of those who take part in it or to their family circle and the community generally."[68] The report also concluded that "whatever the extent of gambling in the country, we have been unable to find any conclusive evidence to support the view that it interferes seriously with production. . . . The conclusion we have reached on the whole from the evidence, is that gambling is of no significance as a direct cause of serious crime, and of little importance as a direct cause of minor offences of dishonesty."[69]

This study thus reached the same conclusions as those drawn in Britain at the beginning of the century, discussed in the previous chapter:[70] most of the appalling poverty was due to unemployment, family size, bad health, low wages, and lack of access to credit. Gambling and drinking were responsible for much less significant secondary poverty and were "themselves often the outcome of the adverse conditions under which too many of the working classes live." McKibbin too, in the previously mentioned study of working-class gambling in Britain between 1880 and 1939, concluded that even gambling on all games of chance lumped together made few demands on the standards of living of those who practiced it. A massive, 111-page 1999 U.S. Department of Treasury study summarizing all the studies examining the relationship between gambling and bankruptcy reached similar conclusions, and did not find evidence that gambling brought about increased bankruptcies (casting doubt on what defines a gambling addiction).[71]

In Sweden, England, Ireland, Gibraltar, and Norway there was no evidence that gambling and crime are related. Nor was such evidence found in the United States, where the myth that gamblers are criminals seems to prevail. The evidence is that the American bettor is not involved in criminal acts other than the placing of the illegal bet itself.[72]

Cornish summarizes additional similar evidence. In England a 1951 study carried out by the principal medical officer in Wakefield's prison showed that out of eight hundred consecutive admissions examined in 1948, in only 2 percent of cases was gambling "a factor in the offender's downfall." Even among this 2 percent, gambling was considered merely one aspect of a "generally slack and dissolute life," and in only seven cases was betting a significant factor.[73] Similar studies of criminal populations have been carried out more recently. Sewell (1972) found, also in England, that the frequency of gambling for a sample of short-term prisoners at Pentonville was not really different from that of comparable groups from national samples, such as those provided in Gallup's (1972) and Borill's (1975) surveys. Of course, if one examines the relationship between crime and gambling when gambling is outlawed, the results are tautological (we shall say more about the link between prohibitions and crime in later chapters).

The Swedish experience is revealing. When gambling was outlawed (up to 1930), Swedes gambled on English soccer games, thereby smuggling substantial amounts of Swedish currency from the country. But once gambling was legalized, the criminal elements of smuggling and gambling disappeared. Similar evidence exists for every country, as is shown in Chapter 7, where we discuss the impact of prohibitions. A final note on crime and gambling, before we summarize the findings: that crime increases when suddenly a city legalizes gambling and attracts millions of tourists, as happened in Atlantic City, for example, is hardly surprising and has nothing to do with gambling. It is easier to commit crimes when there is a large increase in transient population. Indeed, when the number of crimes is adjusted for the number of tourists in cities, the link between gambling establishments and crimes disappears.[74]

Briefly, the picture of the typical lottery player that emerges from all the evidence presented up to this point is close to the description reported by Campbell:

He is . . . earning between five and ten thousand dollars a year. He worked regularly, steadily, dependably, wearing a blue or a white collar. Yet the frontiers of his career expectations have been fixed since he reached the age of 35, when he found that he had too many obligations, too much family, and too few skills to match opportunities with expectations.[75]

Gambling allows people to bet on a possible – not the most probable – outcome and sustain hope, however short-lived, from one week to the next for a better life. What alternative financial instrument does anyone past fit have to keep this opportunity open? For $1, the price of giving up a drink, people pay for that chance of one in a few millions that they drew the right numbers in the probability distribution. Abstaining from buying tickets and spending the few dollars on a drink, a movie, or a T-shirt will not change anything. People just preserve capital. The lottery prize, though, may bring about the significant change that some dream about.

Rich people's behavior is not different, but their gambles do take a different shape and form. Rich people invest in sophisticated financial instruments that similarly allow them to preserve capital and gamble with only a small fraction of their money. McConnell and Schwartz (1993) summarize the way Lee Cole, the options marketing manager at Merrill Lynch, came up with the new financial instrument LYON, liquid yield option note. He noticed that retail customers who were holding large sums in accounts invested in short-term government securities (CMA accounts), which had little interest rate risk, virtually no default risk, and made few equity investments, but were buying with a small fraction of their money calls on common stocks. He noticed that the amounts were limited roughly to the interest earned on the CMA accounts.

Cole's inference was that investors were willing to risk all or a fraction of this interest income in the options market – so long as the principal remained intact. With his introduction of the LYON, corporations could tap a new segment of lenders and lower capital costs by roughly replicating the returns from a combined CMA and option account. The LYON turned out to be one of Merrill's highly successful products, raising $11.7 billion between 1985 and 1991. The popularity of the so-called principal-protected notes today, each with its special structure, should not come as a surprise: an aging population, (and aging lottery players) wants to preserve capital and bet only what it can afford to lose.[76] As Mark Twain once observed, the rich are not really different: they only have more money. Instead of allocating a small fraction of their wealth to playing lotteries, the rich can allocate a similar fraction and play the options and derivative markets.

As we shall see in later chapters, the U.K. government and banks around the world noticed the same behavior pattern among segments of the population as Lee Cole noticed for Merrill Lynch's richer clients. These segments of people wanted to save – but also to gamble with a fraction of their money. As a result, the U.K. government offers the extremely popular premium savings bonds, where people relinquish some basis points for the right to regularly take part in lotteries. Banks around the world offer equally popular savings accounts with similar characteristics, only instead of a lottery, they allow account holders to bet on sport events.

What Do Winners Do with the Money?

Is it true, as many writers have claimed, that winners of big prizes waste their money, don't work, gamble more, abandon their families, and generally go to the dogs? The answer is no.

The facts, once again, confirm the boring, stable image of these small-scale lottery players. For example, Kaplan has done several studies.[77] Although in the first one (based on interviews with one hundred winners), he agreed with the critics of lotteries and concluded that, indeed, the winners stopped working, in the later more precise and reflective study, he gives a very different interpretation of the winners' actions. The more recent research is based on information about 576 winners in the United States who won prizes of $50,000 and more. Of the sample, 25 percent won $1 million or more, 29 percent won between $200,000 and $1 million, 38 percent won between $100,000 and $199,999, and 8 percent won between $50,000 and $100,000.

The average age of the winners was fifty-four: 64 percent were fifty or older, 16 percent were between forty and forty-nine, and only 20 percent were under the age of forty. Thus, it is not surprising that the majority of those who won large prizes either retired early or quit their jobs. What would one expect from people fifty-four years old or older who suddenly become rich and who have worked hard all their lives? If they stop working at this age, after a long life of hard work, does that imply anything about their work ethic? Not really.

The following quotes from winners are typical and provide us with a flavor normally hidden by dry statistics. A fifty-seven-year-old clerk in the New York subway system who won $3.5 million said, "I was able to retire from my job after 31 years. My wife was able to quit her job and stay home to raise our daughter. We were able to travel whenever we want to. We were able to buy a co-op, which before we could not afford." Another winner said: "Since we have raised *eight* children and educated them in Catholic schools in the amount of 112 years tuition paid, it was a help to be able to pay without depriving ourselves for years as we did . . . We feel very secure that we can travel more, and have helped our family." Yet another winner said, "My husband retired in 1981, as he had cancer surgery in 1978 and we wanted to enjoy the remaining years of the income. The end of this year, we expect to turn our home to the ones left at home, travel for six month – which we could never have done." A sixty-year-old woman from Massachusetts said, "A year after I won the money, my sister had an operation and had a year to live. I was able to retire and care for her," and a sixty-eight-year-old winner said "winning the lottery was a Godsend for us. My husband was sick for two years . . . and passed away this year. I had to close . . . my shop and make bedrooms for my mother and sister-in-law." In 2006 the New York Lottery produced one hundred millionaires. The last one, Winston Barnett, fits the preceding profile of winners' characteristics like a glove. He is a fifty-seven year old electrician, married, with two children in their twenties. He announced that he would spend part of the prize to buy a house, another part to escape the winter blues in Florida, and part to help his kids play their college debt.[78]

These answers all come from winners of an age where they can hardly be expected to launch new careers. In terms of education, 45 percent of winners were only high school graduates and another 25 percent had not reached high school graduation. The majority of the winners were laborers who had put in long hours of work for years. Their retirement has nothing to do with the erosion of a work ethic. Their retirement should not be interpreted as a sign that this group of players was in any way predisposed toward unstable participation in the labor force, as many observers have reasoned without ever bothering to just check the ages of winners.

At the time they won, these people had worked at their jobs an average of thirteen years, and 25 percent of the winners had worked for twenty years or more. (In contrast, the American labor force as a whole has job tenure of an average of four years.) This is a sign of stability, but it can also be interpreted as a block to career opportunities, with no chance to raise one's income significantly. A worker does not have much salary-negotiating power after so many years at a relatively low-paying job. Kaplan also found, as one would expect, that the higher were a winner's education and income, the more likely it was for him or her to continue to work.

What did the winners do with their money and the leisure it bought? Eighteen percent spent more time to their family and children, 32 percent worked more on their houses (as one would expect, a large percentage of winners bought a house, made improvements to the one they owned, or bought furniture), 5 percent did more volunteer work, 4 percent entered graduate studies, and 32 percent devoted themselves to various leisure activities.

Indeed, after reviewing this evidence, Kaplan also calls into question the popular myth about marriages and family lives being destroyed after winning. In fact, winning seems to stabilize marriages and families. Although there were few divorces among respondents, they admitted that their home lives were boring and bad before they won (winning, in fact, "stabilized" husbands and wives and enabled them to live more happily apart). But it is the stronger ties reflected in the previous quotes from winners that were typical. And what else did the winners do with their money? As noted, they spent it on housing and travel – but less on gambling.[79]

What do younger people do when they win a large windfall? We found only one study from which we can infer an answer to this question. Thomas Lindh and Henry Ohlsson, in an article titled "Self-Employment and Windfall Gains: Evidence from the Swedish Lottery," found that when people receive windfall gains in the form of lottery winnings and inheritances, they are more likely to become self-employed.[80]

In conclusion, none of the evidence we have presented so far lends the slightest support to explain why gamblers, of large prizes in particular, are often condemned. Indeed, Rubner has already noted that

gambling, particularly in Britain, is clouded by hypocrisy, cowardice and sanctimoniousness . . . Like Anthony Crosland [a once well-known British politician], I, too have come across the mixture of Puritanism and paternalism so curiously common among the British intelligentsia, which is exemplified in the "pubs, pools and prostitutes" argument. It combines a belief in the moral virtues of abstinence with the conviction that the working class wastes all its surplus income on alcohol, tobacco and gambling, if not actually women. Crosland defiantly says this himself: "If I suddenly had a large increase in income, I have no doubt that I should spend a large part on it on smoking, eating, drinking, gambling, and similar deplorable recreations; and I decline to debase myself on that account.[81]

It is the wrongheaded extrapolation of the relatively fortunate – their inability to enter into the minds of the relatively poor or of those who fall behind – that explains, in part, their bias toward this unique financial market and the unique financial instruments it offers. The less fortunate do not think at all in these terms when they buy lottery tickets. They think about educating their children, buying a house, and buying household products; and when they win the big prize, this is indeed what they do.

Recall winners' articulation of the benefits of winning quoted previously and contrast them with the benefits perceived by Crosland. The latter captures the view from above, the way some of the fortunate may think: when they already have their cottage, when they have already provided for their children's education, for their retirement, for their vacations – then, indeed, what will they do with still more money? The fortunate may attribute the negative effects of being bestowed with sudden, large unearned income when they are already accustomed to a comfortable life. They know how difficult it is to raise kids who grow up in affluence, educating them to be as hard-working and entrepreneurial as perhaps their parents and ancestors were.

But such a situation should not be confused with that of the less fortunate, who can better appreciate the value of money and decide to husband sudden winnings for themselves and to give better chances to their kids.

This contrast is illuminating for another reason. Receiving a sudden $1,000,000 inheritance for someone who is twenty, grew up in a middle-class home, and expects an annual income of $100,000 or more is not bad. But this sum is insufficient as a nest egg for one's lifetime, and it may be spent recklessly. Devereux described the following case: "A college student inherited a modest fortune of $250,000 on his twenty-first birthday, and set about quite deliberately to spend it all within a year. He rationalized . . . that the fortune was too trivial to live on permanently, but that its presence would . . . deflate his motivational drives toward academics and pecuniary success, would 'ruin his character' and spoil his life. So he took a year off, with a few college friends, and 'blew the works' in riotous living."[82] Although we could find no systematic evidence showing how typical such behavior is perhaps most parents should include better constraints in their wills about how their children can spend the money they inherit.[83]

Compulsive Gamblers: An Aside

As the data clearly show, compulsive gamblers are a tiny fraction of the gambling population – the majority of those who gamble do so in hopes of becoming richer – and those who commit crimes are an even smaller fraction of this subgroup.[84]

Yet, obviously, compulsive gamblers are the ones who capture the writers', journalists', and filmmakers' attention. Ashton's 1898 *History of Gambling in England*, Chafetz's 1960 *Play the Devil: A History of Gambling in the United States*, and Sullivan's 1972 *By Chance a Winner* are full of stories about compulsive gamblers. Dostoyevsky's *The Gambler* is about a man who left his mark on people's imagination. And movies, such as *The Gambler* (1974), *Lost in America* (1985), and *Atlantic City* (1980), to name just a few, present gamblers as losers, somewhat at the margins of society, even if some succeed in better managing their lives at the end.[85]

However, such histories can hardly be viewed as attempts to understand gambling. The authors have chosen interesting stories, and such stories are not provided by the lives of moderate, average, older people who go on their weekly trip to Atlantic City to eat cheap cucumbers, but rather by the lives of those who in one way or another have deviated from the norm, who have had volatile lives.

Although Dostoyevsky's book certainly captures one side of human nature, his own life reveals that the picture is more complex and not necessarily consistent with the moral of the book. His brother's death, the demise of the review he was editing, and his passion for gambling left Dostoyevsky bankrupt. Nevertheless, he immediately and voluntarily assumed the care of his brother's family. To cope with these burdens, Dostoyevsky did not commit crimes but instead bet on entrepreneurial ventures. He worked feverishly, and his most famous works, *Crime and Punishment* (1866), *The Gambler* (1867), *The Idiot* (1868), and *The Possessed* (1872), were, according to Nabokov, written under the constant stress of having to pay his gambling debts.[86] Whereas people know of the gambler in his book, a weak man who promises every evening to abandon his addiction but cannot, few know about Dostoyevsky, the gambler. Even fewer know that once he married his stenographer, Anna Snitkina, in 1867, she took control of the finances. He had a happy marriage and children, and by 1871 he stopped gambling. It was also the end of his creative period. There have been plenty of adaptations of Dostoyevsky's novels but we do not expect that any movie will be made showing him overcoming the problem and settling into calm domesticity. Calm domesticity does not sell newspapers or movies – or anything. Routine does not sell. The vast majority of people try to escape it; they do not want to pay to relive it in a movie theater.

We noted that official statistics on gambling are largely off the mark, not only because statistics bureaus do not seem to double check data, but also because many people gamble illegally. As noted in this chapter, analysts and law-enforcement officials put sports betting alone in the $96 billion range in 2006, only $3 billion of which is offered legally in Nevada, where people must be physically present to wager.

But the problems with interpreting numbers concerning betting must pale in comparison to those with interpreting numbers thrown around with respect to pathological gamblers, problem gamblers, and at-risk gamblers. The American Psychiatric Association introduced the term "pathological gambler" back in 1980, and since then each subsequent edition changed the diagnostic criteria for this definition, which, considering the vagueness of the association's definitions and methods of classification to start with, should not come as a surprise. At present there are ten criteria. In order to diagnose a person as a pathological gambler, an "appropriately qualified and experienced clinician" must determine that a patient meets five or more of the following ten indicators:[87]

1. Preoccupied with gambling
2. Needs to gamble with increasing amounts of money in order to achieve the desired excitement
3. Restless and irritable when attempting to cut down on or stop gambling
4. Sees gambling as a way to escape problems
5. After losing money gambling, returns to chase losses
6. Lies to family members and therapists
7. Has made repeated, unsuccessful efforts to control, cut back on, or stop gambling
8. Committed illegal acts to finance gambling
9. Has jeopardized or lost a significant relationship, job, or educational or career opportunity to finance gambling
10. Relies on others to provide money to relieve a desperate financial situation caused by gambling

Because gambling is about money, unless someone declares bankruptcy, or steals to cover his or her bankruptcy, it is hard to know what the meaning of any of these "pathology" indicators means. If the indicators have not lead to bankruptcy or theft, then it seems that the gambler disciplined himself or herself in one way or another.[88] The definitions of problem gambling and at-risk gambler are open to even more question, because the clinician would use less than five criteria to make that determination. The numbers associated with addiction suggest scientific precision. But, as can be inferred from the preceding criteria, they are anything but.

The media, by putting the unusual – and rare – stories of addicted gamblers on their front pages, bias perceptions. Stories of delusional gamblers are fascinating and memorable – though exceptional. In a society often recognized as a money culture, stories about making or losing money fast are sensationalized and sell more papers than does yet one more story about a person ending up in jail for drunk driving, a drug bust, or a young woman suffering from bulimia. And, of course, stories about a writer marrying his secretary, having kids, and living a normal life, and then hardly writing anything of interest anymore, do not sell any newspapers either.

There will always be isolated tragedies. Modern media's distribution capabilities would suggest that rather than compulsive gambling being an exceptional event, it represents a problem of epidemic proportions that poses a threat and requires significant government intervention. Yet even with over-regulation (i.e., prohibition) and billions spent on enforcement, no society entirely eliminates the adverse effects of living. We are forgetting a wise eighteenth-century writer, John Butler, who observed that "probability is the very guide of life."

We do not doubt that compulsive gamblers impose a cost on their families, and thus on society. But can their existence as a tiny minority be used as an argument against lotteries and gambling? There are compulsive eaters, compulsive drinkers, compulsive workers, reckless drivers, compulsive watchers of television, and compulsive womanizers. Their lives and their families' lives may be as miserable as those of the compulsive gamblers, and they too impose a cost on society. But prohibitions on drinking in the West are rare by now (though they prevail in Islamic countries).

And whereas eating, drinking, working, and watching television are activities recommended in moderation, excesses are not legally forbidden, though obesity and smoking seem to be on the way to becoming not just pathologies, but new vices. But whereas the point where some of these behavior patterns lapse into danger zones is hard to pinpoint with precision, gambling excesses should be relatively easy, because they signal bankruptcy.[89] Anything short of that suggests that the gambler is spending within limits that he or she somehow manages, no matter how excessive the spending may seem to outsiders or even to family members.

Recent public debates have raised fears concerning the ease with which people, minors in particular, can become addicted to gambling online. First successfully tested software exists to prevent minors from accessing gambling sites (even CBS's bright inquisitors from *60 Minutes* could not find a flaw in it). True, one sixteen-year-old kid in the United Kingdom succeeded in stealing his parent's credit card and geting through to an online gambling site (though even he was caught quickly). But the problem in this case was theft, not a flaw in the software.

As for compulsive behavior, an argument could be made that controlling compulsive behavior online, using these tools, may be more successful than it is offline. In a windowless, land-based casino, where every marketing tool imaginable, including drinks and beautiful women, is used to keep gamblers at the table, there is nobody to tap gamblers on the shoulder to suggest that they should call it a day. Available software keeps track not only of how much the player spent, but also of how much the player will spend if he or she continues to spend at such a rate. If the player does not trust him- or herself, the software can be a reminder and help set limits. Slot machines today have a feature allowing players to keep track of both their spending and the odds of winning "the big one." The machines also tells players how much they will spend on each game if they make a particular choice, and inform them of the rate at which they spend per minute and per hour of play. Software with similar performance can be downloaded too.

Conclusion

The category of gamblers discussed in this chapter mainly are either poor people or people who fell on hard times and want to become rich by allocating a small fraction of their portfolio to games in which they have a chance to win large prizes.[90] These gamblers are not criminals, they do not spend recklessly on games, they do not seem to differ significantly from nongamblers in their leisure activities, and they do not seem to be ignorant of their small chance to win big prizes. (How can they be when articles on the winners of big prizes are front-page material and always point out the tiny probability of winning?) These facts, then, cannot explain the condemnation of gambling, nor can it be explained by the tiny minority of compulsive gamblers. Consider too that heavy drinking, though it has consequences similar to heavy gambling, is not condemned today in such severe terms. Few recommend banning all alcohol consumption because of a small percentage of heavy drinkers.

In the previous chapters we showed that religious and other objections to gambling have been misguided and that objections to gambling as entertainment had no foundations. Here, we showed that condemnations of gamblers do not hold up to closer scrutiny. Gambling on lotteries or games to win a large prize is a unique financial instrument. The next chapters show that, indeed, one can best understand many nonentertainment-related features of gambling as part of the financial market, the roles it has played in government finance in particular. The evidence and sequence of events will also show what happens when people's risk-taking and gambling are misunderstood, leading to prohibitions! Governments and central banks bring about a wide range of unintended consequences.

*When I was young, people called me a gambler. As the scale of my operations
increased I became known as a speculator. Now I am called a banker. But I have been
doing the same thing all the time.*
Sir Ernest Cassel, private banker to Edward VII

FOUR

Betting on Futures and Creating Prices

Reuven Brenner

*Which shows how conventional wisdom about futures markets was often wrong, and
the relationship between these markets and gambling and insurance.*

To gamble.
To bet.
To speculate.
To invest.

All these terms and other phrases ("to take a chance," "to challenge luck,"
or "to take risks") have been used when people put money in stocks, futures
markets, and derivatives, or have bought and sold land, houses, or other
tangible assets. As we saw previously, both England and the United States
passed at various times in their histories laws that made contracts to wager
unenforceable. The problem that often came up both before the courts
and in public policy debates was how to distinguish between contracts that
allocated risks and rewards legitimately in productive sectors and gambling
or wagering contracts.

This chapter shows that the source of the confusion – still with us today,
even in the United States and the United Kingdom, sophisticated financial
markets notwithstanding – is the false idea that the "real" economy can be
divorced from the financial, betting one, and still function well. This idea
permeates most societies to this day – bringing about restrictions on risk-
taking and financial markets that make them function less well and allow
the impacts of mistaken decisions to compound.

The debate about gambling was also part of the broader view of managing
risk in society, which has led to harmful laws and regulations to this day.
During the nineteenth and twentieth centuries courts distinguished among
gambling, insurance, and futures markets; although we have a better understanding of the latter two in parts of the world, the same cannot be said

about gambling. Innovations in telecommunications in the United States played a role in bringing about a better understanding of futures markets. We believe that the Internet will now play this role, and eventually help to eliminate misunderstanding surrounding gambling, because the popularity of gambling and betting on events online will spread and create an ever-increasing range of futures markets. Tradesports.com is one example of this trend.

False Ideas: Bad Laws, Bad Policies

It is embarrassingly easy to debunk ideas about the sterility of money, usury laws, and Ponzi-scheme accusations against financial markets. Never mind the thousands of tomes written about these topics; we shall devote just a few paragraphs to them.[1]

As the previous chapters showed, it is easy to understand why, when a population was small and dispersed, there could be little specialization and no formal insurance (because the law of large numbers did not apply). Families and tribes provided insurance, enforced by custom, tradition, and a variety of institutions.[2] Anthropologists have labeled these societies as "traditional" because each generation lived as the preceding one did.

As the population and its density and mobility grew, people specialized, built statistical tables, entered into complex contracts drawing on probability distributions, created new institutions, and eventually standardized contracts to establish markets for them. The contracts, backed by a variety of institutions, came to substitute for the trust and implicit contracts that both families and small immobile tribes offered before. Yet intellectuals' debates have remained firmly rooted in vocabularies of the past, with utter misunderstanding of interest rates, pricing risks, and the essence of financial contracts. Some Islamic countries ban charging interest to this day, though they have ways to design financial contracts without calling the payments "interest." Recall that it was just in the 1970s, when the United States experienced high inflation, that usury laws came into effect, with state laws controlling interest rates in consumer credit contracts and fixing interest rate ceilings. It has only been since the early 1980s that state legislatures relaxed statutory controls on consumer credit and finally realized what they should have known all along: controls only make it more difficult for newcomers – people with shorter credit histories – to have access to credit (at higher interest).[3]

Why have such ideas that limit the democratization of capital markets had such long lives, impeding the markets to this day? The answer is, once again, simple, in line with the findings in the previous chapters, and linked to gambling.

Through which channels can capital be allocated in any society, at any time? There are just these four channels:[4]

1. Governments, which raise taxes (or sell natural resources they own) and then distribute the money
2. Family, which saves and passes on money to others in various shapes and forms (e.g., giving to voluntary organizations, inheritance)
3. Crime, which involves taking money by force and redistributing it
4. Capital markets

When capital markets are absent, capital is distributed only through the other three channels, though, as the next chapter shows, people come up with ways to access capital that we do not consider today part of capital markets. For most of world history and in most countries to this day, these three channels – the first and second in particular – have dominated. (In some countries, though, it is difficult to distinguish the government channel from the criminal one).[5] But let us compare here just the government and the capital markets as financial matchmakers.

The problem that both institutions solve is that they match people with capital and make all sides to a transaction accountable. But who the matchmakers are matters, and the degree of accountability is different in government from that in competitive capital markets. As the latter developed, bureaucracies became threatened as it became evident that financial intermediaries could better match people with capital and hold all sides accountable. If capital markets find ways to finance expeditions, explorations, and infrastructure, and are ready to finance anyone judged competent to start an enterprise (even the penniless, as banks did in Scotland during the eighteenth century[6]), there is less need for bureaucracies. It served government bureaucracies' interests to eliminate capital markets or to slow down their development by laws and decrees, and to finance an army of priests and so-called intellectuals to rationalize the restrictions.

Because developed capital markets also disperse power, there were plenty of other interests in spreading false ideas about capital markets.[7] Treatises written since biblical times that display abstract reasoning but utter ignorance of contracts and business risk, and affect laws and regulations to this day, are testimony to this basic conflict between controlling the flow of funds or permitting their dispersal. Gambling, linked to the process of pricing risks, was often the firing rod in this conflict.

How did the Romans put it when they saw odd things happening and looked for an explanation? *Cui prodest*? That means, "Who benefits?" Who indeed?

Back to Basics

One of Demosthenes' orations condemned with aristocratic contempt the manner in which the Greeks of his time insured marine cargo. The insurer advanced somewhat less than the value of the ship and its cargo, and received, when the voyage was successfully completed, a much larger sum.[8] Religious authorities scrutinized these contracts and their objections were similar to those raised toward derivatives and gambling today.

Jean Favier, a French historian, writes about the rise of commerce during the Middle Ages, emphasizing the risk of weather- and pirate-related dangers that vessels faced.[9] Entrepreneurs solved the problem in various ways. In Venice the merchants could opt either to use private ships without escort or to sail under the protection of the city-state's official vessels for a fee. Shipowners in Marseilles spread the risks by forming partnerships.[10] Favier's description of contractual solutions negotiated between Genoese merchants and financiers is particularly useful because it shows where commentators on financial markets got it all wrong.

In 1298, the merchant Benedetto Zaccaria wanted to ship thirty tons of alum from Aigues-Mortes to Bruges. Two Genoese financiers struck the following deal: Zaccaria sold the financiers the alum at an agreed-upon price, once the alum was loaded on the vessel. If the vessel arrived safely to Bruges, Zaccaria had to buy it back. If something went wrong and the ship did not reach the destination, the merchant owed nothing to the two financiers.

Would the transportation of alum have occurred if there were no people willing to finance it and bear the risks? Unlikely. Without the financial transaction, the real transaction would not have happened – unless, as in Venice, the alternative of the merchant paying a fee for state-owned official vessels existed. In other words, one needs either private financiers or government programs for business to be brought to life in the real economy. In the first case, the risk is allocated and priced on the basis of merchants' and financiers' ability to bear risk and their negotiating power. If the transaction took place under the auspices of government, as in Venice, we do not know how the transaction would have been priced or who would bear the risks. It makes no sense to separate the real from the financial – even if thousands of tomes say the contrary.

Daston (1987) notes that Pope Gregory IX's thirteenth-century decree *Naviganti* prohibited the most popular form of maritime insurance as usurious. This prohibition led jurists to discussions about the distinction between insurance and usury on the basis of risk. The decree also covered topics such as how to allocate gains obtained from labor and others that were perceived to have been obtained without labor. Zaccaria's Genoese transaction passed muster because it fit within the concept of *damnum emergens*, meaning that because there was a physical risk, there could be legitimate compensation. In fact, the deal was structured as a sale and repurchase contract to fit the ecclesiastical demands, even if the financiers were never in the alum business. They owned the alum only while it was on its way from one port to another, when they could not do anything with it. Although on paper the financiers were in the business of alum during the voyage, in practice they never were. They were in the business only because regulations required them to structure that facade.

If this same transaction were translated to the language of finance today, it might be called a loan with an option of default, a loan combined with a weather derivative, venture capital, or insurance. Calling it by these names, though, means that suppliers of capital were not interested in owning physical assets, but in the business only of pricing and properly allocating risks then and over time. These nontangible considerations, though, would not pass muster for centuries to come. The idea that people could buy and sell property rights to price ranges was condemned (what people to this day call speculation). And the fact that some would bet not on the most probable result but on other possibilities, such as tails in pricing distributions (what lottery buyers do too), is misunderstood to this day. Indeed, the idea that information about prices is property, that private companies rather than invisible hands can occasionally produce prices and have rights to them, appeared first in an opinion that U.S. Supreme Court Justice Oliver Wendell Holmes wrote for a 1905 case discussed later in this chapter.

With the expansion of commerce during the next three centuries, civil and canon lawyers used notions of risk to defend suspicious commercial practices. They had to prove that the risk was large enough but could be controlled and avoid suspicions of usury, but not so large and uncontrollable as to bring suspicions of gambling. By the mid-sixteenth century, it had become customary to argue that those who shared risks deserved a share of the profit as much as those who shared labor. Yet the aforementioned ideas about risk, usury, and suspicions of gambling continued to impose constraints not only on casinos but also on insurance companies and purely financial transactions.

As late as 1777 England passed usury legislation that made any loan for interest greater than 5 percent illegal unless it involved "genuine" risk. Such laws explain, in part, the initial reluctance of insurance companies to use probability theory and pricing based on known probability distributions, because "the quantification of risk seemed to presume too much certainty for the venture to be genuinely risky."[11]

Note too that usury laws, going back to the Bible, not only prevented ventures that existing companies might have wanted to pursue, but also prevented poorer ranks in society, with no credit history, from having access to credit and starting an entrepreneurial venture. Although the declared purpose of usury laws was to protect the poor, there are probably few laws that harmed them more. After all, those without credit history have to pay higher interest in one form or another when they want to start an entrepreneurial venture. Establishing credibility does not come free. With no access to credit, dreams stay dreams, the poor stay poor, and the establishment is not threatened. There is nothing that threatens established companies more than having hungry potential competitors with easier access to capital. They also weaken the standing of governmental or religious bureaucracies in managing the problems of the poor. For centuries labeling transactions as "usurious" or as "wagers" were ways to limit freedom to contract and allocate risks through financial instruments, and the advancement of the talented but lowborn.[12]

Navigating between the previously mentioned constraints, marine insurance developed and, according to Thomas (1971), had taken root in England by the mid-sixteenth century. Other types of enterprise linked with notions of risk fared less well. The 1570 Code of the Low Countries outlawed both gambling and life insurance, and put them in the same category: insuring the lives of people and "wagers . . . and similar inventions" were banned. All ordinances regulating insurance prior to 1681 that mention life insurance prohibit it. This was the case in Amsterdam (1598), Middleburg (1600), Rotterdam (1604), and Sweden.[13] Life insurance remained illegal in France until 1819.[14]

Daston shows that until the sixteenth and seventeenth centuries, the notion of probability was linked with gambling devices like dice and lotteries. Even the mathematicians who had developed probability theory up to the eighteenth century – Pierre Fermat, Jacob Bernoulli, and John Graunt (who built the first mortality table in his *Natural and Political Observations upon the Bills of Mortality*) among them – did not explain how probability applied to mortality. Wasn't death a matter of divine will? In fact, great mathematicians, such as Gottfried Leibniz, objected to applying probability distributions to human affairs because they held such a religious out-look. Indeed, the major objection to insurance, life insurance in particular, came from religious institutions. They viewed insurance as sacrilegious, and because it profited from the death of loved ones, as "a speculation repugnant to the law of God and man."[15]

In spite of these confusions and reservations, the insurance industry expanded rapidly in England between the sixteenth and eighteenth centuries. As we have noted, marine insurance was first prominent, although the law relating to arbitration of insurance disputes remained unsatisfactory (and merchants insured themselves by dividing both the ownership of the ship and the value of the transported goods among several individuals). The situation changed in the early eighteenth century with the development of Lloyd's Coffee House as a regular meeting place for underwriters and as the foundation of two substantial joint-stock companies devoted to marine insurance in 1720, the London Assurance and the Royal Exchange. Fire insurance first emerged in London in 1680, and the Amicable Society for mutual insurance of lives was established in 1706 (with a tontine-type arrangement). This was the only insurance company, from among fifty established between 1699 and 1720, that survived the crash following the South Sea bubble in 1720.[16]

How did people deal with misfortune during these centuries? When populations were smaller, more isolated, less mobile – when warfare, plagues, and disease were major sources of misfortune – family, kin, community charity, and religious institutions offered insurance. Magic and witchcraft offered additional "insurance" – though tolerated, socially sanctioned blackmail is perhaps a better way to describe actions based on such beliefs. These beliefs induced the relatively fortunate to redistribute wealth toward those falling behind, so as to insure themselves against evil eyes.[17] But, as Keith Thomas documents in his book on the decline of magic, "at a lower social level, the eighteenth century saw the launching of pioneer insurance schemes by industrial forms for their employees and the proliferation of working-class friendly societies. Nothing did more to reduce the sphere in which magical remedies were the only form of protection against misfortune."[18]

Before we continue examining the relationships among insurance, futures, and various gambling acts, let's take a small detour on another misinterpreted sequence of events in futures markets, the illuminating tulip-mania. We examine only the end of this seventeenth-century event here, the events of 1635–7. What happened in the tulip market between 1605 and 1635 we discuss in the next chapter, as the volatility displayed during these two distinct periods is not related.

The Tulipmania That Never Was: Part 1

A dramatic confirmation of both the misunderstanding surrounding gambling, future markets, and the impact of laws making gambling and futures contracts unenforceable is the famous tulipmania episode in the seventeenth-century Dutch Republic. People remember two things about tulipmania today: that fantastic prices were paid for tulip bulbs and that all ranks of society were caught up in frenzied speculation that led to a crash. Closer examination shows that this is not quite what happened.

Let's start with the broader picture. Tulip prices rose continuously between 1605 and 1635 (the next chapter will explain why). Futures markets developed for rare tulip bulbs, but a modest one developed for the common bulbs. The "mania" refers not only to the high prices paid for the exotically patterned, rare bulbs, but also to the two years when the price of common tulip bulbs went up and then crashed in 1637. The market for rare bulbs was not significantly affected – these bulbs remained scarce. Only in 1920 did researchers find the virus that brought about the spectacular patterns in these rare bulbs, which to this day can fetch into the $500,000 range.[19]

But the sudden increased demand for the common bulbs between 1635 and 1637 is not hard to explain. During these two years the plague devastated the republic. One-sixth of Amsterdam's population and one-third of Leiden's population were wiped out. If that wasn't enough, the Dutch also faced the prospect of Spanish invasion. Facing death and war, why wouldn't people gamble on tulips – or on anything for that matter?[20] When life suddenly is expected to be short, why live modestly with solid possessions?

It was during these two years that commoners, people of modest means and little if any understanding of financial markets and instruments, entered the tulip market.[21] Their entry is not surprising, and has nothing to do with greed or the madness of crowds. If people made money, they could have a bit more fun during the shortened lifetime they expected. And if they lost, the prospect of a short lifetime meant not too much added hardship. Or, perhaps, people expected that they might not have to pay their debts, as Dutch laws on debt arising from trading options were similar to English statutes concerning gambling debts and were not enforceable.

Why were these latter statutes passed and what was their impact? The Dutch, who had the world's first stock market in Amsterdam and the world's most sophisticated financial market, were preoccupied about finding solutions to guide investments to satisfy both those who demanded safety and those who wanted to take risks. The Dutch understood that growth was a consequence of risk-taking. But what type of risk-taking should be legitimate? Financial markets and many financial instruments were novelties at the time. How much credit and in what shape and form should it be advanced to buy these instruments? How much risk-taking was good? These questions preoccupy the Federal Reserve and regulators of financial markets to this day, as they preoccupied the Dutch authorities then.

In 1610 the Dutch passed an edict that prohibited trading in the wind, or trading shares the investors did not possess (a reminder of similar events that took place centuries later in the United States, as we shall see later in this chapter). Sales for future delivery were permitted only for investors who owned shares. Whereas futures for hedging were legal, the authorities condemned futures trading as immoral gambling, and the edict, renewed once in 1630 and again in 1636, precluded the civil enforcement of contracts.

However, as we will see in England and in Italy in the next chapter, futures trading and selling short thrived and were enforced privately. Traders trying to rely on the law were excluded from the bourse, and most traders honored their contracts. Only on rare occasions, as when facing bankruptcy, did some traders dishonor the contracts. Private enforcement worked before the plague- and war-induced brief 1637 bubble, and worked afterward. Christian Day (2004) describes the way the futures market in tulip bulbs worked in 1636, at the peak of the plague, as follows:

Traders met in groups called "colleges" in taverns. Buyers were required to pay 1/20 guilder per contact with a maximum of 3 guilders for each deal . . . Margins were not required for either party. Typical buyers didn't possess the cash until closing. Sellers didn't possess the bulbs. Neither party expected delivery on settlement. Payment of the amount between the contract price and settlement price was required. Contracts were not repriced according market fluctuations; there were no margin requirements to prompt compliance; commitments were to individuals rather than an exchange.

When tulip prices collapsed in February 1637, they were followed by a suspension of settlements for contracts. However, Day (2006) notes that growers proposed that contracts made before November 30, 1636, be executed and honored, whereas later contracts would give buyers the right to reject the contract upon payment of 10 percent of the sale price. Dutch authorities did not accept the proposal, and in April they outlawed futures contracts on terms that let professional growers keep both the bulbs and the gross amounts of money paid for them. Because bulbs might have been resold dozens of times, this was a fantastic windfall (although mostly not collectible, as traders were forced into bankruptcy because they owed money on bulbs they bought, but then could neither get the bulb nor collect money on bulbs they sold).

Although the courts did not uphold the contracts, the parties worked out settlements in private, through arbitration, and the brief frenzy and crash soon ended. The plague disappeared, the risk of Spanish invasion was over, the tulip markets returned to their normal state of affairs, and Amsterdam and the Dutch Republic returned to their status as "the miracle of the seventeenth century" – until England emerged to replace it a few decades later.[22] The quick return to normalcy happened without any regulatory procedures. If anything, the interventions mentioned earlier only aggravated the volatility in tulip prices during those few months. Briefly, the years 1635–7 do not illustrate any irrational bubble in futures markets: it seems a rational reaction when suddenly people fear that death is near. Some may take drugs and others may bet on getting rich quickly and try to enjoy more intensely the little time left. Magic against misfortunes can take many shapes and forms, and the 1635–7 tulip volatility was just one particular shape.

More on Insurance and Gambling

Legislation passed in England between 1764 and 1774 (the Gambling Act) made insurance contracts illegal as wagering agreements – unless the policyholder had an insurance interest in the contract.[23] The interest had to be in proportion to the amount insured otherwise the policy would be declared null and void. (One would identify such a requirement today as the principle of mitigating moral hazard).

At the same time, the biggest question preoccupying companies and the aforementioned societies offering insurance was of an actuarial nature. Nobody knew what the probability of sickness was or whether this was a valid notion to start with.[24] Only at the end of the eighteenth century did the British enact laws to determine premiums for life insurance and annuities using the Northampton Tables, which were based on records from that city providing information on the law of mortality. These numbers became standards for a century, although by 1820 they were known to be inaccurate and to misprice the premium (by putting life expectancy at birth at twenty-four rather than thirty). But for a century, the tables became the standard and the law.

At the same time that this legislation passed, the debate about insurance was dedicated to distinguishing sharply between insurance and gambling:

The extraordinary success of the Equitable [an insurance company] is the result not only of its exploitation of the mortality statistics and the mathematics of probability to fix premiums . . . but also of its creation of an image of life insurance diametrically opposed to that of gambling...Long-term life insurance was aimed at a growing middle-class of salaried professionals – clergymen, doctors, lawyers, skilled artisans – who were respectable but not of independent means. In a world where apparently even the clergymen could not count upon commercial charity, the sudden death of the provider could topple the family from the middling ranks of society to the very bottom. Such reversals of fortune were the proper fate of the gambler, not the good bourgeois.[25]

Briefly, insurance gained ground at the expense of both charity and beliefs in magic and, echoing Adam Smith, it came to be perceived as a "precise, scientific, and, at the same time practical form of that unconscious solidarity that unites men."[26] By the third decade of the nineteenth century, the divorce between insurance and gambling seemed final. Gambling was outlawed to a large extent, whereas insurance became a pillar of social order, guaranteeing that "a man who is rich today will not be poor tomorrow."[27]

Legal Confusions and Political Debates: Property Rights and Prices

Although there cannot be any formal or analytical distinction between regular business contracts with embedded options and speculative and wagering ones (as illustrated previously by the thirteenth-century maritime transaction), during the nineteenth century and to this day such contracts have received severe scrutiny. Occasionally the courts declared such contracts illegal and categorized them as gambling; elsewhere governments outlawed them, drawing on a combination of prejudices and misunderstanding, some of which prevail today too.

In 1896 the German government prohibited futures trading.[28] The Farmers' Party passed the law, claiming that speculation in agricultural commodities depressed prices. What were the consequences? Commercial experts at the time estimated that the prohibition kept the price of wheat in Germany at six to ten dollars less than where it would have been otherwise. This, according to them, led first to excessive exports. Afterward, the shortfall had to be made up by imports. Contrary to expectations, the farmers were worse off: the statute diminished their negotiating power relative to that of millers and traders, because they lost information upon which to base their decisions about the production of grain. In turn Berlin merchants lost power relative to that of the Berlin bureaucracy. For, with the tacit approval of members of the German government – nobody knows how much they were bribed to keep their eyes wide shut – some merchants speculated through agents in Liverpool, New York, and Chicago. On April 2, 1900, Germany abolished the law, and futures trading was relegalized.

In the United States, legitimizing futures markets took different twists and turns. The debate took place not only in the media but also before the court, where the Chicago Board of Trade, Western Union, and bucket shops locked horns for some twenty-five years. A 1905 decision recognizing the Board of Trade's property rights in prices put an end to part of the debate. But it left the issue of recognizing gambling as a productive force open to questions. Although all futures transactions, regardless of motivation or intent to carry out a physical sale, have become by now an integral part of the economy, and few in the United States and United Kingdom question their effect on diminishing volatility in the real economy, gambling has stayed suspect to this day.

In the 1876 case *Rumsey v. Berry*, the Supreme Court of Maine held:

> A contract for the sale and purchase of wheat to be delivered in good faith at a future time is one thing, and is not inconsistent with the law. But such a contract entered into without an intention of having any wheat pass from one party to the other, but with an understanding that at the appointed time the purchaser is merely to receive or pay the difference between the contract and the market price, is another thing, and such as the law will not sustain. This is what is called a settling of differences, and as such is clearly only a betting upon the price of wheat, against public policy, and not only void, but deserving of the severest censure.[29]

Similar misunderstanding is reflected in courts' decisions in other states as well. In 1865 the Indiana Supreme Court held that dealing in futures was not illegal gambling. Later, however, the same court changed its opinion and declared that commodity speculation was illegal gambling if, at the time of entering into the contractual agreement, neither party intended actual delivery.[30] In 1887 the Illinois legislature passed an act declaring that participants in futures contracts, referred to as "gambling contracts," would be fined a thousand dollars and imprisoned for up to one year. Seven members of the Chicago Board of Trade were arrested under this act. The act was repealed a year later, but in 1874 all futures contracts were again banned in Illinois.

In 1875 the prohibition was canceled, but in 1889, in *Schneider v. Turner*, the court held once again that all option contracts were unlawful, stating explicitly that the rationale for the decision was to "break down the pernicious practice of gambling on the market prices of grain and other commodities."[31] Apparently the statute was ineffective, for a year later, in *Soby v. People*, the court stated that the practice was becoming more widespread. Cases similar in nature came before the Quebec's Court of Appeal (*Forget v. Ostiguy*, 1883) and later in 1895, on appeal, to the Imperial Privy Council, in the House of Lords. But one should note that cases arriving before the courts where the issue of gambling was brought up were not necessarily morally driven, but were driven by people who did not want to pay their debts. What's better than dressing up a real issue into a moral cloak and bringing the gullible on board?

The debates and confusion surrounding futures markets were apparent in political debates too. More than a hundred bills were introduced in the U.S. Congress to abolish futures trading. In 1893 a bill recommending a prohibitive tax on all futures trading in farm products failed to pass only because final action before Congress adjourned required suspension of the rules of the House of Representatives, and the necessary two-thirds majority failed by a vote of 172 to 129. A similar bill in 1894 passed the House but failed to gain approval in the Senate. The attacks on futures contracts reflected the same confusion that marked legal decisions.[32] In 1890 a Kansas representative described futures markets as follows:

Those who deal in "options" and "futures" contracts, which is mere gambling, no matter by what less offensive name such transactions be designated, neither add to the supply nor increase the demand for consumption, nor do they accomplish any useful purpose by their calling; but on the contrary, they speculate in fictitious products.[33]

And in 1892 a senator declared:

At least 95% of the sales of [the Chicago Board of Trade] are of . . . fictitious character, where no property is actually owned, no property sold or delivered, or expected to be delivered but simply wagers or bets as to what that property may be worth at a designated time in the future . . . Wheat and cotton have become as much gambling tools as chips on the faro-bank table. The property of the wheat grower and the cotton grower is treated as though it were a "stake" put on the gambling table at Monte Carlo . . . Between the grain producer and the loaf eater, there has stepped in a "parasite" between them robbing them both.[34]

The flagrant misunderstanding shows that not much changed between the thirteenth and the nineteenth centuries as far as political debates are concerned about the link between the real economy and the financial one, and the notion of allocating risks, derived from price volatility in particular, remained elusive. To get around the legal requirement of intent of delivery, for the contract not to be classified as gambling, bucket shops made bettors sign a document stating that they agreed to take or make deliveries of commodities or stocks.[35]

Only in 1900, in *Booth v. People*, was it explicitly stated that the prohibition of "market gambling" (by which term reference was made to bucket shops) need not embrace all contracts for options to buy or sell, but only contracts that threatened the public safety and welfare.[36] Though a step in the proper direction, this was still a vague decision, open to interpretation. It was not until Justice Oliver Wendell Holmes, in *Board of Trade of the City of Chicago v. Christie Grain & Stock Co.*, that one found a better understanding of the issues. Holmes acknowledged both that legal reasoning cannot lead to distinctions between speculative gambling contracts and legitimate business ones, and that gambling is necessary for financial markets to operate, providing both insurance and liquidity for the real economy:

As has appeared, the plaintiff's chamber of commerce is, in the first place, a great market, where, through its eighteen hundred members, is transacted a large part of the grain and provision business of the world. Of course, in a modern market, contracts are not confined to sales of immediate delivery. People will endeavor to forecast the future, and to make agreements according to their prophecy. *Speculation of this kind by competent men is the self-adjustment of society to the probable.* Its value is well known as a means of avoiding or mitigating catastrophes, equalizing prices, and providing for periods of want. It is true that the success of the strong induces imitation by the weak, and that incompetent persons bring themselves to ruin by undertaking to speculate in their turn. *But legislatures and courts generally have recognized that the natural evolution of a complex society are to be touched only with a very cautious hand, and that such coarse attempts at a remedy for the waste incident to every social function as a simple prohibition and laws to stop its being are harmful and vain.* (198 U.S., pp. 247–8, italics added).

The case in which this paragraph appears was also the one in which Justice Holmes established the principle that the Board of Trade owned the price quotations produced there and had the right to prevent bucket shops from using them. The decision established the principle of property rights in prices, and it concerned the telecommunications business too, as is explained in the next section.

It is worth quoting one additional court decision from 1942. In *Albers v. Lamson*, when a party contested the obligation to pay a debt, claiming that commodity transactions were wagering contracts, the Supreme Court of Illinois relied on Holmes's reasoning and, by then, on the congressional regulation of commodity exchanges, when it stated:

The titles to the various acts of Congress make it clear that our public policy now recognizes the desirability and necessity of maintaining open markets, even if they sometimes be used for gambling, in order to stabilize values in commodities and securities. *As briefly mentioned in the Monroe case, every human transaction is a gamble, which all must take whether they wish to or not. From the time he plants his seed until he sells his crop every farmer is gambling. From the time he makes a contract of sale until he delivers the flour, every miller is gambling.* The public policy has been declared to be that these contracts for future delivery are necessary to the commerce of the people of the United States in their domestic interstate economy, and since no one can tell with what intent they are entered into, it is impossible to pick and choose among them (italics added).[37]

So, it took a few thousand years for reasoning to catch up with deeds on the ground – at least to some extent – and acknowledge that without gamblers and the financial contracts they trade, the real economy would be far worse, and part of it would not exist. And yet the Albers decision is not quite the end of the story.

The onion futures market, active since 1949, was banned in 1958. An index of seasonal price variations for a period of active trading before 1949 and a four-year period following the prohibition of futures trading reveals that the before-and-after indexes were nearly identical, ranging from a harvest low of about 75 to a spring high of about 145. In contrast, while the futures market existed, the index had a harvest low of 87 and a spring high of 118.[38] False ideas, articulated in ancient words whose original meanings are lost in the mist of time, can have lives longer than even thousands of years, and unless constantly debated, they can lead repeatedly to bad policies.[39]

Although Justice Holmes's majority opinion established good precedent, other parts of the opinion reflected the same prejudice against ordinary people reflected in the condemnations of gambling. As we saw previously, Holmes believed that speculation was beneficial, adjusting society to the probable, a "means of avoiding and mitigating catastrophes, equalizing prices and providing for periods of want." But these outcomes happened only when undertaken by "competent men," and "incompetent persons bring themselves to ruin by undertaking to speculate in their turn." Whereas there were some much-publicized cases on the front pages of newspapers, as with gambling, the fact that they appeared in headlines suggests the relative scarcity of such events.

Stabilizing and Destabilizing Speculations

The head of the House of Rothschild in Paris was asked why he was buying French government bonds when the streets were running with blood. He replied that he could buy the French bonds for twenty-five cents on the dollar only *because* the streets of Paris were running with blood. Was the impact of the Rothschilds' bet on the price distribution of these bonds stabilizing or destabilizing? By buying the bonds, they showed confidence in the eventual restoration of stability in France. By this expression of confidence they checked panic selling, prevented the price of bonds from falling farther (thus having a positive effect on people's savings), and may have affected people's expectations as to France's future in general. Some may have thought, "If the Rothschilds have confidence in France's future, so should we." The question is, then, Who helped restore the country's stability? The few speculators who bet on the upside or the majority who was selling?[40]

Was the Rothschilds' eventual monetary success due to avoidable ignorance (a term economists use today to imply that if information were diffused, more people would become somewhat richer rather than a few becoming significantly richer)? The answer is no. They just believed in a future in which the majority of French people did not. And, as in bets on football games where those who win large prizes are always those whose predictions are out of line with the other forecasts, the Rothschilds won the large prize for backing their own opinion.

Were the Rothschilds taking advantage of the French terror when buying the bonds at panic prices? "Taking advantage" has a negative connotation, suggesting that somehow the Rothschilds had inside information, and could be sure the terror would end and France would be restored to some measure of glory. But this way of posing the question is erroneous, because it confuses consequences with expectations. Yes, it turned out that they profited handsomely from their pricing bets, which reflected their belief in the future of France. Most other French people did not share this belief (so who was the greater patriot?). But no, they did not take advantage of anybody, because they could not be sure of the future. So, their bets on the bonds' price distribution (i.e., speculation) was not destabilizing but stabilizing, whether we look at the narrow effect of their actions in the bond market or at the broader one of affecting people's belief in a more stable future.

The language of Justice Holmes's decision implies that betting on price distributions can generate false information if the general public, who lacks special knowledge, was allowed to participate, because this means that they would be gambling. Holmes was wrong. The issue is not lack of special knowledge, but something else, which Irving Fisher identified correctly. He wrote, "Were it true that each individual speculator made up his own mind independently of every other as to the future course of events, the errors of some would probably be offset by those of others. But . . . the mistakes of the common herd are usually in the same direction. Like sheep, they all follow the same leader . . . A chief cause of crises, panics, runs on banks, etc. is that risks are not independently reckoned, but are a mere matter of imitation."[41] He shares Mackay's views in the latter's classic (but much misinterpreted) *Extraordinary Popular Delusions and the Madness of Crowds.* Not in vain does the title refer to "*popular* delusions" and "crowds." The book neither condemns speculators nor suggests that speculation in general is bad. In the "money mania" episode, linked to the 1719–20 Mississippi scheme – which the next chapter explores in some detail – Mackay emphasizes that John Law, the financial entrepreneur behind the scheme, was an outstanding one, who "was more deceived than deceiving, more sinned against than sinning."[42]

When are people more likely to imitate another or to act as a herd? The answer is straightforward: when they do not have access to independent, diverse, dispersed sources of capital. Without such dispersion, there cannot be independent sources of information, and people are more likely to bet on the same ideas, following a single leader. But the solution to this problem is not prohibition, but allowing capital markets to develop and become deeper, to democratize capital, that is. This is the only way to create independent sources of information and to prevent the herds from betting on mistaken ideas, political ones in particular.[43] As the United States has the deepest financial markets, some may ask: What about the technology bubble? Well, what about it? There were no crises or panic. People made mistakes about how quickly entrepreneurs would find ways to commercialize the new technology. But why would one call a mistake a bubble? Investors corrected this mistake very quickly and the U.S. economy continued to thrive. If many people making grave mistakes, reflected in the allocation of capital and people, is a bubble, then communism and fascism qualify too. And on smaller scales, Keynesian economics and a wide range of academic fads could be bubbles, making the term rather irrelevant. The reason observers single out financial markets as associated with bubbles has an implicit ideology hidden behind it. After all, if financial markets are unstable, susceptible to the crowd's follies and leading to mismatching people and capital, wouldn't it be better instead if governments started making those matchmaking decisions?

Confucius was right when he wrote, "If names are not correct, language will not be in accordance with the truth of things." When this happens, language shapes reasoning, which in turn shapes reality when laws and regulations apply reasoning that uses the outdated language and then these laws and regulations are enforced. In the June 22, 1987, issue of *Newsweek*, an article titled "Thatcher's Two Britains" read: "And although a few of the new middle class have made it as entrepreneurs, many have simply followed the upper classes into lucrative but unproductive fields such as law and banking."[44] In 1988 James Gibney, the managing editor of the *New Republic* at the time, commented on the civil case against Michael Milken, the financial entrepreneur who created the high-yield-bond market. Gibney wrote, "Mind you, part of me wants to see Milken suffer not out of any highfalutin sense of moral outrage over securities law violations. No, like the millions of Americans who gloated over the fall of plutocrats Adnan Kashoggi and Harry and Leona Hemsley, I want Milken to suffer because he is filthy rich. What better way to close an eight-year era of officially sponsored greed than to go after one of its prime movers? I only hope that Donald Trump is next. As far as ritual sacrifices of the rich and powerful go, that would be quality.'"[45]

At least some observers state explicitly how envy clouds their views, rather than hide behind jargon that rationalizes increased roles for central authority based on lofty principles.

Telecommunications and Speculation; or, How to Outlaw the Competition

After 1880 the combination of two technological innovations – the ticker, invented in 1867 by E. A. Callahan,[46] and the quadruplex (which Thomas Edison invented, allowing four messages to travel simultaneously over one telegraph wire) – allowed Western Union to market its ticker service and private wire leases. They became the company's most lucrative activities, brokers and bucket shops being the main customers – much as English newspapers once found betting news to be their most lucrative business. In 1910 Western Union abandoned this market when courts of law established that the exchanges owned the price information they produced.[47]

For some twenty years, though, the Chicago Board of Trade struggled with the question of how to distinguish trades on its exchange floor from transactions in the bucket shops. It had the incentive to find a distinction because, by 1880, the Board of Trade became aware of the competition from bucket shops and asked telegraph companies to cease transmitting ticker quotations to them.

Bucket shops were small brokerage houses that flourished between about 1880 and 1905. They bought ticker services from telegraph companies, and with a few dollars people could bet on price fluctuations in the Chicago and New York exchanges, and trade on margins. People could bet just one, two, or five dollars on price fluctuations in commodity markets, though most transactions were between ten and fifty dollars. The bucket shops did not deliver stock certificates or commodities (neither did the Chicago Board of Trade for the vast majority of its transactions). These are familiar and legitimate ways to make financial transactions today, but they were less understood at the time. Bucket shops were financial intermediaries, enticing customers with investors' guides and tip sheets, and they made money the way casinos do. Just as people pay a fee to a casino and bet on probability distributions in card games, bucket shop customers paid a fee to bet on stock and commodity price fluctuations transmitted through Western Union's ticker network.

According to Hochfelder, there were five thousand bucket shops in the United States in the 1890s, two hundred in New York, one hundred in Chicago, and at least one in each town with a population of more than ten thousand. There were claims that bucket shops traded more than 90 percent of all commodity trading in the countryside. The term "bucket shop" may be a misnomer, because there was consolidation: by 1887 four companies controlled the shops in Manhattan – and possessed millions of dollars in working capital. From 1880 to 1890, the value of a seat on the New York Stock Exchange dropped from $34,000 to $18,000, and one on the Chicago Board of Trade from $2,500 to $800.[48] Hochfelder notes that though bucket shops did not leave financial records, these prices may not be surprising because estimates at the time suggested that the exchanges were losing millions in commission trades. The spreading bucket shops provided "the only venue for the million [of so-called middle and wage-earning classes] to participate in financial markets."[49]

For twenty years the Chicago Board of Trade went before both state and federal courts to get an injunction against bucket shops' obtaining of price quotations. They tried to rationalize their request by making moral and economic distinctions between transactions that took place on the exchange and those of bucket shops. But the courts upheld the bucket shops' rights to the quotations. They made it repeatedly clear that they saw no distinction between the transactions. Three judges in a 1903 case before a federal appellate court explicitly stated that "in all essentials [these were] gambling transactions," and the board itself was violating an Illinois statute banning such transactions, which implies that the board was little more than a bucket shop itself. The antigambling reformers singled out bucket shops for attacks, claiming that their transactions hurt the farmers, which was not true.

The fact that for twenty years the bucket shops succeeded to defend themselves before the courts, arguing that they were democratizing speculation, suggests too that there was no factual basis for accusations of fraud or dubious dealings. Considering the antigambling lobbying at the time and the board's power, if there were an unusual number of fraudulent transactions, the courts would have long outlawed the shops. Although the board could have stopped supplying pricing data through the wires, board members were aware that the competition in New York and St. Louis would have supplied them. These fears also suggest that the bucket shops were not doing anything to harm the board's credibility. They were actually in the business of democratizing capital markets, because anyone could bet those small amounts.

The bucket shops paid only Western Union for the services, but not the Board of Trade. But Western Union and other telegraph companies paid the New York Stock Exchange, the Chicago Board of Trade, and other exchanges high fees to get access to the trading floor and to transmit their quotations.[50] This is the arrangement that the 1905 decision put an end to, recognizing the exchanges' ownership in the price information they produced, giving them the authority to deprive bucket shops of their quotations. Bucket shops ceased to exist soon after, not only because the 1905 decision deprived them of ticker quotations, but also because they were prosecuted under state and federal antigambling laws, whereas the Board of Trade and the large brokerage houses became exempt.[51] Predictably, exchange officials and brokerage houses catered then to bucket shop clients, and, as Hochfelder notes, by 1920 the bucket shop "gambler" became an "investor." The number of Americans owning stock between 1900 and 1922 went, according to some sources, from 4.4 million to 14.4 million, or from 5 percent of the population to 12 percent.[52]

Innovations in telecommunications technology – especially the ticker – led to the 1905 decision, which solved the problem of defining and enforcing property rights in prices, because prices were now acknowledged to have been produced like any other item in the real economy (showing clearly just how wrongheaded all those theories were that separated the real economy from the financial sectors). This was a novel idea then, and it still seems so today – we shall come back to this point in the next chapter.

Gamblers and Speculators: More Confusions

Women's disproportionate buying of lottery tickets in the seventeenth and eighteenth centuries provoked much interest. Observers of the time came to the conclusion that they were searching for dowries to compensate for the lack of other charms. As a poet put it at the time:

> A country girl that stood below,
> To the same Tune her sighs let flow;
> Oh help me to a lumping Prize,
> To shine in my dear Dicky's Eyes.
> Without the pence, alas poor Nan,
> I fear thou'lt dye and nee'er taste Man.[53]

Recall the discussion of lots in the Bible in Chapter 1, where their use in ceremonies was referred to as *payis* or "pacified." The choice of this same word for Israel's lottery company today – Mifal Ha'payis – seems quite appropriate. Lotteries and the ability to stake small sums on futures with the chance of large rewards pacify those who are down on their luck, or perhaps those who just never had any luck to start with.

It is this basic leapfrogging instinct that has been widely misunderstood, and has led to so much long-lasting misunderstanding and confusion among gambling, insurance, and speculation. As late as 1898 Ashton remarked:

> Paradoxical as it may appear, there is a class of gambling which is not only considered harmless, but beneficial, and even necessary – I mean Insurance. Theoretically it is gambling proper. You bet 2s.6d to 100 pounds with your fire insurance; you equally bet on a marine Insurance for the safe arrival of your ships or merchandise; and it is also gambling when you insure your life. Yet a man would be considered culpable, or at the very least, negligent and indiscreet did he not insure.[54]

Ashton failed to see the sharp distinction between gambling and insurance. By gambling (on games with chances with large prizes), people try to restore or increase their wealth. By insuring themselves, they try to protect what they have already achieved or would customarily expect. Thus, although there is a sharp distinction between the two, there is no inconsistency in people's paying for both.

To this day many economists consider insurance natural, whereas they consider gambling irrational and a puzzle, drawing on so-called risk-aversion theory.[55] According to the theory, gambling and insurance are simply a matter of taste, a reflection of mathematical features of the utility function. Milton Friedman suggested that the natural bias of academics against gambling and in favor of insurance, which is reflected both in esoteric elaboration of risk-aversion theory and in negative attitudes toward gambling and speculation, is due to the following:

> It is natural for [academics] to regard futures market . . . as a market in which "legitimate" producer hedges his risk by transferring them to a "speculator"; the producer is viewed as buying "insurance" from the speculator. But granted that this is a possible and indeed likely interpretation of an actual futures market, it is not the only possible one. May such a market not be one in which the "legitimate" producer engages, as a side line, in selling gambles to speculators willing to pay a price for gambling and knowingly doing so? And if so, putting moral scruples about gambling aside, is any economic loss involved?[56]

Friedman puts his finger on the right point when he uses the word "legitimate." For, as we saw (and as the next chapter discusses in further detail), authorities and various groups questioned the legitimacy of markets where property could change hands such as to change social rankings by betting on price ranges (call these people speculators, if you wish). This questioning was the source of another confusion: the view that only attempts of producers of real things had legitimacy but not of those who produced prices.

The inability to understand that the real world cannot be divorced from the financial (the part that produces price information in particular), and if done by legislation has a disastrous outcome, has been the source of another error made in discussions about gambling and speculation. Irving Fisher, for example, wrote: "the distinction between a speculator and a gambler . . . is usually well marked. A gambler seeks and takes risks which are not necessary to assume, whereas the speculator is one who merely volunteers to assume those risks of business which must inevitably fall somewhere."[57]

This line of reasoning is not useful because both the person betting on price distributions and the gambler assume risks that fall somewhere. For the gamblers, the risk falls on them: gamblers find themselves down on their luck being leapfrogged. Gamblers do not create additional risks: they respond in one particular way to risks inherent in society. If they did not gamble, who knows what other risks they might have taken? Consulting an astrologer? Betting on a blissful afterworld? Betting $5 on television evangelists? One cannot say that a gambler seeks and takes risks that are not necessary to assume. What does "necessary" mean anyway?

The risks associated with chances of leapfrogging are assumed, if not by gambling, then through other channels. Thus, the distinction between a gambler and a speculator (betting on price distributions) is not that one takes risks and the other volunteers to assume them, but that the gambler (in games of chances with large prizes) assumes risks associated with ranking by wealth. The speculator assumes risks associated with trade. This distinction may explain why although both gamblers and speculators have been frequently condemned, speculators were still tolerated when gamblers were not, as futures markets became legalized and antigambling laws stayed on the books. Those engaged in futures, if they were successful, climbed up the ladders of wealth through a channel that benefited trade. The gamblers who won large prizes did not make a visible contribution.[58]

As the effects of telecommunications helped sharpen the debate about futures, perhaps the Internet will lead to a sharpened debate about betting markets in general, for which the Internet is an ideal technical vehicle. It may bring about the realization that gambling and betting are as much part of the real economy as futures markets have always been. The present debate about gambling, sparked by the UIGEA, which prevents financial institutions from transferring funds to online gambling and betting companies, may lead to a better understanding of the issues at stake.

The debate may also lead to the recognition that gambling and betting have always been productive activities, offering entertainment options to some and channels of hope, of getting rich by chance, to others – much as bucket shops once did. As the following two chapters show, this does not imply, however, either that the government should be the bookie or that there are no situations of too much gambling: the latter can happen when governments pursue mistaken monetary and fiscal policies.

But during relatively normal times, gambling in all its incarnations fulfills productive roles. For those born without genetic accidents of beauty, athletic prowess, wonderful vocal cords, unusual eye-hand-leg coordination, stunning intelligence – having ways to challenge luck sustains hopes. The vast majority of these people always bet with their head and not over it, whether on lotteries, in casinos, or in bucket shops.

Venture capital can be viewed as the more respectable brother of gambling, except that the chips on the baize table, the galloping horses or the scampering dogs are entrepreneurs seeking financial clout, an exit or a float.
Marc Barber

FIVE

Gambling as Banking: Poker, Junk Bonds, and Central Banks

Reuven Brenner and Aaron Brown

Which shows how gambling was banking, and how it is linked to the development of clearinghouses, central banking, and creating wealth in a country.

How do you sell a relatively expensive property in a society that does not have banks or developed financial institutions? How can the owner of this property raise money to reinvest it elsewhere? How can entrepreneurs raise money in a world where there is no venture capital and there are usury laws that prevent banks from giving loans to newcomers with no credit rating?

The answer is – surprising perhaps – by gambling, whether selling lottery tickets, or around the gambling table.

Merchants in Italy, the German states, and England discovered during medieval times that they could make more money if they auctioned off their relatively expensive goods as prizes in lottery drawings.[1] This practice gained currency later in the New World, where relatively large property, which could not be divided, was the prize. Thomas Jefferson explained the rational for such financing:

An article of property, insusceptible of division at all, or not without great diminution of its worth, is sometimes of so large a value that no purchaser can be found . . . The lottery is here a salutary instrument for disposing of it, where men run small risks for a chance of obtaining a high prize.[2]

Shortly before Jefferson died, when he was eighty-three years old, he tried to pay debts totaling $80,000 by disposing of land through a lottery. He failed to sell enough tickets to liquidate the debt before his death, in 1826. Security markets were then still in their infancy: before 1790 there were only three incorporated banks in America and, of course, no venture capital as we know it today. Lotteries, and gambling tables, where entrepreneurs could meet with richer people, the venture capitalists of the times, reallocated capital from consumption or hoarding and formed capital. They fulfilled two roles that financial institutions play today.

Such lotteries are illegal in the United States today, so people instead sell homes and businesses in, for example, essay contests. In a typical situation, there are no interested buyers nearby. The cost of inspection for faraway buyers is a significant fraction of the value of the property, and the new owner would have to change residence to take possession. The local cash buyers available offer low bids because they know the situation. The owners hope to collect more by charging $100 or so for entries to a contest to win the property. Although requiring that entrants write an essay is sufficient in most states to avoid antigambling laws, the decision based on short essays (typically less than 125 words) is random for most practical purposes.

Here is how the flow of funds works. Say there are one thousand people, each with $100 hoarded or available for discretionary spending on entertainment. Offering a lottery at $100 per ticket for the chance to win one large prize of $100,000 results in the following outcome. The owner of the property receives $100,000 and then reallocates it. The lucky winner gets the property valued at $100,000, but 999 people lose $100, which they recoup by forgoing a few drinks or a new garment. If the lottery was prohibited, the property would remain dormant, in the hands of owners who no longer knew what to do with it.

Is this type of lottery a zero-sum game? The answer is no. People who buy into the lottery expect to do something with the property, and the seller expects to do something with the $100,000. We saw in previous chapters that most winners of lotteries spend the money prudently, investing in houses and in their kids' education. If the property and the money raised are put to better use, society becomes richer and happier. After all, these are all voluntary transactions.

It may be true that 999 people will temporarily spend less on discretionary items, such as drinks and clothing. That is probably why retail and entertainment establishments have been against gambling. But the arguments they have brought forward against it – that it is a zero-sum game – have been inaccurate from no matter what angle we look at them. And it seems equally likely that the losers may work a bit more rather than spend less, in which case the economy gets a double benefit.

Gambling Is Not a Zero-Sum Game

At first sight, the zero-sum perception of gambling seems logical. After all, whatever one player leaves on the table, someone else takes away. Taking into account that someone also charges an entrance fee to use the facilities and the gambling tables and to organize the game, gamblers must expect negative monetary returns. That is the case even if the game of chance was what economists define as fair; that is, the expected monetary benefit from the game is equal to the expected cost, even without considering the costs that addiction imposes.

However, this reasoning is irrelevant when gambling has entertainment value for the players and they do not perceive it as a financial transaction. The flow of funds in gambling is not different from the one in any other entertainment business. The moviegoer pays $10 for the ticket, and the movie theater owners, studios, and distributors split the money. True, people enjoy a movie, but then, when gamblers play poker or bet on horses, they enjoy the game and the time spent too. And just as people lose $10 at the tracks, so they lose $10 at the movies.

This point is even more salient when we consider that gambling is always bundled with other services. Even a basement craps game involves the sharing of minor luxuries like cigarettes and liquor. Commercial gambling establishments offer extravagant entertainment of all kinds. Consider a person who loses $10,000 playing roulette in a week at Las Vegas, but is treated to first-class airfare, a luxurious hotel suite, gourmet food, expensive wine and liquor, spectacular shows, sporting events and good-looking women and men, as the player's taste dictates. Compare a player to a brother- or sister-in-law who spends $10,000 on a vacation to a high-end resort in the Caribbean. Who got more value for their money? *De gustibus non est disputandum.* But if the casino offered a significantly worse deal, and was patronized only by fools and gambling addicts (until the latter go bankrupt), then it would be a more profitable business than a resort. In competitive markets casinos earn normal rates of return.

In entertainment the whole can be different from the sum of the parts. McDonald's does not offer fine wine and the Metropolitan Opera House does not have hot dog vendors working the crowd. Movie theaters sell popcorn, not caviar. For many people, gambling increases the enjoyment of other luxuries, and other luxuries add to the appeal of gambling (just as window-shopping and store displays add to shoppers' fun). Casino customer service is the best in the world, for people who lose big anyway. Some other high-end service providers pride themselves on haughty customer service. After overpaying and getting rude service at a top restaurant in New York or Paris, a casino may start to seem like a more attractive way to get the same meal at the same dollar cost.

Another appeal of the casino is the separation of luxury consumption and payment. Some people find that the thought of paying hundreds of dollars for a meal ruins the enjoyment. Gambling makes the link between consumption and payment indirect: customers get the same fine treatment on trips when they win and when they lose (in fact, casinos are particularly solicitous of long-term losers after a winning trip, because the house wants that money back). This behavior pattern is not different from the one people display before getting married: they do not negotiate the price of every future service, be it preparing meals, taking out the garbage, having sex, raising kids, and being explicit about the link between inheritance and good behavior toward parents during rainy days. The veneer of civilization is sustained by separating consumption from payment – never mind economic orthodoxies.

Betting has a negative externality in the shape and form of a tiny minority of addicted players, who impose burdens on their families and society. The fashion industry has a similar negative externality, if not more significant, in the shape and form of anorexic women, and the millions of other women made unhappy by today's ideals of beauty, ranging from size zero to a maximum of six, pushed by the fashion industry and the media. Add to this the rapid depreciation of cloth that fashion brings about, foot and ankle damage from high heels, and cruelty to animals. One may raise, then, questions like: if we examined this industry in the same way as most examine gambling, would we not reach the conclusion that fashion imposes far more costs on society than gambling?

We are not saying that we agree with the preceding analyses – we do not. Mao's China showed that regulating dress codes would bore people to death. What the parallels suggest is that if people applied the same analyses to the entertainment business as they do to gambling, they probably would recommend shutting them all down. Mind you, communist and theocratic regimes have been doing that, just as the Puritans did on North American soil, and the Amish and, to an extent, the Mormons do to this day (although we have to note the difference between people who renounce a pleasure for themselves and those who seek to ban it for everyone). Yet at all times and in all places, the vast majority of people choose from a variety of entertainment options to escape boredom. They may remain believers in their faith, but they have revealed a preference for spending time and moderate sums on betting, drinking, dancing, and window-shopping rather than on visits to religious institutions or lectures on various "isms."

Others reveal their preference for betting instead of spending on the newest fashions. Books and movies portray weekday gamblers at horse-race tracks wearing cheap, outdated polyester clothes – unless they are at Ascot. Casual observation may suggest that the portrayals are accurate. But if gamblers prefer to bet on horses over wearing Ralph Lauren and extravagantly feathered and flower-filled hats, how can we object to their choice? Of course, retailers, fashion magazines, and those with a fashion herd instinct will make fun of them. But the critics would benefit if their ridicule induced gamblers to spend less on gambling and to adopt stylish Ralph Lauren or conservative Brooks Brothers classics to go watch models stride up and down a catwalk rather than horses running around a track. We see no argument in favor of the fashion business when compared with, say, raising horses and the racecourse business. Some may prefer to display their status and have fun by dressing up, and others may prefer to bet at the races and invest in horses. Both industries use farmers, technicians, and computers. The difference is that because of many prejudices, one gets better press today than another (stunning models look better in media, no doubt, than do horses). Briefly, the zero-sum view of gambling does not hold up to scrutiny when approached from these angles.

Whereas the preceding analyses compare gambling with other entertainment-related activities, let us look at gambling now from the purely financial angle. Consider this question: how is gambling different from any financial institution, such as a bank or an insurance company? Many believed for centuries that there was no difference between gambling and financial intermediation at all because money was sterile. This has been the basis for condemning lending, usury, and futures markets.

Let us look at how funds flow through these various institutions, to show that the zero-sum view does not hold up when we look at it from this angle either. Banks accept deposits and promise to pay interest. They expect to pay interest from their returns from loaning the money, after they pay their own administrative expenses. Borrowers pay more interest than depositors receive, so the game is either zero-sum, if we include the bank as a player, or negative sum, if we do not.

Compare this with the flow of funds in gambling. After subtracting its expenses, the casino pays winners with money lost by losers. The game is zero-sum if we include the casino; otherwise, it is negative sum. In lotteries players in the United States get back, on average, 53 percent of the money they bet. The government bureaucracy then decides to whom to give the rest of the money, after it defrays administrative costs. This is similar to insurance: when people pay premiums, most do not get back anything, and a few get relatively large awards if the event they insured against happens. A private poker game is zero-sum; there is no house to take a fee. This is similar to a rotating credit association like the Korean *kye* and Mexican *tanda*. Whether the institution is zero-sum does not depend on whether we call its activities gambling or financial intermediation. *The positive sum comes from winners who use their winnings productively, to generate more money, and losers who work harder to earn more and indulge their passions.*

The facts presented in Chapter 3 leave little doubt that, as far as lotteries are concerned, players behave exactly as depositors or lenders do. The winners invest the money prudently, buy houses, and pay for their kids' education.[3] The losers invest only small amounts.[4] George Orwell, in his *The Road to Wigan Pier*, refers to gambling as "the cheapest of all luxuries" – and that is what it has been, buying a chance to riches, and it is often some people's only option to become rich quickly.

There is one difference between gambling and financial intermediation – the speed with which winners get the money and others lose it.[5] Another difference is that whereas financial institutions do due diligence before lending money or investing, winning gamblers get the money without going through such a process. However, people seem to spend far less time researching stocks than they do researching buying a car or appliances. Perhaps, deep down, most people know that, for them, buying stocks is a gamble after all, never mind the seriousness of the financial jargon.

There are other differences between banks and a gambling table in terms of explicit and implicit contractual agreements linked to the flow of money. People who borrow from a bank pay it back, unless they default or steal. They usually (but not always) agree to use the money for some reasonably prudent, productive investment. But there is no contractual agreement that requires winners either to play the game of chance again with the same players or to invest their winnings prudently. In this sense, though, gambling is more like other parts of financial markets – such as stock and commodity exchanges, where people make transactions, winners keep their winnings, and losers bear their losses.

Imagine neighboring suites in a New York hotel. In suite A, bankers and businesspeople are sitting around a table to hammer out a loan agreement. In suite B, people are playing poker. Neither group is doing anything "real": no ore is being mined; no food is being grown. The activities financed in the two suites would certainly not qualify for advancing credit according to the old real bills doctrine, which utterly derailed the Federal Reserve during the 1930s and kept it from broadening the definition of collateral.[6] Viewed in isolation, both are zero-sum activities: no one will walk out of the room with anything tangible that someone else did not bring in.

But we all know that the group in suite A is engaged in productive economic activity, because bankers expect that the loan will stimulate activity outside the suite. The borrowers will walk out of the room knowing they have more money, which they will use to, say, expand production of a business.

But the bank lenders will not think that they gave away the money. They will keep the loan on their balance sheet as an asset. In fact, they will book a profit when they sign the note. Although the cash on their balance immediately following the transaction will decrease, their total assets and net assets will increase, and the deal they struck may increase the bank's share price, thereby making it easier for the bank to raise money. In this case, the bank will have more money available after making the loan than it did before.

In the same way, an individual thinks of stocks and bonds in a brokerage account as money available to spend (albeit with some cost and delay compared with cash in a pocket). An individual will plan finances assuming that money is there (despite the old adage, "Spend on stocks as much as you can afford to lose"). But traders and businesses use this money at the same time. When expectations work out – the bankers have made good matches between capital and talent, so that people want to buy the products and services that the matchmaking created – businesses can pay back their loans and return dividends to their shareholders. The individuals are vindicated in their faith. When the bankers make a mismatch and develop no product or service that people want to buy, some businesses stop repaying, the banks get in to trouble, and the customers suffer unpleasant financial surprises.

For centuries, and in some societies to this day, people argued that this type of matchmaking process was immoral. It seemed obvious that there was only a fixed supply of money, and if two people were using it at the same time, at least one of them had to be a fraud. But we recognize today that the demand for liquidity is not fixed, and that working to increase it, as the bankers and borrowers are doing in suite A, is productive economic activity. When these matchmakers – whether in venture capital or in private equity – between capital and talent are successful, it improves the economy for everyone. Although, as we shall see later, the Federal Reserve managed to bring about the Great Depression in the 1930s in part by implementing a policy based on a variation of misunderstanding when it is warranted to expand liquidity. Perhaps if the chairman of the Federal Reserve and its board members were casual poker players, they would not have made these mistakes.

Now let's look at the poker players in suite B. Are they changing expectations of future cash flows? Certainly they are, because there is no poker without changing expectations of future cash flows. Will these changing expectations result is a net increase in economic activity? Usually. The winners in the game walk away thinking that they have more money, as do the borrowers in suite A. The losers are more straightforward than the bankers are. They know that they do not have a poker losses asset and that they will not book a profit (though the losers may not admit to anything more than,

"I lost a little"). But like the bank, they do not cut productive spending the way someone who suffers a nongambling loss might. We are talking here about risk-takers. Some continue to spend as if they had not lost, expecting to recoup losses next time; others make efforts to earn the money back. Thus, we have the same two economic effects in suite A and suite B: concentration of assets and expansion of economic activity, though, depending on the circumstances, by different magnitudes.

If a Martian observed both hotel rooms, it might conclude that the poker game was the more sensible financial institution. Money changed hands, rather than legal documents (because poker players trust one another, trust substitutes for legal documents and formal enforcement). In the poker game, people measured one another as risk-takers instead of arguing about words. The words people did use were common speech and technical slang, the way people talk when they want to get work done. Suite A dealt in words from dead languages and often impenetrable legal boilerplate, and numbers were written in words (due to a medieval prejudice that arabic numerals were too flexible for calculation to be trusted). Suite B was quick, and suite A was mind-numbingly slow. The Martian would guess that suite A was engaged in some intensely conservative religious ritual with no financial substance while suite B was running the economy.

Observation across countries and time reveals that there were times when there was no doubt that gamblers who lost expected winners to come back to the table and recoup their losses, and the same players would repeatedly face one another. When that did not happen, laws were passed to prevent gambling with emerging, mobile gamblers. England, Italy, and the United States passed such laws, with the explicit intention to prevent "gentlemen" (who had previously gambled regularly among themselves) from becoming venture capitalists (though who else could be a venture capitalist at the time?) by playing with hoi polloi newcomers who would then get access to capital. The goal was to sustain distinctions of rank and prevent the transfer of capital around the gambling table, land in particular.

The laws were not effective, and the players developed their own codes of conduct – not surprisingly accompanied occasionally by violence. Violence accompanies prohibitions because disputes cannot be settled in the open, before courts. However, such correlation between gambling and violence does not imply that gambling causes crimes, but that bad laws bring about the correlation. One problem has been that people often saw the correlation and read superficial newspaper headlines, but the laws and regulations that brought about the correlation were long forgotten.[7] Misperceptions and prejudices have long lives.

This prejudice is mistaken in another way. The vast majority of gambling debts in history have been paid voluntarily, without violence. Many people who feel no qualm about taking extra change from a vending machine, cheating on their taxes, or leaving town with an unpaid telephone bill would rarely consider reneging on a gambling debt, a debt of "honor." Those who are ready to use violence to get money have no need to go through the charade of gambling first. The increase in violence associated with the legal prohibition of gambling came about rarely, when some players (the losers) suddenly treated the debt as a legal matter because the laws allowed them to not pay it back. The other players continued to treat the debt as one of honor. Except for those rare occasions, people agreed to forget about the gambling debt laws and settle disputes privately and in nonviolent ways.

Gambling has been part of the financial market across countries and time, when played privately, and the clearinghouses and other institutions we now associate with the financial sector have their origins in gambling. Far more important, in a broader sense, is the relationship that exists among "soft money" banks, "poker" banks, and where the Federal Reserve went wrong by pursuing a narrow view of the real bills doctrine.

Preventing Financial Intermediation by Law: Protecting Noblemen

The word for a gambler in Rome was *aleator*, which had a negative connotation, and laws were passed to limit bets. The laws prescribed that money lost at play could not be recovered by the winner, whereas money already lost and paid out could be recovered by the loser.[8] These were laws that England rediscovered in the seventeenth century.

In 1664 a statute of Charles II aimed to limit fraudulent and excessive gambling. Whereas punishment for cheating or fraud is not surprising (though one should ask why cheating in gambling should be singled out for different treatment from cheating in other walks of life), we have to point out the intent of these laws, for they seem counterintuitive at first reading. The laws were introduced to protect estate owners from losing their holdings by chance. The fear was that significant gambling losses would make it visible that ranks and riches are not eternal or divinely ordained, but man-made. With gambling, how could the existing institutions then be sustained, based as they were on unquestioned acceptance of rank and the rights and obligations that came with rank?[9]

The statutes had nothing to do with protecting the poor from succumbing to temptations or from allowing gambling to create a something-for-nothing frame of mind. The poor did not have the sums that the new laws on gambling debts referred to. And if having a something-for-nothing frame of mind was the worry, legal authorities and moralists should have been advocating the taxing of inheritance at 100 percent. There are far more people who inherit significant wealth than those who become wealthy by gambling. The statutes' thrust was, in fact, to prevent creating a frame of mind that people change from gentry to pauper in a flash – which could only happen to gentry and not to paupers. In other words, in the seventeenth century the gambling table suddenly became a financial intermediary, allowing some people to access capital and others to lose it. The statutes tried to outlaw this capital market channel, so as to ensure that those born to the manor stayed there, or at least did not transfer property or significant amounts of money or land at the gambling table.

The statutes declared that gaming debts secured on credit in excess of £100 became judicially unenforceable if incurred "at any one Time or Meeting" – and £100 was a relatively large sum then. Contracts relating to the payment of these debts were "utterly void and of no effect." The statutes declared that any securities conveyed in relation to such debts were also void. In the case of excessive gaming, any person could sue the winner for a penalty similar to the one imposed for cheating, even though there was no cheating involved. Thus, the law tried to prevent the redistribution of significant amounts of wealth by gambling.

"An act for the better preventing of excessive and deceitful Gaming," passed in 1710 under Queen Anne, shows this intention clearly. The first section of the statute made "all Notes, Bills, Bonds, Judgements, Mortgages, or other Securities or Conveyances Whatsoever" given in payment of gambling debts "void, frustrate, of no Effect to all Intents and Purposes." The statute diminished the sum for which a loser could sue to £10, and it even allowed anyone not in collusion to sue for treble the amount lost. A section of the statute provided that any person instigating a gambling-debt-related quarrel would forfeit all possessions to the Crown and serve two years in prison.

When were these laws passed? As the next section shows, during a time of upheaval in English history, when lower ranks started to percolate up and the higher ranks to trickle down, and the gambling tables became banks – a place where financial intermediation took place; it was the infancy of formal financial markets, backed by real estate, which became more liquid. Until then people had gambled within their class: they were gamblers linked by social ties and acquainted one with the other. Such games did not raise problems because the justified expectation was that what gamblers lost one day, they would likely win back in the future – this was "gentlemen's flow of funds." But what happened when one of the gamblers joining the game was, heaven forbid, not a gentleman and moved away? With gamblers from lower classes, and people starting to move more often, the flow of funds became different. A poorer person could become rich, and the gentleman could lose his manor.

The law did not have its intended impact of diminishing interactions among ranks while gambling. Instead, people continued to play and develop their own moral codes, finding ways to make oral, implicit contracts when gambling contracts became unenforceable – a recurrent, predictable consequence of prohibitive legislation everywhere and at all times.

The Volatile Road to Democratized Capital

The hundred years between 1540 and 1640 were unique in English history up to 1880 for the speed at which manors changed hands, and because there was more gentry rising and falling than at almost any other time in English history.[10] These times were also unique in another respect. With respect to the writings of Protestant theologians, Keith Thomas remarked that the common theme was the denial of the very possibility of allowing chance and accident to have any effect on who would be rich or poor.

Recall Calvin's 1559 *Institutes of the Christian Religion*, where he condemned the apparent widespread belief in chance:

Who, likewise does not leave lots to the blindness of fortune? ... For although the poor and the rich are blended together in the world, yet, as their respective conditions are assigned to them by Divine appointment, he suggests that God, who enlightens all, is not blind, and thus exhorts the poor patience ... Those who have learned this modesty will neither murmur against God on account of past adversities."[11]

Recall too texts such as the Anglican Homilies, which emphasized that to make fortune into a goddess was a grave mistake, and the Elizabethan bishop Thomas Cooper's writings. "That which we call fortune, is nothing but the hand of God, working by causes and for causes that we know not. Chance or fortune are gods devised by man and made by our ignorance of the true, almighty and everlasting God," wrote Cooper. Lewis Bayly's writings made similar points. In his influential devotional *Guide the Practice of Piety* (1613), he blamed fires on people's practice of making preparations for market day on the Sabbath. Sickness too was attributed to God's will, and it was argued that "health came from God, not from doctors."[12]

The avalanche of numbers, in particular those focusing on statistics concerning illness, had significant effects on decisions and pricing only after the population grew and after the Industrial Revolution. Only then, with the law of large numbers in effect, could governments and insurance companies use statistics for insurance purposes. Before that, family and religious and voluntary organizations offered safety nets. Every Christian had been taught that life was not a lottery, but reflected the working out of God's purpose: the events of the world were not random, but ordered. These were the teachings of most theologians and moralists, and they gave intellectual support to legislation against gambling at least until the later seventeenth century. And they make sense, but in a small, largely immobile world.

A few documents have survived from the seventeenth century to suggest that there were observers who looked at preserving ranks and at gambling differently. In his treatise *Of the Nature and Use of Lots*, Thomas Gataker, a Puritan divine, tried to eliminate objections to the use of lotteries and to justify their use in routine, secular events. He argued that the fall of the dice was no more an immediate providence than the daily rising of the sun. He also distinguished between the two types of games of chance: one where large sums were at stake and others played for entertainment. He concluded that wasting one's estate on games was to be avoided, but the use of lots in games of recreation, including card games, was legitimate.[13] When stakes were so small in proportion to the player's wealth that loss would not cause anxiety and gain would not constitute a source of unearned income that would be more than trifling, Gataker did not condemn gambling. But even such mild views about gambling were contested by religious objections against gambling, and as late as 1687, Gataker's ideas were unrepresentative of the main body of theological opinion at the time.[14]

Volatile Ranks and Taking Chances

England's population as a whole had been increasing significantly since 1520, though the growth rate was erratic. Historians still view the doubling of the population in the 120 years before the Civil War as the variable that sheds light on the main events of the sixteenth and seventeenth centuries.[15] In England the increase in population and its mobility brought about major changes in agriculture, trade, industry, urbanization, education, social mobility, and overseas settlement.[16] From 1650 there had been dramatic growth in trade with the Americas and the Indies; consumption of sugar, tea, coffee, and tobacco soared. The import of new textiles from the East increased and led to outcries from the defenders of English woolens, who predicted the ruin of the English economy because of the new addiction to luxury (what's new?).[17]

Manors were managed in new ways. Much that was regarded as new in the eighteenth century – such as the growing of root crops, the introduction of clover and new grasses, systematic crop rotation, and beneficial leases – was well established in eastern England and elsewhere by the reign of Charles II.[18] The hundred years between 1540 and 1640 saw the growth of wealth, of the size of the landed classes, and of professions, as well as a massive shift of wealth away from both the church and Crown and from the very rich and very poor toward the upper middle and middle classes.

Such leapfrogging provoked reactions from among the ranks of those falling behind – the church, the land-based nobility – who tried to slow down those who got ahead by words and swords. Those who jumped ahead tried to ensure their position – again, by swords and words – by rationalizing the new order. Belief in Providence and in the idea that people usually get their just rewards resonated among members of the rising groups: the merchants, the shopkeepers, the aspiring artisans and craftspeople.[19] Lower down the ranks, the doctrine of Providence, the teaching that the poor had only themselves to blame, that it was their idleness that had landed them where they were, found no acceptance.[20]

Secular notions of chance and unjustified privilege could account for misfortune (in a world where access to either capital or insurance was limited) and raise questions about discrepancies between merit and reward. "Since the World is but a kind of Lottery, why should gamesters be begrudged the drawing of a Prize? If . . . a Man has his Estate by Chance, why should not my chance take it away from him?" wrote Jeremy Collier in his "An Essay upon Gaming" (in the 1713 *Dialogue between Gallimachus and Delomedes*).[21]

It is not surprising either that the poor turned not only to gambling, as both entertainment and a way to receive financing, but also to non-religious modes of thought, such as magic, witchcraft, and divination. These activities offered the idea that people could live easier than with religious beliefs telling them to meekly accept that some people prosper and others suffer.

When the Rich and Poor Intermingle, Lessons for the John Laws

Until the sixteenth century it was customary for the rich to play sports or games of chance with the poor during holidays, with the rich having the right to start and stop the games.[22] The arrangement preserved the distinction of ranks. But during the seventeenth century there were changes in the rituals, and gambling was singled out for condemnation. The objection was that people from lower classes now interacted with the higher classes, that winners from lower classes were accepted – once they won – and the richer lost their standing. A text published in London in 1700 had this to say:

Lantrillou is a kind of republic very ill-ordered, where all the world are hail-fellow well met; no distinction of ranks, no subordination is observed. The greatest scoundrel of the town, with his money in the pockets, shall take his turn before the best duke or peer in the land, if the cards are on his side. From these privileged places not only all respect and inferiority is banished, but everything that looks like good manners, compassion and humanity. Their hearts are so hard and obdurate that what occasions the grief of one man, gives joy and satisfaction to his next neighbour.[23]

Notice, however, that the worst accusation concerns the poorer ranks' manners. Similar condemnations of gambling, of bringing together the higher and lower ranks in one venue – which would allow one to lose wealth and another to gain – continued well into the eighteenth century. In 1769 Sir William Blackstone, a leading commentator on English law, said:

Taken in any light, [gaming] . . . is an offense of the most alarming nature . . . Among the persons of superior rank, it hath frequently been attended with the sudden ruin and desolation of antient and opulent families, and abandoned prostitution of every principle of honour and virtue, and too often hath ended in self-murder.[24]

Gambling was condemned because of the effect it had on the rich, not on the poor. Commentaries lamenting such interactions continued during the nineteenth century. The following, from 1870, shows the rather representative way of thinking:

Distinction and personal merit being but little regarded – in the low moral tone that prevailed – there needed but to support certain "figure" in life (managed by the fashionable tailor), to be conversant with a few etiquettes of good breeding and sentiments of modern or current honour, in order to be received with affability and courteous attention in the highest circles. The vilest sharper, having once gained admission, was sure of constant entertainment, for nothing formed a greater cement of the union than the spirit of *high gaming*. There being so little cognizance taken of the good qualities of the heart of fashionable assemblies, no wonder that amid the medley of characters to be found in those places the "sharper" of polite address should gain too easy admission.[25]

There were occasional voices advocating the abolishment of all antigambling laws, explicitly emphasizing that the laws *protected* the wealthy and the status quo and not the poor because they slowed down the movement of capital. One noted explicitly that "gaming . . . abhors Perpetuities, property is in constant circulation, but then, like the Sea, what it loses on one shore, it gains in another."[26] This quote recognizes accurately the role of gambling as a financial intermediary.

Such voices appear to have been rare. Perhaps those who wrote and were critical of gambling did not understand financial markets, which would not be surprising. Another reason for the disproportionate amount of documents focusing on rank when criticizing gambling may be that the reallocation of property happened when innovative ways to pass the time competed with visits to the church, and so went against a main tenet of the Protestant ethic. How can one raise money while playing, while having fun, and not through hard, manual work to manufacture something tangible?[27]

The terms we are familiar with and that constitute the vocabulary we use to explain why some places prosper and others fall behind (e.g., "managing risk," "correcting mispricing," and "reallocating capital") had not yet been invented. They were hardly on the horizon. To do any such financial work requires talents that are intangible – it is more art, intuition, and guts than science. The causes of prosperity and poverty were perceived very differently from how many perceive them today. The prism of risk-taking and leaps into the unknown was yet to be invented, and the fact that the financial world and pricing were intimately linked to the real world was out of sight and out of most minds.

A particularly dramatic example that shows both that the fears about ranks intermingling were not idle and that capital markets played a role in the process of bringing about volatility in ranks is the career of John Law. Law was the son of a Scottish goldsmith, a commoner with some money and minor social accomplishments. Yet Law parlayed his success as a professional gambler into becoming the most sought-after economic adviser in Europe in the early 1700s, despite his common origins, "incorrect" religion, disreputable profession, and unconventional living arrangements (open adultery, that is). He was entrusted with running the economy of France, which he did so successfully that the word "millionaire" had to be invented (before Law, there were not enough of them to require a word).[28]

The economic stimulation created social upheaval. Servants became richer than masters, ancient manor houses were purchased by the *nouveaux riches*, and the highest nobles of the land had to bow and scrape before the Scottish upstart, who, as if all this were not enough, enjoyed the nobles' wives' sexual favors too. Reactionary forces in France crushed the economic revolution and blackened Law's name. Only recently was he rehabilitated as an important early economic thinker and doer, his occasional mistakes notwithstanding. Nobody is perfect. His influence survived in an unlikely place, as we will see later in this chapter.

The Tulipmania That Never Was: Part 2

Another dramatic confirmation of the misunderstanding surrounding gambling, futures markets, and the impact of laws that made gambling and futures contracts unenforceable is the famous tulipmania episode in the Dutch Republic in the 1630s. People remember two things about tulipmania today: fantastic prices paid for tulip bulbs and all ranks of society being caught up in frenzied speculation that led to a gigantic crash. However, these are two unrelated facts that occurred at different times.

Tulip prices rose continuously between 1605 and 1635. The fantastic price stories are from the first half of the period. The buyers who paid those prices made money. However, the buyers were not paying for a single bulb, but for a monopoly on a new variety of exotically patterned tulip. For example, if you owned the only Admiral Eck bulb, and fashion decreed it to be the most beautiful of tulips, you could sell its annual flower for a large sum (think of a Picasso painting today).

The bulb grows slowly and can be split every two or three years. Each split doubles your production. Of course, the price per flower goes down as the supply increases and new bulbs arise to attract fashionable attention, but you can still get many years of high revenue either until the bulb falls out of fashion or until it becomes so common that it commands no premium over the cost of production. The present value of that revenue stream can add up to what seems like a fantastically high price for one flower. In inflation-adjusted terms people still pay large amounts today for new varieties of bulbs that catch the public fancy (though lilies are now more likely than tulips to fetch the top prices).[29]

The mania did not begin until the early 1630s. The term refers not to the high prices paid for the exotically patterned, rare bulbs, but to futures trading in partial interests of common tulip bulbs. Futures prices accelerated, especially after 1634, and then crashed in February 1637. Although observers lumped all the period together, we showed in the previous chapter why the increase in prices between 1635–7 is quite understandable, and has nothing to do with particular exuberance. Rather, it has to do with fear of death due to the plague. When that fear disappeared, the market for rare bulbs experienced only a mild, short-lived contraction – these bulbs stayed scarce. And Amsterdam continued to prosper.

But why did so many middle-class people in the Dutch Republic trade tulip futures in the early 1630s?[30] The key lies in the transition from static and medieval economies to reformation ones. Medieval society had few ways to finance innovations. Both church and secular authorities worked to keep things as they were, and to sustain distinctions of rank rather than give opportunities to create wealth. That is why usury laws played such central parts in the theological debates of the sixteenth and seventeenth centuries, especially in Martin Luther's and John Calvin's writings. Although the Bible condemned usury, the debates started to question whether prohibitions on higher interest harmed the poor, the start-ups, those without proper collateral, and how to reinterpret ancient texts so as to justify the paying of interest.[31]

There was a sharp distinction between honorable income, which came from land or offices, and trade – never mind moneylending, which only Jews were allowed to practice. Aristocrats could earn rates typically around 2 percent per year by owning land or purchasing offices that paid in fees or bribes. Merchants could earn much higher returns, often 20 percent or 30 percent or more per year, by accepting a low social status. With easy – and not stigmatized – access to capital, returns like these would have been competed away quickly. But medieval society made it very hard either to save or to raise capital. With entrepreneurial determination and collateralizing even a small stake, people could get rich. But few people could get even a small stake, and even fewer could borrow money.

As Europe began the transition to what historians call modernity, attitudes toward self-made wealth began to improve, especially in the Dutch Republic. After the revolt against the Spanish in the sixteenth century, the Dutch Republic and its policy of religious toleration, which was far in advance of the times, attracted considerable immigration of merchants, craftspeople and financiers from not only Europe but also the rest of the world. Jews (thrown out of Spain) and Huguenots (thrown out of France) were prominent among them. The result was a population leap from 1.2 million in 1550 to 1.9 million in 1650 – a 60 percent increase. Amsterdam's population grew from 30,000 in 1570 to 215,000 in 1630, and it soon became known as the "miracle of seventeenth-century Europe."[32] Much of the capital active in Amsterdam was foreign owned, or owned by Amsterdammers of foreign birth.

Amsterdam began to develop institutions like stock markets and corporations to support the businessmen's activities. Although unlocking the potential of these skilled immigrants allowed the Duth Republic to leapfrog Spain, still a medieval power at the time, it created tensions within the new Dutch society. As in other European societies, laws were passed to prevent ordinary citizens from emulating the wealthy by eliminating small and highly leveraged financial transactions. The money supply was kept extremely tight.[33]

The partial interest tulip future was created in taverns and coffee houses, without any organizing body. The transactions often involved barter: goods and services were occasionally exchanged for futures, though most of the time people bartered in futures. No one was building up large portfolios of tulip holdings: people bought the futures only to sell them. Market participants were likely to have no if any holdings of tulips. The contracts were used as money – like chips at a poker table – allowing ordinary citizens to bet and some to get richer. These contracts had no more to do with tulips buried in some grower's yard than trading in bucket shops had to do with interest in commodities. Most people were not making huge bets on tulips. They held small net long or short positions, or were fully hedged. If some made large bets long, others had to bet short.

However, viewed either as a form of money or as a futures contract, tulip futures had some grave defects. There was no clearing mechanism and no mark to market. Still, it is impressive that tavern-created poor person's money consistently rose in value (for quite a while), whereas money backed by the full faith and credit of great governments and ministered by those passing for the wisest economists eroded in value either slowly or quickly (for example, since 1913, when the Federal Reserve was created, the U.S. dollar has lost roughly 96 percent of its purchasing power – and the dollar is considered one of the world's better currencies).

The tulip futures market (in common tulips, not the exotic ones) probably would have collapsed eventually because common tulips, unlike gold, are not scarce. However, we will never know for sure when this would have happened, because reactionary forces in the Dutch Republic managed to have the contracts declared illegal in a piecemeal and confusing way that worked to the disadvantage of almost everyone. Accidental events, such as the plague that struck Amsterdam and Leiden between 1635 and 1637, only sped up the end of this experiment to invent a medium of exchange not backed by the government.

The view that futures contracts with low intrinsic value can become money (only as a liquid medium of exchange) may first seem unusual. But consider the well-known story of the monetary system of a small island in Micronesia that Milton Friedman describes in his book *Money Mischief*. At the end of the nineteenth century, the inhabitants on the island used stone wheels as a medium of exchange and as a store of value. The colonial government imposed fees on disobedient district chiefs by painting black crosses on these stone wheels, thus confiscating them. This induced the locals to change their ways and work harder to erase the marks and get back their stones. Friedman concludes that this example illustrates how important appearance, belief, or myth become in monetary matters.

Our interpretation is different. This story is similar to that of tulipmania: Dutch commoners bet on using bulb futures as money, just as Micronesians used the stone wheels. Only with Micronesia we do not know how the arrangement came about, or how it came to be stable and trusted by all the islanders. The Dutch experiment shows how commoners invent private money – and how the arrangement is destroyed by a combination of misguided legislation and bad luck.

If we smile at the fact that the Micronesians were ready to work harder to recoup their confiscated stones, or that Dutch commoners could believe that futures contracts could become money, consider what people do in our supposedly better-informed age. Governments have regularly imposed taxes by inflation, wiping out significant amounts of people's wealth. People then started to work harder; only in cases of hyperinflation have they discarded the fiat money. With milder inflation, the dollar remained the dollar, despite that it has lost 96 percent of its value since 1913. What are the differences among Micronesians and their stone wheels, the Dutch and their tulip contracts, and U.S. citizens and their greenback – backed often, indeed, by green ink? There aren't any. In the years before and after the tulip crash, the Dutch government published satirical pamphlets attacking the social mobility that resulted from bulb trading. These pamphlets remain the main source people rely on today for accounts of tulipmania.[34] Very few have taken a closer look at either the broader picture or the details to ask the following: What exactly was traded? At what prices? What happened when commoners entered financial markets? And why and how did private enforcement of contracts work when laws made them unenforceable?

It is easy to believe in false things, especially when they are repeated often and when beliefs strengthen the prejudice that commoners cannot manage the allocation of capital unless – hold your breath – politicians, central bankers, and academics overcome commoners' animal spirits or irrational exuberance. Of course, the prejudice, which often passes for social science or economics, excludes the possibility that politicians, central bankers, and intellectuals are themselves subject to the uncivilized sentiments of the hoi polloi.

Gambling in Venice

In a meticulous study about gambling and noblemen in Venice between 1500 and 1700, Jonathan Walker (1999) shows that there too governments were concerned with the richer and the poorer gambling around the same table because nobles could be defeated by commoners.

Venice also passed laws to preserve distinctions of ranks. Gambling among the nobility was not an issue. On the contrary, nobles' behavior while gambling became "an examination in the noble virtues of magnanimity and self-control."[35] Because chance did not distinguish among players, gamblers's reactions to the monetary outcomes became a test of character. The issue arose when nobles lost to commoners, as in England, and the transfer of capital, land in particular, resulted in fluctuations in ranks.

The Venetians were quite the innovators in gambling. Betting on elections was popular (as it was in Genoa) – a market that has been reinvented during the past few decades in the rest of the world. In the United States, it is legal to bet on election results only at the Iowa Electronic Exchange (at http://www.biz.uiowa.edu/iem/markets) under strict regulations and under academic auspices. The Venetians, however, could wait near the ducal palace or even inside the basilica of San Marco for the results.

Not only the nobility played the game, and not only in Venice. In the seventeenth century Italians came up with opportunities to gamble that mimicked electoral procedures in other trading cities. Although laws allowed only members of the nobility to be elected, people perceived this method of choosing elected officials as conducive to political stability. Lobbying was less effective, because people did not know which noble's name would be drawn from the bag. In Genoa, for example, the choice of two councilors to serve in higher office from among the 100 or 120 sitting on the Council of Genoa were chosen by lot. Because of gamblers' interest in the elections, the state, together with a group of entrepreneurs and bankers, set up a parallel lottery with many options.[36]

It is useful here to make a brief deviation and note that whereas betting on elections soon disappeared from Italy, it reappeared in China in the nineteenth century. There people could bet on the surnames of candidates in civil service examinations. Those who hit the most surnames of successful candidates won. Although such betting was very popular, the government prohibited it in 1875. The gamblers promptly moved to Macao and continued to run their business from there. Ten years later, China abolished the prohibition and taxed the activity. If today's online gambling companies had looked to others' experience and negotiated with U.S. states, perhaps they could have prevented the 2006 UIGEA.

Another point on China is worth mentioning before we turn back to Italy and gambling's role serving as venture capital. Whereas in Europe the various religious institutions were against gambling, and implicitly and explicitly against the development of financial markets, in China the first four money-raising institutions established there – pawnshops, lotteries, mutual financing associations, and auctions – all originated or had close connections with Buddhist temples and monasteries.[37] In light of this, it may not be as surprising that under communism, a newer "religion," the Communist Party keeps financial institutions under its control.

Financial services available to gamblers in Venice were complicated because laws set legal limits for bets in cash and defined the assets that could be put up as collateral. Because usury was illegal, Christian moneylenders often put a clause in the contract that any borrowings could not be used for gambling. Also provisions dating back to 1560 prohibited minors and wards from giving assets – including anticipations of inheritance – as collateral to moneylenders and pawnbrokers, without their fathers' or guardians' approval.

As in England, sixteenth-century legislation in Italy stated that while "gentlemen and citizens of 'honest recreation'" could gamble one with the other, other people could not. As gambling among the nobility spread, statutes in 1567 started to make explicit reference to prohibitions of some places (*ridotti*) where nobles played and apparently interacted with outsiders. Anyone who denounced those who gambled for greater sums than was allowed would receive half of the money involved.[38] In 1634 the statutes reiterated that no one could play beyond certain amounts, "neither in cash, nor with their word, not with pledges of any sort." Legislators saw gambling as threatening to dissipate inherited wealth. To prevent such dissipation, entailings were used to control the descent of property in the male line, to prevent gambling from "accelerating the turnover of wealth."[39]

Cardano, a controversial jack-of-all-trades of the Renaissance (he was a physician, an astrologer, and, according to some, among the outstanding figures in mathematics), labeled "the Gambling Scholar" today, wrote in his biography that the "odium of estate and a desire to escape . . . compelled him to play."[40] He speculated about both types of players who gambled and the consequences. The gambler, he wrote, did not believe in chance, but regulated his behavior through contractual agreements with players. To Cardano, the risk-taker, "fortune" meant fatalism and passivity. In his probability theory, he argued that whereas most people are passive and submit to probability distributions, there are a few who could – and should – struggle to change them. His distinction between the active risk-takers, or gamblers, whom we would call entrepreneurs – who succeed in changing probability distributions by leaping into the unknown – and those who passively adjust to existing distributions anticipates debates centuries later about ways to distinguish between risk and uncertainty.[41]

Gambling was at its height in Venice while it was a vibrant trading city. In his majestic history, William McNeill (1974) summarizes Venice's transition from a trading and manufacturing center to a rentier economy by 1675. The traders left the city, with some buying land and retiring in the countryside and others moving to northern Europe. The population of Venice stood at around 170,000 in 1563, dropped to 100,000 in 1633 (following the plague), and even at the end of the eighteenth century was only about 140,000. With the gamblers and risk-takers moving out, the city settling down, and the nobility playing among themselves, gambling ceased to be an issue. McNeill captures perfectly the change of mind:

A managerial elite that lives by trade and manufacture must maintain an active, inquisitive, energetic mode of life. Merchants deal, mostly, with equals, buying from and selling to men of power in their communities. To prosper in such encounters a man must perpetually respond to new situations, . . . calculate margins, take risks. Men so engaged constantly experience new things, whether at home or abroad. Landlords and tax collectors who squeeze goods and services from a sullen and resentful peasantry have a far less stimulating experience in life . . . Men's minds quite naturally close up when new experiences cease to be a normal part of life; this, as much as the plague of 1630–31 and the missionary persuasiveness of Catholic reform, accounts for the narrowing of Venetian outlook. (p. 227)

It is not surprising that, as in the Netherlands, following the drastic drop in population due to the plague, greater interaction among commoners and the nobility suddenly became an issue, gambling and carrying out financial transactions among them in particular. Once the plague was over, Venice, with its vital few gone, returned to the preplague trends and maintained things as they were before – until a ruthless Corsican upstart shattered the order at the end of the eighteenth century.

In North America, where many risk-takers from northern Europe eventually moved, the opposite of Venice's eighteenth-century hibernation happened. Was it the stimulation of new experiences that broadened the outlook? Or did gamblers and risk-takers make the trip? No doubt the answer to both questions is yes, but there was a third factor as well. An active, inquisitive, energetic native population awaited them. The collision created the modern derivative economy.

Banking on Gamblers

Anglo-American settlers worked on the basis of an old economic system of adventurers and planters. The words are confusing. "Adventurers" – from the same linguistic root that gives us the term "venture capitalist" – put up the money for a new colony or town. The "planters" settled the new places and were led by professional town founders, skilled in administration and in dealing with the indigenous people.[42] The planters had the adventure, and the adventurers planted money in hopes of making a profit.

This worked well enough on the eastern seaboard because the transportation system was organized around rivers and roads that led to ports. The first planters settled the ports and developed the local economic resources. When population growth exceeded local opportunities, the former planters turned adventurers and financed their children's new towns. Roads and rivers connected the new towns to the eastern ports. A few years later, the process repeated itself, but the tree never forgot its roots: the port, and deeper than that, the country of the original adventurers.

For several geographic and historical reasons, this pattern did not describe the interior of the continent. There was a mix of indigenous and nonindigenous people and they pushed ahead of the transportation network. The river system (later augmented by canals and railroads) provided the only practical long-distance transportation. It was not settled in an orderly, gradual progression; there was a free-for-all race for opportunities, and lands were occasionally distributed through lotteries.[43]

A limited amount of capital had to be agile to finance literal and figurative gold rushes. The planters were not settled townsfolk, but entrepreneurs – and, yes, renegades and outlaws too – in a land where anything was possible and legalities were a gray area. As in any place where that is the case, relationships and networks substitute for contracts and enforcement.[44]

The planters could be miners, farmers, ranchers, or lumberjacks. They arrived with skills, tools, provisions, and livestock. Someone had to match people and assets and induce them to work together. This is what developed financial markets achieve. Entrepreneurs raise capital by borrowing money and issuing stock, and then they hire people and buy assets. They repay the borrowings with interest and pay dividends to the equity holders. But before 1790 there were only three incorporated banks in the New World, and all three were on the East Coast.

A common local solution was for a person with a small amount of gold and silver to set up a bank. These were "soft money" banks because they issued banknotes far in excess of their hard capital. If many people tried to redeem their notes, the bank would fail. The bank was backed by expectations of future earnings – different from either banks or governments today, because banks are subject to many regulations and governments are subject to the discipline that bond markets impose. Governments' debts are backed by future tax revenues, and they, in contrast to banks, have the option to default through inflation and devaluation (neither of which today is defined legally as default, though they should be).

People use the small bank's notes in their town. If the local economic activities are profitable, the town becomes successful. It sells goods to outside markets for gold and silver and attracts newcomers. The soft money bank may then evolve into a "hard money" bank. Meanwhile, using banknotes is less risky for the town than extending credit to individual entrepreneurs. Why?

The banknotes offer liquidity that alternative arrangements cannot. Instead of borrowing from a bank, the person running the logging camp or mine could promise to pay suppliers and workers only when he sells the logs or ore. The problem is that if the business fails, there is immediately less liquidity. Economic activity ceases and assets and workers are stranded. Only a very persuasive new entrepreneur could hope to get everyone to write off their losses and start work again for another promise of future payment.

However, if banknotes are issued to fund loans, the amount of banknotes in circulation is not affected if one business fails. Suppliers and workers have already been paid. People with money can buy up the bankrupt business's assets and redeploy them to maximum advantage. On a small scale, the soft money bank plays the role of a bank, a venture capitalist, and a central bank, whose currency – the banknotes – is partially backed by gold or silver.

What sustains the banknotes' value when a venture does not work out? The soft money bank takes over the failed business and may either reorganize it or sell the assets. As long as the townsfolk trust that new ventures are pursued and some will be successful, the velocity of the banknotes' circulation goes down and sustains their value. Of course, if nothing comes out of the ventures and no new opportunity is found, the banknotes are less acceptable. The soft money bank is then on shakier ground and unable to pay back in terms of silver or gold if everyone shows up with the banknotes at once. If there are too many business failures relative to the profits generated from successful loans, the bank can fail – and soft money banks often did fail.

Essentially, this is a variation of what economists call the real bills doctrine of a banking system, combined with a soft commitment to convert the notes on demand into specie, be it gold or silver. In rough terms, the doctrine implies that banks give loans backed by future production, and inflation happens if there is inadequate backing. Adam Smith was among the first to uphold this doctrine, but he insisted on subjecting banks to the regulatory requirement to convert their notes to gold.

In other circumstances, poker games fulfilled the same function as the soft money banks. If people converted their assets into poker chips and played, the winners could acquire enough assets to start businesses. Poker chips took the place of banknotes. As were the notes, chips were in limited supply, and no one held significant wealth in them for long – people bought them only to play poker and exchange them for real assets at the conclusion of the game (as the Dutch did with tulip contracts). The losers could then work for the winners to get enough chips to try to win businesses in the future.

An apparent disadvantage of the poker game over a soft money bank is the randomness of allocations. The best or luckiest poker players would run the businesses. In contrast, a banker decides who gets loans on the basis of experience, honesty, and ability. However, in the times we are talking about, of the American frontier (and earlier times in Europe), there were not many experienced bankers around to make these decisions, or records on which to base them. Skill at the gambling tables, such as displaying good ability with people and probabilities – rare skills even today – was probably as good a qualification as any.

A clear advantage of the poker game is that it does not need a banker or matchmaker between capital and the people who receive it. Whereas today one player or the house acts as banker, on the early frontier, they played poker with a check system instead. All players had their own chips, which were identifiable. At the end of the game, players bought back their own chips. Winners would have the losers' chips left over, and they had the task of collecting the money. Players with fewer chips than they started out with owed money to the players with excess. That meant that no one had to act as a bank, and no one had to bring large amounts of cash to the game. If a loser could not or would not pay, it was the winner's problem, not the whole table's.[45] For the most part, people willingly paid their poker debts.

This last point is critical, and related to some of our previous points. Unless you gamble or work in finance, it is easy to forget that financial rights and obligations represent relationships among people, not just numbers and theory. It is not enough to know who owes you money and how much: the nature of their obligation can mean the difference between whether or not you are paid. Recall how both the Dutch and the Italians settled their implicit contractual agreements privately: they had no legal recourse.

Another difference between a soft money bank and a poker game concerns the distribution of profit if the town succeeds. With the soft money bank, the bulk of the money goes to the people who were selected for bank loans and who then established successful businesses. The biggest cut goes to the banker and bank investors. Poker randomizes such rewards, in the sense that it both gives everyone a chance to be the business owner and spreads the profits among a broader group.

If there is a gold rush or land opening or new railhead, losers in the game or in an unsuccessful town move on and try their luck again. Many people who were leapfrogged will move on and bet again. Such an arrangement was documented in the Yukon gold rush camps.[46] It may have happened elsewhere too. Miners would work all season and play poker all winter. The winners could leave, having accumulated as much gold as they could carry and as much as they needed to be settled for life. The losers would continue to mine for another season and try their luck again. This is an agile system, where assets and people are allocated more quickly than under alternative arrangements. It concentrates assets in the hands of a few who can then move on, and their move opens places for newcomers who want to try their luck.

In this sense, the poker bank was a more dynamic institution than a bank, as we understand them today. It had its advantages in mining or when exploring new frontiers, intangible ones in particular. A bank has advantages when a society depends on farming or ranching, or whenever there are such large investments that people are less likely to move.[47]

It did happen, however, that towns that started with poker games evolved into permanent settlements. The next step was an outside gambler who arrived with significant capital. Professional gamblers were typically excluded from poker games: Players had to participate in local economic activity to play. But at a certain point, professional gamblers offering faro, chuck-a-luck, and roulette were welcome. Such gamblers would provide safe-deposit services and import luxury goods and necessities. They also provided a degree of rough law enforcement, because they had to defend their own property. As the town grew, it probably attracted a professional gunman in exchange for the faro concession. Wild Bill Hickok, holder of the famous deadman's hand of aces and eights, did this for a living. Finally, the town would likely reach the point of collecting taxes and hiring a sheriff – who might even be directed to shut down the gambling halls and poker games.[48] That is what often happened on much larger scales, not in towns, but in states.

Briefly, for more than a century, the southern and western United States had soft money banks and poker banks. The soft money banks would take in small amounts of capital and lend it out a hundred or a thousand times. They failed frequently, but they also did more to commercialize the natural resources of North America than did the hard money banks.[49] Soft money banks arose spontaneously when people gathered on the frontier. They lent the money needed for development. If the town succeeded, the bank prospered and became a hard money bank. The investors who put up the bank's risk capital became extremely wealthy. If the town failed – if the adventurers and explorers did not stumble on gold, silver, or other resources – the bank failed, and people moved their digging holes elsewhere. As people settled, both poker banks and soft money banks diminished in importance, and soft money banks were replaced by hard money banks and a central bank.

But it may not be accidental that in 1931 – during the Great Depression – Congress effectively outlawed soft money banks and the California poker rooms were reinvented and Nevada legalized gambling. And it is not surprising that gamblers and risk-takers usually have become more accepted during periods of hardship. Cardano said as much centuries ago, when he noted that "in times of great anxiety and grief, [gambling] was considered to be not only allowable, but even beneficial.[50]

But it is not surprising that a place with no natural resources, or a place that has lost them, often legalized gambling or opted for financial experimentation.[51] Amsterdam, for example, was below sea level, well endowed with natural disasters, and needed heavy infrastructure to protect against them – and had the world's first stock market in the seventeenth century. The city became the so-called miracle of that century, having attracted financial minds and risk-takers from around the world. And it is no wonder that places such as Hong Kong, Singapore, Nevada during the Great Depression, or Antigua and the Cayman Islands, all lacking natural resources, were jurisdictions betting on either financial institutions or gambling to develop. What else can make deserts and relatively isolated places – geographically or politically – flourish, except for attracting risk-takers, gamblers, and tourists?[52] It is perhaps not surprising that tribes located in the middle of deserts bet on pilgrimage (tourism by a different name) before they stumbled on natural treasures.[53]

From Poker Banks to Clearinghouses

Let us consider briefly where poker banks came from and where they went. First, recall John Law. At the height of his success, Law wrote that he had developed a scheme far greater than his work in France. He had an idea to stimulate tremendous economic growth in France's Mississippi River possessions.[54]

Basically, Spain exploited Native Americans by force: it relied upon involuntary exchange. The English used money exchange that appeared gentler, but it invariably reduced Native Americans to abject dependence within a generation or two. Those who refused to accept dependence either assimilated or moved west.

France tried both of these schemes and failed. The Native Americans insisted on gift exchange. The French would make them a present of trade goods, and they would reciprocate with presents of grain and hides. Gift exchange can be between equals: there is no forced dependence. Moreover, things received as gifts have a value beyond the same things we buy or steal. The Native Americans of the Mississippi River system remained independent and a significant military force until 1890, centuries after the great empires of the Incas and Aztecs collapsed, and more than a century after the mighty Iroquois Confederation was defeated by English and American forces.

Law knew that slavery and dependence could not create a society of dynamic risk-takers. He tried several creative approaches. The most successful was to draft a boatload of faro dealers, complete with cards, and send them to the region to set up a string of gambling trading posts. There are four kinds of exchange (a classification that parallels the four sources of capital discussed previously[55]): involuntary, equal value (money or barter), gift, and gambling. Because the first three did not work, Law tried the fourth.

We do not know for sure that poker was invented at these trading posts, but we do know that it was invented at this place and time, although it was a century later that the game entered recorded history. By that time, it had acquired characteristics that distinguish it from any earlier gambling game. Those characteristics provide an essential clue as to where the poker banks went.

One characteristic is that for all of history, gambling always involved cash (or other physical stake) or someone acting as a bank to guarantee payments. Poker was different. It was rarely played for cash, and rarely with a bank. Players used chips (checks). This was not bilateral credit. Everyone's chips went in and out of pots with everyone else's. But at the end of the session, people offset gains and losses until the remaining obligations were all bilateral.

In the 1840s futures exchanges sprang up in virtually every city in the Mississippi region (the trading region for Law's faro dealers), and not anywhere else. Although nothing like them had ever existed, no one thought them remarkable. No one mentioned their invention or development. It was as if they were a natural idea. One of their key features was that at the end of a day's trading, market participants gathered in a ring and traced trades around to the ultimate buyers and sellers. Offsetting trades were canceled. So after a day with perhaps ten thousand trades, the obligations were reduced to perhaps one hundred bilateral contracts. This is called ring clearing, and it first appeared in poker. Today futures exchanges have evolved the idea further into a clearinghouse, but it remains one of the essential techniques of modern financial markets.

Another unique feature of poker is that every player remaining in the pot at the end of every betting round has put exactly the same amount of money in the pot, both in the latest round and in all earlier rounds. Earlier gambling games either structured all bets as bilateral or had complex rules about contributing money to a pot and taking money out, allowing for unequal contributions.

The financial term for this, "marking to market," is the other distinguishing characteristic of futures contracts. If I enter into a futures contract to buy wheat for $1 per bushel, and the price of wheat rises to $1.10 by the end of the day, I am paid $0.10 and my contract is rewritten to buy wheat at $1.10. I am no better or worse off: a contract to buy wheat at $1 is exactly the same as $0.10 plus a contract to buy wheat at $1.10. But when all wheat contracts are marked to the same price, the standardization makes trading much simpler. Moreover, credit risk is limited to one day's price move. Because I get my gains and pay my losses in cash every day, no one is at risk of longer-term price movements.

Of course, a futures market is more than a poker game, and we do not know for sure that it evolved directly from the game. We do know that it shared two very important ideas, and that both of those ideas can be traced back to the writings of John Law. Maybe Law stimulated the development of poker so that it evolved into modern futures exchanges. Or maybe Law shared some ideas in the air in France and Mississippi, and these evolved along different branches to animate poker and futures exchanges. But the spirit of gambling exchange, with self-organizing credit, clearing, and marking to market, rose up only once in world history, in one time and place, and we are still feeling the shock waves.

Poker Banks and Junk Bonds

Poker declined as an economic institution at the end of the nineteenth century. Antigambling laws were part of the reason, but more important were improvements in conventional financial services. Poker remained an important business and political networking tool, but it retained direct economic importance mainly for people on the fringes of society, especially single men fighting wars or working in isolated places like oil fields or mines.

That changed with the economic dislocations of the 1970s. President Richard Nixon took the world off the gold standard, and currencies immediately began to inflate or hyperinflate. Statutory marginal federal tax rates reached 70 percent in the United States (and greater than 90 percent in the United Kingdom, at which rate, the difference among isms becomes fiction). In Italy, effective tax rates often exceeded 100 percent – a sure recipe for corruption.

The idea of money is that you can keep it in your pocket and spend it how you please. If the government takes 70 percent every time you take it out of your pocket and 20 percent in the form of inflation if you leave it in, money functions neither as a medium of exchange nor as a store of value; and it is not much good as a *numéraire* either. How well you lived depended more on your tax lawyer than on your nominal income.

But inflation and taxes are old problems. People respond by evading taxes (Italy, Greece, and Belgium have been prominent), resorting to barter, or finding an alternate form of money. And there were other, deeper causes that drove people to gambling in general, poker in particular, in the 1970s.

Improvements in information technology, coupled with a de facto abandonment of privacy protections, made it far more difficult to run out on legal judgments. The problem was exacerbated by overproduction of lawyers in the 1960s and 1970s, just when demand for traditional legal services declined. The dramatic increase in regulation and complexity of the tax system compensated for this problem and increased the price of legal services. As a result, people with tax problems, bitter divorces, health problems, or failed businesses found themselves cut off from mainstream financial institutions or economic arrangements. They were joined by people on fixed incomes (many pensions were fixed in nominal terms as late as the mid-1970s) and by those whose investments were wiped out by the predictably terrible bond and stock markets of the decade, predictable outcomes of high taxes and high inflation.

Some of these people made it to the legal poker card-rooms of California (an influx of Vietnamese refugees with similar needs for different reasons followed them about a decade later). To most economists, the cardrooms were simply places to organize underground economic activity, that is, undocumented cash employment and purchases that escaped taxes and regulation. In that explanation, poker was just a cover; it could have been replaced by pool, bowling, or just hanging around.

In fact, poker was more important than this view implies. To see that clearly, let's strip away the tourists. These people came rarely, played poker for entertainment, and lost as a group. They represented the large majority of players by number, but were only a minority in terms of the time they spent playing. These people did come for the poker as entertainment, like casino players today. Another group that lost consistently included action players or riskers. These people were invariably small-business owners or professionals who did a lot of cardroom business. They bet big and lent money freely. Lose to them and they would let you work off the debt at their business. When you won they would offer you discount appliances, cheap apartment rentals, and all manner of goods and services under market price, all for cash.

Many of the remaining players were part of a loose group who borrowed from and lent to one another freely, always without interest. The effect was that as long as you showed up regularly and did not lose too consistently, you could get credit to keep playing. If you kept playing, you could work and get goods, often without cash changing hands and always without legal record. Another reason that poker was important is that it helped guarantee the loans. If you lent someone money, you knew where and when they played. You could show up there and collect when they had a good night, or even a good hand. If they stopped showing up or did not pay promptly when they had chips and were asked to pay, their credit disappeared quickly. Outside bill collectors could not do the same thing.

Of course, many people did fall into debt and disappeared from the poker network. The half-life of regular players was about four years (about half of the regular players disappeared and were replaced over a four-year period). Most of them left without leaving debts, and their defections were slow enough that the poker-financed economy survived. When a poker player skips out, he leaves behind his friends, his recreation, and most of his life. It is not something people do lightly. A gambler's urge to gamble is deep and ancient, as worthy of respect as a homeowner's urge to keep his or her home. The poker table is the gambler's only collateral.

This whole poker banking system was an informal speculative bills doctrine at work – true, taxes, laws, and regulations were evaded. But these banks came into existence because of the high taxes and the unexpected high inflation to start with. This is a lethal combination that has always led to tax evasion and decay. The United States was not an exception during the 1970s.[56]

When the government destroys money, people invent their own alternative, and many real and perceived solid things melt into thin air. Inflation and high taxes were not the only problem that the U.S. banking system faced in the 1970s. Regulation Q was on the books, preventing banks from charging the higher nominal interest rates justified by inflation, and it brought about disintermediation. If all this was not enough, banks continued lending to third-world countries, which would soon go sour. By 1989 the cumulative losses to third-world countries, realized and unrealized, amounted to $1 trillion. With these bad loans on the books, banks lent less to domestic companies – opening the doors to Michael Milken's junk bonds. The late 1970s and 1980s situation became similar to that of the nineteenth-century American West.

There was great economic opportunity – but no credit. While Milken created a liquid market for bonds of less than triple-B-rated companies, reinventing the role soft money banks once played, others, on much smaller scales, took whatever assets they had, money or goods or a business, and played poker. Everything ran on credit, making the poker checks and IOUs a form of a banknote, but one inaccessible to outside creditors and tax collectors. The volatility kept everyone in the game and disguised how little underlying capital there was. And, in both cases, it worked. And, in both cases, when financial institutions improved, most (but not all) poker players went back to using banks and money.

From Banking on Gambling to Gambling on Central Banking

The poker banks and soft money banks both worked on the speculative bills doctrine. In poker banks, the players had their own limited supply of chips, whereas soft money banks created notes (only nominally backed by and denominated in species) as a by-product of their lending operation.

Under the real bills doctrine, a banking system that restricts its lending to discounting short-term, self-liquidating commercial bills of exchange arising from real transactions of goods and services only – that is, productive rather than speculative use of credit – cannot overissue. Thus, a banking system that adheres to this doctrine will not lead to inflation. As noted previously, Adam Smith was among the first to uphold this doctrine (and he was right), though he thought it necessary to subject the banks to legal requirements to convert their notes into species. This was the mechanism through which, if bankers made the mistake of over- or underissuing, mistakes toward inflation and deflation would be corrected.

There are variations on this doctrine, and it has its critics too. We shall not get into that, but rather discuss how the doctrine was applied in the United States during the 1930s. Notice that if monetary policy draws on the doctrine, it requires a definition of what is productive and what is speculative use of credit. One can debate whether searching for gold and silver in America's West or pursuing innovations today qualifies as a productive use of credit. Also, whereas credit advanced to buy rare tulip bulbs may qualify for such credit, credit advanced to buy options even in such rare bulbs would not. The doctrine came about long before the notions of producing prices and of establishing property rights in prices – both productive activities – were on the horizon. To this day, though, the latter is defined as speculation, somehow implying an activity that is tolerated, but not particularly useful.

In 1929, following the death of Benjamin Strong, the influential governor of the New York Fed, the Federal Reserve went on a rampage under Adolph C. Miller, a Fed board member, and his pursuit of a rigid, outdated interpretation of the real bills doctrine. Strong believed in price-level stabilization policy, which Miller opposed. The gold standard was by then a facade, in the sense that reserve bank credit became the equivalent of gold in its power to serve as the basis for commercial credit. The central banks ran the show, and did not automatically adhere to the gold standard.

Miller may not have understood this. In contrast to Strong, he believed in a strict implementation of the real bills doctrine, which condemned many forms of bank lending – long-term loans, mortgages, and especially "speculative" loans that, according to this view, fueled real estate and stock market bubbles.

Combined with Miller's and the board's opposition to price stabilization, and the nonadherence to gold standard principles, the federal banks stopped rediscounting or otherwise acquiring eligible paper. Warburton described years later the Fed's tactics to achieve this goal: "This [policy] ... was due to direct pressure [from the Fed Board] so strong as to amount to virtual prohibition of rediscounting for banks which were making loans for security speculation, and a hard-boiled attitude towards banks in special need of rediscounts because of deposit withdrawals ... Federal Reserve authorities had discouraged discounting almost to the point of prohibition" (quoted by Timberlake 2007, p. 341).

Miller's and the Fed's argument was that banks would manage to return to responsible lending and offer the right amount of money only if speculation was crushed.[57] There was speculation in the 1920s – as always – no doubt. But adherence to a gold price signal and to price stabilization, rather than to the Fed's theories about what type of loans would have been productive, could have prevented the Great Depression.

What, then, are the lessons, far beyond gambling, of the sequence of events presented in this chapter? One is that – once again – a central authority's adherence to a rigid dogma – the real bills doctrine in this case – and an utter misunderstanding of financing risk-taking brought about long-lasting devastation. If in previous centuries opposition to risk-taking took the shape and form of usury laws, of condemning futures markets, and of condemning many financial innovations, during the 1930s, the same opposition was articulated under the real bills dogma. This doctrine, rather than the gold standard, to whose principles the Fed no longer adhered anyway during the 1920s or early 1930s, brought about – predictably – the stock market crash. Insisting on its application prevented the remedy. Friedman and Schwartz, and later Schwartz with other collaborators, concluded that the "expansionary open market operations at two critical junctures of the Great Depression would have been successful in every scenario in averting the banking panics without endangering convertibility."[58]

This brings us to the Fed's present chairman, Ben Bernanke. In a review, Bernanke praised an academic treatise about the gold standard in which the author suggested that gold was the culprit in the events that unfolded during the 1930s. Bernanke is wrong on this point, but, to his credit, he raises a basic question in his review – but he leaves it unanswered: "Why was there such a sharp contrast between the stability of the gold standard regime of the classical, pre-World War I period and the extreme instability associated with the interwar gold standard?"[59] The answer is, of course, easy. As with the Cheshire cat's enormous grin in *Alice's Adventures in Wonderland*, where the cat disappears leaving only its smile hanging in the air, so are we with names and doctrines. The words stay, though they have long lost the meaning of what they stood for. Interwar observers might have called the practice a gold standard, but it was not, and the "real bill doctrine" too got a rigid meaning.

The lessons of the 1930s are also that decisions to go after gamblers, speculators, and risk-takers with far-fetched arguments and doctrines, suddenly prevents leveraging of their collateral (accountably, we should add), and the result is that the economy becomes undone. If you want to prevent that, and still decide to gamble on central bankers too, at least prevent the latter from pursuing academic fads and constrain them by golden fetters. Imperfect as they might be (after all, nothing is perfect), they are better than the alternatives.

The mode of taxation is, in fact, quite as important as the amount. As a small burden badly placed may distress a horse that could carry with ease a much larger one properly adjusted, so a people may be impoverished and their power of producing wealth destroyed by taxation, which, if levied in another way, could be borne with ease.
Henry George, Progress and Poverty (1879)

SIX

Lottery Is a Taxation, and Heav'n Be Prais'd, It Is Easily Rais'd

Reuven Brenner and Gabrielle A. Brenner

Which shows how gambling has been part of public finance, how lottery finance led to investment banks, how lottery bonds have been a major savings vehicle for the past few decades, and how lotteries financed major western museums, universities, monuments, and wars.

It's not the money. It's not the money.

It's the money.

The title of this chapter is part of a song in Henry Fielding's 1732 farce *The Lottery*. There is not much new under our sun, except words we use to help disguise what we are talking about.

Indeed, only by looking at governments' attempts to protect their monopolies on lotteries and casinos in various parts of the world can we understand the present gambling landscape, especially the passage of the myopic and ill-advised 2006 UIGEA. The U.S. Congress attached the act at the last minute as section 7 of the Port Security Bill. Go figure. With terrorism and Islamic fascism on the horizon, Congress had nothing better to do than allocate resources to prevent millions of U.S. citizens from gambling online.

Supporters of the act drew on arguments that, at close inspection, hold no water and relied, in part, sincerely or not (we do not know), on outdated and misguided laws, such as the Wire Act. It was attorney general Robert F. Kennedy who fought to pass this act in 1961. His view was not so much that interstate gambling transmission was the problem, but that people could make a good living from illegal enterprises. He could have reached two conclusions: either to legalize and regulate gambling or to pass a law that would make it easier to catch those involved in what was then an illegal activity. He chose the second option for reasons that do not hold up to close scrutiny, one being that the enforcement would bring back respect for laws.[1]

It is surprising that with the experience of Prohibition any attorney general in the United States would reach such a conclusion.

The UIGEA is, in fact, not as surprising as the act passed in 1961, or as surprising as it might seem at first reading. Countries without legislation similar to the Wire Act on their books have been reacting in a similar manner. A look at governments' money trails gives a better answer for the rationale of the UIGEA's passage.

Laws and regulations often treated lotteries separately from other forms of gambling. Lotteries' unusual feature of needing no significant capital expenditure and, when properly structured, raising money quickly offers an explanation. Governments have known since medieval times that they could raise money fast and with relative ease by selling lottery tickets. Paying taxes by buying into lotteries at monopolistic prices (as other forms of gambling were prohibited) was even fun – how often do taxpayers have fun paying taxes?

In 75 percent of the cases in the United States during the past thirty years, referenda and initiatives led to decisions to introduce such lottery monopolies – which is not surprising. For people who want to play, even monopoly prices are an improvement over prohibition, and they are the equivalent of lowering taxes, or of lowering prices. It is not the case, as is often stated, that lotteries are a voluntary tax that people love to pay. They are no more voluntary than any other indirect tax: after all, we may decide to refrain from drinking alcoholic beverages or buying cigarettes and thus avoid paying excise taxes. And people love to pay the monopoly price only in contrast to the alternative of not being able to play at all. The move from prohibition to monopoly is still the equivalent of lower taxes.

If people had been asked to vote on the question, "Do you want gambling to be a sector like all others, taxed and regulated rather than being a monopoly?" they probably would have done so with even greater enthusiasm. We can make this guess because we know that people continue to bet hundreds of billions of dollars illegally on types of gambling that are either prohibited or priced at monopolistic levels.

For the moment this question has not been raised during U.S. elections, because the United States does not yet rely systematically on the tools of direct democracy to decide on taxing, spending, and regulatory issues. We have to touch briefly upon direct democracy, not only because in 75 percent of cases this was the institution used to reintroduce lotteries in the United States, but also because economists have often asked whether lotteries are a good tax and have written incoherent treatises answering the question.

As we point out, only referenda and initiatives could answer this question,[2] in the sense that these are the political institutions that could prevent fiscal and regulatory errors from persisting.[3] Models and theories will not do. If voters find out that they were mistaken, whether on gambling issues or anything else, they can change their minds and reverse their decisions through an initiative. Only Switzerland has relied on these institutions of direct democracy systematically for centuries, on federal, canton, and municipal levels, and to make decisions on taxes, spending, regulations, and matters of public interest in general. After introducing gambling through this mechanism, perhaps U.S. voters will go the next step and take the initiative to rely on it to get out from the present confusing state of affairs in many matters, those concerning gambling in particular.

L'Estrange Ewen gives the most detailed survey of lotteries, public and private, over centuries, as well as of sweepstakes in England, Scotland, and Ireland until 1932, reprinting the main features of the initial prospectuses of each government- and private-backed lottery issue. The examination of the conditions surrounding issuance led Ewen to conclude that the "main reason for prohibitive ordinances [against lotteries] were at first to clear the way for State monopoly, the Exchequers very soon realizing the possibilities of the lottery as a revenue-producing machine."[4] The English treasury was not the first to go through these motions. In 1561 Bruges passed a prohibition against private lotteries, as a step toward the institution of the state lottery.[5] Indeed, after occasional broad prohibitions against gambling, governments soon carved out exemptions and monopolies on specific games – frequently to themselves – exactly as various U.S. states have been doing over the past few decades.

Such monopolies in the past were often abused. However, these were "outside vices," as Ewen puts it, having nothing to do with lotteries or gambling, but with monopoly, as part of the returns were used for bribes both to sustain such powers and to obtain other privileges. Nevertheless, moralists indicted gambling, rather than monopoly powers – and governments and pliable intellectuals did not seem too eager or alert to correct the error.

Isn't it surprising that behind the rhetoric of competition today, we are encountering the same problems that Adam Smith's 1776 book, *The Wealth of Nations,* was really about, namely the fight against monopolies? Only then Smith was talking about monarchs granting "patents," and now we talk about democratically elected governments doing the same.[6] Hiding behind moralists' unfounded accusations, western governments (and the rest of the world to an even greater extent) continue to create and sustain, explicitly or implicitly, monopolies, be they in gambling, health, education, first-class mail, electricity, oil production, or, as in Quebec, liquor stores. Western governments avoid much-needed debates about just how much they could spend to start with, what would be the best ways to raise revenues to sustain such spending, and what type of political institution other than those that exist today are needed to better answer these questions.[7]

Ewen also concluded that governments gave way to objectors to gambling and gave up revenues from time to time because both administration developed and direct taxation became easier, which meant less need for intermediaries specialized in marketing and distributing lotteries. Also, as the banking system and financial markets developed, they could raise money quickly by issuing bonds instead: banks became the new intermediaries that raised money for governments. False views about the effect of lotteries gained currency, especially claims that the poor were succumbing to the temptations of lotteries and gambling with devastating effects.

There is no evidence to support this view, and there never was, as the previous chapters show. The facts are probably the clearest and sharpest in the United Kingdom today – and suggest the contrary. The same English people who buy lottery tickets also save a lot – and they do so with the same financial instrument, so-called premium savings bonds, which contradicts much fact-free theorizing and moralizing. During the past few years, the English allocated roughly £7 billion of their portfolio every year to this financial instrument. Twenty-three million Brits, almost 40 percent of the population, hold such bonds in their portfolios. This English innovation, backed by the government and dating back centuries (though in its recent incarnation going back only some fifty years), offers savers a few basis points less in interest rates than ordinary government bonds. In return, savers have the right to take part regularly in lottery drawings, where winnings are free of both income and capital gains tax.[8] This innovative financial instrument is one indication of what might happen if, instead of sustaining monopolies on lotteries, governments allowed any corporation to issue them in combination with customary debt instruments. Financial entrepreneurs would come up with a wide variety of innovations, combining debt instruments with lottery features and thereby lowering the cost of capital – actually reinventing what has been popular for centuries in the United Kingdom.

It is not surprising that lotteries have reappeared since the 1970s, in spite of large bureaucracies administering every possible tax imaginable, liquid bond markets, and the Mafia's gambling mythologies.[9] As governments took on expanded commitments, when they faced the choice of further explicit tax increases or implicit increases through legalizing lotteries and casinos, they opted for the latter. As more states adopted gambling, hoping to attract tourists from other states and to tax them, every state that did not legalize gambling lost tax revenues. Today, with forty-eight states having one form or another of gambling, and with lotteries providing, on average, 2 percent of state revenues (varying between a low of 0.5 percent and a high of 7 percent), the threat suddenly struck them all from online gambling companies, which are located in low-taxed foreign jurisdictions.

The UIGEA's impact has been to protect the states' tax base and, for a while, to strengthen the states' monopoly powers on lotteries and other forms of gambling for which the online companies posed a threat. In the United States, historically, gambling regulation, with the exception of Indian gaming, has been the purview of the states. But Senator Jon Kyl, a sponsor of the UIGEA, has been saying since the 1990s that state attorneys general have been asking for Washington's help, which is "simply responding to the states' requests to help them enforce their existing state policy."[10] When suggested in a 1999 interview with the *Wall Street Journal* that the states have an interest in prohibiting Internet gambling because, already in 1997, state lotteries earned a combined $56 billion in sales, Senator Kyl called the number a pittance. He added: "It would be cynical in the extreme to attribute to these attorneys general a motive that they are trying to protect state revenue streams." Instead, Senator Kyl has been repeating customary arguments against gambling to rationalize his stand, which, as has been pointed out, do not hold up to closer scrutiny.

However, for centuries, governments and rulers were not shy in acknowledging that, indeed, they outlawed private lotteries in order to increase their revenues. Moreover, Senator Kyl's sponsored act exempts gambling activities from which the states profit – lotteries, horse racing, and dog racing. This makes it hard to accept the interpretation that the states' efforts have little to do with stamping out potential – untaxed – competition from online gambling, that the legislative efforts are pursued instead to eradicate a vice, or that the act would mitigate other risks. In fact, we can safely predict that the impact of the UIGEA will be, as has always been with prohibitions, that fly-by-night operators will replace brand-name operators, such as Party Gaming, that withdrew the sale of services after the passage of the act. These small operators will offer less in prizes, they may not pay what they promise, and they certainly have no incentive to prevent minors from playing or to put software in place to warn players about their spending patterns. Our first book on the topic, published in 1990, made several predictions, all of which held up. Only time will tell if the previous predictions will hold up.

But now back to the present. Tennessee's governor Phil Bredesen, in his State of the State address in February 2007, put forward a proposal to pledge part of the state lottery money as collateral for bonds to finance schools in cities and counties that do not have a good bond rating. In Illinois, the state government hired Goldman Sachs to advise on leasing the state lottery, looking to obtain $10 billion in funds, and it promised to spend parts of it now, on just about anything. In 2006, the state lottery made $630 million, on revenue of $2 billion.

In Texas, Governor Rick Perry made the centerpiece of his State of the State speech in February 2007 the spending of $1 billion dollars to help the uninsured and to fight cancer – and to pay for it by selling the state lottery. The Texas lottery reported $3.77 billion in sales in 2006. The states are by no means alone in advocating restrictions on online gambling, or in following up such legislation with the securitiziation of fast net revenues from the monopoly on lotteries. The states are doing what Italy did in 2001, when it raised €3 billion by selling revenues from Lotto and SuperEnalotto for five years to two Dutch foundations.[11] In 2001 Greece privatized its national lottery and sold equity stake to institutional investors and the public. The resulting entity, OPAP, had a market capitalization of roughly $11.7 billion in March 2007. Yet when a company goes public, the government explicitly acknowledges a business interest. Such acknowledgment is inconsistent with statements that the service such companies offer represents some intangible higher principles.

Perhaps states may now follow the Greek, Italian, and other U.S. states' examples. Forty-eight states (all except Hawaii and Utah) have some form of legalized gambling. Forty-two states have lottery monopolies. As authorized by the federal Interstate Horseracing Act, thirty-seven states currently allow bets on horse and dog racing to be placed online. Oregon, for example, currently hosts hubs for these forms of online gambling among state residents, which generated more than $200 million in revenue in 2005. As noted, the UIGEA exempts online bets on horse racing, Internet state lotteries, and some fantasy sports within states, as well as Indian intratribal transactions, which are subject to the Indian Gaming Regulatory Act. Perhaps it is not surprising either that in February 2007, both Standard & Poor's and Moody's upgraded $100 million worth of Oregon lottery–backed bonds to triple A from AA3 (this happened just three months after the passage of the UIGEA). The Oregon State Legislature is already looking into an additional $100 million in infrastructure investments financed by lottery-backed bonds.

Such ratings upgrades and securitization are not necessarily beneficial. Greater assurances about monopoly powers, now offered by the UIGEA, will always bring about higher ratings.[12] And immediate securitization allows governments to immediately spend money and buy votes. They may finance current spending (never mind if governments label them "investments"), but people did not vote for the increased monopoly powers of the UIGEA, for increased spending at the state level, or for redefining governments' roles as far as the gambling sector is concerned. Actually, millions of law-abiding citizens were voting with their pockets to gamble online, using sites of companies listed on the London stock market. The end result may be that the issuers – the state's taxpayers – are left with large liabilities.

History may be repeating itself. In 2003 California sold $3 billion worth of bonds, backed by future receipts from the 1998 settlement between the four biggest U.S. tobacco firms and state governments. Earlier, in 1999, New York City raised $709 million by selling bonds backed by the same settlement. These four companies agreed to pay $206 billion over twenty-five years in return for exemptions from state claims. Although these bonds were designed to get A ratings, some of the bonds' yields varied between 6.5 and 7 percent. Similarly rated securities to finance toll roads, for example, yielded only 5 percent (additional evidence that rating agencies' grading may be important for regulatory purposes, but does not offer reliable information on pricing). A possible reason for the greater spread is that, as the states sold their exposures, their interest in maintaining the demand for cigarettes was weakened. New York mayor Mike Bloomberg's policies of both increasing taxes on cigarettes and imposing additional restrictions on where people can smoke should not come as much of a surprise. But what this sequence of events and pricing means is that raising money through tobacco settlement–backed bonds does not come cheap.

Can a similar sequence of events happen with bonds backed by lottery monopolies? Probably. The states may be raising the money now to finance current spending. Once the bonds are issued, the states will have less inter-est in sustaining the monopoly and the rating agencies may give A ratings to these bonds, but their yields will be another matter. Taxpayers may not immediately recognize in them the relatively high costs of current spend-ing. And when future taxpayers pay for them, it will be too late. By then the politicians under whose tenure the bonds were sold will be long gone, together with the underwriters.

We do not know when voters will impose an initiative to reexamine the legislative and regulatory gambling landscape, the one concerning online gambling, and the issuance of bonds backed by future lottery revenues. This chapter, by focusing on gambling and public finance, hopefully, will help provide an impartial debate when the time of such initiatives comes. After all, in recent surveys, 83 percent of U.S. citizens were in favor of the statement, "Gambling is a question of personal choice. The government should not be telling American adults what they should or should not be doing with their own time or money." Only 13 percent disagreed, and 4 percent either said that they did not know or refused to answer.

Lotteries and Public Finance

The Roman emperors understood the contribution that lotteries could make to state coffers. Both Augustus and Nero used lotteries regularly to finance their massive monument buildups. Lotteries also financed the rebuilding of Rome after Nero burned it down. The famous Chinese general Cheung Leung invented keno, a Chinese lottery, in 200 BCE. He did so to finance his army that faced a rebellion. Keno was so successful that it was then used to finance the building of the Great Wall of China, a military infrastructure that, as so many other ancient military monuments around the world, is bringing an unexpected return as a tourist attraction millennia later.

When there was neither developed administration nor developed financial markets, lotteries were the means to raise money quickly to finance infrastructure, military, or other needs. Flanders used lotteries in the fifteenth century to build ports and poorhouses.[13] The first recorded use of lotteries in the fifteenth century is in the town of Sluis, in the Netherlands, in 1434, to strengthen the town's fortifications.[14] Middleburg later raised funds through lotteries for the same purpose. In Amsterdam in 1592 lotteries paid for the building of a hospital. In 1695–6 twenty-four cities in the Dutch Republic organized lotteries with large first prizes. In 1726 lotteries became a state monopoly and financed many infrastructures.[15]

In Italy, Venice created the first successful government monopoly in lotteries,[16] with Florence, Milan, Turin, and Rome following suit.[17] Lotteries, as a method of public finance, took root in France after the courtiers of Catherine de Medici introduced them. Francis I immediately saw their potential for generating revenues and proceeded to issue the first patent letters (monopoly, by another name) for a *loterie* in 1539 in exchange for an annual right to two thousand livres.[18] During the same century, the proceeds of a lottery financed the building of the Parisian Church of Saint-Sulpice, as well as that of the Military School of Paris.[19] In 1572 a lottery in Paris provided dowries for impoverished but virtuous young women.[20] Before the tickets were drawn, on Palm Sunday, Mass was celebrated with great pomp, and Pope Sixtus V granted promoters of the lottery remission of sins. Lotteries were so successful in France that they became important fiscal instruments.[21]

In 1776 all public lotteries in France were consolidated in the Loterie Royale, modeled on the successful lottery of the Roman states sponsored by the pope (which helped to maintain Rome's public monuments and create the museum of the Vatican).[22] All private lotteries were outlawed – which is a way to increase taxes without being explicit about it – thus allowing the government to charge monopolistic prices for the lottery tickets. The state lottery then offered significant support for the chronically insolvent French treasury. It even survived the French Revolution.

Whereas the revolutionary government in 1793 first abolished lotteries on the ground that they exploited the poor, the decision was reversed a few years later.[23] In 1799 the lotteries were reborn under the name Loterie Nationale. During the few years of prohibition, the French played foreign lotteries illegally.[24]

With Napoleon Bonaparte's coming to power, the Loterie Nationale was renamed Loterie Impériale, and it helped finance Napoleon's wars and projects.[25] The lottery survived both Napoleon's fall and the restoration of Louis XVIII. The legislature abolished it in 1836, while at the same time creating savings banks – an unsurprising result, repeated in many countries, as is shown later in this chapter.[26]

Stephen Stigler, in his 2003 Ryerson Lecture "Casanova's Lottery," gives a thorough description of events leading up to the 1836 prohibition. (And, yes, the title refers to *that* Casanova: he had ideas about innovating lottery offerings too, not only about seducing women). He too finds that there was no evidence whatsoever that people bet over their heads or were ignorant of the exact probabilities of winning. In fact, much of his lecture is about the detailed statistics he found in the rare 1834 book *Almanach romain sur la loterie de France*. The book gave all the winning numbers of every draw in France between 1758 and 1833. Both the winning numbers and the geographic distribution of winners were random, and so there could not have been fraud.

Stigler also found that the true odds were widely known to all levels of society because they were widely advertised and disseminated. It is not accidental that Stigler found too that the golden age of French lotteries was also the golden age of French probability theory, between 1783 and 1836. His only puzzle remains why lotteries were prohibited: he misses the link to the emergence of competing financial institutions to raise funds and to attract discretionary income for deposits, and to the expanding administration, which could manage a variety of taxes.

Following the 1836 prohibition, lotteries to promote the arts or for charitable purposes were still authorized. Also, municipalities such as Paris,

Lyon, and Marseilles frequently sold premium bonds, where part of the accumulated interest was pooled and allocated by lot, similar in structure to present-day premium savings bonds in the United Kingdom.

Today in France, the gambling industry brings to the state coffers roughly € 5 billion – a number "threatened by the online gambling companies," as recent headlines in the French press declare. A September 28, 2006, major article in *Le Point* by Romain Gubert, titled "War of Gambling Has Started," notes that France has tried to block the "barbarians at the online gates," though Brussels has tried to fight the national monopolies, and promises that the new industry will level the field across Europe. At the time of the writing of this book, the monopolies are standing – just as the U.S. states' monopolies do.

Lottery Finance by English Governments

English rulers relied on lotteries as a significant source of public finance. Queen Elizabeth chartered a lottery that was drawn in 1569 and offered a variety of prizes in goods as well as money.[27] In addition to the first prize of £5,000, there was another prize that rendered the buyer free from arrest for seven days except for major crime. This first lottery was not a great success though, in spite of its apparently heavy advertising.[28] Less than one-twelfth of the tickets were sold, and the prizes were reduced. The next drawings took place in 1569, 1585, and 1612, when James I authorized them to raise funds for the Virginia Company to finance settlements in the New World. This lottery was successful, and the Virginia Company used the proceeds to raise lotteries in the following years.

Cities and towns were at first very happy with the lottery. But some began to complain that the excitement of the lottery had demoralized business and industry. Given all the evidence presented in the previous chapters, one cannot exclude the possibility that these were sour-grapes competitors who saw a decline in their business when people preferred to spend more discretionary income on lotteries. Indeed, from the 1621 declaration, when Parliament halted lotteries until "we shall be more fully informed of the inconveniences and evils of [lotteries] . . . and may ordane due remedy to the same,"[29] we can infer again that there was no obvious demoralization in the land. Private lotteries continued to flourish in spite of the prohibition. The only occasional objection against them has been that "the meaner sort of people are diverted from their work,"[30] a statement that should not be taken at face value, but as reflecting class prejudices concerning people's choices of entertainment.

The 1621 act did not last for long. The king granted monopoly privileges to his courtiers, and in 1627, 1631, and 1689 lotteries were used to finance the supply of London water.[31] In 1693, though, Parliament passed legislation to ban public lotteries again, this time "to eliminate competition prior to launching its own scheme," as Anne Murphy shows.[32]

The year 1694 saw the return of the state lottery in a new guise, not dissimilar to today's premium savings bonds. To replenish the Exchequer, depleted by French war expenditures, the state sponsored a lottery whose tickets were state bonds to be repaid sixteen years later. The interest rate to be paid, above a minimum of 10 percent (a rather low rate for that period), was drawn in a lottery.[33] Also, the nonprizewinning tickets entitled holders to a yearly 10 percent return until 1710, and they had a liquid market.[34] This new financial instrument was very successful, and was repeatedly issued until 1769. The 1693 ban against private lotteries was lifted too, and the last decade of the seventeenth century also saw a wide variety of private lotteries, as part of a competitive market of selling almost anything.[35] This may well have been the best way to dispose of items when financial markets were in their infancy and mobility and information were costly.[36]

Both the private and the state lotteries were sold under a variety of names, each lottery having some distinguishing characteristics, much as bonds do today. They went by the name of "adventures," "lottery annuities," "contingent lotteries," and so forth. Actually, as Natasha Glaisyer points out, "overwhelmingly the term used to describe lottery ticket purchasers was 'adventurer.'"[37] The only surviving variation on these types of bonds reappeared in the 1950s as premium savings bonds, and gambling laws were the obstacle for innovations in this class of financial instrument.

If lotteries had not been the monopoly of governments, financial markets would have probably long ago reinvented a wide variety of debt and lottery combinations, allowing for cheaper financing for both governments and companies – and, as Aaron Brown once put it, even "putting the 'fun' back into funded debt." The U.K. lotteries were themselves modeled after various Dutch innovations: recall that Amsterdam had the first stock market and became the financial center of the world.[38] Among the financial innovations were the "class" or "Dutch" lotteries, which consisted of a sequence of drawings, with each class – often called the adventurer – becoming eligible for later and more desirable classes, as the number and value of prizes increased. English lotteries emulated the Dutch lotteries and made innovative variations around them.[39]

Still, subsequent English rulers occasionally banned lotteries. The preamble of a 1699 statute, for example, noted that lottery promoters had "most unjustly and fraudulently got . . . great sums of money from the children and servants of several gentleman, traders, merchants...to the utter ruin and impoverishment of many families."[40] There is no evidence to back this opinion, and in 1709 the British government abolished the ban. Actually, there is plenty of evidence to suggest the contrary about lottery promoters. They used a variety of ways to assure lottery buyers that the drawings were honest, and they went to great lengths to publish probabilities, as in France.

The promoters appointed prominent men as trustees. Once it was clear how many tickets they issued and what prizes they awarded, marketers publicized the probabilities and regularly published lottery manuals.[41] Anne Murphy notes that "the odds of winning a lottery were generally listed in each advertisement and the *Athenian Mercury*, at least, defined the likelihood of receiving a prize in numeric terms." As an example, she notes that in 1695, "the paper suggested that . . . the best chance of winning a prize was offered by Unparallel'd Adventure because 'you are sure for 21 *l.* to have Three Prizes, which is at least 15 *l.*"[42] Imagine if all stocks and bonds today were promoted with information about their statistical characteristics, which could then be compared with those of other financial instruments.

During the eighteenth century and until 1826, the government continued to authorize annual lotteries as a means of financing the Exchequer, and it allowed the sale of expensive items through private lotteries. In 1721 private lotteries were outlawed, but publicly sponsored ones continued to flourish. As always, eliminating the competition was a way to raise taxes, by increasing the state's monopoly powers on pricing its own lotteries. Five Westminster Bridge Lotteries between 1737 and 1741 financed the building of the bridge, and one, in 1753, financed the British Museum.[43] The archbishop of Canterbury was the trustee of these lotteries. There were also the South Sea Company lottery annuities and the navy lottery annuities. Altogether, between 1694 and 1768, there were forty-three state lottery issues, each with its own features, that raised roughly £140 million.[44] This number does not include the large number of private lotteries that were marketed with flair, or the drawings taking places in theaters and associated with entertainment. After 1790 lottery revenues represented roughly 2 to 3 percent of government revenues (a range similar to that of today), reaching 7 percent during the war with the North American colonies.[45]

As in France, lotteries became a main topic of conversation among mathematicians and scientists during the seventeenth and eighteenth centuries in England. One scientist writing to Isaac Newton about lotteries commented: "almost extinguished for some time at all places of publick conversation in this towne, especially among men of numbers, every other talk but what relates to the doctrine of determining between the true proportions of the hazards incidents to this or that given chance or lot."[46] As in France, the eighteenth century in the United Kingdom saw a revolution in the literature on gambling and the publication of several books on probability and card games. Books covered quadrille, piquet, and whist (the forerunner of bridge). Edmond Hoyle was one prominent writer, and between 1740 and 1770 his books about gambling ran quickly through several editions, sometimes up to fifteeen.

Although there was no evidence of vice, each year the passage of the Lottery Act, which allowed the sale of lotteries for that year, became the occasion of severe criticism. In 1808 a committee of the House of Commons was appointed to inquire into the evil consequences of lotteries and the remedies that could be obtained from regulating them. Its final report concluded by saying that "the foundation of the lottery system is so ... vicious ... that under no ... regulation ... will it be possible ... [to] divest it of all ... evils" (Ashton, 1969, p. 161). Yet, as Raven points out, the moralists were speaking, as there was no evidence of such ill effects:

Lest one take the language of the debate too seriously, it must be said that working-class gambling did not pose the threat to social order or self help alleged by almost every parliamentary critic. Fraud was certainly evident, but not on the scale claimed by many commentators ... [M]ost working class gambling was free from extensive fraud because it was self regulating and answerable to a far from ignorant clientele. There is also little evidence to support alarmist contemporary accounts of the amounts lost by the gambling poor.[47]

The 1823 Lottery Act made provisions ended the practice after a last drawing in 1826.[48] This epitaph was written for the occasion:

In Memory of
THE STATE OF LOTTERY
the last of a long line
whose origin in England commenced
in the year 1569,
which after a series of tedious complaints
Expired
On the
18th day of October 1826.
During a period of 257 years, the family
flourished under the powerful protection
of the
British Parliament;

The Minister of the day continuing to
give them this support for the improvement
of the revenue.

As they increased, it was found that their
continuance corrupted the morals,
and encouraged a spirit
of Speculation and Gambling among the lower
classes of people . . . [49]

Why was the lottery canceled? Again, one gets a better understanding if one follows the money trail rather than take the moral debates at face value. A couple of events took place. With the end of the revolutionary and Napoleonic wars raising money quickly through lotteries – be it as a "tax" or a "loan" – became less needed. The returns from this source of funding diminished because there were more lotteries being offered (in part because laws against private gambling were not enforced) and the administrative costs of raising money by other means was relatively diminished. Before 1810 gross lottery revenues contributed 3 percent to public incomes, but they never exceeded 2 percent after 1810. This also happened because of larger official salary lists and the lack of transparency of the lottery administration. Raven concludes that "from the late eighteenth century the lottery administration took on a practical independence, its efficiency and contribution to the exchequer often too complicated to appraise. The intricacy and autonomy of both Lottery Office management and the contractors' operations were a formidable shield against full investigation."[50] This happened, in part, because the market price of the tickets derived from contractors' secret tenders and negotiations with the treasury.

The lesson from legislative history is that problems associated with gambling happened when lotteries either were monopolies or were not managed transparently at arm's length. But such problems have nothing to do with gambling per se. Whether lotteries should still be a tool of public finance, as was the case when there was neither a developed administration nor developed capital markets, is one question. As we pointed out, the best way to answer this question is by direct appeal to voters. The evidence suggests that the best way to deal with this fast-changing industry is along the lines of the United Kingdom, following exactly the recommendations that Ewen spelled out some seventy years ago:

In the event of the Government not preserving a monopoly, but resting content with a stamp duty, as with other entertainments, possibly a Board of Control might have to be set up, certainly each private scheme would have to be examined before being licensed, and guarantees taken, preferential treatment guarded against. [51]

The 1823 act marks the end of lotteries in England untill 1956, except for their use to promote the arts and some other special purposes. In 1836 the advertising of foreign lotteries was also prohibited.[52] And what did people do? A select committee in 1844 found that working-class gambling had transferred to the racecourse.[53]

Lottery Finance in the New World: Origins of Investment Banking

Lotteries came to the New World as an import from the Old World.[54] Recall how the Virginia Company financed the early settlers with the help of lotteries and that the banking system was undeveloped.

Although there were groups such as the Quakers of Pennsylvania whose objections against lotteries resulted in the passage of laws against them, and other groups repeating arguments that the poor may be tempted to play too much, the colonial governments did not outlaw lotteries. They needed this source of public finance, because the fiscal needs of the colonies were large and taxation was poorly organized. The colonial governments waged wars against both Native Americans and the French, but the population resisted increased taxes.[55] The lotteries then financed the protection of the seacoast against the French (1744, Massachusetts), paid for fortification (1746, New York City), helped to build colleges (Yale, Harvard, Princeton, and the University of Pennsylvania), and provided for the construction of churches (1765, Pennsylvania). One reason for the delay of Harvard's lottery was to prevent it from competing with lotteries to support British troops fighting the French and Indian War.

The price of tickets was relatively high. Another Harvard College Lottery sold twenty-five thousand tickets at $5 each – when the dollar was a dollar and per-capita annual income for the white population was estimated at $60. It is as if the price of the ticket were some $1,500 today.[56] The revenue from these lotteries can be compared with today's, which are earmarked to finance culture and education. Indeed, in 1892 a historian remarked:

Lotteries organized for public projects...were not regarded at all as a kind of gambling; the most reputable citizens were engaged in these lotteries, either as selected managers or liberal subscribers. It was looked upon as a kind of voluntary tax for paving the streets, erecting wharves, buildings, which a contingent profitable return for such subscribers as held the lucky numbers.[57]

Between 1744 and 1774 the colonies sanctioned approximately 158 lotteries. One-third financed the building of canals and roads and twenty-seven financed the building of churches (if you can't beat them, join them); thirteen helped educational institutions; and five financed the start of new industries. These lotteries were high priced and respected. As in England at various times, community leaders promoted lotteries as they promoted charity drives.[58] George Washington promoted lotteries to finance westward expansion. Benjamin Franklin launched one to erect a steeple at Christ Church in Philadelphia, and, in 1748, another to buy cannon for the city. John Hancock was behind a lottery in 1762 to rebuild Faneuil Hall, and recall Jefferson's favorable view of lotteries that we quoted in Chapter 1.

Following the debates in England, the British administrators of the colonies called for the abolition of lotteries. A circular sent to colonial governors in 1768 forbade them from licensing further lotteries, stating:

Whereas a Practice hath...prevailed...in America for passing laws for raising money by instituting public lotteries;...such practice doth tend to disengage those who become adventurers therein from that spirit of industry and attention to their proper callings and occupations on which the public welfare so greatly depends.[59]

Was there some truth in this statement? Perhaps, although the implications should have been different. Some adventurers (today we would call them venture capitalists) who occasionally won at the poker tables or in lotteries may have used the money to settle down, actually giving opportunities to new adventurers to challenge their luck. Still, the condemnation smacks of class distinctions and of wrongheaded ideas about the law of labor. It appears that the adventurers who chose to come to the New World were expected to work relentlessly, and were not given the option to win big and then retire to the pastoral, gentry life they aspired to. That lifestyle was supposed to be the prerogative of inherited rank.

But the days of the English were numbered, and during the Revolutionary War lotteries were again a means by which a hard-pressed Continental Congress hoped to finance its war expenses, establishing the U.S. lottery. The first drawing was successful; the following was less so.

Lotteries flourished in the independent United States as they had in colonial America. The people were wary of taxes (they had, after all, just waged a war to not pay them). So, both the federal government and the states used lotteries to finance public projects – recall that monopoly prices mean lowered taxes when compared with the alternative of prohibition. Counties and municipalities used them to finance public buildings, to repair streets, to ensure the water supplies of cities, and to build roads, canals, and bridges.

At the same time, banking developed. Still, lottery financing continued to be combined with what we now view as conventional methods of finance. For example, after the Revolution, John Adams negotiated Dutch loans for the new country. Because the credit rating of the United States was not top notch, the lenders required sweeteners – bonuses beyond the negotiated interest payments. Adams arranged for a lottery to pay the bonus.[60] Although by 1810 there were nearly ninety incorporated banks, up from three twenty years earlier, lotteries continued to be important sources of funding.

From Lotteries to Banking

According to the *Boston Mercantile Journal*, in 1832 approximately 420 lotteries were drawn in eight states (New York, Virginia, Connecticut, Rhode Island, Pennsylvania, Delaware, North Carolina, and Maryland). The tickets sold in these lotteries brought in a gross revenue of $66 million that year, more than five times the expenses of the federal government.[61] This sum was four times the federal expenditure in 1832. Gribbin and Bean (2005) note that by the mid-nineteenth century, New York City had 160 lottery shops and Philadelphia more than 200. In the South too, lotteries were seen as a legitimate way for public finance. When revenues from crops were volatile and banking institutions undeveloped, lotteries offered a solution to raise money from time to time, substituting either for explicit taxes or for issuing bonds. Governments authorized lotteries when crops were sold and cash was available.

As lottery activities expanded, their character changed. Governments and other institutions outsourced the marketing and sales of lotteries. A group of intermediaries, ticket brokers, and lottery contractors developed. The contractors took over the management of lotteries and hired brokers to sell the tickets. The brokers bought large blocks of tickets at a discount and resold them at face value in all the states. Just as gamblers brought about the development of clearinghouses, this network of lottery contractors and ticket brokers set the foundations for modern investment banking and stock brokerage services by initially tapping people's savings to finance big public works.

Lottery brokers founded both the Chase National Bank and the First National Bank of New York City. The lottery brokerage firm of S. & M. Allen transformed itself into a banking and stock brokerage firm. This company was also where Enoch W. Clark, a relative of the Allens, who later established E. W. Clark & Co. of Philadelphia (which became the largest dealer in domestic exchange in the 1840s and 1850s), started his career. By 1823 two entrepreneurs, John B. Yates and Archibald McIntyre, had the privilege of handling nearly all the sales of New York's authorized lotteries.[62] By the time midwestern towns and states needed capital for major improvements, the newly chartered banks of New York and other eastern cities provided the necessary loans, and local administration was more developed. Local governments then saw fewer benefits in raising money through lotteries, which they realized could substitute for taxation only if the competition of private lotteries was restricted.[63]

Toward Prohibition

One lottery scandal occurred in Washington, D.C. In 1823 Congress authorized the Grand National Lottery to pay for improvements to the city. After selling the tickets, but before distributing the winnings, the private agent that organized the lottery fled town. The winner of the $100,000 grand prize sued the government of the District of Columbia, and the Supreme Court ruled that the district was liable.

Instead of pointing out that such occasional fraud happens in every sector and that there were no facts to back various outlandish accusations drawing on few observations, Pennsylvania became the first state to abolish lotteries in 1833, followed by Massachusetts in the same year. By the beginning of the Civil War, all but Delaware, Kentucky, and Missouri had similar laws on their books.[64]

The Civil War and its financial consequences for the southern states brought their revival. Once again, lotteries financed the construction of roads, bridges, and schools. One difference between these lotteries and previous ones was that the tickets were sold nationally, whereas previously they were sold locally. However, by 1868, three years after the end of the war, Congress forbade any sale of lottery tickets by mail, and by 1878 all states except Louisiana had prohibited lotteries.

In Louisiana, the lottery (known as "the Serpent") started in 1868 helped reconstruction. By the late 1870s tickets for the Louisiana lottery were sold illegally across the nation, and the lottery generated apparently extravagant profits for its monopolistic marketers. In the late 1880s almost 50 percent of all mail coming into New Orleans was connected with the lottery.

When in 1890 the charter that authorized the running of the Louisiana lottery was about to expire, the operators bribed state officials. The bribes were widely reported. State legislatures called on Congress and President Benjamin Harrison to prohibit the lottery. In 1895 Congress strengthened the law, preventing interstate transportation of lotteries by use of federal mail – an early version of the Wire Act and the UIGEA, which outlaws transferring money to online gambling companies. The Louisiana lottery stopped in 1895. Although, as so often before and since, the problem was because the lottery was a monopoly, the rents from which paid for bribes, and not because of anything linked to gambling.

This was the end of legal lotteries in the United States until 1963, when New Hampshire reintroduced the first one. This did not mean that Americans stopped buying into lotteries. Whereas English people spent more on races, Americans bought into Canadian lotteries, which we examine next. Prohibitions never had the impact that legislators expected.

Lotteries as Public Finance in Canada

The colonies of the North did not escape the lure of lotteries.[65] Whereas Quebec's authorities prohibited all games of chance, they allowed a few lotteries to dispose of some expensive property (as in the United States) or to raise money for charitable purposes or public projects. Again, the reason for lotteries was to substitute for an undeveloped banking system or for a nonexistent administration and bureaucracy that would collect taxes effectively.

The first lotteries in Quebec were severely regulated. Experts had to evaluate them, and the organizers had to obtain authorization from the government. During the Revolutionary War in the United States, the British governor in the North used lotteries to distribute land to Loyalist soldiers and to immigrants fleeing from south of the border.[66] In addition to property disposal, lotteries were used for public works: the new prison built in Montreal in 1783 was financed by a lottery. Moreover, revenues from American lotteries were used to finance large projects in Canada. An American lottery financed the Welland Canal between Lakes Ontario and Erie.[67]

But, apparently, there were no signs of excitement for lotteries in the Canadian provinces as they existed in the United States in the 1810s. The 1817 law outlawing gambling passed in Lower Canada did not seem to steer any particular attention. The official reason given for the law was, again, to prevent lower-class people like workers and servants from ruining themselves,[68] though, as everywhere else, there seems to be no evidence to back such opinion.

One form of lottery that continued to flourish in Lower Canada during this period was the raffle, a common fund-raising tool in many churches. Canadians who wanted to buy lotteries could buy into American ones. But, as one American state after another was outlawing lotteries during the 1840s, Canadian promoters of lotteries appeared, and between 1845 and 1856 many private lotteries in Canada were sold.[69] In 1856, as in other countries where financial institutions and administration to enforce taxes developed, a law was passed both outlawing lotteries and forbidding the sale of foreign tickets.

This was the end of legal lotteries in Canada too, except for Quebec, until the 1960s. In Quebec, under pressure from the Catholic Church, the law was amended to permit lotteries for charitable purposes in which the prizes were objects but not money.[70] But, using loopholes in the law, private lotteries continued to flourish until 1892, when the federal government amended its criminal code to outlaw lotteries. This law spelled the end of lotteries even in Quebec.

The Rebirth of Lotteries

As we have seen, France, England, and the United States all outlawed lotteries during the nineteenth century as their financial institutions took hold and governments found ways to collect taxes through tariffs, income taxes, excise taxes on alcoholic beverages (from 1860), or proceeds from sale of land and property taxes.

Belgium also outlawed lotteries in 1836, and Sweden in 1841.[71] Everywhere the official stand was that the lower classes are – or could be – tempted to play too much. This opinion has been repeated so frequently that to this day it seems to pass for fact, though there is absolutely no evidence to support the view that at any time poorer people were playing too much. True, as we saw, poor people did spend a greater fraction of their wealth on lotteries than did rich people. This is predictable. But they prudently allocated a small proportion of their wealth, shifting marginally either from consumption or from charities, which are often the competition for the small change that people decide to spend on lotteries. (This explains why many charitable organizations – self-declared cultural ones among them – oppose gambling or its privatization: when gambling is a government monopoly, they are vocal about getting a share of the revenues because most charities are in the small-change business.)

Sweden reintroduced lotteries in 1897 and legalized pari-mutuel betting on soccer games in the 1930s. Elsewhere, a few lotteries survived during the nineteenth century. The Spanish lottery, founded in 1763 to build the Madrid hospital, was never outlawed.[72] In 1769 Spain created the Lottery of New Spain, later renamed the National Lottery of Mexico, which still exists.[73] Portugal has had a lottery since 1783, when a royal charter created the Santa Casa da Misericórdia, an institution charged with collecting money for charitable purposes, in part through lotteries.[74] Italy never outlawed lotteries either, and the pope sponsored a successful lottery in the Papal

States. Germany has had lotteries since the Middle Ages, and in spite of calls for abolition during the nineteenth century, the German states continued to promote them for fiscal purposes, as did the Netherlands.[75]

The trend changed in World War I, when governments were left with empty coffers and huge debts. To attract subscribers to state loans, the governments of Austria, Belgium, France, Germany, and Italy introduced variations on premium bonds, which had the characteristics of a lottery: people gave up some points in interest for the right to participate regularly in lottery drawings.[76] It was also the burden left by the war that spurred France to reintroduce a lottery in 1933 earmarked to pay the pensions of war veterans.[77] Belgium introduced a national lottery the following year. The Irish Sweepstakes also had its origin at the end of World War I, when a ship sank off the Irish coast leaving the families of the drowned sailors destitute. A special lottery organized for their benefit was so successful that it led to the foundation of a permanent lottery.[78]

The Great Depression of the 1930s, when the price level in the United States dropped from 1929 to 1932 by roughly 30 percent and the unemployment rate increased to roughly 30 percent, saw the rise of gambling fever in the United States. Churches and charitable organizations were at the forefront of requesting the decriminalization of bingo parties, as they were received as a "healthy substitute for gossip teas, lovesick movies and liberal-minded chapters." Massachusetts decriminalized bingo first in 1931, followed by Rhode Island in 1937. Bingo then became popular at amusement parks, firefighters' carnivals, and church socials. Pari-mutuel betting was next, and New Hampshire, Ohio, and Michigan legalized it in 1933.[79]

Another rationale given for the relegalization of lotteries was that they would prevent the flow of U.S. funds to foreign lotteries or untaxed underworld coffers. *Time* magazine (April 20, 1936) wrote about the efforts of Mrs. Oliver Harriman, the head of an organization called the National Conference on Legalizing Lotteries Inc. She stated that there were no moral issues involved, that taxation had reached its limits, and that revenues from lotteries would actually help the poor.[80] During the 1930s, when interest in lotteries was at its height, the legislatures of New York, New Jersey, Massachusetts, Pennsylvania, Maryland, Louisiana, Illinois, Maine, New Hampshire, Connecticut, California, and Nebraska all considered bills legalizing them. In Massachusetts in 1935 the bill was rejected on a tie vote of 110 to 110.[81] Edward A. Kenny even introduced a bill in the House of Representatives, but he died in 1937, just before the matter was to be brought up for vote. Almost every subsequent session of Congress discussed the issue, but the war started, and more important matters were on legislators' agendas.[82]

Additional information on the increased interest in lotteries during the Depression comes from various polls. In October 1935 *Fortune* published the results of a national poll answering the following question: "Do you think that lotteries similar to the Irish Hospital Sweepstakes and conducted only for charity or taxation should be allowed in this country?" Fifty-five percent answered yes, 33 percent answered no, and 12 percent answered "don't know." There were wide regional variations in the answers. On the industrialized Pacific coast 79 percent favored lotteries, whereas in the northeastern states 58 percent favored it.[83] In fact, every poll taken after 1938 showed support for the legalization of lotteries. Meanwhile, illegal lotteries flourished, and during the 1930s an estimated 13 percent of Americans bought into Irish Sweepstakes illegally.

If Not Lotteries, Then Sweepstakes

Although lotteries were forbidden, substitutes were invented. The Great Depression was the period when contests swept the United States. The game involved buying a relatively cheap product, which gave the right to participate in the lottery, with prizes varying between $25 and $100,000. The legal loophole that allowed for these lotteries was that buyers had to answer a "skill" question, such as how much is two multiplied by two.[84] Three thousand contests were sponsored, and hundreds of millions of entries were submitted. After 1933 the volume of contests leveled off, though they remained popular until the 1940s.[85] Most contests offered monetary prizes, though those offering to sponsor the winners' children's college education were widespread. Contests offering radios, cars, fur coats, and diamonds were less common than contests offering monetary prizes in similar price ranges.[86]

The Depression years also brought in their wake the chain-letter craze of the 1930s and variations on the numbers racket. Another invention during the Depression was the movie house "bank night." Tickets bought not only admission but also a chance to win prizes. Charity organizations and private businesses gave away cars, refrigerators, and stoves as prizes, and chambers of commerce, representing the majority of merchants, engaged in these drawings. A contemporary commentator noted that whereas in the 1920s business looked down on contests, considering them cheap and circusy, during the Depression years, the contests became respectable.[87] This is not surprising: when the law prohibited lotteries, this tie-in arrangement satisfied a latent demand, and helped businesses move relatively expensive items, just as lotteries have helped sell expensive items since medieval times.

But does such a joint offering necessarily increase the price of products, as some claimed at the time? It is useful to take a small detour to answer this question, because it shows that antigambling laws may prevent not only a wide range of innovative debt and lottery financial instruments but also various innovative pricing schemes.

Assume that during "normal" times, a pack of cigarettes sells for $10 and $10 million is spent on ads. With the introduction of contests, the company may decide to spend $5 million on expenses involving the lottery (prizes and administration), and only $5 million on advertising. Such a change in the composition of advertising may be beneficial for businesses when, during periods such as the Depression, people prefer the product-lottery tie-in rather than the customary product-advertising tie-in.[88] Indeed, by 1931 contests were rapidly displacing special offers and premiums, and Eric Bender (1938) remarked that the "nation went contest-crazy." Slot machines were very popular too. Another contemporary observer estimated that in 1939, the national take from these machines exceeded $500 million, and a Gallup poll taken the same year indicated that one in three adults played slot machines (Blakey, 1977, Chapter 6). Horse racing and gambling on other types of races prospered during this period, for laws prohibiting racing and bookmaking were not enforced.

The fact that people gambled more during the 1930s – a period of Depression in England too – was not lost on English observers. Whereas the twentieth century saw a slow but steady decline in the proportion of income spent on drink, the reverse is true for betting and gambling, as expenditures on both grew quickly during the 1930s. An inquiry concerning office and warehouse workers in a number of firms in the city of Birmingham found that 80 percent were gambling regularly, legally or illegally.[89] Others noted that gambling increased during the period of economic and industrial depression between the wars "when the fascination of possibly winning something by luck did undoubtedly make its appeal to men and women who were living under conditions of financial stringency."[90]

It was, in part, the proliferation of dog tracks, following their establishment in the 1920s, and the gambling opportunities they offered to the depressed urban workers that led to the investigation of the 1932–3 Royal Commission into the whole issue of gambling.[91] Another reason for convening the commission was that in the 1930s, the Irish Free State began to promote the Irish Hospital Sweepstakes both in Ireland and in the United Kingdom. The Royal Commission seriously considered the revival of state lotteries, and recommended the legalization of off-course cash betting.

The most eloquent view of gambling comes from this period. An anonymous article, titled "Chance," had this to say:

The next best thing to a fortune is the chance of a fortune... To purchase a ticket in a lottery, indeed, is to buy a kind of fiction in which oneself is the hero. It is to see oneself, in one's mind's eye, happy and rich, free from all the cares and anxieties involved in earning a living, able to buy a cottage in the country, to take as long a holiday as one wishes... It may not be the most heroic of ideals, but it is among the most innocent... Besides this, the desire for money won without labour does not exclude dreams of nobler kind. It might even be maintained that anyone who longs to live a noble life should wish to obtain money without labour so that he may be released from the material struggle for gain and be able to devote himself to loftier pursuits... Getting and spending we lay waste our powers, says Wordsworth, and getting wastes even more of powers than spending. Day after day, hour after hour goes wastefully by in the effort to provide our families and ourselves with the necessaries of existence... It turns most of us inevitably into materialists. Let one of us win a first prize in a sweepstake, however, and he will have time to sit down and read the philosophers.[92]

This is certainly one possible extension of the ancient Latin proverb that well describes a majority of the lottery-buying public at all times: *Primum vivere, deinde philosophari.* Or, as Bertolt Brecht put it more recently, "Food first, ethics later."

Although there had been discussions about introducing lotteries in England during the war, they were avoided. Only in 1956 did the Macmillan government introduce a lottery in the budget in the form of the already-mentioned premium savings bonds. All other forms of betting, including lotteries and casinos, were legalized in 1960, taxed, and regulated, as the United Kingdom experimented with the entire betting business rather than with prohibitions.

Gambling Today in America

Groucho Marx once said, "Politics is the art of looking for trouble, finding it everywhere, diagnosing it incorrectly, and applying the wrong remedies." Politicians certainly seem to have found such perfect trouble in gambling.

Yet despite the trouble, some real, most imagined, in 2006 Americans could place bets legally in almost 900 casinos, 455 privately run in 11 states, 406 on Indian reservations in 29 states, and 29 racetrack casinos – called "racinos" – in 11 states. Another nine states were considering licensing casinos or racetrack gambling in 2006. Forty-one states, the District of Columbia, and Puerto Rico have lotteries.[93] Although some states, such as

Georgia, Nebraska, West Virginia, Maine, and Texas, have permitted private concerns, such as Scientific Games and G-Tech, to operate the instant-game portion of their lotteries, the vast majority of lottery operations are conducted by the state.[94] Moreover, until October 2006 Americans could bet online too and participate in many poker competitions.

These numbers do not take into account illegal sports betting and number games, wherever they take place.

The gross revenues from legal gambling, including Internet gambling but excluding illegal gambling on sports, amounted to roughly $84 billion in the United States in 2005. Gross revenues refer to revenues left after distributing the prizes. The gross from all lotteries amounted to almost $23 billion, while Indian reservations reported almost $22 billion and casinos nearly $32 billion. The rest was split among cardrooms, charitable bingo, charitable games, and legal bookmaking (including sports and horse books), amounting roughly to $4 billion. Internet gambling amounted to roughly $6 billion.[95]

The vast majority of U.S. citizens gamble. In 2005, 73 percent played the lottery, 67 percent played in a commercial casino, 36 percent wagered on a horse or a dog, and 33 percent played slots or casino games at a horse or a dog track. Only 3 percent of the U.S. population said that they had not taken part in any of the above, and 1 percent refused to answer. These numbers and observations recall the findings of the third Royal Commission in the United Kingdom, chaired by Lord Rothschild between 1976 and 1978, which observed that "the percentage of our adult population that gambles some time or other is about the same as the percentage of adults who engage in sexual intercourse."[96]

The commission also could not come up with anything that contradicted the finding of a 1949–51 commission that examined gambling, which drew conclusions on "gambling's relative social and economic insignificance."[97] Indeed, the numbers mentioned previously and all the surrounding noise concerning gambling laws and regulations should be put into perspective. With a roughly $12 trillion gross domestic product, the amounts spent on gambling total to about 0.8 percent, in the ballpark with spending on alcoholic beverages and tobacco.

The U.K. commission also concluded that though state intervention was necessary, it should be kept at minimum "to discourage socially damaging excesses, to prevent the incursion of crime into gambling, and to ensure that facilities offered should respond only to 'unstimulated demand.'"[98] Whereas the United Kingdom applied these principles and went from industry prohibition to regulation (and today has the most open betting markets in the western world), the United States, in spite of the aforementioned evidence, seemed to be stuck in prohibition rather than regulatory mode.

Much of the debate in the United States seems to be out of focus. Numerous articles discuss whether lottery is a tax, and others conclude that it is, and that it is a bad one. Still others examine whether moving from prohibition to monopolies on lotteries and licensing gambling establishments created employment and revenues. The predictable answer is, "Of course they did." But none of these issues are relevant for setting a solid, impartial foundation to a discussion of whether the gambling sector should be a sector like all others, though with a regulation fitting the specific features of the industry.

But let us also not forget that with the roughly 80 million retiring baby boomers, health-care programs are becoming more popular, and with both the increased focus on children and the low level of public education, higher teachers' salaries are pursued as remedies (rather than privatization). The selling of assets is viewed as preferable, because tax increases are unpopular. In 2003, following the early 2000 recession and constitutional requirements to balance budgets, the National Governors Association reported that the states were undergoing their worst budget problems since World War II. The sale of public assets – including lotteries – though, may not be the solution. Their sale, protected by promises of monopoly that may not last, will create obligations that are not backed by future revenues. In this sense, critiques of lotteries that they are a form of tax have a point – the monopolistic price is a tax. The reason that people still prefer this form of not-quite-transparent taxing to alternatives of direct taxes is that without the lottery monopoly they would not have any lottery. Those who attack government lotteries do not advocate a private gambling sector.

The best political process for moving from the present confused state of affairs in the United States to the one practiced in the United Kingdom with great success, is a sequence of initiatives. Voters would be asked whether they want the various state monopolies in the gambling sector to continue and, on the federal level, whether the Wire Act and the UIGEA should be discarded. Present disagreements about interpreting the Wire Act are related to debates over whether transmitting bets and wagers wirelessly is covered by the act or not, but the debate should be about whether this outdated act should be discarded altogether.

It is not the heavy taxed realm that executes great deeds, but the moderately taxed one.
Ancient Asian proverb

SEVEN

Politics and Prohibitions; or, What's a Good Tax Anyway?

Reuven Brenner

Which shows why prohibitions on gambling have been wrongheaded, often serving narrow political interests, their effect at all times in all countries having been the creation of extensive black markets rather than withdrawal from betting.

By the twentieth century, old theories blaming poverty on poor people's propensity to gamble and drink and on gambling violating the law of labor disappeared from both academic and political vocabularies. But it did not take long for new well-intentioned but inaccurate arguments against gambling to emerge. Some of these new vocabularies and models suggested what other jargons and models had suggested before: that gambling should either be prohibited or be a government monopoly both to prevent too much vice, fraud, corruption, and involvement of criminal elements and to control the populace's occasional irrational urges to gamble.

Other models have condemned government monopolies of lotteries or casinos, though without drawing the arguments to the logical conclusion or providing any alternatives. They condemned lotteries and some forms of gambling not on the grounds that monopoly rents could be spent on bribes or that monopoly prevents the development of a wide variety of innovative financial instruments and innovative betting markets. Instead, they stated that lotteries are both a regressive tax and a nontransparent one. Still others condemned gambling because of fear of addiction and fear that minors were in serious danger of corruption from easy and uncontrolled access to Internet gambling. This chapter takes a closer look at these assertions (some of which we have looked at before already) and, after dismissing most of them, examines their implications.

The conclusions reinforce those we reached in previous chapters; namely, that the best solution is to let the gambling sector – the online businesses in particular – operate as most others, neither prohibited nor a government monopoly, but properly taxed and regulated. Because government-owned enterprises that charge monopoly prices charge a form of tax, even if by another name, we have to raise the question of what a good tax is. We show how the political process of referenda and initiatives answers this question – the process used in most U.S. states to legalize lotteries and gambling.

Lotteries as a Regressive Tax: An Irrelevant Argument

We saw that, indeed, those people with diminished opportunities to "make it" – whether sixty-year-olds who recognize their only chance to become rich or others who are down on their luck – spend a higher proportion of their wealth on lotteries. When prohibition closes this venue, it is these people's hopes, dreams, and options that are severely taxed. Do these people then find refuge in religion? Do they escape into a drunken stupor or drug-induced hallucinations? Do they just live quiet, hopeless, desperate lives? Do they bet illegally or on foreign lotteries? It turns out that most often people do the latter. What we also know, from the previous chapter, is that when people are given the option of getting rid of prohibition, with lotteries and gambling promised to become government monopolies, the majority often votes for such a policy through referenda or initiatives. Relative to prohibition, a monopoly represents a lower tax.

The fact that people with fewer opportunities play lotteries or other games with relatively large prizes, priced at monopolistic levels, does not necessarily imply that lotteries and such gambling constitute a regressive tax, as far as taxation is concerned. Unless those who criticize government monopolies on such grounds recommend that lotteries be a private business and not taxed at all. Let's see why.

First, a move from prohibition to legalization means that implicit and explicit taxes – on hope and ways to become rich – become less regressive than they were before. As we saw already, people also paid explicit regressive taxes when they gambled illegally under prohibition. They bet on horses, sports, foreign lotteries, or other substitutes. This meant that when lotteries and many forms of gambling were prohibited, these people paid regressive taxes to foreign governments, to criminal elements, or, at best, to domestic racetracks.

What, then, is a logical conclusion of those who argue against lotteries on the grounds that they are a regressive tax? One might be that lotteries should be privatized and become a taxed and regulated business as most others. But would the taxes on lotteries in this case become any less regressive? The answer is "Unlikely."

After all, if lotteries or casinos ceased to be monopolies, competition would bring about lower prices and a wide variety of gambling and betting options. At the lower prices, people could gamble on lottery-type games even more than they did before. The companies in these businesses would make profits, and the government would collect excise taxes. The same people would continue to gamble – and be likely to buy more tickets than before. They would be paying the excise taxes instead of the monopoly price on the greater number of tickets. Neither the total amount of taxes transferred to governments nor the categories of people paying them would change. Taxes on lotteries and some forms of gambling would be just as regressive if the sector was competitive as they were before. Thus, viewed from this angle, even if the argument of regressivity has foundations,[1] it is an irrelevant consideration as far as gambling is concerned.[2]

Perhaps those who criticize lotteries on the basis of regressivity would like them to be privatized and exempt from all taxes, so as not to burden at all people down on their luck. If so, none of the studies arguing against regressivity makes this recommendation – which could follow logically from the studies' arguments – yet this is the only situation when a private lottery business would not imply regressive taxation.

Another possible conclusion of those who criticize government monopolies by drawing on regressivity arguments is prohibition. But, as we have noted, most critics of the present government monopolies are not explicit about the alternatives, and do not examine the impacts of prohibitions. However, prohibition implies regressivity too (because the same people gamble anyway, or, if they escape to beer, that is taxed too) – and worse.

Still other critics suggest that the average 2 percent tax revenues in U.S. states' budgets from lotteries should be replaced by another better tax, though they never say which one or examine the consequences. We have found no study relying on the regressivity argument that considers the alternative that government should diminish spending and be explicit about alternatives, once it prohibits lotteries.

Nor did we find any studies that raised the basic question of just what constitutes a good tax and good government spending to start with. After all, one can argue that the best tax and best spending associated with it is the one that a large majority votes for rather than one derived from an abstract economic model. The fact that people voted in referenda and initiatives to introduce lotteries and various forms of gambling in 75 percent of U.S. states suggests that, as an alternative to prohibition, people prefer the government monopoly. The initiatives, though, did not offer citizens the option to vote to allow gambling to become a private, regulated industry as all others, to get rid of the Wire Act, or to determine what exactly should happen to government spending.

Let's examine additional implications of the three options for government policies:

(1) continuing with the confused state of affairs as it is;
(2) prohibition; and
(3) moving toward the abolishing of monopolies and prohibitions and then properly taxing and regulating the industry, the online one in particular.

The conclusion is that moving toward a regulatory or fiscal framework – through a sequence of initiatives – that would allow the gambling sector to become a "normal," private one is the best path.

If the majority vote against this option, so be it (though the polls suggest otherwise). The beauty of applying the tools of direct democracy to certain fiscal and regulatory questions is that they are more flexible than alternative methods of political decision making. If people realize that they have made a mistake, they can vote in another initiative, reverse the decision, and thus prevent the persistence of erroneous policies.[3]

Theories of Taxation without Foundations

The argument of regressivity is entirely irrelevant to lotteries and gambling because the alternatives imply similar regressivity, even more harmful consequences (in the case of prohibition), or letting the lottery business be free of indirect taxes altogether. Nevertheless, it is useful to briefly point out the flawed foundations of the economic theories that rationalize stands against lotteries on the basis of regressivity.

Regressivity means that the poor pay a relatively higher fraction of their wealth as a tax on certain items than do the rich. Models suggesting that such taxes are bad are superficial, to put it mildly. However, they have been disguised by a veil of mathematics and jargon, included in textbooks, and taught at universities; otherwise, they would have been ridiculed and sent long ago into well-deserved oblivion. This does not imply that, overall, the rich should not pay a higher proportion of their wealth as a tax than the poor, or that taxes on wealth should not be progressive. Relying on the "leapfrogging" view of human nature, it is easy to explain why that should be the case, and why this would benefit the poor and the rich (though it has nothing to do with fairness or other vaguenesses).[4]

The previous statement means only that the models economists now use to argue against regressive taxation have no foundations, as they are applied to attack lotteries and gambling in particular. One of the assumptions behind the view that regressive taxes are bad is that the resultant redistribution of wealth (by relying on lotteries to raise revenues) brings about greater inequality, because the poor spend disproportionately on lotteries. Such redistribution makes a society unhappier than it was before; the contrary, a redistribution of wealth from the rich to the poor, makes society happier. The models reach this conclusion by making several explicit and implicit assumptions.

The higher taxation of the rich does not alter any incentives in this model, and total wealth before and after the redistribution stays the same. The diminished happiness of the rich, from whom wealth has been taken away, is more than compensated for by the increased happiness of the poor, who get the money (for the mathematical translation of this theory, see Appendix 1). Hope, incentives, and reference to age all are absent from these models (as is any discussion on the movement of people and capital from more progressively taxed shores to less progressively taxed ones).

The following questions are also left out entirely from such models. How can we compare people's happiness? In many economists' theories, comparing people's utilities is not just excluded but also considered invalid. Who makes the comparison? How much would it cost to administer a tax and enforce it? Wealth is somehow there, unaffected by taxes or bureaucracies. Incentives and hopes – or the effects of taxing hopes and ambition – are absent. Moreover, implicit is another strong assumption: everybody in society is exactly the same; that is, from equal amounts of wealth, at the same levels of wealth, everyone derives equal satisfaction.

Condemning states' monopolies on lotteries on the basis of these models is wrong for additional reasons. It is true that mainly those who perceive themselves as having fewer opportunities to become rich spend a higher proportion of their wealth on lotteries. But this is also the group that wins the prizes, which represent roughly 60–70 percent of the total revenues. Thus, wealth is redistributed among those who perceive fewer opportunities for advancement. A few achieve, thanks to the prizes, a standard of living that welfare payments, no matter how generous, can never provide (there were one hundred millionaires in 2006 in the state of New York alone). Economists' static model, even if it had some validity (which it does not), does not apply at all to lotteries for this same reason. People gamble and make bets for the chance, no matter how small, of having a better life. Welfare payments, no matter how generous, do not offer this option.

Other critics of the states' monopoly of the sale of lottery tickets have argued that raising income taxes can generate the same revenues as the sale of lotteries; this time, they point to the relatively large collection costs of taxation through lotteries. But this argument is wrong too, for a number of reasons. First, comparing collection costs is valid only if one assumes that the only function of lotteries today is to generate revenue. That is not quite the case now.

The lottery provides a service that people desire as an alternative to prohibition – even at the government's monopolistic prices. There would be collection costs too if the sector was privatized, only they would be called operating expenses – though they would probably be lower than they are now, when lotteries either are state-owned enterprises or have monopoly powers.

As we emphasized earlier, people voted in initiatives and revealed their preference to pay monopoly prices rather than continue to live with impacts of prohibition. A comparison between the operating costs of lotteries and those of generating revenues by other forms of taxation is thus not valid. The logical conclusion is to allow lotteries to be an ordinary, regulated, and taxed private business, not singled out for tax-generating purposes or state-owned enterprises. The latter can lead governments to become "pushers" and overrely on this source of tax revenue.[5]

Briefly, the arguments against government monopoly on lotteries and on lotteries as state-owned enterprises can be justified. But it should not be confused with criticism against lotteries and gambling.

Some economists rationalize their opposition to lotteries, gambling, and regressivity by using the term "risk aversion," which has a different meaning in economics than it does in everyday language.[6] In its current form in which mathematical economists need to assume risk aversion to reach a cherished, static general equilibrium where, actually, nothing happens (there are no innovations of any nature at such point) – the risk-aversion model cannot say anything about gambling. For, if people were risk averse in the economists' sense, there would be no gambling whatsoever and no lotteries at all. People would only seek insurance and never buy lottery tickets. What the popularity of this model says about academic research, what it says about the model being taught for decades as if there were not daily evidence to refute it, I let readers decide.[7]

How Do Governments Spend the Money?

Another attack from the regressivity angle raises the issue that governments either spend the net revenues from lotteries on items that disproportionately favor the richer or do not spend them as promised on, say, education, which might benefit the poor. To an extent, this criticism is accurate, in the sense that there is plenty of evidence that the entire earmarking exercise is little more than a political gimmick. But one cannot conclude that if governments relied on other taxes, then the composition of overall government expenditures would change at all, toward less regressivity in particular.

It turns out that earmarking revenues from future lottery revenues for some causes results in lesser amounts being allocated to those causes to start with in the general budget. The sequence of events concerning earmarking also invalidates the criticism of governments' lottery-based financing from the regressivity view.

Back in the 1980s, Steven Gold, director of fiscal studies for the National Conference of State Legislatures in Denver, stated that, because of gains from lotteries, education programs sometimes lose equal amounts of money from general appropriations. More recently, in New York, state officials confirmed that over the twenty years of the lottery, the proceeds had substituted for other funds. Paul C. Reuss, director of budget studies for the state's Senate Finance Committee had this to say: "The primary debate in New York has been whether lottery funding become a supplementary source. The truth is that it is just one of the funding sources, but if we didn't have lottery, taxes would have to be increased by $650 million."[8]

Indeed, when New York instituted its lottery in 1967, the profits were set aside for education. But when the state faced a budget crisis in 1968, the legislature shifted the net revenues from lotteries into the general fund. A similar event took place in Connecticut. Until December 1975 lottery revenues were earmarked for education. But then a special session of the legislature voted to allocate the revenues first to education, with "the balance to become part of the general fund."[9] In a recent examination of these patterns, Gribbin and Bean (2005) conclude that funds that would have been used for public education are frequently replaced by lottery funds, rather than the latter increasing education spending, and they describe in detail the political gimmicks and machinations behind the scenes.

Often governments point out the projects on which the net revenues from lotteries are spent, but they make curious statements. An official communication in Japan reports that "gambling or lottery has never been considered as a taxable item in Japan," but then mentions that lottery profits were used "for the development of educational equipment, road construction or repairs, construction of dwelling houses, expenses for public prosperity and welfare." (Is there any item in the governments' budgets that would not fit in?) The famous Irish Sweepstakes, conducted by the Hospitals Trust, was required by acts of Parliament to pay out the net proceeds to 410 institutions that provided free medical and surgical services. The trust's communication declared that the proceeds did not appear in the government's budget. Although corporations' accounting practices have been subject to intense scrutiny during the past few years, governments for the moment have escaped similar scrutiny, though with baby boomers retiring, questions about diversions from pension funds have been coming up more frequently.[10]

Statements about the worthy projects on which net income from lotteries is spent are common in the United States, Canada, and the United Kingdom. In some states (e.g., Connecticut, Delaware, the District of Columbia, and others), legislators had the good sense to provide that the net income from lotteries go to the general fund. There are other states and provinces that earmark net revenues for education (e.g., California, Michigan, and New Jersey), conservation, and parks and recreation (e.g., Colorado, and Alberta).

It is on such declarations of specific uses that studies examining regressivity of revenues from governments' sale of lotteries have been based, and have argued that the revenues are spent on items that benefit the richer.[11] However, as government actions make clear, earmarking cannot be taken at face value, and its examination cannot confirm regressivity. What it does imply is that politicians often promise anything to gain voters' support for a new revenue source. But voters should not believe in the promise of specific spending, or that the new revenue source, relying on a government-induced slack in the system (because of existing prohibition) to increase revenues, will solve fiscal problems. Governments are quick to spend the additional revenues and impose liabilities on future generations, as the previous lottery-revenue-backed bonds discussion showed.[12]

Gamblers at Opera's Gates

Although our arguments show that regressivity should have no place in discussions about lotteries and gambling, it is useful to examine closely one area in which governments often state they would increase spending from lottery revenues: culture. We shall take a closer look at what is probably the most exclusive area of culture: opera. We will take politicians' statements on earmarking at face value for the sake of argument. The reason for doing so is twofold. One is that the financing of opera houses has a close connection to gambling, as we have briefly noted. The other is to show why arguments against lotteries based on regressivity, this time focusing on spending, lead to only one logical conclusion: gambling in all shapes and forms should be legalized. We reach the conclusion that people must live with regressivity if they want this art form to survive.

Data from the U.K. Department for Culture, Media and Sport show that between the inception of the national lottery in 1994 and 1997, £1.13

billion was distributed to the arts. The two main recipients were drama (£329.41 million) and music (£201.17 million), the latter of which includes opera houses. Since when have governments ventured into subsidizing opera houses?

Recall the previous discussion of the great Italian opera houses – from Naples's San Carlo to Milan's La Scala, which were all once privately run and profitable – sustained by their gambling saloons. Monte Carlo is a reminder of what once was a typical arrangement. The saloons adjoined the theaters, and faro tables and roulette were the most popular games. These were the entertainment complexes of the times. Domenico Barbaja, the most famous impresario of the times, commissioned young composers' operas and ballets from the profits of the gambling saloons' banks attached to the opera houses. The profits from the tables, coming from the rich, also financed Salvatore Viganò's highly praised ballets at La Scala.

But the opera houses combined with casinos were not only entertainment complexes for the rich at the time. They were also among the few public places where people of all ranks could congregate lawfully. It is this uniqueness that eventually led authorities to close down the casinos, when governments considered the gathering of crowds in opera houses to be politically too dangerous. An unanticipated consequence was that, since then, opera has come to depend on government financing.

That a revolution could have started in an opera and casino complex is not as far-fetched as it might seem today. It may be difficult today to imagine the audiences of the Metropolitan, La Scala, or Covent Garden running out from their jewel boxes, climbing barricades, and turning into flag-waving revolutionary mobs. But on the evening of August 25, 1830, a riot started in Naples's opera house following a performance of Daniel Auber's patriotic opera *La muette de Portici* (strange name and subject for an opera, with a mute as the heroine, but strange things do happen in opera). The libretto was written to fire national fervor: it is the story of Masaniello's uprising against the Spanish masters of Naples in the seventeenth century. A duet, "Amour sacré de la patrie" ("Sacred Love of the Homeland") became the signal for the revolution.

The crowd poured into the streets after the performance, shouting patriotic slogans, and swiftly took possession of government buildings. Italy quickly closed down the casinos in the opera houses. These were revolutionary times in Europe, and censorship of opera in particular was severe. But people are good at overcoming such prohibitions too. When people's passion could not be expressed in words, composers found ways to express it in music, fomenting revolutionary and nationalist fervor. Giuseppe Verdi, the great Italian composer, eventually perfected this particular musical vocabulary. To this day, the chorus of the Hebrew slaves in *Nabucco,* Verdi's first success – an allegory for Italians under Austrian rule then – resonates.

After the casinos attached to opera houses were closed, Monte Carlo remained the only place where the traditional arrangements survived uninterrupted to this day. In becoming the financier of opera, governments even gained for a while more control over what opera houses could produce. Imagine what would happen to movie theaters today if governments prohibited the sale of "unhealthful popcorn and soft drinks" (which bring in a significant percentage of net revenues). Most would close – unless governments then started to finance them. What movies would end up on the screen? Entertainment complexes must sell more than one thing to be commercially viable, and not everything can be priced in separation.

Assume, then, that part of government lottery revenues today are earmarked for culture, in our case to sustain opera houses. Let us take earmarking at face value for argument's sake (that means that unless governments raised revenues from gambling, they would not spend the same amount on opera from the general budget). Could we then conclude, under this unrealistic assumption, that lotteries are a regressive tax, as far as this spending is concerned? The answer in this case is yes – but only relative to the alternative of letting opera houses reopen their casinos. If the latter was allowed, governments would no longer be involved in the opera and casino business, and taxes would be a marginal issue, if one at all. If the nineteenth-century financial arrangements were reinvented, the richer would play in the casinos linked to the opera. The losses at the gambling tables would start to again finance this entertainment business, and to indirectly subsidize the rest of opera audiences. It is the prohibition of such an arrangement that makes the financing of opera houses by lotteries a regressive tax.

But if critics do not draw their arguments to the logical conclusion or argue for the privatization of culture, then their criticism of the regressivity of government spending remains invalid. For, without the legalization of casinos, opera houses might not find alternative financial arrangements and would continue to rely on government funding. It does not matter then how the sums are earmarked: as far as regressivity is concerned, nothing would change.[13]

With casinos prohibited, nobody came up with an alternative form of private financing for opera houses. The choice the public and governments faced – once the private option was outlawed – was the following: let the art form fall into oblivion or take over the financing of opera houses. Governments chose the second option, and financing first came from the general fund. In an awkward way, since the legalization of gambling and lotteries, governments have reinvented a financing option that entrepreneurs found and practiced with great success centuries ago. In this sense, the earmarking exercise has some logic.

True, it would be better if today's governments allowed any shape and form of private financing for opera or other cultural institutions. If the Metropolitan Opera wants to make a deal with Donald Trump, and sell him the right to open a casino near its premises, so be it. There are small signs that we are moving in this direction anyway. During the past two decades, Las Vegas and other casino towns have been rediscovering the casino-entertainment combination in various incarnations. For example, Celine Dion, Andrew Lloyd Weber and Broadway musicals, the many Cirque de Soleil options, and Pavarotti's arena concerts may not be perceived as high culture (only Monte Carlo continues to finance opera and ballet from its casino revenues), but they are a few steps up from the type of shows Las Vegas offered a few years back. With the Met now broadcasting opera performances in high definition to movie theaters around the world, and London's theaters soon to join in, they might all move to the Strip, to reinvent nineteenth-century financial arrangements.

The French also had discovered the link between casinos and opera. In 1907 France passed a law exempting spa towns and seaside resorts from the ban on gambling. In 1988 France allowed casinos to open in tourist towns with more than five hundred thousand people – but only if they had a successful opera house already and if the city was not called "Paris." The rationale was that Paris is the symbol of the hardworking French, who should not be distracted. Or if they are, they should only be distracted by opera. I would not be surprised if museums and national monuments did not have a hand in the decision. If given a choice, most people – the French too – prefer to play games now and plan for the future rather than just revisit the past.

Russians, after getting rid of their disastrous seventy years of central planning, reinvented the theater-casino combination with some flair. In 1977, still under communism, Moscow's Jewish Musical Theater was financed and controlled by the government of Birobidzhan, the region Joseph Stalin created on the border with China as the new Jewish homeland. With the fall of communism, Birobidzhan stopped paying the rent, and the theater had to come up with the financing. In 1995 the Vinso Grand casino agreed and invested $1 million in renovations. The new casino and theater entertainment complex offers classic theater (in Yiddish) until ten o'clock at night. Then, the theater space is transformed into a nightclub that puts on erotic shows (not on biblical themes though). The food reflects this innovative combination: in 1998 one could get gefilte fish for $6 and Dom Perignon starting at $350.

The more things change, the more they stay the same – unless governments' regulations set up obstacles and bring a chain of unanticipated events in their wake.

What this section suggests is that government financing of culture today may be a distant, poor substitute for the unintended effects of outlawing forms of private financing. If casino-related financing had continued, perhaps opera would have been long transformed, rather than turning into a government-financed museum of roughly the same seventy Italian and German operas being performed all around the world. But one cannot draw conclusions on whether such spending is regressive or not. We do not know what the alternative is to this spending that critics, drawing on the regressivity argument, have in mind. If governments did not spend on this or other culture and still prohibited financing through lotteries and casinos, how much music would have been produced to start with – music on CDs or DVDs, or listened to on radios by the poor segments of the population?

Legalizing Gambling to Bring Prosperity

Others who analyze the impact of lotteries and casinos have focused on whether they create employment and bring prosperity to areas when legalized, whether they will continue to do so, and just how big the sector should be.[14]

The answer to the first question is positive, as one would expect. Whenever governments legalize a service that people want to buy, they will record increased employment and increased prosperity, however measured. Public knowledge about both legal gambling around the world and significant illegal gambling wherever it has been outlawed, shows that people have always wanted to have these entertainment and portfolio options.

Governments will record increased prosperity and employment when gambling is partially legalized, even if the real size of the gambling sector does not change at all relative to its size under prohibition. As employment and businesses move from the underground to the surface, to legal ground, statistics bureaus will capture the move. If a 1948 *Business Week* study is to be believed, in the 1940s in the United States, one of every 250 employees also worked as an agent for gambling operations, earning fifty times their weekly legal wages. In larger plants, 10 percent of employees gambled regularly and 50 percent occasionally. In smaller ones, either all did or none did. People bet on numbers, horse races, and sports.[15] Once these activities were legalized, official statistics would reflect these numbers – even if the sector did not expand. The statistics would record growth and increased employment.

McKibbin draws similar observations about Britain. He notes that mass betting was the most successful example of working-class self-help in the modern era in Britain:

It was at every stage a proletarian institution and bore all the characteristics of the British working class. *Although illegal it was almost entirely honest* ... To some working class families ... it brought great wealth, to others some money to throw around and a certain flashy style: "they have now a bank account and enjoy the luxury of clean linen and water-tight boots" ... To the unemployed it sometimes meant a temporary job, and young boys were able to scrape a bit of extra by operating on its margins. It is very difficult to say how many were employed in any capacity at all by gambling: the whole of the full and part-time fraternity at most numbered 100,000.[16]

Does the previously described behavior really reflect a flashy style? Having clean linen? A bank account? At the time, one hundred thousand people represented about 1 percent of the labor force, which is not negligible, considering the fact that they came from among the poor only.

The fact that the underground gambling sector provides opportunities for the poor can be inferred from many other sources. Louise Meriwether, in her book *Daddy Was a Number Runner* (1970), shows how the numbers game in New York's Harlem gave hope in the midst of despair and poverty.[17] A windfall was used for family expenses, and her father's employment as a numbers runner provided an irregular but important source of income. The leaders of Chicago's underworld in the 1930s, involved mainly with gambling and bootlegging, consisted of young, ambitious immigrants. Thirty percent of bosses were Italian; 29 percent, Irish; 20 percent, Jewish; and 12 percent, African American. There was not a native-born white American among them.[18]

Briefly, part of the leap in employment statistics at the moment of legalization is, to an extent, a statistical illusion. Of course, the sector becomes much larger and innovative than it was under prohibition. Prohibition means that casinos have to stay small, tight, Spartan-style operations, as illegal operations cannot explore the many options to expand that legal enterprises can.

David Schwartz (2005) drew a parallel between the sequence of events following the legalization of lotteries and pari-mutuel betting in the United States, in their ability to bring revenues to the states in particular. He notes that the expansion of gambling in the twentieth century started with the permission of pari-mutuel wagering in the 1920s and 1930s, suffered set-backs in the 1940s and 1950s with antigambling movements, and regained footing in the 1960s. Pari-mutuel wagering brought benefits to those in the horse breeding and training business. For the states, legalization offered new sources of revenue. The betting public could pursue a pastime they liked without breaking the law. Every party benefited from the expansion. By the early 1970s, thirty states permitted pari-mutuel betting on horse racing, greyhound racing, and jai alai. It was also in the 1970s that their popularity started to decline, reflected in lower attendance, smaller purse sizes, and diminished state revenues.

This is when the operators instituted legal off-track betting – illegal book-making far from the tracks was thriving by then. Because the state was losing revenues, and New York City faced a fiscal crisis, there once again were common interests in legalization. New York voted in a referendum in 1963, and the first state law to permit off-track betting was passed in 1970. By 1974, as Schwartz notes, the New York City OTB became the city's largest retailer, with a hundred branch offices serving 100,000 to 150,000 people a day, and created additional employment because of the use of a telephone service to permit account wagering.[19] Next, tracks installed video lottery terminals, which proved popular, and track operators transformed their sites into entertainment complexes, adding shops and sports activities too.

By 2005 U.S. commercial casinos alone employed more than 350,000 people, paid $12.6 billion in wages, contributed almost $5 billion in direct gaming taxes, and earned $30 billion in gross gaming revenues.[20] These numbers do not include the impact of either lotteries or sports betting, much of it illegal. Nor do they include effects on creating employment and opportunities in telecommunications, sports, retail, and other businesses.

As for the second question – just how big the gambling sector should be, and whether its present composition is a good one – is impossible to answer for two main reasons. One is that when gambling is outlawed, people find ways to gamble illegally. Spending on illegal sports gambling in the United States is estimated in the $90 billion range (others put much higher figures on it[21]). The UIGEA has outlawed online options since October 13, 2006. Will people gamble more as a result at land-based casinos, on lotteries, or at racetracks because of the UIGEA? Probably, though, as we saw in Chapter 3, people do not see all forms of gambling as substitutes. Playing poker online is no substitute for socializing with others whether widows in bingo halls, playing the lottery, or when betting on sports to extract more fun out of the game. What would the size of the gambling sector be – online and on land – if it were legalized and privatized? What shapes and forms would it take? These are questions we can speculate on. But such speculation is not the subject here.

What we can say is that the composition of the sector would be different; that people would gamble more online than at video terminals; that, perhaps, fewer people would go to see horse and dog racing; that more would learn games online and then visit land-based casinos with greater confidence. We can also predict that people would bet on a variety of events, from elections and politics to the weather, and put real money on the Hollywood Stock Exchange, where at present people can only bet with pretend money on which movies will be successful, which scripts should be financed, which stars should be cast, and so forth. People could bet on just about anything. A few ideas would resonate and some betting markets would become deep. Perhaps by changing the name from betting markets to aggregate information markets, where "information" means opinions backed by money – which such markets really are – antigambling laws on the books would be eventually discarded. The present prohibitions, whether the Wire Act or the UIGEA, prevent the development of these broader information-generating markets.

But since entrepreneurs and vital young talent rarely work for government-owned enterprises, or heavily regulated ones, it is not surprising that occasional new gambling ventures initiated by governments did not go in the aforementioned directions, but failed. In 1976 Delaware launched a football lottery offering two games: Football Bonus and Touchdown. It had an esoteric bet structure, less than favorable odds, and those who won more than $600 had to pay income taxes – rewards that could not compete with those of illegal sports betting at the time. Delaware abandoned the football lottery. Oregon tried in 1989 football and basketball lotteries, which folded for similar reasons. Although in the ban against sports betting passed in 1991, the U.S. Congress carved out exceptions for Oregon, Delaware, and Nevada, no further innovative experiments in sports betting were made. Illegal sports betting nevertheless continued to thrive, whereas legal betting is still marginal in the United States, pursued from Nevada.[22]

In general, after decades of prohibition, lotteries and most gambling turned out to be successful in raising revenues for the states, and by now almost every state has them. As more states adopted lotteries, they experienced declining rates of revenue growth. The states then turned toward casinos and licensing new forms of games either to sustain tax revenues or to bring in more. Each such expansion, done by easing regulations, so as to protect the state tax base, has been a threat to the neighboring states' tax base, and at times, unexpectedly, it has cannibalized existing gambling revenues within a state. Reacting to the expansion of gambling in some states, neighboring states respond by either introducing similar games or easing regulations, and all responded by spending heavily on advertising.[23] Mitt Romney, the governor of Massachusetts, reacted in probably the bluntest way, extending the idea of noncompete fees from the corporate world to that of state governments. In 2003 he asked casino and slot operators in the neighboring states of Connecticut and Rhode Island to pay Massachusetts $75 million. If they did not, Romney said, he would push to legalize more gambling in the state.

Because lotteries are not a private business and because much of the gambling sector is outlawed or regulated, it is impossible to say whether there is too much gambling (recall the conclusion in Chapter 5, reached from a different angle). There may be too much of some forms of gambling, and too little in other shapes and forms. The situation in the gambling sector recalls the days of AT&T's monopoly. Although U.S. phone service then was the best in the world, few thought that the phone business could expand vastly. Only when MCI succeeded to dismantle the de facto AT&T monopoly did the telecommunication sector suddenly explode in many unexpected directions. Actually today, regulations prevent phone companies from fulfilling banks' functions, and from being involved in gambling. Again, we can speculate about how big the gambling and betting sectors would become and what shapes and forms they could take if there were no antigambling laws on the books, no government monopolies, or no lotteries managed by states.

Briefly, critics of state monopolies of lotteries and various forms of gambling must raise and answer these questions:

- Is the fact that those with fewer opportunities spend a relatively greater percentage of their wealth on lotteries under criticism?
- Is the criticism that expenditures on lotteries are taxed because of the government's monopolistic pricing?
- Or, is the criticism that governments relying on this monopolistic source of taxation spend too much, and if gambling were prohibited that spending would be curtailed? Or, do critics imply that government spending should stay at the same level, only raise money differently?

Though there is a massive amount written on the subject of governments and lotteries, I have not come across anyone who has raised these questions and answered them properly. Most of the vast amounts written on lotteries and gambling are superficial rationalizations of prejudices, articulated in new pseudoscientific jargon, that at closer inspection are invalid

or entirely irrelevant as applied to this topic. Here is a typical conclusion of
one such recent study in the United States:

No state has abandoned the lottery in the past century, and, unfortunately, none is
likely to do so soon ... If they did, however, they would improve their tax system by
increasing accountability, transparency and economic neutrality, as well as decreasing regressivity. Legislators would find that they do not truly need the tax revenue
raised by lotteries; they would either get by without it or raise it through explicit
taxation enacted legislatively. They could allow lotteries to continue in the private
market or even ban them entirely, but, in either case, the cessation of state-run
lotteries would result in more principled state tax systems.[24]

What is a "principled tax system" anyway? And were state taxes and regulations any better before lotteries were legalized through referenda and
initiatives?[25]

What Is a Good Tax; or, Who Guards the Guardians?

As the previous sections show, examining this topic inevitably touches on
a fundamental question that economists have examined for centuries: what
is a good tax?

There is a relatively easy answer to this question, which is out of sight
and mind of the economic profession, but reflected in practices that have
become more widespread during the past two decades in the United States
and the rest of the world. Because the notion of a good tax is intimately
linked to the ways the tax is spent, why not let people reveal their thoughts
about it through referenda and initiatives – as they did to legalize gambling?

Actually, it is happening. People vote now on a wide range of issues concerning regulations, taxation, and gambling – although, for the moment,
there is only one country in the world where decisions on good taxes (and
good government spending or good government in general) are made in this
way at all levels: Switzerland.[26] Below, I summarize briefly evidence from
the United States only.

From 1901 to 2001, according to Dane Waters, president of the Initiative
and Referendum Institute, the United States had 1,902 statewide initiatives,
of which 787 were adopted. For the first twenty-five years, initiatives worked
well. With the two world wars, the Great Depression and the Cold War,
however, the system became a marginal form of lawmaking. The initiative
process came back in 1978 with California's famous Proposition 13, which
cut property taxes from 2.5 percent of market value to 1 percent. Within
two years, forty-three other states had implemented property tax limitations,
and fifteen had lowered income taxes.

In 1996–97 alone, the Minnesota legislature (to use just one example), considered 6,656 laws, of which it adopted 422 – half as many as were accepted by citizens of their own initiative in twenty-four states over one hundred years. In 1998 the twenty-four states adopted just thirty-five laws using the initiative process. During the same year, the same states adopted fourteen thousand laws after considering more than seventy thousand. One can guess which laws received more attention and scrutiny. The abuse of power these latter numbers represent could be prevented if the initiative and referenda process was formally made part of the political process, subject to various constraints.

The initiatives covered a wide range, besides fiscal and spending issues: as we saw that is how gambling was relegalized in 75 percent of the U.S. states. In 1992, for example, voters in various parts of the United States responded to sixty-nine ballot initiatives – more than ever since 1932. In fact, in California any issue can now be put to a statewide vote, if 615,958 signatures are collected. In 1996 voters there passed Proposition 218 (to require voter approval for increases in local taxes) and Proposition 210 (to increase state minimum wages), and defeated Proposition 217 (to increase the top income-tax rates). Californians also passed Proposition 209, abolishing affirmative action, and Proposition 215, legalizing medical use of marijuana.

Were some of the voters' decisions mistaken? Maybe. But this is the strength of this trial-and-error process. If people are mistaken, they have the option to correct their mistakes with another initiative, be it on a fiscal, regulatory or other matter that can be subject to the process. And if they stick to a decision some do not like, the latter can vote with their feet and move to another state. Or have the right, as in Switzerland, through a sequence of local and federal referenda, to carve out a new state, or to join another. Instead of moving with one's feet, people move the borders on paper. Jura was carved out of the Canton of Bern in 1979 through a sequence of referenda to become Switzerland's twenty-third canton.[27]

This process is a better way to answer not only the question of what is a good tax, but also the broader one that has preoccupied observers since antiquity: "Who guards the guardians?" In the corporate world, takeovers, hostile or not, and all the mechanisms falling under the term "market for corporate control" (as Henry Manne coined the term) are solutions to this problem. In the government taxing and spending sphere, referenda and initiatives appear to be the best. The evidence suggests so. Is the process perfect? Nothing ever is. But in no field of life has there been a better process invented than the one that relies on trial and error in separate, clear issues, and on holding decision makers accountable – having such institutions allow people to vote on values they believe in. Betting, futures, and financial markets could price the rest.

No abstract models can substitute for any trial-and-error mechanism, whether in politics, business, or finance, and no linguistic or mathematical acrobatics will ever allow anyone to answer the question of what a good tax is. When regulations prevent such trials and errors, whether in financial or futures markets, then governments manage taxes, spending, regulations, and errors last. As we discussed in Chapter 1, governments then rationalize and legitimize decisions with various intellectual fads that have long-term, unpredictable consequences. Some, though, are predictable and are examined next.

Impacts of Prohibition

If it is prohibition that critics of lotteries and various gambling businesses have in mind, then an accurate analysis to back such opinion requires that we raise these questions: Would governments reduce their spending; if so, on what exactly? Or, would they maintain their spending; if so, what would they tax instead? But the most important questions are, What would people do if they were prohibited from playing? And how will governments enforce the prohibition?

We know not only that there is much illegal sports betting going on in the United States, but also that there are other thriving forms of illegal gambling. This should not come as a surprise: high-priced monopolies (and high taxes) bring about such markets, in the case of lotteries because they give better odds than the government lottery.

Sharon Sharp, director of the Illinois lottery, estimated that the state was losing about $200 million a year to illegal lotteries in 1988. This sum represented about 30 percent of Illinois net lotteries at the time. When in 1989 the Chicago Police Department discovered an illegal lottery operation, the investigation summarized its advantages relative to the legal options. The report said that "the illegal operators had bigger pay-offs, winnings were delivered each day in cash, wagers were taken over the telephone, credit was extended and bettors could avoid reporting their winnings for income tax purposes."[28]

These reactions are the same as those we discussed in Chapter 5, when examining the impact of inflation and bad fiscal policies. A government monopoly, on lotteries in particular, is a tax by another name, and unsurprisingly brings in its wake similar reactions to those of bad fiscal and monetary policies, black markets being one of them. But claims that illegal gambling was often fixed or otherwise fraudulent should be taken with a grain of salt. The preceding report suggests, and David Schwartz concludes, "state and federal prosecutions of illegal gambling became less a crusade to protect an unwitting public and more a drive to liquidate potential competitors."[29]

Prohibitions in the United States and Elsewhere

Prohibition, though, has bad impacts; worse than betting on illegal games and occasionally stumbling on fly-by-night operators or buying adulterated beverages illegally. Some governments have quickly realized that prohibition was a mistake, but others took decades or even centuries, during which they brought about much harm.

In 1739 the House of Commons outlawed faro, basset, ace of hearts, and hazard. However, the city of Bath, the Las Vegas of the times, relying on tourists, found ways to circumvent the law. They appropriated the French three-dice game passe-dix and called it passage. In 1740 the Commons outlawed this too, the law referring to any game or instrument using numbers. The law also stated that "all persons playing and betting at any lawful games . . . shall be deemed rogues and vagabonds." But again the law was evaded. A man named Cook invented a game called EO, which was much like modern roulette, but without the numbers. In the numbers' place on the revolving wheel there were letters: forty slots marked alternately "E" and "O" (signifying "even" and "odd") and two slots, called bars, which gave owners an average gain of 2.56 percent of every wager placed on the circular table. The law forgot to mention "letters."[30]

The revolutionary government in France abolished all lotteries in 1793, but the government revised its decision a few years later. The reason was that, being deprived of national lotteries, people played the foreign ones. As a result, the French government was losing both revenues and foreign currency, and the police then, as later, could not enforce the law.[31] Before the French Revolution, baccarat used to be played in illegal gambling halls. Antoine de Sartine, chief of the French Sûreté, persuaded the government to legalize the game, as he saw no way to enforce the prohibition.[32]

When governments sold lottery tickets at monopolistic prices, there was, apparently, much illegal gambling too – the Illinois government could have predicted the undesirable outcomes of its policy. Between 1760 and 1826, when the price of a state of lottery ticket in England was £13 (a prohibitive price for the less than rich), insurance was invented, and hundreds of offices sold it to the relatively poor. In 1793 the practice was outlawed, which created both a black market and, as one would expect, protection rackets to enforce the distribution of prizes. Once lotteries were outlawed at the beginning of the nineteenth century, illegal private lotteries multiplied, and the poor continued to buy into them – though numerical evidence is obviously lacking.[33]

When Sweden outlawed gambling (in effect until 1930), the Swedes gambled on English soccer games, apparently smuggling out substantial amounts of Swedish currency. Once Sweden legalized gambling, the criminal elements that were involved with smuggling and gambling disappeared. China inaugurated a state lottery on July 31, 1933. But the Chinese were familiar with lotteries: until then, they had played hwo-wei illegally, the poorer in particular.[34]

Similar patterns can be detected in the United States. In 1851 the New York Association for the Suppression of Gambling was established, and the Green Law of 1851 was the harshest antigambling law that had been passed up to that time. It imposed fines on anyone found guilty of keeping a gambling establishment, exhibiting gambling devices, or assisting in any game. This legislation too turned out to be ineffective. According to estimates, thirty thousand people in New York made their living from gambling at the time.

The law's lack of impact was due to several reasons. Members of the Protestant establishment passed the law. Yet in the years between 1825 and 1855 New York State's population doubled, primarily because of the immigration of penniless non-Protestants who wanted to gamble. It also turned out that politicians had interests in the gambling industry. Eventually the police commissioner, who claimed to be ignorant of the law, refused to enforce the law – a sequence of events that happened repeatedly around the world.

Surprising as it may sound today, Nevada passed a comprehensive law prohibiting all forms of gambling in 1909, and gambling remained a criminal offense for two decades. Authorities did not expect the consequences, though they were entirely predictable. Government revenues dropped, people continued to gamble, and corruption and protection became widespread, as bribes became little more than getting a license. Commentators reached the following conclusions:

The fact that the Nevada gambling prohibition had to be enforced along with the national liquor prohibition did not do much good in Nevada for either law enforcement program. The speakeasies had gambling tables and slot machines. The people who wanted only to gamble or only to drink felt a brotherhood. Both groups, of course, were outnumbered by that mass who wanted to both drink and gamble. One of the byproducts of all this was the creation of a lawlessness in attitude for a whole generation of Americans, and a class of dishonest law enforcement officers and public officeholders such as the nation has never seen before.[35]

Nevada legalized gambling in 1930. The change can be attributed not only to the crash of 1929, but also to the recognition that people gambled anyway and there was no evidence of the desperation and ruin that gambling was supposedly bringing about.[36] And what can people do in a desert, which lacks natural resources, except use their brains or attract tourists?[37]

The impact of the legalization was, as one would expect, that eventually the criminal elements associated with gambling disappeared.[38] The fact that for a while they stayed involved is not surprising. When anything is outlawed, only criminals know the business – by definition. When communism fell, many entrepreneurs were those the previous regime had labeled black marketers and criminals. But because all business transactions were illegal, these people were the only ones who knew something about the business and about enforcing contracts. To this day, many once-communist countries require private enforcement, because the legal enforcement is in its infancy and corrupt.[39] When previously outlawed businesses are legalized, one would expect people with "criminal" backgrounds to stay involved.

Antigambling laws also had some unexpected effects. When gambling was outlawed in California, enforcement of the law became discriminatory. At the time there were many gaming houses and types of lotteries that catered to the population of Chinese background only. Apparently, gaming laws were enforced more vigorously against Chinese establishments.[40]

In spite of such evidence and in contrast to the easing of antigambling legislation in England by the 1960s, New York's legislature in 1960 passed a series of tough new antigambling laws. Their purpose was to facilitate convictions and, by increasing the penalties, have a detrimental effect on gambling. The law was passed in spite of the fact that public opinion in New York City did not condemn gambling. This is what one can infer from the fact that a public opinion survey in 1963 revealed that few New Yorkers worried about the morality of betting on races.[41]

This law did not seem to achieve its intended impact. Organized crime associated with prohibition persisted, though there were few convictions. If the law had a significant effect, it was on the police, for whom, the Knapp Commission found, gamblers' protection money became the main source of bribes. A typical police officer on the gambling squad was able to earn $300 to $1,500 per month, and the superiors got their bribes too.[42] These revelations led to the decision by New York City's police commissioner Michael Murphy to stop enforcing certain aspects of the gambling laws. He also argued that dismantling the gambling squads would not bring about any great increase in gambling. But it would, he argued, have the beneficial effect of diminishing corruption, thereby enabling the police to concentrate on controlling violent crime and improving the morale of police and public.[43]

Other Impacts of Prohibition in the United States

Until the reemergence of lotteries in the 1960s and 1970s, the dominant illegal games were numbers and insurance (also called policy). The latter got its start with the drawings of authorized lotteries, which took time and were expensive.[44] The reason for the time lapse between the issuing of tickets and the drawing was that each new lottery had to get a license from the government, and there was always the possibility of not getting it. Insurance disappeared with the abolition of lotteries at the beginning of the nineteenth century, but people continued to play the numbers game in the poorer districts of large cities. None of these patterns seemed to attract much attention. By this time, both in the United States and in the United Kingdom attention was focused on gambling linked to horse racing.

Throughout the nineteenth century, the bookmaking industry in the United States was illegal – yet very popular.[45] In spite of its illegality, Western Union provided communications services to disseminate race results and odds (just as today sports broadcasts widely disseminate prompt information on players' injuries, which only matter to gamblers, not fans). When in 1904 Western Union was put under increasing pressure to comply with the law, the result was that, just six months later, John Payne, of Cincinnati, had an illegal monopoly to provide the desired information.[46]

A similar sequence of events later took place in Australia.[47] Legislation in Queensland in 1936 and in New South Wales in 1938 that prohibited off-track betting in newspapers or through broadcasting led to the organization of illegal means of communication. People were employed to signal from the courses and used telephones to handle transactions. The organization also bribed police officers and employees of the phone companies. Because transactions were arranged by phone, a credit system was necessary: its enforcement had to depend on threats and use of violence to enforce the oral contracts.

During the early 1920s pari-mutuel wagering was legal only in Kentucky, Maryland, and Louisiana. Yet horse racing and gambling on the races continued to prosper in other states, because the laws prohibiting racing and bookmaking continued to be unenforced. They could not be. Whereas the entrepreneurs involved with gambling quickly used new technologies, it took years for government agencies to catch up with the innovations. Bookmakers in New York used telephones fifty years before the state authorized wiretaps.[48]

Moreover, the law itself was ambiguous. Because bookmaking was illegal, track managers invented a system of oral betting, which in the case *Ex rel. Lichtenstein v. Langan* (1909) was held to be exempt from the bookmaking law under the argument that successful bookmaking required "the writing out of list of odds laid on some paper or material so that they can be seen by those who are solicited to invest." Thus, went the decision, oral betting did not constitute bookmaking.[49] Perhaps some lawyers will use this as precedent to argue that betting through wireless is allowed, because it does not contradict the Wire Act, which Congress passed in 1961 to prohibit people from using phone lines to receive bets, because no wires are involved. Play on words in legal decisions related to gambling has other precedents. Already in *Van Valkenburgh v. Torrey* (1827), the court exempted racing on the grounds that it was a sport, not a game. The decision said that trotting was different from racing, and so the antigambling laws did not apply.

Lack of enforcement was also a consequence of the fact that in some southern states hostility toward gambling was found more in judicial opinions than in legislative enactments. Blakey speculates that this phenomenon may be because whereas many judges received their legal training in the East, where features of the frontier life were frowned upon, legislators reflected the will of voters, who were not concerned about gambling at all.[50] An additional reason for the lack of enforcement was, as we implied earlier, that gambling had close links with urban politics. Gamblers, police, and politicians were frequently of Irish-Catholic background in many American cities, and "it was not simply that gambling syndicates influenced political organizations, but that gambling syndicates *were* the local political organization. Local bookmakers or policy writers served as precinct captains, while the leaders of syndicates became ward leaders and often won elections as aldermen or state representatives."[51]

Taxing Foreigners

Americans, as did the Swedish and the French, gambled on out-of-state lotteries when forbidden to play within the states. As we noted, this was the reason for the Louisiana lottery's spectacular success during the nineteenth century. Louisiana was the only state with a lottery by then. Australians too gambled on out-of-state lotteries when forbidden to play within their own states, thus diminishing local tax revenues. As a result, New South Wales, Victoria, Queensland, and Western Australia passed laws prohibiting the post office from carrying lottery tickets, thus putting serious obstacles in the way of Tasmania's attempts to export and market its lotteries.[52] Today, instead of imposing prohibitions on the post office, governments impose restrictions on their present substitutes – banks and telecommunications companies – to prevent them from transferring payments to online gambling companies.

Notice though that though the UIGEA of 2006 claims to protect the poor, it actually carved out exemptions for buying state lottery tickets or betting on horses online while denying the playing of poker online. Yet the facts are that the online poker players are relatively young and well-to-do (and their winning of the poker contests suggests that there is skill involved too), whereas lottery-ticket buyers and those betting on horses are not. But it is true that the online poker companies have not been paying U.S. taxes, whereas the lotteries bring in tax revenues. As we have seen repeatedly, following the money trail offers better insights into what is happening than does following politicians' and easily gullible or even sincere observers' statements and opinions. These exemptions led the World Trade Organization to rule twice (first in April 2005, and then in March 2006) against the United States on Antigua's and Barbuda's request. The ruling said that whereas countries can impose restrictions on imports on public, moral grounds, the same rules must apply to domestic and foreign providers. The increase in the stock prices of online gambling companies around the world (as they are legitimate public companies, many listed on London's stock exchange) since the ruling suggests that people speculate that the United States will repeal the ban. Now, in 2007, the European Union is being lobbied to join Antigua to negotiate a compensation deal from Washington to the tune of $100 billion, as a result of the plunge in the mainly London-listed Internet gambling companies and the value of business lost.

The fact that prohibitions in other states or nations could be used to raise revenues, thus imposing taxes on "foreigners" was and is perceived by politicians as an attraction of lotteries and gambling that attracts tourists. With only six hundred thousand inhabitants in 1964, New Hampshire's lottery officials knew that to succeed they must appeal to out-of-state people. They succeeded: in 1964, 80 percent of the tickets were sold to residents of Massachusetts, New York, and Connecticut, even though out-of-state buyers had to travel to New Hampshire's border towns to purchase the tickets (as use of the mail was prohibited). After 1964 the residents of these three states had to travel less, because New York and Massachusetts introduced successful lotteries of their own.[53] Residents of other states were traveling some distance too in hopes of the large prize when few states had lotteries. Delaware residents drove more than twenty miles twice a week to buy into the Maryland lottery – even though Delaware's lottery gave out prizes, but only small ones. Delaware then decided to collaborate in plans to offer a four-state lottery with Maine, New Hampshire, and Vermont, with first prizes varying between $1 million and $10 million, competing with New York's prizes at the time.[54]

Prohibitions in the United Kingdom and the United States

Whereas England outlawed lotteries in the first half of the nineteenth century, both on- and off-course betting flourished, with the latter appealing to the working classes. There were numerous off-course betting shops, and carrier pigeons relayed the results (they were the Federal Express of the times, which the Rothschilds were the first to use to obtain speedy, reliable information to make pricing bets). Before the widespread use of the telegraph, avid bettors – working-class entrepreneurs, in fact – hung over bridges to catch the name of the big race winner from the firefighter as the train flashed through.

The 1853 Betting Houses Act prohibited the use of "a house, office, room or other place" for betting. The act did not forbid betting itself – just as the UIGEA does not prohibit online gambling, but the processing of transactions to an online gambling site. Lawyers, with their customary skill, interpreted the 1853 act as implying that betting transactions could still take place – but only in public places. But prohibitions had more serious consequences than illegal gambling, invention of less reliable substitutes and finding loopholes in the wording of laws, which brought about increased complexity and misallocation of police force.

One reason the poor could bet even in England after the passage of the 1906 class law was that enforcement of the law was not taken seriously.[55] In Scotland the law was to be used merely to raise revenues through penalties rather than to suppress illegal bookmaking.[56] The lack of enforcement resulted from several reasons. Not long after the law passed, members of the police force criticized the law on the grounds that it was "antiquated, obscure, illogical, ineffective and falls unevenly upon different classes of the community."[57] Because the poor did not equate legality with legitimacy, the police, in attempting to enforce the law, were faced with a hard-to-execute task. The bookmakers had developed a tight organization, and the buyers sympathized with the bookmakers rather than with the police. Bookmakers bribed members of the police, and the corruption led journalists to declare in the 1920s that confidence in the police was at its lowest ebb in half a century.[58]

The U.K. Royal Commission on Lotteries and Betting, in 1932–3, recognized that "it was impossible to ignore either popular demand for betting facilities or popular objectives to discriminatory legislation which had led to 'mass disobedience' of the 1906 Act." The commission also "noted the perception of the 1906 Act as 'class legislation' and 'the opinion commonly held by a very large number of people that gambling in moderation, and within a man's means is a pardonable habit . . . which may fairly be reckoned among his amusements.' "[59] When police witnesses appeared before the commission and were asked how street betting could be stopped, the deputy police commissioner Trevor Bigham answered, "I am afraid that I cannot make any suggestion which will be practically effective for stopping betting of any kind. Perhaps that answers the question."[60]

The commission decided that the law not only was ineffective, but also brought about the corruption of the police and disrespect for laws. For a number of reasons, the commission did not repeal the prohibitions. But, as Dixon concludes, although the "enforcement of the law was not abandoned, it became increasingly ritualized into a process of regular arrests and insubstantial penalties. Realizing that 'it would be only a matter of time before the law was changed,' the police preferred to devote interest and resources to duties which were more important and less likely to provoke problems of corruption and difficulties in police-public relations."[61]

Similar trends characterized the United States. Although efforts to enforce antigambling laws in 1971 and 1972, for example, yielded roughly one thousand convictions each year, the prosecutors found that judges gave convicted defendants probation and that "the game was not worth the candle. They therefore shifted resources into other areas of investigation."[62] The 1978 *Gambling Law Enforcement* reported that there was a 70 percent conviction rate for gambling offenses (higher than for other crimes). But most of the cases involved plea bargains and reduced charges. The report estimated that only 15 percent of the gambling cases went to jury trial. As Schwartz (2005) notes, prosecutors entertained strong doubts about juries' willingness to convict gambling operators. The same report also found that people rated other crimes, such as selling heroin, pornography, and drunk driving, as more important priorities, and demanded enforcement of these matters rather than of gambling offenses. The survey also revealed that people believed that gambling was thriving anyway because the police had been paid off.

The second Royal Commission on Gambling, which looked into all aspects of gambling between 1949 and 1951, concluded that remedies to gambling could not be found in prohibitions or restrictions and that gambling did not bring any serious social or economic problems. The solutions were to provide legal ways to gamble and to educate people about the games. The question was just how exactly to replace the prohibition.

The commissioners looked at the Irish experience, where betting was legalized in 1926 (for fiscal purposes), which led to the recommendation of a policy of administrative regulation. The police officers' testimony was even blunter than that before the previous commission and carried more weight. Sir Harold Scott, the metropolitan police commissioner, described the gambling laws as "illogical, chaotic and ... absurd."[63] He criticized governments' appointment of commissions but failure to implement reforms, and their neglect of the view of the police, who "are more closely attuned to the ideas of the man in the street than many of our legislators." Conditions during World War II also had an effect on the police's view. A police federation representative told the commission, "It was a common comment that persons who shirked work to attend racecourses were respectable while the loyal citizens who remained at work and had a bet in their dinner hour were regarded as lawbreakers ... The war made a big difference in that the working man engaged in intensive war work demanded betting facilities convenient to his work without interference."[64]

In spite of the commission's recommendations, it took almost ten years for them to be implemented, as opposition came from a variety of lobbies and interest groups that were threatened by competition. As has happened often in the past and today, the opposition, from the racing lobby to smaller bookmakers, brought up every possible argument, some familiar (the old religious objections and that there would be more crime) and some newer ones about the way the government would allocate licenses and possibilities of monopolization. Today in the United Kingdom, bookmaking is a large and respectable industry. Whereas at one time there were more than 15,000 betting shops, through consolidation they have been reduced to about 8,500 today, with four major bookmakers dominating: William Hill, Ladbrokes, Coral, and the state-owned ToteSport.

By the time of the third Royal Commission on Gambling (1976–8), which was established to look into only specifics of lotteries and the allocation of profits from gambling on various sports, its report was clear and sharp on the impact of prohibitions. It concluded that "the strategy of prohibition has been a notable 'folly' in the 'chequered and unhappy history' of gambling legislation ... Instead of suppressing betting among poorer people, the law produced resentment and attempts to corrupt the police, contempt for authority and a bookmaking trade operating outside the law, prey to protection rackets and gang violence."[65]

Similar conclusions, worded nearly the same, were heard in the United States some forty years before, when the issue was getting rid of the prohibition of alcoholic beverages in the United States. The commissioner of prohibition, Henry Anderson, concluded that "the fruitless efforts at enforcement are creating public disregard not only for this law but for all laws. Public corruption through the purchase of official protection for this illegal traffic is widespread and notorious. The courts are cluttered with prohibition cases to an extent which seriously affects the entire administration of justice."[66]

Although before reaching that conclusion and abolishing the prohibition, the effects were predictably disastrous and similar to the impact of prohibitions on betting. Mark Thornton notes that the death rate from poisoned liquor was high, as alcohol was adulterated. In 1925 the toll was 4,154, compared to 1,064 in 1920. Although prohibitionists argued that the benefits of Prohibition would affect the young, what happened was that the average age of people who died from alcoholism fell by six months between 1916 and 1923, which was otherwise a period of improvement in the health of young people.[67]

As with gambling, the prohibition of alcohol became a major source of corruption. (The legal beneficiaries were foreigners – Canadians – as the money flows to the alcoholic beverage industry contributed significantly to establish lasting family fortunes, such as that of the Bronfmans.) Politicians and police officers took bribes from bootleggers, crime bosses, and those involved in the import and distribution business of the beverages. The Bureau of Prohibition was then reorganized to reduce corruption. Prohibition not only created the Bureau of Prohibition, but increased the size and power of other government agencies as well. Thornton notes that between 1920 and 1930 employment at the U.S. Customs Service increased 45 percent, and the service's annual budget increased 123 percent. Personnel of the coast guard increased 188 percent during the 1920s, and its budget increased more than 500 percent between 1915 and 1932. Those increases were primarily due to the agencies' role in enforcing Prohibition. Its repeal in 1933 dramatically reduced crime, including organized crime and corruption. Adulteration of alcoholic beverages became a thing of the past, and Alcoholics Anonymous, a voluntary organization, began in 1934.[68]

With the spread of legalized gambling in the United States, crime in this area – as defined by estimated arrests – declined significantly too. According to the Bureau of Justice Statistics's *Sourcebook of Criminal Justice Statistics* (1974–2002), the arrests went steadily down from about forty thousand (roughly three thousand for bookmaking, six thousand for numbers, and thirty-one thousand "other") to about ten thousand in 2002.[69]

Why Do American Sports Leagues Oppose Sports Betting and Online Gambling?

The legality of sports betting varies from country to country. In the United States, for example, sports betting is generally forbidden except when associated with horse racing and on-the-spot legal betting on a few sports in Nevada. In Europe bookmaking is regulated and bets on soccer and horse racing are extremely popular. But the major American leagues – the National Hockey League, the National Basketball Association, the National Football League, and the National Collegiate Athletic Association – have all repeatedly expressed their opposition to any sports betting.

Yet neither these sports nor those in Europe would be as popular if not for gambling. People bet on sports to have fun, to get a better kick out of life. Some people pay a few bucks more to buy a souvenir mug on vacation, to make life more beautiful on a cloudy morning at home. Others pay a few hundred dollars more for the aesthetics of Apple's round and transparent computers. The same principle holds for sports betting. People always get more involved when they have even a few dollars at stake, and they back their opinions with money. Daniel Seligman (2000) has pointed out that many football games are boring blowouts, rather one-sided games that nonbetting fans would rapidly decide not to watch. But bettors are more likely to stay and watch. So the audiences are larger, the television rights are worth more, and the associations selling those rights take in more revenue: in 2000 the National Collegiate Athletic Association received $6 billion in broadcasting rights. It would seem, then, that the leagues should be in favor of legalizing sports betting: more people would bet, and that would bring a larger number of more enthusiastic fans.

The leagues, however, state that they fear corruption. Yet, as we noted, in 2006 the estimates were that whereas U.S. citizens bet about $3 billion legally on sports a year, about 100 million U.S. citizens bet another $93 billion illegally. These numbers and the European evidence of regulated sports betting suggest that if people wanted to fix the games, they would not need legal bookmakers across the United States. In Canada betting on U.S. sports is quite popular. British Columbia's Lottery Corporation allows residents to wager on them. The corporation ran promotions for March Madness with the following text: "It's all about hoops: 64 teams, 61 games, March 16–April 3. Bet on all the big games with Sports Action Oddset and

Point Spread below." Briefly, there is much betting on U.S. sports, online in particular. In fact, sports betting accounted for more than half of Internet gambling revenues in 2001. In 2005 it constituted about 35 percent of the revenues (roughly $4 billion). Virtually all online sports books cater to the American market by accepting bets on U.S. sporting events. Yet bribing scandals and fixed games have been rare.

But it is not difficult to understand the associations' stand on the two issues. They have an interest in keeping sports betting illegal but honest, so that the value of broadcasting rights is not jeopardized. Mandating that teams disclose all injuries immediately through the media is a service to bettors, not fans. Schwartz notes that, at times, sports commissioners inadvertently make statements that clearly reveal that they are pursuing policies to sustain the sports betting markets. For example, in 1975 Pete Rozelle, the National Football League commissioner, stated explicitly that the league maintained the practice of mandatory publication of player injuries to prevent "suspicion when odds suddenly shifted."[70]

If fixing games is not the issue, why not argue for legalization? The answer is simple. In an illegal market neither the bookies nor the winners are taxed. If the league succeeds in sustaining the perception that the games stay honest in spite of the illegality, they get the best of both worlds. They get the large market – and significant broadcasting revenues. Once sports betting becomes legal, the taxation issue comes up, and, as experience shows, politicians cannot be trusted to tax the business properly. Italy, for example, imposed an 8.5 percent betting tax on revenue, rather than net profits. Gribbin and Bean (2005) note that in states where casinos became a prosperous business, state taxes and the regulatory framework were reasonable. Mississippi taxed low, and allowed the market to determine the number of casinos. Illinois taxed high, and the state set the number of licenses. This led to a process that took years and millions of dollars. Illinois assessed the highest casino taxes in the country – at first 35 percent, compared with 6 percent in Nevada, 9 percent in Atlantic City, and roughly 20 percent in other states. In 2004 the Illinois legislature raised the casino tax from 35 percent to 50 percent. After all, what may seem to be the sports associations' cynical stand has a rationale: better to keep the betting market illegal and honest than subject it to fiscal and regulatory whims that may destroy it.

Have there been occasional bribing scandals and fixed games? Yes, as we show in the next section, and some recent much-publicized ones too. But just as the few gambling addicts whose unusual stories have ended up as front-page news suggest just how rare they have been, the occasional fixed games ending up on front pages also may suggest the rarity of such events.

At least the rarity of those that authorities discover. When occasional fixing of a game happens, the legal European bookmakers notice the unusual trading patterns and notify the authorities. This is actually the pattern one should expect – unless governments pursue mistaken fiscal and regulatory policies.

With the point-spread system and the bookies locking in a fixed 5–7 percent profit on all bets, they have no incentive to fix games. They have all the incentive to keep it honest, so as to attract many bettors and more spending and to expand the market. (In fact, customers have incentives to fix the games in this case, not the bookies).

However, if there are debates about governments considering the imposition of ill-conceived taxes, such as Italy's 8.5 percent betting tax on revenue rather than net profits, we should expect more corruption. Operators and players become more likely to fix games, so as to grab as much money as they can and exit the business before the tax is imposed. It is the tax that turns them into fly-by-night operators. We would expect exactly the same outcome as soon as governments start talking about prohibition or stricter enforcement of antigambling laws. Paradoxical as this seems, the mere prospect of ill-conceived taxes, regulations, and prohibition increases the chances of corruption, scandals, and fraud.

Once prohibition is in place, the situation gets worse. In a recent study of illegal bookmakers in New York City, Strumpf (2004) found that these bookmakers behave according to the principles previously outlined. They try to extract money quickly and, because bettors cannot run price comparisons, they misprice the bets. In New York, the mispricing took the shape of charging more for the New York Yankees' bets, because they knew that their clients were fans. They extract money fast by advancing short-term credit to bettors, and Strumpf found that these were mostly compulsive gamblers. When betting is outlawed, the bookies cannot be held liable for selling their services to, specifically, compulsive gamblers.

The associations' opposition to the legalization of online gambling is equally understandable. Until October 2006 online gambling companies were not taxed because they were located in tax havens and the income the illegal bookmakers declared was most likely less than what they made. Gamblers could choose between spending time and money on untaxed (illegal) sports betting and watching games or on untaxed online poker games. It appears that relatively young, well-to-do males have been playing both games. Immortal as many youngsters believe they are, even they have only twenty-four hours in a day and limited funds. Prohibiting online gambling restores the advantage of betting illegally on sports. As we have often stated, one gets a better understanding by following money trails than pious declarations.[71]

But wouldn't both the sports associations and the online gambling companies be better off if sports betting and online gambling became legal, properly regulated, and taxed?

First, this is a big "if," and sports associations know that ill-conceived taxes and regulations can bring about corruption, destroy the market, and diminish interest in the sports. It is much easier to point fingers at fixed games than at the bad fiscal policies that may have brought them about. But suppose that the regulatory and fiscal mistakes did not happen. Then, the answer is yes – as we point out in the next section.

Still, there are a wide variety of other interests that suddenly come then into the picture, interests that would have much to lose if both sports betting and online gambling were properly taxed and regulated businesses. It appears that, unfortunately, these interest groups, with shortsighted views, have won the upper hand in the U.S. political arena for the moment.

Sports Betting Update: The Donaghy File[72]

To paraphrase Claude Raines in *Casablanca*, we are then shocked, shocked to find out that so many people pretended to be shocked by the charge that National Basketball Association referee Tim Donaghy fixed some games. Let us make it then as explicit as possible: the entire issue is being analyzed backward not only because of the refusal to see the impacts of prohibition but also because of the refusal to acknowledge gambling's link to sports.

Let's start with two factual statements:

1. People bet on sports. (Although we could go further and show that professional sports were originally organized by and for professional gamblers, let us just make the lesser claim).
2. People's bets affect the sport.

One obvious effect is that gamblers may try to fix the sport. Remember Paulo José Danelon, Marie-Reine Le Gougne, Robert Hoyzer, Edilson Pereira de Carvalho, and Eugenia Williams? (And if you don't, Google the names). These are referees caught fixing major international sporting events or mired in related controversies. The recent case of Tim Donaghy is not an aberration. Of course, given how hard it is to detect referee cheating, it is a safe assumption to make that there are more referee fixes than proven cases. In sports like boxing and skating, judges are often assumed to be biased at best, completely fixed at worst.

But fixing is only one influence of betting on sports. Betting affects fan interest and media coverage, and influences the organization of sports, as the previous section showed. Does anyone read the daily *Racing Form* out of interest in horses? Would daily newspapers devote a third of their reporting budgets and news pages to sports, including many pages of data in small print, if no one bet on games?

One of the distinctions between economics and finance is the following. Economics emphasizes real transactions in the financial trading markets: new issuance of stock by corporations, physical delivery of commodities in futures markets, long-term investment by households. Trading itself is assumed to provide intangible benefits such as liquidity, capital formation, and price discovery – with no attention devoted to what the gamblers bring to the table. Yet those who practice finance believe that betting in the financial markets exerts a profound influence on the real economy. Although it is "just money" changing hands among these speculators (who may have little knowledge and no interest in or direct link to the businesses or consumption of commodities they bet on, as Chapter 4 showed), to say that the real economy could function as well without such betting is wrong. Similarly in sports, the gambling markets affect the game, even if no gambler ever meets anyone physically involved in the sport.

The obvious goal is then to harness the influence of betting in positive ways. The usual pretended goals are either to eliminate betting altogether or, no less unrealistically, to eliminate any effect of betting on the sport. Both of these not only are impossible, but also would be wasteful if accomplished, as we showed. Properly taxed and regulated and backed by the right institutions, bettors could supply significant revenue to a sport, leading to lower ticket prices, higher salaries for athletes, and more profits for owners. No one follows the minutiae of a sport more than bettors, and their oversight can be put to good use.

Consider again the example of horse racing. To combat undesirable gambling influences on the sport, the pari-mutuel system was introduced. All bets are placed in a pool, the track takes its cut (say, 15 percent), and the rest is distributed among people who bet on the winning horse in proportion to their bets. All betting totals are displayed in public as bets are placed. A clear advantage of this system is that all the parties producing this sport get a cut of the revenue, without the organizers having a stake in the outcome of the race. The money from betting means that tracks can be beautiful and admission can be cheap or free, while the people involved in the sport can make a nice living. Bettors pay for all the record keeping and analysis that help define the sport. Another advantage is that the odds are determined in public, in an informed way. All bets are aggregated and paid off at the same rate; no one gets favorable or unfavorable odds. There have been many scandals in horse-race betting, but they took place off-track, with gamblers who attempted to use the track odds to quote their own bets. The pari-mutuel system removes the problem of fixes from the sport. As a result, horse racing can be freed from the intrusive enforcement of other antifixing measures.

Owners, trainers, and jockeys routinely bet using their inside information. It is common for owners to hold their horses back in some races, resulting in poor performances and better odds when the owner decides to bet and push the horse for maximum performance. Although this might be regarded as a fix in other sports, the pari-mutuel system means that the owner's betting (along with that of trainers, jockeys, and others in the know) is distinguishable on the pari-mutuel board. Horse bettors know to look for the same two things that work in all trading markets, value (a horse with better odds than its historical performance would suggest) and momentum (a horse with odds that get worse as track time approaches, which indicates that money with inside information is going on it).

This system is not a good model for the National Basketball Association. It works because essentially all the interest in horse racing is betting interest (except for a few marquee events like the Triple Crown and some major stakes). No one cares that some of the horses are not trying to win, as long as everyone has an equal opportunity to exploit that information. That is not true in competition among humans.

The innovation of point spread in human-sports betting in the twentieth century solves this problem. Instead of betting on which team will win and adjusting the payout odds to make it a fair bet, whether on the favorite or the underdog, the betting is on whether the favorite will win by more than the point spread and get even odds. (A standard 5 percent commission to the bookmaker is subtracted). Bookmakers were coerced into a national organization that matched off the bets. Like the pari-mutuel system, this meant that the organization running the betting had no stake in the outcome of the bets, and it just took a fraction of the amount wagered.

Although organized football and basketball have not profited directly from gambling, they have gained by having a monitoring service provided for free. Another indirect profit was from the sale of information services to gamblers. There were nonfinancial benefits as well. The point spread created interest in all games. A midseason one-sided contest between dull teams has the same betting potential as an evenly matched late-season contest between exciting teams. Without gamblers to monitor things, it would have been difficult for the league to ensure that teams played hard every game. Moreover, gambling interests result in television and newspaper coverage of the less exciting games, and that attention in turn attracts new nongambling fans.

Professional football acknowledges these realities, and works with legal and illegal gamblers to keep the game honest for everyone's benefit. The National Football League releases extremely detailed data about players, teams, and game situations, so there is no inside information to sell. Although the league tries to distance itself from gambling in public, in private it seems to recognize the value of gambling to the popularity and integrity of the game. The gambler is the sport's conscience. The purist sports fan cares only that the game is well played, and the partisan fan cares only that his or her team wins. It is only the gambler who cares that the outcome is decided fairly. In the long run, unfairness ruins the game for everyone, but only the gambler brings single-minded intensity to monitoring the fairness of every game, early or late in the season, even match or blowout, popular or obscure teams. People agree that public stock trading provides an essential monitor of the performance of corporations. Why is it less obvious that point spreads are useful to monitor the performance of sports teams? One answer is that perhaps there is too much misinformation and prejudice about gambling and gamblers.

The National Basketball Association's attitude may be attributed in part to this too, in addition to the other possibilities we suggested in the previous section. It guards basic competitive information jealously, which creates incentive for leaking. It monitors only legal gambling, thereby missing most of the market. As a result, its games are less appealing to gamblers. Players do not play hard every night. Referees exercise too much influence on the outcome, and they often do poor jobs. Obvious cases of information leakage, inconsistent officiating, and erratic play go uninvestigated.

The problems created by the National Basketball Association's see-no-evil attitude toward gambling are getting worse because of changes in the sports betting industry. The Internet plus federal crackdowns on organized crime have created a new type of gambling entity in the past decade: bookmaking entities that take risk. Some are offshore companies that take bets on the Internet; others are telephone bookmaking firms. Rather than try to match bets and take commissions, they try to predict winners, a much riskier but potentially more profitable activity. They appeal to bettors who shop point spreads, because the company is willing to give slightly higher or lower spreads to attract action on the side it expects will lose.

These companies have strong incentives to get inside information and fix games. Although they are smaller and less powerful than organized crime, there are many of them, which makes them much harder for law enforcement to monitor.

How do you put these people out of business and convert gambling from a negative to a positive influence on the game? Make the betting market more efficient, make the official point spreads more accurate, release more information, encourage publication of analysis and spreads. All these reduce the risk-adjusted profit of trying to beat the spread. On the other side, try to increase the appeal of the game to bettors, which increases the total betting interest, which makes commissions more profitable.

A still better solution would be to legalize gambling and have an affiliate run a worldwide operation to consolidate all betting activity. This would provide revenue to the league, give bettors a fairer game and discourage game fixing and other corruption while maximizing the oversight benefit of gambling. Unofficial betting would still take place, of course, but the people engaging in it would do so at their own risk. But this solution seems now out of sight and out of most minds, probably for some of the same reasons that people view all betting with suspicion.

To combine the best attributes of pari-mutuel systems and point spreads, the league could borrow a system from the U.S. Treasury market. Most bettors would simply pick the team they wanted to bet on (or another item like the total number of points scored or which team would have more rebounds). They would take whatever the consensus spread was, which would not be known until the betting cutoff time, say ten minutes before tip-off. Other bettors would specify a spread at which they were willing to bet. The league would set the spread at the level that equalized the amount of money bet on both teams. All bettors, both market orders and limit orders, would get the same spread.

We do not expect to see anything like this in the near future. In fact, we expect that the Donaghy story will make things worse. It will lead to more pressure to get rid of gambling, and more strictures to separate sport from gamblers. Both of these are hopeless and counterproductive. There is a positive approach, which is proven, but it requires admitting obvious facts. But it is safer to pretend to be shocked, shocked again and again – for hundreds of years – than to admit to having made big mistakes. After all, admitting them would mean giving up power and wealth. Nobody does that voluntarily.

Online Gambling

Between July and October 2006, online gambling companies trading on the London Stock Exchange with U.S. exposure lost $5 billion from their market value.

For many years, there have been repeated attempts in the U.S. Congress to pass bills outlawing online gambling directly or indirectly, by making it illegal to receive their funds by credit cards, checks, or electronic funds transfers. But many investors believed until July 2006 that such bills had few chances of turning into law, and they were caught by surprise.

Internet gaming companies started to be listed on public exchanges (the Toronto Stock Exchange, the Over-the-Counter Bulletin Board, and the Australian Stock Exchange) in the late 1990s. Because of the existing laws in Canada and the United States (in the latter the Wire Act in particular[73]), these companies were mainly involved in the back-office business. They specialized in payment processing, software, and marketing services for companies that offered gambling online.

Although from the 2006 UIGEA one would infer that online gambling companies are located in obscure places with criminal associations, a closer look suggests that that is not the case. Atlantic Lottery Corporation operates in Nova Scotia, Prince Edward Island, Newfoundland, Labrador, and New Brunswick and offers its services online, as does the British Columbia Lottery Corporation, which offers not only online sports betting but lottery products and keno too. The Kahnawake Mohawks (in Canada) host a large number of online gambling companies, and the United Kingdom is a big hub, with public companies in this sector, dozens public and regularly traded. Stewart (2006) notes that eighty-five jurisdictions around the world currently regulate some form of online gambling, though most companies are clustered in a few places, such as Antigua (536), Costa Rica (474), Curaçao (343), Gibraltar (111), which hosts PartyGaming, and a few others.

In 2006 there were ninety-seven public companies traded on exchanges around the world with at least some exposure to the online gambling business, and some, like PartyGaming, were in that business only.[74] In July 2005 the market value of PartyGaming alone was £5.7 billion (US $10.21 billion), roughly the market value of the MGM Mirage at the time. Global online gaming revenues were growing rapidly, from about $3 billion in 2001 to $12 billion in 2005, and their share of the total gambling market went from 2.4 percent in 2001 to 5 percent in 2005.

By 2007 the market value of the MGM Mirage doubled, whereas that of PartyGaming and other online gaming companies dropped significantly. It happened after the Congress passed the UIGEA, attached at the last minute as section 8 to a bill on port security and signed into law on October 13 by President George W. Bush. The act made it illegal for financial companies to transfer payments to online gambling companies. Ten days before the signing of the bill was anticipated, in just one day, PartyGaming shares fell 58 percent, losing $3.8 billion of their value.

Whereas this drastic one-day drop shows that the passing of the act caught most investors by surprise, there were some signs that the United States was moving toward a more rigid stand toward online gambling. On July 17, 2006, it was announced that BetOnSports's CEO David Carruthers was indicted by a federal grand jury on charges of racketeering conspiracy in connection with a U.S. gambling probe. Two months later, on September 6, Peter Dicks, the CEO of Sportingbet, was detained at JFK International Airport in response to an arrest warrant issued in Louisiana, related to gambling by computer.

The legal status of online gambling was uncertain for a number of years. In 2002 the New York attorney general required Citibank to block the use of its Visa and MasterCard credit cards for payments to offshore gambling businesses, and other New York–based banks followed suit. Banks in other states did not, though. The New York attorney general also subpoenaed PayPal for records. After paying a $10 million settlement with the Justice Department for violations of the USA Patriot Act, PayPal stopped dealing with offshore gambling companies.

The United States was emanating conflicting signals concerning the prospects of online gambling. As we noted before, it would be a mistake to infer that there is a clear principle behind the preceding actions and the UIGEA, or a proven harm linked to betting online. Actually, on the basis of the federal Interstate Horseracing Act, thirty-seven states allow online bets on horse and dog racing. Oregon, recall, has been a hub for such online gambling, which generated $200 million in revenues in 2005, and is contemplating issuing bonds backed by future monopoly profits. Yet adding to the confusion, on April 5, 2006, the Justice Department stated that the horseracing business violates the federal law (the Wire Act) by allowing online bets. The question is, of course, whether either the Department of Justice or the Treasury and the Fed would enforce the law (the latter two about payments to online gambling companies) – whatever the interpretation of the law turns out to be.[75]

Adding even more to the confusion, in 2005 Nevada governor Kenny Guinn signed Bill 471, which allows betting using wireless devices in the state – once the gamblers are on the premises of a licensed casino. In March 2006 Nevada regulators approved and designed the detailed rules. The facts concerning betting online are even more flexible in Nevada than this bill would imply. Station casinos are allowed to operate a virtual private network for sports betting by Las Vegas area residents. Once they open an account in person, bettors can direct wagers through that account through cable, dial-up service, or telephone.

The following section briefly summarizes arguments against legal gambling, all brought up before the passing of the October 2006 UIGEA, and discards all those that we have not already discarded.

Problems and Solutions

There has been much speculation about the reasons for passing the UIGEA. Some said that land-based casinos feared competition. Others blamed religious groups. Still others invoked fear of money laundering and criminal involvement. As we have shown already, none of these views holds up to closer scrutiny.

Land-based casinos would actually benefit from having online gambling subsidiaries. One reason is that many online players (many women among them) bet a few hundred dollars to learn the games – so they can head to a land-based casino with some confidence. Whereas one may never convince religious fanatics that they misread and misinterpret thousand-year-old texts, they are in the minority. If lobbyists were not fueling private beliefs toward politics, and if the instruments of direct democracy were better established, it is not clear just how active this minority would be on this issue to start with.

As to money laundering and criminal involvement, there is no evidence whatsoever of online gambling companies' involvement. However, nobody should be surprised that with the passage of the UIGEA, there would be more fly-by-night operators online, paying out less in prizes, or perhaps not paying at all. These are predictable adjustments we identified when we looked at sports betting in particular. We also would not be surprised to learn that, considering the extent of illegal sports betting, entrepreneurs (whom the law turned into criminals) would get into the banking business and become honest (though illegal) brokers between U.S. players and online gambling companies. Similar arrangements have happened in the past.

People have always distinguished between criminality and dishonesty. The fact that from time to time ill-conceived laws turned people into criminals does not imply that these people became dishonest just because a politician signed a piece of paper. It does not imply either that the general public and the police and the courts quite perceived them as being a threat to society. What it does imply is that once criminalized, people who were prejudiced against gambling could say that criminals were in charge of the business. In these days of terrorist risks, wouldn't scarce resources better be spent on protecting people against such crimes rather that go after companies who offer people a small ray of hope, moments of even-fleeting pleasurable anticipation, and some amusement?

Worrying about minors – another frequent objection against online gambling – has merit, but it has solutions too. Software is available for identification, verification, and automatic monitoring of players. The software can help people stay within their limits and even bar gambling if requested or necessary. In fact, controlling compulsive behavior online by using such tools may be better than off-line controls. In a windowless land-based casino, where every marketing tool imaginable is used to keep gamblers at the table, there is nobody to tap them on the shoulder to call it a day. On one occasion in the United Kingdom, headlines screamed about a teenager who had stolen his parents' credit cards and spent tens of thousands of pounds on a gambling site before he was caught. Notice, though, that the issue here is stealing, not gambling. But how many times do teenagers steal cars and credit cards with far more devastating consequences, such as accidents or death, and never make the front page? As with stories of addiction, the fact that this one case ended up in the headlines just shows how rare such theft is, in part because software that identifies teenagers has been tested and works.

There are several age and ID verification systems available and being used by the online gambling industry. They include Experian and Verify Me, for example, which search governmental and financial records to find evidence that people are registered at the address they claim and are older than eighteen. Of course, now that they are outlawed, online gambling companies have fewer incentives to install such software.[76]

There will always be isolated tragedies linked to gamblers. Modern media's distribution capabilities suggest that rather than being an exceptional event, they represent a problem of epidemic proportions that poses a threat and requires significant government intervention. Yet even with overregulation (under prohibition) and with billions spent on enforcement, no society entirely eliminates the adverse effects of living. We are forgetting that wise John Butler, who observed that "probability is the very guide of life." There will always be sensational stories involving unfortunate events and accidents. Yet exaggerating fears and fictionalizing the past can ruin the future. The key is to find a balance between regulations and freedoms. Otherwise, we risk abdicating more and more personal responsibility. Preoccupied with ensuring rights, societies at times forget that rights must come with obligations. What Blaise Pascal once said about wine – "No wine, no wisdom / Too much wine – the same," holds equally true for gambling and for risk-taking in its many incarnations too. Indeed, as we have seen, the vast majority bet with their heads and not over them. People never needed either bureaucrats or academics to remind them to do so. As for the addicted minority, they will not heed to advice in any case. The solution for this tiny minority may be found in medical rather than legal treatment.

Many have raised the specter of increased bankruptcies due to gambling. The Department of Treasury looked into this claim in 1999 in a massive 111-page "Study on the Interaction of Gambling and Bankruptcy" to determine whether there is evidence that legalization draws people into betting over their heads. The study concluded that there was no connection between state bankruptcy rates and the extent or introduction of casino gambling. This result was supported by a nationwide analysis that showed "no statistically significant casino effect (proximity to casino) with regard to county bankruptcy rates." (p. I). Also, as we already noted, research on crime, when adjusted for tourism, whether violent, against property, or total, found no significant differences among cities. Crime rates did increase when suddenly, after the legalization of casinos, tourists showed up in massive numbers.

Another issue often raised in public debates concerns lost revenues by the states, the subject of this chapter and the previous one. It is not surprising that, today, prominent among the states favoring prohibition are those where casinos and state lotteries bring in high revenues to the states' coffers, to which the present untaxed online gambling businesses are a threat.[77] A solution to this problem is to require online gaming companies to incorporate and operate their businesses in the United States. Software exists to identify the players. Thus, taxing them and bringing the properly allocated revenues to state coffers is not an issue either – though negotiating such a deal might not be easy. But the software is there to deal with it.

European events offer a hint, perhaps, of how events may unfold eventually in the United States too. In April 2007 William Hill, the U.K. bookmaker, launched a challenge against gambling monopolies in Europe by requesting a license to open betting shops in Greece. It based its step on a March ruling by the European Union in Brussels that barred Italy from using criminal law to keep out foreign bookmakers. The public company OPAP, which derives its revenues from gambling, has a monopoly agreement with the Greek government (thus, its revenues are backed in ways similar to bonds floated by U.S. state governments). Its management stated that it expects the Greek government to respect the monopoly agreement. However, William Hill declared that because OPAP is a publicly listed company, it is clear that gambling is there for commercial benefit. The barrier to entry cannot be defended on the basis of public moral principles (controlling the urge to gamble through high prices, prohibition, or a combination of both) – the principle the United States evoked before the World Trade Organization (WTO), discussed earlier in this chapter.

The WTO ruled against the United States in 2004, and its appellate body upheld the decision one year later. In March 2007 the WTO upheld the ruling a second time, and declared that Washington was not in compliance with its rules. In May the administration announced that it would remove gambling services from the existing trade agreements. At the time of the writing of this book, U.S. lawyer Mark E. Mendel was representing Antigua before the WTO, challenging the United States and testing the WTO's ability to enforce its agreements. At the same time, Antigua wants compensation of $3.4 billion, whereas European online gambling companies have been lobbying Brussels to back them with demands for $100 billion.

The United States could have avoided the preceding tricky challenges. By legalizing online gambling and regulating it properly, the United States would have helped establish an already thriving global industry, in the United States in particular. Moreover, it would have been able to create attractive new asset classes (emulating the United Kingdom's premium savings bonds, among others). This policy would have attracted investment, retained entrepreneurs and brains specialized in the business, and increased employment and tax revenues – as any high-tech, entertainment industry would (and if tradesports.com is any indication, have the inadvertent effect of expanding vastly, perhaps, the scope of futures markets).[78] Online gambling companies could abide by regulations designed for the online gambling business, by the Nevada authorities perhaps, which are known for their scrupulous checking. It would allow legislators to enforce laws against those gambling businesses that do not comply on U.S. soil. Technically, it is not difficult to shut down access to sites at the level of Internet service provider and control access for users.

It is always better to explain behavior by what it repeatedly achieves – eliminating the competition and ensuring cash flows to entrenched interests – than to pay attention to suddenly rediscovered moral issues or the floating of new fears. By elimination, we are left mainly with one culprit to shed light on the present effective prohibition: the states' and some existing gambling businesses' interest in sustaining their monopolistic revenues (and a minority's misunderstanding of ancient documents). In Europe the battle is brewing along similar lines as it is in the United States. Only there the European Union (in contrast to Washington) seems set to fight the national gambling and lottery monopolies.

All these conclusions do not imply that there is not too much gambling on games with large prizes or too much gambling as a pastime in various countries at various times, in the United States in particular. Under the present regulatory, legal, and institutional framework, it is impossible to say whether there is too much – or too little – gambling in the United States or in Western Europe today. It may well be that there is too much reliance on monopoly lotteries and too little on a wide range of debt or lottery financial instruments that would exist if the states did not have monopolies on lotteries to start with.

Last, but not least. An often-heard accusation has been that the mere presence of gambling brings about an appetite for effortless wealth that undermines the work ethic. Never mind that there is absolutely no evidence to substantiate such an opinion. If those who held it were consistent, they should advocate taxing inheritance at 100 percent. But their criticism brings us to the final chapter, where we show that, yes, there is a relationship between gamblers' minds and prosperity.

As it turns out, though, the relationship is just the opposite of what critics of gambling and those who take chances assumed. Gamblers, with a predisposition for understanding probabilities and prices, "correct the future."

EIGHT

How Gamblers and Risk-Takers Correct
the Future

Reuven Brenner and Gabrielle A. Brenner

Which shows that the story in this book is a history of humankind, told from the perspective of gamblers, risk-takers, and those who finance them. It tells the story of people who leap into the unknown, hoping to leapfrog their fellows.

Since ancient times people have tried to understand what makes some places rich and others poor. Herodotus wrote 2,500 years ago in his *Histories*:

For most cities which were great once are small today; and those which used to be small were great in my own time. Knowing, therefore, that human prosperity never abides long in some place, I shall pay attention to both alike.

Over the past few decades, countries like Ireland, Singapore, Taiwan, and China have leapfrogged others, which were better endowed with natural resources and whose populations had more formal education. At the same time, many oil-producing countries, for example, despite the windfall of money from selling oil, have not succeeded in leveraging their riches into prosperity.[1]

Risk and financial markets play relatively marginal roles – if any – in most views that examine the previous question, and though gamblers and risk-takers occasionally do make their appearance, the link between what is "civilization" on one side and risk-taking, creating liquidity, and financial markets on the other is rarely made. Yet getting to the bottom of facets of risk and uncertainty is crucial to the discovery of these links, and to an understanding of which countries are likely to get ahead and which ones will fall behind.

Implicitly, this broader topic has been the subject of this book, but we described it from the particular angle of looking at actions such as assessing risks, dealing with uncertainty, gambling, financing, betting on prices and sustaining liquidity. These acts have often been singled out for condemnation, and they still are.

It turns out that businesses and institutions brought to life to deal with risks and uncertainty, as societies adjusted to their increased populations, are at the heart of what brought prosperity about. The risk-takers, the ones who deviate, correct the future, and create history – whether in science, business, arts, or politics – are the innovators and the entrepreneurs, once they are financed. And while waiting for financial backers to appear, to ensure that they attract the better matches to a business, gamblers and speculators sustain liquidity – and hope.

Charles Mackay, in his 1841 classic *Extraordinary Popular Delusions and the Madness of Crowds*, explained that dissatisfaction with one's lot in life, far from leading to evil as at first might be supposed, has been the "great civiliser of our race." This human trait, writes Mackay, has tended more than anything else to raise the human race above the condition of brutes. But the same discontent – which is brought about by leapfrogging, according to the view of human nature put forward herein – has been, Mackay continues, the source of follies, speculations, absurdities, and the seeking of remedies that have "bewildered us in a wave of madness and error. These are death, toil, and ignorance of the future ... From the third [sprang] the false science of astrology, divination and their divisions" (pp. 98–9). These are the topics we started with at the beginning of the book. Can we go one step further and determine when it is more likely that people will take constructive risks rather than destructive ones? The book has answered this question too. Democratized, better-understood financial markets and better political institutions to ensure accountability and prevent mistakes from lasting too long – or correcting the future faster – make such channeling more likely.

The view that civilization is the art of adjusting to increased populations through leapfrogging is not quite new, though it has not been articulated or approached in the ways done here. Yet it can be found in the Bible – if closer attention is paid to the words there.

Recall the well-known story of Cain's murder of Abel. Some people take this and other biblical stories literally. Others undertake deep philosophical interpretations, trying to figure out how it is that a murderer is the father of civilization. But what if these texts document oral traditions of illiterate societies, where words were not taken literally? What if these stories reveal patterns of human behavior that we could instantly recognize – if only we translated this story properly?

After Cain, the farmer, kills his brother, the keeper of sheep, the Bible tells us that he settled down, "knew his wife; and she conceived, and bore Hanokh. Now he became the builder of a city, and called the city's name according his son's name, Hanokh." Whereas there has been much philosophizing about why Cain was not punished, little attention has been paid to the fact that the Bible mentions a city for the very first time in this story. It is not accidental either that the word "hanokh" means "to train, to discipline, to educate."

We know now that as their populations grew, societies around the world turned gradually from herding animals to farming, and we also know that innovations in agriculture did not happen randomly, but in response to sudden increases in population, as did literacy.[2] We also know that the transition did not happen peacefully: the keepers of the sheep, used to letting animals graze freely, fought the tillers of the ground, who had to enclose land used for farming. Even those unfamiliar with history can recognize this sequence of events from its musical incarnation in Rodgers and Hammerstein's *Oklahoma*. The biblical story suddenly makes sense, and the fact that the word "city" appears in it for the first time becomes understandable too.

Cities come into existence when population grows – by definition. Their emergence is linked to markets too – places where farmers brought the fruits of the land, merchants traded, fairs were set up, courts were established, and contracts were disputed. People specialized and new occupations appeared. The rest of Cain and Abel's story then becomes recognizable too. Cain's many offspring should not be taken literally either. They describe the new features that come with population growth, mobility, and life in the city: anonymity, diminished trust and specialization. One offspring is Irad (the "fugitive"), another is Mehujael ("smitten by God" – a fanatic, perhaps, trapped by languages of the past), a wife Adah (which means "ornament," referring to "artists," perhaps), and so on.

God's preference for Abel, which explains Cain's jealousy, also makes sense. Abel represented the long-lasting tradition of herding. And across countries and time, there are always groups that hold the past in greater esteem, want to slow down change, and use the priesthood and intellectuals to rationalize their views and cover them with veils of language – patterns we have examined throughout the book. These views found their way into the written text that became the Bible too. Times of transition have always been accompanied by conflicts, with words and arms too. It is also not surprising that the word for "city" in the biblical story (*eyr*) has the same root as "to watch," or "to be alert to dangers."

Listeners or readers of this story might have gotten this message that later generations missed altogether and might have drawn from it the lesson of pragmatic adaptation. After all, what is Cain's punishment? There is none. If the story is not interpreted literally, its message is pragmatic and resonates to these days. Whether one likes it or not, herding belongs to the past. The population is growing. Better that one adjust to it, build cities and the institutions needed to sustain them. Stop mourning for the good old times and move on.

What does this story have to do with leapfrogging? As population grows, herders overgraze and become poorer. Earlier ways of living can no longer be sustained, unless people adapt, become creative, and bring to life new institutions. People fall behind. What will they do? Some will resign to being poor. Others will bet on destructive ideas, like stealing and killing, organizing in bands, and fighting. Others will gamble and speculate. Still others will bet on constructive, innovate ideas, start farming and new businesses, establish cities and trade, become litigators and judges, and debate conflicts that arise with trade to resolve them. They leave herding and pastoral tribes behind. That is where the leapfrogging game started.

Today the narrow confines of arbitrary, accidental academic disciplines of economics, finance, anthropology, psychology, or political science approach the question of why some countries leapfrog others and others fall behind. Such a fragmented view is neither useful nor illuminating.[3] One cannot separate economic determinants from institutional framework and cultural heritage – today's established academic orthodoxy notwithstanding. These matters are linked, and for a simple reason that is also at the heart of what economic change means. Risk-takers and gamblers have been bringing about this change. And it is the financing of risk-takers that make some places rich and others poor. Gamblers, speculators, and risk-takers, and the intense debates surrounding the notions of chance, risk, and the financing associated with them have all played key roles in bringing about the businesses and institutions that are necessary to the way financial markets work today.

We took the long route in this book because we agree with a Chinese political leader's reply to Henry Kissinger, then U.S. secretary of state. When Kissinger asked the Chinese leader what he thought about the effects of the French Revolution, the latter replied that it was too soon to tell. On crucial issues – such as risk-taking and gambling throughout the ages – it is better to take a very deep breath to get a better understanding as to the state of confusion, even in the United States, on these topics. We thus went as far back as we could – to the Bible – where we began this book and, for the sake of coming full circle, we returned to it in this last chapter.

A broader conclusion from this book, which also takes us back to Chapter 1, is that the democratization of financial markets sheds light on the question of what makes some societies click and others fall behind. Societies that allowed their gamblers and risk-takers more scope for experimentation ended up with more developed capital markets, attracting and retaining talents – the "vital few" as the late historian Jonathan Hughes called them.

The societies that did not fell behind. Gamblers, speculators, and risk-takers who originated futures markets and many of the institutions that back financial markets today and sustained liquidity have been among those vital few, though they are rarely, if ever, celebrated. In understanding why some places thrived and others did not, emphasizing the roles of the vital few has little in common with those who emphasize trade as key to such understanding.

Every society since time immemorial has traded. Few societies, however, developed financial markets – the trading of paper securities that entitle owners to fractions of ownership of assets and allowing people to then bet on price distributions. Such securitization requires a complex maze of institutions to sustain it: clearinghouses, futures and free information markets, and the enforcement of complex laws concerning property rights are just some of them.[4] These institutions are all needed to bring about accountability and to build long-term trust (without which financial markets cannot exist). Whereas among relatively immobile, small tribes, families and religion built such trust and enforced decent behavior, once population increased and became more mobile, these institutions lost their potency, and new ones were invented to substitute for the lost accountability and trust.[5] We found that this is the key to understand prosperity, and, as we showed, gamblers played unique roles in bringing these institutions about.[6]

Just as among the most valuable assets of a business is its ability to pursue options, so is the case of countries. But what determines how many options in business are created? What institutions are needed to price them? If allowing people to trade property rights in price distributions (defined as "speculation" or "gambling") is, in fact, necessary to create more such options, what does that imply for monetary policy and policy toward betting markets?

We answered these questions too. In the remaining sections we shall tie some loose ends together and draw the larger picture that emerges from all the puzzles we have solved throughout the book.

Betting on Ideas, and Matters of Trial and Error

Innovations, whether in technology, organization of enterprises, politics, law, science, or culture, define change – economic change in particular. But what does the term "innovation" mean?

Innovation is a deviation from traditional ways of doing things. People take bets on the unknown, and others then can leap into the unknown. By definition, therefore, deviation – and innovation – is relative to the institutional framework or cultural heritage.

It is easy to define innovation. It is hard to bring it to life for a simple reason: new ideas may be good or bad. Some ideas that seem wonderful at first sight may be hard to execute or take far more time than anticipated. Others may seem to be great ideas, but, upon realization, it turns out that the innovative good or service has no commercial value. What is the new business model to commercialize innovations, or what are the new institutions that societies need to bring some innovations to life? These are questions that do not have easy answers. As we showed in the previous chapter, businesses and societies differ in their views about what to do with gambling when the Internet comes along. What innovative, changing societies need, then, are, among others:

- Risk-takers and a maze of institutions that encourage and finance them
- Institutions to continuously reevaluate the experiments and with the right and ability to stop them, preventing a persistence in costly error
- Gamblers and speculators to sustain the liquidity needed during the long years that elapse between the floating of an idea and the time it is brought to life.[7]

These may not sound too difficult, but except for western societies, no others have developed the institutions that encourage wide-ranging experimentation. And, as we saw, it took a very long time for the West to get a grip on the subjects of risk and uncertainty, and occasionally even the United States moves toward prohibition rather than the pursuit of trial and error.

The outlook on life of trial and error, of encouraging and financing risk-taking, and of allowing bets on anything unless it is explicitly prohibited is radically different from that of predestination and everything being prohibited unless explicitly allowed. The risk-taking but accountable society requires introspection, raising questions such as: What did I do wrong? One cannot have an innovative society unless institutions – themselves shaped by trial and error – have come into existence and brought about a culture with a frame of mind that says, "let's try to go for it." An innovative society requires people to both admit to their mistakes (rather than blame others for their misfortunes and believe that everything has a motive and cause) and give to those who failed second and third chances. Some societies stayed intolerant to human frailty: one mistake, one bankruptcy, and people could no longer access capital.

In brief, innovations are a bet and a matter of trial and error. And every trial, every development is a cost – unless something comes out of it. Drug companies spend about $500 million to develop a new drug. They may succeed or they may not. The movie *Titanic* cost $200 million to make. It turned out to be a commercially successful experiment. The movie *Alexander* was estimated to have cost more than $100 million, and it flopped. Somebody must finance all such ventures and others must keep betting on their prospects to eventually reach a commercially successful venture.

Compare two societies. One gambles, speculates, and finances experiments continuously. Some experiments do not lead anywhere and they are a cost. Others find consumers who want to buy the products and services that these experiments gave birth to. Another society does not experiment at all. The same things are done over and over again, generation after generation. The latter society is stable and traditional. The first may occasionally fall behind when nothing comes out of various projects. Eventually, though, a society that finances risk-takers and sustains liquidity will stumble on a successful innovation. This society will change and, over time, grow by creating options and attracting other risk-takers. The other society – which does not experiment at all – falls behind.

But why is it that the West persisted in being an experimental, wagering society? Some answers can be found in features of religious beliefs and others in accidental events, such as the separation of powers, of religious from political ones in particular, which did not happen elsewhere. This book singled out policies toward risk, risk-takers, and gamblers that resulted in the development of financial markets that complement the answer. As we briefly show in the next section, these unique features of western societies are not independent.

How Did Some Societies Come to Tolerate Risk-Takers and Gamblers?

In his two books on the history of western law, *Law and Revolution* (1983) and *Law and Revolution II* (2003), Harold Berman showed what makes western law different from other legal systems. He has also been one of many writers who made the point that the years between 1050 and 1200 were the turning point in western history, brought about, in part, by the sudden significant increase in Europe's population.[8] It was by 1100 that cities grew and filled with traders and merchants, that writing and the building of the large cathedrals spread. Twelfth-century France and Italy became a hotbed of probability theories, though only in the seventeenth century did Pierre de Fermat and Blaise Pascal discover their translation to mathematics. This late discovery is not so surprising: observers will start noticing regularities linked to the law of large numbers only when there are large numbers around them for a while.

Berman found answers in what he calls the Gregorian revolution and the struggle of investitures in the eleventh century. These events in the West sharply separated the church from the secular world of politics and governance, freeing the clergy from the domination of lords, kings, and emperors. This separation (which was accidental, and undertaken without either power perceiving its consequences), Berman wrote, "gave rise to the formation of the first modern Western legal system, the 'new canon law' . . . of the Roman Catholic Church, and eventually to new secular legal systems as well – royal, urban, and others." For centuries after, the church was the only institution capable of resisting royal and feudal authority. It became a bureaucracy of educated celibate clergy (the only institution at the time allowing a better life to the poor) and the seed of universities.[9]

Later, in the late fourteenth and fifteenth centuries, the West experienced a widespread clamor for additional reformation.[10] This happened because the initial separation of powers was circumvented, and abuse of power and corruption persisted. The Lutheran reformation, which abolished ecclesiastical jurisdiction in Protestant kingdoms, brought about a new separation of powers and new institutions independent of both political and centralized church controls. Although later the denial of the church's role and the unification of the legal system increased the power of the secular rulers (who for the first time claimed absolute power), the English Revolution reversed this trend by establishing the supremacy of Parliament over the Crown. The revolution brought about the enforcement of what the Magna Carta promised centuries before, namely, separation of the powers to tax from the powers to spend.[11]

These features – the long history of struggle, of rivalry between the highest political authorities and the church, and then between rulers and their constituents – is a distinguishing feature of the western experience. Even when state and church were not fighting each other, the idea of the legitimate coexistence of the two – first rendering unto Caesar the things that are Caesar's and to God the things that are God's – was almost always in the background.

The preceding features allowed scope for experimentation, as first the existence in each polity of two distinct powers, and later more, allowed for the raising of questions in all domains, even in those judged sacrilegious. The Vatican condemned Galileo for going against dogma, but his ideas were widely disseminated, helped by the secular authorities' interest. Later in

England, the new powers of Parliament came with a reform of the financing of the state – often with lotteries. This led to more secure property rights and to the development of financial markets with land becoming a liquid asset. The existence of and competition between two or more powers also allowed various emerging groups to extract more rights for themselves.[12]

Nothing threatens established powers and cartel-type political arrangements more than the opening up of capital markets. It is access to various independent sources of capital (and power) that offer people alternatives and increase their negotiating power and ability to stand up – to extract rights and to obtain financing in particular. As long as the powers to be keep capital markets closed by, among other things, preventing land from changing hands, government remains the only source of capital, and power is not dispersed at all. One may observe so-called democratic institutions and pro forma separation of powers in such countries. But they are all facades, because votes are not independent. It is not surprising that many countries – be they in Latin America, Africa, the Middle East, or Asia – remain mired in corruption, unstable, and poor.[13]

It is not surprising either that when capital flows through governments and religious institutions, there are restrictions on the flow of information and subsidies to spread teachings that rationalize both keeping capital markets closed and the threat of innovations and risk-taking. (One should not be surprised that the deepest capital markets are in London and New York, which are centers of media too.) Such teachings cast long shadows.[14]

In *Democracy in America*, Alexis de Tocqueville remarked that historical accounts must be affected by democratic tendencies. Historians will put emphasis neither on chance nor on the "deeds and accomplishments of heroes and leaders, but ... upon mass movements and general causes."[15] How is such a uniform viewpoint shaped among historians and social scientists in a society that seems to celebrate individualism and originality? Well, says Tocqueville, the liberty of the American mind is an illusion. He was mistaken there: as long as there are independent sources of capital, independent minds flourish. Once, however, there are few sources of capital, and most of it flows through one institution, then few signs of independent thinking will be visible.[16]

Recall the discussion on usury laws with their biblical origins, which significantly slowed down the development of capital markets in Western Europe. The common interpretation of the text was that high interest rates harm the poor, and should thus be illegal. Yet the poor, the young, and the newcomers were the ones harmed by these laws. It is people without a track record who have to pay initially higher rates until they establish their credibility. Even if there is, say, a risk-taking innovator, and people willing to bet on him, usury laws would prevent the financing of his venture. What can he do then? Work for the establishment as an engineer or move. If he stays, and brings his idea to life within the established institution, though he may get a piece of the pie, it is the unthreatened established company that will reap the riches.

Now if the innovator raises money, even at the gambling table, the story becomes different. Fred Smith is now known as the entrepreneur who built Federal Express. But before he bet on the idea of providing a fast, large-scale, and reliable method of delivering mail (that the state-owned post offices around the world did not) – he went bankrupt. As a last resort, he went to Las Vegas, got lucky, and won $50,000. He did not gamble either before his bankruptcy or after his win. The $50,000 enabled him to restart his venture, and the rest is, well, history. Although today this story is a curiosity, in the past it was not.

Behind the accusations of high-yield bonds being junk bonds and Ponzi schemes just two decades ago, one can still detect these same myths at work. After all, what were these bonds? They were securitized loans to newcomers, such as CNN, MCI, McCaw Cellular and others. The financing allowed them to contest the then establishment of the three networks and AT&T. Without access to the high-yield market (and in Fred Smith's case, the gambling table), we might still be watching a few networks and have the option to choose Bell. Without the ability to access capital, dreams stay dreams – and the establishment stays unthreatened.

It is not surprising, then, that in societies that rationalize the closing of capital markets, most innovations and risk-taking are frowned upon. Joseph Needham showed how the unification under a centralized monarchy back in the third century BCE (whose features persisted into the twentieth century) turned China into what historians have called bureaucratic feudalism, which prevented the rise of a significant Chinese mercantile class – the risk-taking, probability-mindset class. And Landes noted that "in China, even when the state did not take, it oversaw, regulated and repressed," and asked for total obedience from subjects.[17] Although Su Song built a heavenly clock in the 1080s to help the emperor decree the calendar – issuing a calendar was the emperor's prerogative and an unauthorized calendar was lèse-majesté – its use was restricted to the imperial court. The art of clock-making was soon lost in China when a new emperor declared his predecessor's calendar to be faulty.[18]

Although Chinese navigators used compasses much before they were rediscovered in Europe and explored the seas in the 1400s, their goal was not trade, but to sing the praises of the emperor. The voyages ended in 1433 when the emperor forbade the Chinese from exploring abroad. China (and Korea), in spite of having developed many of the innovations – printing press, gunpowder, compass, textile machinery – that centuries later defined the Industrial Revolution in England, prohibited the commercialization of those innovations. Printing was invented in China during the Tang dynasty (sixth century CE), and was used first to replicate Buddhist texts that were then the Confucian classics. But only when Gutenberg reinvented printing and saw its commercial potential – in a society that had an expanding commercial class – was the printing press fully exploited.[19]

The Chinese scholars, employed by the state, were suspicious of science and commerce, any innovations coming from the West in particular. Westerners visiting China in the seventeenth century noted that scholars were interested in local antiquities rather than modern things. They were xenophobic, though by the nineteenth century some started to suggest that China could choose western technologies – but only those that would not bring upheaval to custom and tradition.

The control of printing should not be surprising: it can diffuse information cheaply, and reveal that the content of sacred books may not be so sacred after all. In modern times communists have severely restricted communication channels, access to typing machines, and later computers, and today many countries – China among them – impose severe constraints on information channels, the Internet among them. The Chinese reluctance today to internally open up its financial markets is not surprising either. There would be nothing that would weaken more and faster the communist grip on power.[20]

Capital Markets and Models of Society

The historian Douglass North noted that people make grave mistakes either because they "don't have a correct understanding of reality" or because the "belief system is wrong – communism for example."[21]

These two points, however, only beg deeper questions. No doubt that perception and reality are guiding our lives today, much as they guided those of our ancestors. This is unavoidable and we do not know what, for example, the "correct understanding of reality" is. Does anyone? In fact, futures markets, by aggregating information (once there are many independent sources of capital, and many gamblers and speculators are held accountable) more often than not offer the best available understanding of reality.

When societies have small populations and are relatively isolated, they perceive reality differently from how we perceive it and use a different language to describe it. Their reality *is* different. As we have noted, there cannot be such a thing as the law of large numbers in such societies, and insurance cannot be priced but is offered by the family and the tribe and enforced by beliefs. Small, isolated, relatively immobile societies cannot pursue specialization, such as lawyers and police. Fear of hell and the rewards of heaven, taught from an early age, are among the ways to achieve good behavior. Strict adherence to rituals is another. The language of societies that aim for such beliefs will differ from others. Even when such societies become suddenly more mobile and integrated with the rest of the world, it takes time until their members learn the new languages and view a variety of institutions in a different light.

Let us consider here just briefly the 1920s and 1930s, because many of the ideas that intellectuals came up with then concerning risks and models of society still shape policies today. These were also the decades that the communist regime established its power in the Soviet Union, hyperinflation destroyed Western European societies, and the United States and United Kingdom, among other western countries, faced massive, unprecedented unemployment rates.

Could it have been clear to people at the time that communism was one of the worst models of society they could choose from? Elsewhere, hyperinflation destroyed the middle class in Germany, Hungary, and Austria. It wiped out their savings and destroyed their capital markets. The collapse of property and security and the banking system prevented people in these countries from restarting. Little wonder that European capitals became centers of vice and hedonism at the time, and Europeans bet on crazy ideas with disastrous consequences.[22] With capital markets destroyed, it is not surprising that people turned to government as a source of capital, or that a wide range of theories rationalizing centralization gained currency.

It is true that people did not have a "correct" understanding of reality at the time and did not realize that grave monetary, exchange rate, and tariff policies and ill-conceived postwar treaties (such as that of Versailles) brought about disastrous outcomes. But people wanted to live first and philosophize later. With many traditional institutions bankrupt and gone, people bet on models of society where governments had increased roles in creating employment and managing aggregate demands and borrowed against a few particular futures – as imagined by various isms.[23] Keynes's views do not constitute an ism, but Keynes claimed that businesspeople's animal spirits (risk-taking and speculation) bring about hardship, are unpredictable, and can be corrected only by wise policy makers and bureaucrats. The latter, he assumes, never succumb to such lowly spirits.[24]

In other words, when three sources of capital – savings, inheritance, and financial markets – were destroyed, people predictably turned to government and crime, crime organized by the state, rationalized by what was claimed to be a noncriminal new jargon relying on the notion of "superior races" in particular. With capital markets closed, politicians and government bureaucracies became the matchmakers among capital and talent and financiers, claiming that they could design institutions to hold all parties accountable. They predictably failed. Decades later we still pay the price.

Natural Resources Are No Mothers of Invention

If once it was true that lands, mines, farms, gold, and oil were the sources of wealth in most of the world, this is no longer the case today. The ability to create options, some of which end up being commercial successes, is far more important than acquiring wealth from land or the occasional high prices of exportable natural resources.

However, in societies endowed with natural resources, a powerful elite can keep for longer their outdated notions about the nature of wealth – what it is and how it is created – and sustain backward-looking institutions, keeping their societies immobile and frozen, and preventing risk-taking and the emergence of institutions to back it. The fact that many of these countries have lotteries is not a contradiction. It is perceived as a modern version of fairy tales about poor people stumbling on treasures. In fact, having lotteries implicitly suggests that becoming rich by stumbling on treasures is legitimate, whereas becoming rich through risk-taking and sustaining liquidity is suspect.

Take, for example, Mexico, Venezuela, Brazil, Kenya, Nigeria, Cameroon, Democratic Republic of the Congo, and Angola. All are rich in land, mines, oil, diamonds, and beaches. Occasionally these countries receive high revenues from their natural resources. But trading in these windfalls did not bring about a commercial society. Instead, it subsidized a corrupt elite that used the rents from resources to keep its people immobile, bribing some and forcing others into obedience. The risk-takers left – if they could. The millions of poor who could not bought lottery tickets.

If the former Soviet Union had not been so well endowed with rich agricultural land and other natural resources, it is unlikely that communism could have survived for as long as it did. There would not have been enough resources to sustain a large military and the police that kept most people docile. Although communism had already made the Soviet Union poor, President Reagan's Star Wars and plummeting oil prices during the 1980s brought the Soviet Union close to bankruptcy. In politics, as in business, bankruptcy has been the mother of invention.

It is not surprising, therefore, that South Korea, which has few natural resources, prospers (as Amsterdam did in the seventeenth century). Japan is a small island with little arable land, a large population, and no natural resources either (though it is well endowed with wealth-destroying natural disasters). It prospers too. Taiwan, Hong Kong, and Singapore reflect similar patterns. And it is no surprise that China, with its 1.3 billion people and fewer natural resources, is making faster adjustments to pricing risks than Russia, with its greater endowment of natural resources.

Extreme cases disprove rules. Take the tiny pacific island of Nauru. Because of its rich deposits of phosphates, Nauru became for a time one of the richest nations on earth. In 1983 it had a per capita income of $25,000. The residents either worked as bureaucrats or not at all. For hard-labor jobs they imported workers. By now, half a century of strip-mining has left the island a wasteland. Almost all the phosphate has been mined, leaving the island without a source of income and no topsoil. The island's authorities mismanaged the money that should have been put in trust for this contingency in ventures such as musicals in London's West End, and a national airline. (Why do governments think that painting flags on planes produced and maintained elsewhere, and flown by foreign pilots is a symbol of national power?) Nauru now faces a financial crisis and there are talks of either moving the population to Australia or to another unoccupied Pacific island. The sudden riches brought about by natural resources have also brought about the downfall of Nauru.[25]

On the other extreme, take the example of the Jewish tribe (who are heavy gamblers, apparently disproportionately represented among addicts though light drinkers, and disproportionately represented among innovators, financiers, Nobel Prize winners, traders, and risk-takers).[26] They have never relied on natural resources, and even when they owned immobile property, they repeatedly encountered confiscation and were forced into exile. It is not surprising that Jewish people specialized in mobile professions, linked to financial markets in particular. The latter happened because they were forced into usury for centuries (now banking), which positioned them well to become experts in pricing and assessing credits – the fundamentals of financial know-how.

By the time banking was legitimate, many were well versed in assessing probabilities and prices, as traders are, and think in terms of compounding interest rates, complex contracts, and litigation. The Talmud, much of which deals with everyday legal issues and legal principles, helped. Having often been forced to quit their lands allowed them to have dispersed networks. Their small numbers notwithstanding, they became "globalized" before this term became a cliché. As the rest of the world became more mobile and encouraged risk-taking, all these particular features combined turned out to be good preparation for realizing profits from these skills, skills acquired initially through much suffering.[27]

Briefly, an embarrassment of natural riches does not make countries wealthy.[28] It even gives more power to prohibit all forms of risk-taking. On the contrary, the lack of natural resources does not prevent countries from prospering and leapfrogging their resource-rich rivals. People must rely on their brains and take risks.

What this section shows, from yet another angle, is that one cannot separate economics, the state of capital markets in particular, from politics, frames of mind, or cultural heritage. If countries want to catch up quickly, they should not only encourage their own gamblers and risk-takers, but, to speed the adjustment, allow for easier movement of people, so as to transfer more quickly many of the intangible skills linked to risk-taking, as the next section shows.[29] Gamblers and speculators facilitate this transition.

Creating Wealth and the Movement of the Vital Few

Even though the Netherlands is below sea level, with few natural resources, the Dutch Republic became the miracle of the seventeenth century and has prospered ever since, with Amsterdam the jewel in its crown. The city's rags-to-riches story puzzled observers of the seventeenth century. The puzzle centered not around Spain's and Portugal's riches, which were "found" treasures, but around the republic's sudden wealth.

The Dutch Republic leapfrogged not only Spain and Portugal, but also England and France. Although England had grain, timber, and wool, and France had vineyards and salt, the Dutch, lacking any of these and forced to spend fortunes to build and maintain dikes to prevent towns from sinking, became the exporters of fine clothing. They also became the biggest traders in grain, the builders of better and cheaper ships than England, and the exporters of high-quality salt and wine.

As we saw, the Dutch Republic achieved this by being the first state tolerant toward all religious practices, the most open society of the times. It attracted people from all over Europe, Jews and Huguenots prominent among them. The city saw unprecedented innovations in financial practices, including the world's first stock market, where French, Venetians, Florentines, Germans, Poles, Hungarians, Spanish, Russians, Turks, Armenians, and Hindus traded not only in stocks but in sophisticated derivatives too. Much of the active capital was either foreign owned or owned by Amsterdammers of foreign birth. Amsterdam's entrepreneurs and traders, like those of the Italian city-states before, thought globally before anyone bothered to use that term. The city's influence radiated around Europe and beyond.

But it is misleading to call this a Dutch miracle. The openness of the new republic attracted to Amsterdam skilled immigrants, merchants, gamblers, and financiers with networks around the world. They were the ones who turned Amsterdam into the financial and trading center of the seventeenth-century world. It was not illiterate Dutch fishermen of the time who became scientists, entrepreneurs, traders, and designers of herring derivatives. It is the bias today of thinking in terms of national histories, national statistics, that brings about mistaken analyses in terms of geographically defined entities.

In the twentieth century, Taiwan, Singapore, Hong Kong, Israel, and, of course, the United States and Canada, have been among the places that offered immigrants opportunities denied to them by mainland China, Nazis, communists, or large ethnic groups. Hong Kong benefited from waves of immigrants from China. The city prospered from the inflow of Shanghai merchants and financiers when Mao Tse-Tung "liberated" China in 1949. The effects were similar when Jews fled many parts of Europe, when Cubans fled for Florida, when Toronto became home to English-speaking Montrealers (with almost the entire financial community moving there) who were fleeing the specter of independent Quebec, or when Lebanese Christians (the merchant class) fled Beirut for Paris and Montreal. During the early 1990s, 1 million Russian immigrants, many scientists and engineers among them, arrived in Israel. At the same time, Israel deregulated its financial markets. By now Israel, with about 7 million people, is the third country in terms of number of companies listed on the Nasdaq (Canada is the second).

Shanghai's merchants initiated Hong Kong's textile and shipping industries. These Chinese immigrants also established a network of merchants, traders, financiers, and manufacturers – as Jewish, Italian, Armenian, Parsi, and other immigrant groups did throughout history in various parts of the world. In the 1960s, when Singapore split from Malaysia, Indonesia threatened both countries. However, since the beginning of the 1990s, Indonesia has allowed Singaporean companies to outsource some of their labor-intensive operations into Indonesia's poorer economies, Batam Island among them, where 150 Singapore-based companies made investments. The island prospered. But does it mean that it could prosper without the knowledge of Singapore's people?

Such a sequence of events is again taking place before our eyes. It would be a mistake to attribute the growth of China only to the political changes there without reference to the fact that, with the sudden openness, 55 million expatriate Chinese were involved in most investments, bringing their knowledge and contacts to the mainland. And their entrepreneurship also extends to financing, as Chinese banks lend mostly to the bankrupt state-owned enterprises while informal financing fuels China's economic miracle, Kellee Tsai's book, *Back-Alley Banking* shows. Another recent example is Ireland. In response to lower taxes and the easing of regulatory burdens, some four hundred thousand skilled people from around the world moved there (a 10 percent addition to Ireland's population), turning one of the poorest countries in Europe from sheep to Google in little more than a decade, and making it one of the richest. The "Celtic Tiger" had Polish cubs.

Time will tell how much the spectacular performance of Western Europe, the United States, and Canada since World War II can be attributed to the large movement of ambitious risk-takers, gamblers, and capital from around the world, a world that until about twenty years ago was hostile to initiative and hope. Then one will know how much the transfer of such unmeasured capital helped cover up the many mistaken policies that these countries have indulged in – though these mistakes pale in comparison to those committed by governments in the rest of the world. What should be clear is that when and if the rest of the world retains its risk-takers and allows capital and futures markets to develop, western countries, the United States, and Canada will have to change their ways to sustain their standards of living. They will have to correct their many mistaken policies – starting with those based on a basic misunderstanding of risk, risk-taking, liquidity, and gambling.

Happiness and Luck

Because capital markets and betting on a wide range of events is about the future – which is what values in open capital markets represent – their expansion allows for correcting the future quickly. Those that kept their capital and futures markets closed and limited people's options to gamble and take bets, even if they traded – features of most societies today – are still living in the present and the past. Because their ability to borrow against the future is limited, this should not come as a surprise. They bet on one future, creating few other options, making it harder to correct.[30] Instead of occasional pricing upheavals, such societies need to go through revolutions to correct their future.

All this is fine, some may say. But what about happiness? What if some people are content with maintaining the past and want to bet on just one future that would look very much like that idealized past? A linguistic exercise offers an answer.

The word "happiness" derives from *hap*, which means "chance," "fortune," "a condition due to randomness." This linguistic relationship is not exceptional. Schoeck notes that in Middle High German *gelücke* referred to an aimless, unpredictable, and uncontrollable power that shapes events favorably or unfavorably, and that in German there is today one word (*Glück*) for both happiness and luck.[31] It appears then, that at least in the western tradition, pursuing happiness is identical to pursuing policies that do not prohibit creating options.

We started this chapter with comments on civilization, and these last paragraphs sentence brings us back to them. Most of the Ten Commandments are about what not to do, and so is civilization. Civilization is not about regulating conduct. Civilization is about regulating misconduct, such as murder and theft. Civilization also is defined by allowing people to create options, to give them chances, and, at the same time, having institutions to discipline and hold people accountable for the choices.

It is this principle – of everything being allowed unless being explicitly prohibited – that is the secret of the pursuit of happiness and prosperity, and that defines what we call civilization.

This is all easy to define, but hard to execute and sustain, as this book has showed. And it implies that governments that claim that their goal is to let people pursue happiness but then reduce people's options to take chances do not know what they are talking about or are lying through their teeth.

It is a characteristic of an educated man to look for as much precision in each subject as the nature of a particular area of enquiry admits.
Aristotle, Nicomachean Ethics

APPENDIX ONE

Gambling and Risk-Taking: The Leapfrogging Instinct

Reuven Brenner

Which shows how to translate the view about human nature underlying this book, the words "taking risks" and "leaping into uncertainty" into mathematics, and how this view differs from conventional ones; it also shows why the other views do not hold up to close scrutiny.

Introduction

"A new idea does not come forth in its mature scientific form. It contains logical ambiguities or errors; the evidence on which it rests is incomplete or indecisive; and its domain of application is exaggerated in certain directions and overlooked in others," wrote Stigler in one of his essays on the history of economics.[1]

These sentences summarize the justification for presenting the model of risk-taking and decision making on which the arguments in this book rely, despite that its essential features have been presented in the work of R. Brenner (1983, 1985, 1987). I made various approximations in those early works, omitted details, and overlooked some implications. This appendix presents corrections and compares it with other models that try to explain decision-making and risk-taking behavior, a comparison that earlier works made only in passing.

The points emphasized in this appendix are only those that I judged pertinent to the subject matter covered in this book: gambling, insurance, progressive taxation, decision making in general, and the link to sources and allocation of capital. This model deals with 'jumps' – relatively large changes. The traditional economic models can deal with small changes, where people adapt passively but do not bet on any new idea.

This view of human behavior underlies many historians' and social scientists' work, though neither articulates their views in the way done here or links them to the state of financial markets, to the notions of "necessity" and chance, or to that of uncertainty.

To devote your whole life to keeping stock, or making phone calls, or selling or buying. To suffer fifty weeks of the year for the sake of a two-week vacation, when all you desire is to be outdoors, with your shirt off. And always to have to get ahead of the next fella. And still – that's how you build a future.

Arthur Miller, Death of a Salesman (1949)

Gambling and the Leapfrogging Instinct

Let W_0 be one's wealth and let I_o be an interval in the distribution of wealth, defining a class with mean wealth equal to $\bar{W}_0$. This interval defines one's perception of a certain class, or rank in society, a class to which the individual expects to belong. $\alpha(\cdot)$ denotes the percentage of people who are richer than $\bar{W}_0$ in society. Then I define the utility function as follows:

$$U(W_0, \alpha(W > \bar{W}_0)| W_0 \in I_0), \tag{1}$$

where

$$\delta U/\delta W_0 > 0; \delta U/\delta \alpha < 0. \tag{2}$$

The first derivative represents the usual assumption that the marginal utility of wealth is positive, whereas the second negative one represents ambition, fear (of being leapfrogged by others), envy, or vanity.[2] The names are less important than the actions to which leapfrogging leads. As is shown in the work of R. Brenner (1983, 1985, 1987), this reformulation of the utility function is useful only when risk and uncertainty are taken into account – words that can be precisely defined and distinguished at this departure point. The usefulness stems only from the predictions one can derive from it. Let us consider some of them, starting with the simplest.

Let W_0 be one's wealth expected to be derived from all investment opportunities, excluding gambling. Let h be the price of a lottery ticket where there is a probability p of winning a large prize H that can propel people up the social ladder. On what variables does the decision to gamble depend? The mathematical translation of this question is:

$$\begin{aligned} (1 - p)&U(W_0 - h, \alpha(W > \bar{W}_0)| W_0 \in I_0) \\ &+ pU(W_0 - h + H, \alpha(W > \bar{W}_1)| W_0 \in I_0) \\ &> U(W_0, \alpha(W > \bar{W}_0)| W_0 \in I_0). \end{aligned} \tag{3}$$

$\bar{W}_1$ is the mean of the wealth distribution in the interval I_1, representing a higher class. To keep it simple, I assume that there is no overlap between the two intervals I_0 and I_1. The fact that the conditional statements are unchanged suggests that the parameters of the utility function are the same as long as one does not actually win the large prize. The left-hand side reflects a hope, a dream, an expectation, and does not alter one's preferences.

Note that when people spend amount h on a lottery ticket, they do not take into account either that the mean wealth of the class they belong to changed or that the percentage of people in the various classes changed. These assumptions do not seem strong: if there are a large number of individuals in each class, the individual's expenditure on lottery tickets changes the mean by h/N or H/N, respectively, numbers that are small relative to a group's mean wealth (even if the group is the poorest in society).

Let the utility function be linear in W_0 and α, and let us see under what circumstances this inequality is fulfilled:

$$U = aW_0 + b\alpha(W > \bar{W}_0), a > 0, b < 0. \tag{4}$$

$$(1 - p)a(W_0 - h) + (1 - p)b\alpha(W > \bar{W}_0)$$
$$+ pa(W_0 - h + H) + pb\alpha(W > \bar{W}_1) \tag{5}$$
$$> aW_0 + b\alpha(W > \bar{W}_0).$$

If the gamble is fair, that is $[(1 - p)h = p(H - h)]$ (this is the definition of a fair gamble, because one pays h even if one wins later), Condition (5) is reduced to:

$$(1 - p)b\alpha(W > \bar{W}_0) + pb\alpha(W > \bar{W}_1) > b\alpha(W > \bar{W}_0) \tag{6}$$

(linearity implies risk neutrality in the standard definition, b being equal to zero). Because $b < 0$, one obtains that the condition to buy such a ticket is:

$$\alpha(W > \bar{W}_1) < \alpha(W > \bar{W}_0). \tag{7}$$

This condition is always fulfilled, because $\alpha(\cdot)$, we recall, denotes the percentage of people who are richer than the respective means in the whole society. Because $\bar{W}_1$ is greater than $\bar{W}_0$, the inequality in Condition (7) always holds.

If the game is unfair, that is, $(1 - p)h > p(H - h)$ (and all lotteries are), one gets:

$$a(pH - h) + (1 - p)b\alpha(W > \bar{W}_0)$$
$$+ pb\alpha(W > \bar{W}_1) > b\alpha(W > \bar{W}_0). \tag{8}$$

Dividing by b on both sides (and recalling that it is negative), one gets:

$$\frac{a}{b}(pH - h) - p\alpha(\bar{W}_1 > W > \bar{W}_0) < 0, \tag{9}$$

where $\alpha(\bar{W}_1 > W > \bar{W}_0)$ denotes the percentage of the population the winner would leapfrog if he or she won the prize (notice that the first term on the left-hand side is positive, because b is negative and the game is unfair). Briefly, the first term in Condition (9) reflects the relative subjective cost of gambling, and the second reflects its perceived benefits of jumping ahead. The subjective costs, as we saw, were giving up a drink or other consumption, and allocating the marginal amounts saved to one's portfolio.

There are significant differences between the predictions derived from the model presented herein and the type of prediction derived from others that have tried to explain gambling behavior.[3] One difference is that the evidence needed to test this model cannot be reproduced in any laboratory experiment. There is no way one can become either rich or poor in a laboratory. Thus, the predictions derived from this model can be confronted with data reflecting behavior in the real world rather than with data obtained in artificial experiments.

An additional difference is that in models that view gambling as a matter of taste (i.e., depending on the shape of the utility function only), one cannot explain – in a falsifiable way – why some people may suddenly start to gamble or stop.[4] Yet it is easy to explain such decisions within this model. Suppose that an individual with wealth $\bar{W}_0$ did not gamble on an unfair lottery:

$$U(W_0, \alpha(W > \bar{W}_0)| W_0 \in I_0)$$
$$> (1 - p)U(W_0 - h, \alpha(W > \bar{W}_0)| W_0 \in I_0) \tag{10}$$
$$+ p\, U(W_0 - h + H, \alpha(W > \bar{W}_2)| W_0 \in I_0),$$

where $\bar{W}_2$ is the mean of the upper-class distribution.

Now suppose that one's wealth suddenly diminishes significantly. Will the individual start to gamble on the unfair lottery? Let W_1 be the lower wealth and $\bar{W}_1$ the respective mean value. The question can be translated as follows:

$$U(W_1, \alpha(W > \bar{W}_1) | W_0 \in I_0)$$
$$< (1 - p)U(W_1 - h, \alpha(W > \bar{W}_1) | W_0 \in I_0) \qquad (11)$$
$$+ pU(W_1 - h + H, \alpha(W > \bar{W}_0) | W_0 \in I_0).$$

The reason to not alter the conditional statements is that the parameters of the utility function were determined by the expectation of belonging to the class defined by the interval I_0. When one's wealth drops suddenly to W_1, the translation of Condition (11) to ordinary language is that "aspirations are not lowered instantaneously."[5] As is shown subsequently, when discussing additional predictions of the model, people are expected to behave differently when their aspirations are realized than when they are not, even if they belong to the same wealth class.

When are inequalities (10) and (11) both fulfilled? Let us once again use the linear function defined in Condition (4) and make the calculations. Condition (10) becomes:

$$a W_0 + b\alpha(W > \bar{W}_1) > (1 - p)a(W_0 - h)$$
$$+ (1 - p)b\alpha(W > \bar{W}_0) + pa(W_0 - h + H) \qquad (12)$$
$$+ pb\alpha(W > \bar{W}_2),$$

which, when simplified, turns into the same type of expression as in Condition (9), only with the reverse inequality sign:

$$\frac{a}{b}(pH - h) - p\alpha(\bar{W}_2 > W > \bar{W}_0) > 0, \qquad (13)$$

whereas Condition (11), as in Condition (9), becomes:

$$\frac{a}{b}(pH - h) - p\alpha(\bar{W}_0 > W > \bar{W}_1) < 0. \qquad (14)$$

A necessary condition for Conditions (13) and (14) to be fulfilled is:

$$\alpha(\bar{W}_0 > W > \bar{W}_1) > \alpha(\bar{W}_2 > W > \bar{W}_0). \qquad (15)$$

This condition means that the percentage of people between $\bar{W}_0$ and $\bar{W}_2$ must be smaller than that between $\bar{W}_1$ and $\bar{W}_0$ for the individual to start gambling when a significant part of his or her wealth was lost. Condition (15) requires that there are many people at the bottom and fewer and fewer closer to the top, or a pyramidal distribution of wealth.

For other games of chance, where winnings are small – of a magnitude that keeps individuals within their class – the model presented here is not illuminating. One must deal with those games either in a model where the choice to be explained is about the allocation of one's time, gambling as a pastime, and has nothing to do with taking risks. Models where gambling is a matter of taste and where whether people are involved in the act depends entirely on local properties of the utility function or, as in Kahneman and Tversky's (1979) descriptive framework on deviations between realized wealth and the level of aspiration, are useless. Their predictions cannot be disproved.

I should emphasize that the term "small" in the model presented here is defined relative to one's wealth and thus to whether the losses or gains will move an individual out of his or her class. A prize of $100,000 may be large for some, but a loss or a gain of $100,000 may be small for others. For people who are relatively poor, $100,000 may move them up a rank, and the model presented here may shed light on their attitudes toward gambling. However, for people whose wealth is more than, say, $10,000,000 and when the distribution in their class is defined over a range of, say, $7,500,000 to $12,500,000, winning or losing $100,000 causes no shift in rank. Thus, the latter group's participation in games of chance cannot be explained by the model presented here, but rather by one concerning the allocation of time, or pastime.[6]

Indeed, as we saw in the text, one cannot talk about gambling in general but must look at the different games: bingo is the cheapest entertainment for widows, Las Vegas appeals to all classes of tourists, and lotteries to those down on their luck (as the model predicts).

In conclusion, we derived two predictions. A static one, that the relatively poor have a greater incentive to gamble on lotteries than do the relatively rich, and a dynamic one, that people who do not gamble may start doing so when they either lose a significant part of their wealth or are suddenly leapfrogged by the Joneses. Gambling represents the small hope of getting rich when there are no other options on the horizon. Giving up a bit of consumption and spending the amount saved on lottery tickets represents poor people's portfolio decision. Just as entrepreneurs and businesspeople's decisions are influenced by possibilities other than the most probable result, so are gamblers' decisions.[7] For some deeper, "philosophical" interpretations of this leapfrogging instinct, see Brenner (1983, 1985) and Appendix 2.

Why Do Lotteries Have Multiple Prizes?

Let us describe the factors that determine the individual's choice between participating in a game of chance that gives away $1 million with a probability of one in a million and one that gives away one prize of $500,000 with a probability of one in a million and five prizes of $100,000 with a probability of one in a million (assuming that the price of the ticket is the same at $1).

Translating this choice in terms of the previous utility function, we find that the second prize structure is preferred over the one with one large prize if the next inequality is fulfilled (taking here, for simplicity's sake, the actual wealth rather than the mean in the respective $\alpha(\cdot)$ terms):

$$\frac{1}{10^6}[a(W_0 + 1,000,000) + b\alpha(W > W_0 + 1,000,000)]$$

$$+ \left(1 - \frac{1}{10^6}\right)(a(W_0 - 1) + b\alpha(W > W_0 - 1))$$

$$< \frac{1}{10^6}[a(W_0 + 500,000) + b\alpha(W > W_0 + 500,000)] \qquad (16)$$

$$+ \frac{5}{10^6}[a(W_0 + 100,000) + b\alpha(W > W_0 + 100,000)]$$

$$+ \left(1 - \frac{1}{10^6}\right)[a(W_0 - 1) + b\alpha(W > W_0 - 1)].$$

Condition (16) translates this question: under what conditions are multiple large prizes preferred over one large prize? By rearranging the terms, we obtain:

$$b\alpha(W > W_0 + 1,000,000) + 5[-a + b\alpha(W > W_0 - 1)]$$
$$< b\alpha(W > W_0 + 500,000) + 5b\alpha(W > W_0 + 100,000). \qquad (17)$$

Because a is positive, this holds if:

$$b\alpha(W > W_0 + 1,000,000) + 5b\alpha(W > W_0 - 1)$$
$$< b\alpha(W > W_0 + 500,000)$$
$$+ 5b\alpha(W > W_0 + 1,000,000) \qquad (18)$$

(for an additional number, $5a$, would be subtracted from the left-hand side). Because b is negative, a sufficient condition for Inequality (17) to be fulfilled is:

$$\alpha(W > W_0 + 1,000,000) + 5\alpha(W > W_0 - 1)$$
$$> \alpha(W > W_0 + 500,000) + 5\alpha(W > W_0 + 100,000). \qquad (19)$$

The pyramidal distribution of wealth typical of societies where lotteries with large prizes exist easily fulfills this condition: although there are few millionaires, there are many more people at the bottom. If, say, 1 percent of the population has net wealth greater than $1,000,000, 3 percent have more than \$500,000, 20 percent more than \$200,000, and 50% more than W_0, then the numbers that appear in Inequality (19) would be:

$$0.01 + 5(0.5) > 0.03 + 5(0.2). \tag{20}$$

The existence of multiple large prizes thus suggests that people prefer the somewhat greater chance of belonging to the middle class (with five prizes of \$100,000 and one of \$500,000) to the smaller chance of jumping higher (with just one prize of \$1,000,000) and the greater chance of staying at the bottom. Whether lotteries offer such a prize structure is irrelevant. People often buy tickets together. Even if there were one large prize and no smaller but still relatively large prizes, people could build a type of prize structure that they prefer.[8]

But why are there a large number of small prizes? The \$10, \$100, or even \$1,000 prize will not make people rich, in the sense of moving them out of their class; it will not make the poor belong to the middle classes.[9] If one assumes that these small consolation prizes are essentially refunds that are an inducement to try again, their existence does not contradict the prediction of the model (because the motivation for playing is still the hope of winning the big prize). The issue is empirical: do people rebet the small winnings? Yes.

Insurance: Preventing the Falling Behind

Economists often raised but never solved the problem in the orthodox expected utility framework (of so-called risk aversion) that people could gamble, in which case the second derivative of the utility function had to be positive, or insure themselves, in which case the second derivative had to be negative. But they could never do both because the same utility function for the same wealth cannot simultaneously have a negative and a positive second derivative. But it is a fact that people both gamble and insure themselves.

I should note that this is a difficulty only if one wants to explain both phenomena by relying on a model of risk-taking. If, however, one views gambling as a pastime and insurance as linked with risk aversion, there is no contradiction that the same people are involved in both activities. Gambling, according to this view, has nothing to do with risk-taking. Whereas this viewpoint may offer partial reconciliation of the problem that the same people gamble and insure themselves, it is hard to accept the idea that buying lottery tickets is a pastime. Anyway, the evidence is clear that gambling on lotteries with large prizes is a matter of deciding on allocating a portfolio.[10]

Friedman and Savage (1948) tried to solve the inconsistency differently, namely by assuming that at relatively high and low levels of wealth the marginal utility of wealth decreases, and at middle levels it increases. This additional restriction on the shape of the utility function describes the observation that people both gamble and insure themselves but leads to new inconsistencies. As both Alchian (1953) and Markowitz (1952) have pointed out, if this were the shape of the utility function, the relatively rich would never insure themselves against events in which large losses with small probabilities occur, and they would never gamble. But they do both. Markowitz tried to deal with these implications by imposing further restrictions on the utility function. But he recognized that his views could not be verified. Moreover, Friedman himself recognized that his method of using the existence of multiple prizes to rationalize that the upper-concave section of the utility function was inaccurate.

Yet it is easy to show within the model presented here why the same individual would gamble and insure her- or himself. The first strategy is used to try to get rich and the second to prevent falling significantly behind.

Let h be the insurance premium, $(1 - p)$ the probability that nothing happens, and p the probability that a significant amount, H, could be lost. The condition for taking out this insurance is:

$$a(W_0 - h) + b\alpha(W > \bar{W}_0) > (1 - p)aW_0$$
$$+ (1 - p)b\alpha(W > \bar{W}_0) \qquad (21)$$
$$+ pa(W_0 - H) + pb\alpha(W > \bar{W}_2),$$

where $\bar{W}_2$ is the mean of the distribution in the rank interval I_2 to which $W_0 - H$ would belong. Condition (21) can be rewritten as follows:

$$-ah + paH > pb[\alpha(W > \bar{W}_2) - \alpha(W > \bar{W}_0)]. \qquad (22)$$

If the insurance is fair, that is $(1 - p)h = pH$,[11] one obtains:

$$-pah > pb\alpha(\bar{W}_0 > W > \bar{W}_2), \qquad (23)$$

or dividing by pb (and recalling that $b < 0$), one gets:

$$\frac{a}{b}h + \alpha(\bar{W}_0 > W > \bar{W}_2) > 0. \qquad (24)$$

Condition (24) shows that the decision to insure depends on the relative costs and benefits, h being the insurance fee and $\alpha(\cdot)$ the percentage of the population one prevents oneself from being outdone by when taking out insurance. There is no contradiction between Conditions (24) and (7). The difference between the two is that when insurance is considered, one looks at the distribution of wealth below one's wealth, whereas when gambling is considered, one looks at the distribution above one's rank. The reasons for insuring and gambling have nothing to do with the shape of the utility function, but with preventing oneself from becoming poor and with wanting to become rich.

The same straightforward exercise for gambling can be used to show that if people did not take out insurance in the past, they might decide to do so if they suddenly become rich. The steps for the proof are the same as those in Conditions (12)–(15). Thus, here too we have essentially two types of prediction, one static and the other dynamic.

Stopping Rules: How Much to Gamble? How Much to Insure?

Conditions (9) and (24) can also be used to gain additional – this time familiar – trivial insights. In Condition (9), the more unfair the game is, the greater is the value of the first term and, ceteris paribus, the less likely it becomes that the inequality will be fulfilled. Thus, demand for higher-priced lotteries diminishes. However, the larger is the prize H and the farther one may leapfrog, ceteris paribus, the greater is the demand. Thus, demand for lotteries depends on their price, on the prizes they distribute, and on the distribution of wealth. Also, according to Condition (24), the higher the insurance fee h, ceteris paribus, the less likely it is that the inequality will be fulfilled (because h is multiplied by $\frac{a}{b}$, and b is negative). However, if $\alpha(\,\cdot\,)$ is greater, then, ceteris paribus, it is more likely that the inequality will be fulfilled.

So, even if it is true that losing $5 on a lottery ticket will not change one's rank in society, what happens if one buys a hundred, a thousand, or more tickets?

When does one stop buying them? There are two answers to this question within this model, one referring to the statics and the second to the dynamics. In the static case, the optimal number of tickets, n, is derived from the usual condition, that is, when the expected marginal utility of the cost equals the expected marginal benefit (of jumping to a higher rank).

In the dynamic context, however, the answer is different: if individuals have lost a relatively large amount by playing, they may believe that they cannot restore their position in the distribution of wealth by gambling. They may then lower their aspirations (thus changing their reference point) and gamble less (with lower aspirations the perceived benefits in terms of utility have diminished). Or they may change their risk-taking strategies and bet on entrepreneurial acts. In the dynamic context of this model, the reversal of decisions sheds light on risk-taking in general and provides the necessary stopping rule.

Risk-Taking and Uncertainty: Leaping into the Unknown

Suppose that an individual, content with his or her rank in society, owns wealth W_0 and avoids pursuing some innovative, entrepreneurial, or criminal pursuits. Assume that the individual believes that by pursuing one such strategy he or she may lose amount P and gain amount H. Let us make a number of different assumptions and examine both the consequences and the implicit assumption behind the mathematical translation.

(a) Assume that by losing P the individual would not fall to a lower rank but by gaining H he or she might move to a higher rank (characterized by $\tilde{W}_2$ and $\bar{W}_2$). If the individual initially, when owning wealth W_0, avoided taking such a risk, the condition for the linear utility function at that time must be:

$$a W_0 + b\alpha(W > \bar{W}_0) > pa(W_0 - P)$$
$$+ pb\alpha(W > \bar{W}_0) + (1 - p)a(W_0 + H) \tag{25}$$
$$+ (1 - p)b\alpha(W > \bar{W}_2).$$

Rewriting, one obtains:

$$b\alpha(W > \bar{W}_0) > -pa P + (1 - p)a H$$
$$+ pb\alpha(W > \bar{W}_0) + (1 - p)b\alpha(W > \bar{W}_2). \tag{26}$$

Will the individual pursue this same strategy if his or her wealth suddenly drops to W_D (W_D still belonging to the distribution $\tilde{W}_0$)? The translation of this question is:

$$a W_D + b\alpha(W > \bar{W}_0) < pa(W_D - P)$$
$$+ pb\alpha(W > \bar{W}_0) + (1 - p)a(W_D + H) \tag{27}$$
$$+ (1 - p)b\alpha(W > \bar{W}_2),$$

assuming that even $W_D - P$ still belongs to the interval over which $\tilde{W}_0$ is distributed and $W_D + H$ to that over which $\tilde{W}_2$ is distributed. The answer is no, because Condition (27) can be rewritten as:

$$b\alpha(W > \bar{W}_0) < -pa P + (1 - p)a H$$
$$+ pb\alpha(W > \bar{W}_0) + (1 - p)b\alpha(W > \bar{W}_2), \tag{28}$$

which contradicts Condition (26).

(b) Suppose now that W_D is of such magnitude that $W_D - P$ may even put the individual into a lower class, characterized by the interval I_1, the distribution $\tilde{W}_1$, and the mean $\bar{W}_1$ (though W_D still belongs to $\tilde{W}_0$). Will the individual then bet on the previously shunned strategy? Instead of Condition (27), we now would have:

$$a W_D + b\alpha(W > \bar{W}_0) < pa(W_D - P)$$
$$+ pb\alpha(W > \bar{W}_1) + (1 - p)a(W_D + H) \qquad (29)$$
$$+ (1 - p)b\alpha(W > \bar{W}_2),$$

which can be rewritten as:

$$b\alpha(W > \bar{W}_0) < -paP + (1 - p)aH$$
$$+ bp\alpha(W > \bar{W}_1) + (1 - p)b\alpha(W > \bar{W}_2). \qquad (30)$$

For both Conditions (27) and (30) to be fulfilled, one must have:

$$pb\alpha(W > \bar{W}_0) + (1 - p)b\alpha(W > \bar{W}_2)$$
$$< pb\alpha(W > \bar{W}_1) + (1 - p)b\alpha(W > \bar{W}_2) \qquad (31)$$

(because the terms on the left-hand side of the two inequalities are the same). This would imply that:

$$pb\alpha(W > \bar{W}_0) < pb\alpha(W > \bar{W}_1), \qquad (32)$$

which, because b is negative, would lead to:

$$\alpha(W > \bar{W}_0) > \alpha(W > \bar{W}_1), \qquad (33)$$

which can never be true, for the percentage of people above $\bar{W}_1$, the lower mean wealth, must always be greater than that above $\bar{W}_0$, the mean wealth at a higher rank.

The results in (a) and (b) suggest that if people avoided taking some risks before, they would not take them if they became somewhat poorer ("somewhat" meaning that the loss did not move them to a lower rank or class).

(c) What will the individual's reaction be if the spread between loss and gain (P and H) increases, but the expected value of the strategy does not change (i.e., only the variance increases)?[12]

Here, once again, one must distinguish among several possibilities:

(c₁) If the spread between P and H increases, but in such a way that both $W_0 - P$ and $W_0 + H$, for all possible values of P and H, still belong to the interval I_0, then if the initial strategy was avoided, so will all the rest.

(c₂) Suppose that the spread increases and the values of α ($\cdot$) are such that whereas $W_0 - P_1$ belongs to I_0, $W_0 + H_1$ belongs to a higher rank, defined by I_2, over which $\bar{W}_2$ is distributed. Then for the individual to bet on this strategy, the two conditions that must be fulfilled are the following. The fact that the individual initially avoided the strategy where both $W_0 - P$ and $W_0 + H$ belonged to I_0 only implies that the expected value of the strategy had to be negative. However, if $W_0 - P_1$ belongs to I_0 but $W_0 + H_1$ to I_2, one finds that, to undertake this strategy:

$$b\alpha(W > \bar{W}_0) < -pa P_1 + (1 - p)a H_1$$
$$+ bp\alpha(W > \bar{W}_0) + (1 - p)b\alpha(W > \bar{W}_2), \qquad (34)$$

or

$$a[-p P_1 + (1 - p)H_1] - (1 - p)b\alpha(W > \bar{W}_0)$$
$$+ (1 - p)b\alpha(W > \bar{W}_2) > 0. \qquad (35)$$

But the expected value of the strategy (the term in brackets) is unaltered, and from the initial condition we know that it must be negative. Thus, dropping the indexes under P and H, Condition (35) can be rewritten:

$$a[-p P + (1 - p)H] - (1 - p)b[\alpha(W > \bar{W}_2) - \alpha(W > \bar{W}_0)] > 0, \qquad (36)$$

and this condition may be fulfilled. For though the first term is negative, the second is positive (because both b and the difference in the second set of brackets are negative).

This result suggests that whereas people may avoid taking smaller risks, they may be willing to take bigger ones, the words "smaller" and "bigger" being defined relative to both one's wealth and discrepancies among ranks. An implication of this conclusion is that whereas people may avoid playing some unfair games of chance (where losses and gains would maintain them within their initial class), that does not necessarily imply that they may not undertake some entrepreneurial gambles with a negative expected value.[13]

Briefly, whereas some gamblers may be risk-takers and entrepreneurs, there are risk-takers and entrepreneurs who are not gamblers.

We must emphasise a further point. The mathematical condition describes an open society, one where risk-taking is rewarded. People can expect to bring their ideas to life. What happens when people fall behind but cannot raise money to pursue the commercial ideas that cross their minds? They have two options: lower their aspirations (as in many societies in distant pasts, and under communism in particular) or bet on 'criminal' directions, an option we discuss later.

(c_3) Let us relax the assumption that when the variability of the strategy increases, H moves one up the ladder, whereas losing P does not move one down. Assume instead that by losing P one drops to the interval over which $\bar{W}_1$ is distributed. Then instead of Condition (34), one gets (dropping for simplicity's sake the indexes under P and H):

$$b\alpha(W > \bar{W}_0) < a[-pP + (1-p)H]$$
$$+ pb\alpha(W > \bar{W}_1) + (1-p)b\alpha(W > \bar{W}_2). \tag{37}$$

Rewriting, one obtains:

$$a[-pP + (1-p)H] + pb[\alpha(W > \bar{W}_1) - \alpha(W > \bar{W}_0)]$$
$$+ (1-p)b[\alpha(W > \bar{W}_2) - \alpha(W > \bar{W}_0)] > 0. \tag{38}$$

Whereas the first two terms are negative, the third is positive (as in [c_2]). Thus, in principle, such behavior is possible. Inequality (38) implicitly requires conditions that may provide intuition of what is hiding behind such behavior. For Condition (38) to hold, at least the last term in absolute value must be greater than the second:

$$(1-p)[\alpha(W > \bar{W}_0) - \alpha(W > \bar{W}_2)]$$
$$> p[\alpha(W > \bar{W}_1) - \alpha(W > \bar{W}_0)], \tag{39}$$

which implies that

$$\frac{1-p}{p} > \frac{\alpha(\bar{W}_0 > W > \bar{W}_1)}{\alpha(\bar{W}_2 > W > \bar{W}_0)}. \tag{40}$$

Because from the initial condition (obtained by assuming that the individual avoided the game with the small variance) we know that the expected value of the game must be negative, it must also be true that:

$$\frac{1-p}{p} < \frac{P}{H}, \tag{41}$$

implying that:

$$\frac{P}{H} > \frac{\alpha(\bar{W}_0 > W > \bar{W}_1)}{\alpha(\bar{W}_2 > W > \bar{W}_0)}. \tag{42}$$

For a pyramidal rank structure, the term on the right-hand side is greater than 1, which implies that the loss P must be greater than the gain H and that the probability p must be less than 0.5. For Condition (40) implies:

$$\frac{1-p}{p} > 1. \tag{43}$$

Pursuing such a strategy may be viewed as obsessive. It suggests an individual who undertakes ventures with a negative expected value to reach the top. Yet it may happen.

(d) Consider now another possibility when an individual reacts to a sudden drop in wealth. Suppose that W_D is such that it moves the individual out of his or her class. If the individual pursues the strategy, one must have:

$$\begin{aligned} a\,W_D + b\alpha(W > \bar{W}_1) &> pa(W_D - P) \\ &+ pb\alpha(W > \bar{W}_1) + (1-p)a(W_D + H) \\ &+ (1-p)b\alpha(W > \bar{W}_2), \end{aligned} \tag{44}$$

assuming that $(W_D - P)$ belongs to the interval I_1 but that H is large enough so that $W_D + H$ belongs to I_2, which characterizes the rank above that described by $\bar{W}_0$. Let us see the condition under which both Conditions (25) and (44) are fulfilled. First, let us rewrite Condition (44):

$$\begin{aligned} b\alpha(W > \bar{W}_1) &< -pa\,P + (1-p)a\,H \\ &+ pb\alpha(W > \bar{W}_1) + (1-p)b\alpha(W > \bar{W}_2). \end{aligned} \tag{45}$$

Let us now rewrite both Conditions (28) and (45):

$$\begin{aligned} (1-p)b\alpha(W > \bar{W}_0) &> -pa\,P + (1-p)a\,H \\ &+ (1-p)b\alpha(W > \bar{W}_2); \end{aligned} \tag{46}$$

$$\begin{aligned} (1-p)b\alpha(W > \bar{W}_1) &< -pa\,P + (1-p)a\,H \\ &+ (1-p)b\alpha(W > \bar{W}_2). \end{aligned} \tag{47}$$

Because the terms on the right-hand side are the same, it follows that:

$$b\alpha(W > \bar{W}_0) > b\alpha(W > \bar{W}_1), \tag{48}$$

an inequality that is always fulfilled (because b is negative and $\bar{W}_1$ is smaller than $\bar{W}_0$), whatever the subjective values given to P, H, and p. Once again, note that an additional implicit assumption behind this exercise is that though the individual's wealth dropped to W_D, the parameters of the utility function do not change, implying that the conditional statement is still that the individual's aspirations (of belonging to the class characterized by $\bar{W}_0$) have not been altered.

   (e) Let us weaken the assumptions in *(d)* and assume that $W_D + H$ is just expected to restore one's rank rather than increase one to the class represented by the distribution $\tilde{W}_2$. Then instead of Condition (45) one obtains:

$$b\alpha(W > \bar{W}_1) < -paP + (1 - p)aH \\ + pb\alpha(W > \bar{W}_1) + (1 - p)b\alpha(W > \bar{W}_0). \tag{49}$$

For Conditions (26) and (49) to be fulfilled, a necessary condition is that:

$$b\alpha(W > \bar{W}_0) - b\alpha(W > \bar{W}_1) > pb\alpha(W > \bar{W}_0) \\ + (1 - p)b\alpha(W > \bar{W}_2) - pb\alpha(W > \bar{W}_1) \tag{50} \\ - (1 - p)b\alpha(W > \bar{W}_0).$$

(This is obtained from Conditions (26) and (49) by the following operation: if $m > n$ and $p < q$, then $m - p > n - q$.) Reorganizing Condition (50), one gets:

$$\alpha(W > \bar{W}_0) > \frac{1}{2}[\alpha(W > \bar{W}_1) + \alpha(W > \bar{W}_2)]. \tag{51}$$

   (f) Are the predictions different if one assumes that a fraction of the group to which the individual aspired to belong becomes suddenly richer?

   Assume that initially an individual avoided taking a risk when $\alpha(W > \bar{W}_0) = \alpha_0$. Let $\alpha_1(W > \bar{W}_0) = \alpha_1$ (as some of the people belonging to the distribution $\tilde{W}_0$ became suddenly richer and now belong to the distribution $\tilde{W}_2'$). Assume, however, that though $\tilde{W}_0'$ and $\tilde{W}_2'$ are the new distributions, their means did not change; that is, $\bar{W}_0' = \bar{W}_1$ and $\bar{W}_2' = \bar{W}_2$. Assume also that no other shifts occurred, so that $W - P$ belongs to the interval I_1, which is thus unaltered. For the inequality to be reversed, we must have:

$$aW_0 + b\alpha_1(W > \bar{W}_0) < pa(W_0 - P) \\ + pb\alpha_1(W > \bar{W}_1) + (1 - p)a(W_0 + H) \tag{52} \\ + (1 - p)b\alpha_1(W > \bar{W}_2).$$

By rearranging Condition (52), one obtains:

$$b\alpha_1(W > \bar{W}_0) < -paP + (1 - p)aH$$
$$+ pb\alpha_1(W > \bar{W}_1) + (1 - p)b\alpha_1(W > \bar{W}_2). \tag{53}$$

Recall that the condition for avoiding this same risk was:

$$b\alpha(W > \bar{W}_0) > -paP + (1 - p)aH$$
$$+ pb\alpha(W > \bar{W}_1) + (1 - p)b\alpha(W > \bar{W}_2). \tag{54}$$

For both Conditions (53) and (54) to be fulfilled, by making the same operation as for obtaining Condition (51) we obtain:

$$b\alpha(W > \bar{W}_0) - b\alpha_1(W > \bar{W}_0) > pb\alpha(W > \bar{W}_1)$$
$$+ (1 - p)b\alpha(W > \bar{W}_2) - pb\alpha_1(W > \bar{W}_1) \tag{55}$$
$$- (1 - p)b\alpha_1(W > \bar{W}_2).$$

$\alpha(W > \bar{W}_1) = \alpha_1(W > \bar{W}_1)$, as we assumed that there were changes only in ranks above that identified by $\tilde{W}_1$, $\alpha_1(W > \bar{W}_0)$ equals the percentage of people who jumped from the rank previously characterized by $\tilde{W}_0$ to the one previously characterized by $\tilde{W}_2$ (and who are now characterized by $\tilde{W}_0'$ and $\tilde{W}_2'$, with the means unaltered). Assume that people who moved to the distribution $\tilde{W}_2$ are equally distributed around $\bar{W}_2$. Then the difference between $\alpha(W > \bar{W}_2)$ and $\alpha_1(W > \bar{W}_2)$ equals $\frac{1}{2}[\alpha_1(W > \bar{W}_0) - \alpha(W > \bar{W}_1)]$. Thus, Condition (55) is reduced to (recalling that $b < 0$):

$$\alpha(W > \bar{W}_0) - \alpha_1(W > \bar{W}_0)$$
$$< (1 - p)[\alpha(W > \bar{W}_2) - \alpha_1(W > \bar{W}_2)]. \tag{56}$$

Because $\alpha_1(W > \bar{W}_0) > \alpha(W > \bar{W}_0)$ and $\alpha_1(W > \bar{W}_2) > \alpha(W > \bar{W}_2)$, we obtain:

$$1 > \frac{1}{2}(1 - p), \tag{57}$$

which is always fulfilled. Thus, although the conditions are different, we still find that when individuals are leapfrogged by others, even if their wealth is not changed, they might now take a risk that previously they were unwilling to take. More will be said on the implications of this result when the subject of information is discussed.

(g) How can this model be linked with discussions of changes in relative prices? A significant change in relative prices has two effects. First, it alters the benefits, *H*, and costs, *P*, of pursuing some ventures, if in particular the benefits of finding substitutes for the product whose relative price has increased have also increased. At the same time, such a change in relative prices may also change people's positions in the distribution of wealth. This is the mechanism through which, within this model, equilibrium may be restored when an innovation that substitutes for the product that became scarcer is found.

Briefly, in open societies, when people either lose part of their wealth or are leapfrogged by others (even if their wealth did not change), they may start betting on new ideas and pursue strategies that crossed their minds but that they did not act on. This conclusion gives a precise meaning to the adage, "Necessity is the mother of invention." Here it seems that necessity acquires the precise meaning of falling behind. For business and politics the implications are straightforward: default or fear of default are the mothers of invention. (Brenner [1983, 1985, 2002]) explored these broader implications, showing when it is more likely that the bets on new ideas, political in particular, would go toward constructive, rather than destructive directions).

I noted before that, implicitly, many historians held similar perceptions of human nature, even if they did not articulate it in this way, and linked it explicitly to either financial markets or gambling and insurance. Democritus, the Greek philosopher, once said, "Everything existing in the universe is the fruit of necessity and chance." The view of human behavior we have discussed gives meaning to both terms and shows that the two cannot be separated in the human mind.

Recall Mackay, who, in his 1841 classic *Extraordinary Popular Delusions and the Madness of Crowds*, explained that dissatisfaction with one's lot in life, far from leading to evil as at first might be supposed, has been the "great civiliser of our race." According to him, this characteristic has tended more than anything else to raise the human race above the condition of the brutes. The same discontent – which in my view is brought about by leapfrogging – has been, Mackay wrote, the source of follies, speculations, absurdities, and the seeking for remedies that have "bewildered us in a wave of madness and error. These are death, toil, and ignorance of the future ... From the third [sprang] the false science of astrology, divination and their divisions."[14]

Another well-known observer who held a similar view of human nature and influenced both Adam Smith and Keynes, was Bernard de Mandeville. His *Fable of the Bees* argues – seriously – that "Envy Itself, and Vanity/ Were the Ministers of Industry" (and at the time the terms "ambition" and "emulation" were used interchangeably). In the last chapter of his *General Theory*, Keynes quotes extensively from *Fable*, and argues, surprisingly, that it underlies his view of how societies prosper. This statement comes as a surprise because there is nothing in Keynes's confused, obscure chapters that come before to suggest the clear language of the last chapter and this view of human nature. Whereas the rest of the book says explicitly that it does not deal with innovations of any kind, de Mandeville's fable is exactly about what makes people ambitious and innovative, and what makes them lower their aspirations and become passively content with their fate. Appendix 2 briefly summarizes additional writers from a variety of disciplines who express, implicitly, similar views of human nature.

Doing Their Best: What "Maximization" Means

The assumption of maximization has been implicit in the calculations up to this point, and, as shown, it is not inconsistent with the assumption that *movements* in relative ranks – leapfrogging, that is – determine people's welfare. Leapfrogging plays the central role in explaining one's attitudes toward gambling and insurance, and one's willingness to take risks or avoid them. The assumption of maximization is implicit in the conditions obtained for reversing the initial inequalities. How does the model relate to discussions in the economic literature?

In the concluding chapter of his book *Uncertainty in Microeconomics*, Hey, for several reasons, criticizes the traditional approaches to the subject of risk:

Consider . . . the optimisation problems that economic agents are supposed to be solving. Most of these problems are so complicated that the economic theorist who publishes the model has probably spent several months finding the solution (and the few readers who bother to check his mathematics will probably find it equally difficult). These optimisation problems are so complicated that the "as if" methodology of economics is stretched to breaking point. Are we seriously suggesting that we are modelling economic behavior?[15]

The answer to the last question seems negative and is linked with the next issue that Hey raises.

He remarks that "the essential feature of von Neumann-Morgenstern utility theory [is] that it conceives of choice as being a once-and-for-all affair. (A sequence of choices is reduced essentially to a single choice – strategy.) Is this how we economic agents actually behave?".[16] The answer he gives is negative and suggests that the way we behave is that we make a decision now and, depending on how it turns out, may or may not revise it. Such a sequential decision-making process is indeed one of the characteristic features of the dynamics in this model.

It should also be noted that it is only when risk and uncertainty are taken into account that the model presented here makes predictions that may be disproved. Otherwise, including the additional variable in the utility function (α (·) with a negative sign) leads to no useful insights. The interpretation given to this variable is that it may reflect one's ambition, one's fear of falling behind or of being outdone by one's fellows, or one of the seven deadly sins – envy. (More philosophical interpretations of the utility function are given in R. Brenner [1983, 1985]).

Risk, Uncertainty, and Information

In spite of the similarity between the mathematical expression of an individual's decision to gamble and that of the decision to pursue some strategies that he or she has never tried before (or, indeed, that no individual has tried), there are significant differences between them.

For lotteries, the value of the monetary prizes and prices of tickets is the same for everyone who plays the game. In contrast, when a venture is pursued, the value of the prize, H, as well as that of the cost, P, differs among individuals. Also, the probability here represents a subjective judgment by an individual, and there is no way to prove whether he or she is right or wrong: the venture may never have been tried before. This contrasts with lotteries and insurance, in which probability is defined in terms of processes that can be repeated many times and in which comparisons can be made between the probabilities facing different people.

Let us, then, distinguish between two situations. Suppose that in one the distribution of wealth is maintained; that is, no shift among ranks occurs. (By what mechanism such stability is maintained is explained in R. Brenner [1983, ch. 2; 1985, ch. 2].) In such a society (of small numbers) people still take risks. They may gamble on games of chance where the outcomes are relatively insignificant, they may buy a defective product, and so forth. Yet people are insured against major losses, losses that could lower their rank. The provision of such insurance – evidence about the various forms insurance takes is presented elsewhere[17] – diminishes incentives for undertaking new ventures in general and entrepreneurial and innovative ones in particular. An outsider looking at such a society will perceive equilibrium or stability as having been achieved and maintained; no innovations of any nature take place. Generation after generation, the same products are produced, and no additional wealth is created (see Brenner 1983, Ch. 2).

Consider a situation in which people can move up and down the social ladder. This can happen in societies with relatively democratized capital markets (see Brenner 2002, Ch. 2). In such a situation, innovations and ventures of all types take place (criminal and entrepreneurial). Wealth is both created and destroyed. An outsider may characterize such a situation as that of either disequilibrium or dynamic equilibrium. Entrepreneurial ventures represent, from the individual's viewpoint, a search for ways to adapt to the new circumstances imposed by shocks that are not under his or her control.

Another way to distinguish between the two situations is to call the first risky and the second uncertain. This distinction recalls the work of Keynes (1921), but in particular that of Knight (1921), who also argued that only the latter situation results in economic profits. The link between such profits and uncertainty in this model is simple. Only in the latter situation are innovations brought to life by entrepreneurs, whose rewards for discovering demands are measured by others as economic profits.[18]

These distinctions also lead to a better understanding of the various meanings that can be given to the word "information." Suppose one examines a "risky" or "stable" situation, where no innovations or entrepreneurial acts, only imitations, take place. In such circumstances the decision of whether to adopt a technique has nothing to do with an inclination to take risks, but with other variables: one's wealth or ability to learn and process transferred information.

In contrast, suppose we are in an uncertain situation, where people bet on new strategies and bring their ideas to life through an entrepreneurial venture (in particular, speculating in financial markets, as discussed in Chapters 4 and 5). In such a situation one cannot just speak about the transfer of information. Information is created when an individual bets on a new, noncustomary idea and pursues it.

Suppose that during this process an individual strikes it lucky and outdoes his or her fellows. Success provides to the outdone members the information of some strategy that may not have crossed their minds before but is now feasible. Such a revelation not only provides information about new opportunities, but also changes the opportunity cost of staying within the initial rank. The successful person becomes a permanent reminder of the outdone people's timidity and induces some of the leapfrogged to now challange their luck.

Wealth, Risk, and Uncertainty

The fact that the rich avoid gambling on lotteries and instead insure themselves, and the fact that those who fall or fear falling behind are more likely to innovate than those whose realized wealth provides them with a rank that exceeds their aspirations, does not imply that the rich do not take risks or will not take risks that a poor person may avoid.

On the contrary, they may take risks, though the types of risk discussed here are different in nature from those discussed when deviations from traditional behavior were examined, and fit into a framework defined as "risky" in the preceding section.

Suppose that a new practice or a new technology was adopted, knowledge about it spread, and both the probabilities of its being used and the monetary costs and benefits involved in adopting it are known. At such a point, the practice is no longer an innovation, and inclination to risk may not be the major element in a decision to adopt. Rather, differences in wealth may explain different attitudes toward adoption of such now-customary investment opportunities.

To make this point clear, consider the following examples. Suppose that there are a hundred independent investment opportunities. The monetary cost of each project is $10,000 and each has a probability of success of 0.1 and a probability of failure of 0.9. Success results in the individual benefiting in the amount of $200,000 at present value. Then the decision to invest in one such project depends on whether the term in Condition (58):

$$0.9U(W_0 - 10,000, \alpha(W > \bar{W}_0)) \\ + 0.1(W_0 + 200,000, \alpha(W > \bar{W}_2)), \tag{58}$$

is greater or smaller than $U(W_0, \alpha(W > \bar{W}_0))$, where W_0 takes into account all the alternative investment opportunities.

The decision to invest in more than one project is, however, different, as the probability of finding oneself with more wealth than one started with increases. The probability of breaking even in the preceding numerical example is 0.9763; the individual needs just five successes out of a hundred. Thus, for somebody who can find $1 million to invest in a hundred projects, instead of a 0.9 probability of being worse off and 0.1 of being better off (probability defined in terms of the individual project), there is a 0.9763 probability of success (defined in terms of the profitability of the whole portfolio) and a probability of 0.003 of losing the whole $1 million invested:

$$P(0 \; success) = \frac{100!}{0!100!}(0.1)^0(0.9)^{100} = 0.003. \tag{59}$$

Thus, the explanation for why one individual rather than another may pursue one or more risky projects may have more to do with differences in budget constraints (including the ability to obtain credit) and the related ability to diversify the portfolio and lower risks than with differences in an inclination to take risks. However, neither the calculations made here nor the preceding comparison can be used when innovations – that is, deviations from customary behavior – are taken into account. The latter are about creating options, which deep financial markets allow to create (see discussion in Chapter 8).

Stability, Redistribution, and Progressive Taxation of Wealth

The mathematical conditions examined previously look at the circumstances in which people may suddenly deviate from traditional behavior and bet on a risky strategy, which may be of either an entrepreneurial or a criminal nature. By just looking at the mathematical conditions, one cannot distinguish between the two.

At first sight, it seems as if it would be easy to distinguish between the two strategies by looking at the final outcomes – criminal acts redistribute wealth or even destroy it, and innovative, entrepreneurial ones create it. But, for several reasons, it is not easy to make the distinction. First, the final outcome may be observed only long after the act takes place. For example, acts that may destroy some goods now may lead to expectations of greater wealth in the future – consider debates about outsourcing or the value of a currency going up. But also consider something close to the topic of this book: by prohibiting alcohol, gambling, or drugs, people involved in any aspect of trading them can be classified as criminals. But another society may view them as entrepreneurs.

Was Robin Hood a criminal, an innovator, or a social reformer? Suppose that his actions both redistributed and destroyed stocks of goods while also leading to expectations of reforms (tax reforms in particular). Such expectations may lead a majority to expect more entrepreneurial acts in the future. Do Robin Hood's actions increase or diminish wealth? The definitional problem in this example and the ambivalent answer arise because it is assumed that people do not agree with the present laws or distribution of wealth. Where there is such disagreement, people fight not only with swords but also with words. (That is why the same person can be considered an innovator and a criminal.)[19]

Assume, however, that there is agreement as to what the term "crime" means, and that the criminal acts examined are such that either a monetary reward or destroying the wealth of others is possible. (There is no such agreement on gambling. Few people bet legally on sports through Nevada bookies, the only legitimate way to do so. Millions bet illegally on sports through different channels. Those managing the bets are criminals by definition in the United States, but not in the United Kingdom, for example.)

Then, the previous predictions concerning the bet on risky ventures in general holds true for criminal acts in particular.

Once again, the probability p and the value of the cost, P (which includes the effects of loss of, among others, reputation, loss of trust, a prison term), are subjective. Thus, within this model no predictions can be made about the propensity of the poor to commit crimes. Instead, those who either suddenly fall behind or are leapfrogged are those whose propensity to commit crimes increases. This prediction should not be surprising. The evidence is consistent with it (after all, the great majority of the poor during so-called normal times do not commit crimes).[20] And many writers have given, intuitively, the answer that "unthinking obedience" (Knight's words, which receive a literal interpretation in this model)[21] explains why most poor people do not commit crimes.

It is a straightforward exercise to link this result with the willingness to either redistribute wealth or allocate money for enforcement so as to change the probabilities of being put away for committing a criminal act. Suppose that everybody in society realizes that this is how people behave; that is, those who are suddenly leapfrogged are more likely to commit crimes or, in a broader context, to undertake revolutionary acts (see Chapter 2). Because such acts threaten the wealth of others, people may be ready to pay higher taxes. Such redistribution benefits both groups: those who get the money and those who pay the taxes, as the chances of crime against property (or its confiscation) diminishes.

The formal translation of this argument is the following. Let π_0 and π_1 be, respectively, the probabilities of a rich person being the victim of a crime before and after the introduction of a tax. Let W_0 and W_1, respectively, be the person's expected wealth when he or she is not the victim of a crime before or after the introduction of a tax. Let H_0 and H_1 be, respectively, the average expected costs from crime before and after the introduction of progressive taxation on wealth (not income), where the following relationships must hold true:

$$\pi_1 < \pi_0; W_1 < W_0; H_1 < H_0. \tag{60}$$

Then, for those who stayed relatively rich to prefer the introduction of a tax, the following condition must hold (for simplicity's sake we omit the conditional statements):

$$\pi_0 U(W_0 - H_0, \alpha(W > W_0 - H_0)) + (1 - \pi_0)$$
$$U(W_0, \alpha(W > W_0)) < \pi_1 U(W_1 - H_1, \alpha(W > W_1 - H_1)) \tag{61}$$
$$+ (1 - \pi_1) U(W_1, \alpha(W > W_1)).$$

If π_1 and H_1 are sufficiently diminished by the tax scheme, this condition can be fulfilled even if W_1 is less than W_0. Thus, everybody's welfare increases. This conclusion is reached without making an interpersonal comparison of utilities, assuming diminishing marginal utility of wealth, or assuming the existence of any social-welfare function.

However, this argument, while justifying a progressive tax scheme on wealth in particular, does not say anything about just how progressive the scheme should be. This depends on the responsiveness of π (the probability of a rich person being a victim of crime) to changes in the tax rates, on the effect that redistribution of wealth has on both crime rates and total wealth, and on the responsiveness of the probability of detection to an increase in expenditure on enforcement.

Traditional explanations of such redistributive taxation are based on other arguments (for an excellent critical summary, see Blum and Kalven [1953]). One is that the marginal utility of wealth is diminishing; that is, a dollar is worth less to a rich person than to a poor person. According to this argument, both the rich person and the poor person have the same utility function:

$$U = U(W), \tag{62}$$

where W is wealth. If U' denotes the marginal utility, and one assumes that it is diminishing, then:

$$U(W_R) > U(W_P) \quad \text{and} \quad U'(W_R) < U'(W_P), \tag{63}$$

where W_R and W_P denote, respectively, the rich and the poor person's wealth. These assumptions lead to the conclusion that welfare increases if wealth is redistributed from the rich to the poor people.

These arguments have been criticized for several reasons. The first is that such a justification for redistribution relies on an interpersonal comparison of utilities that, in general, is not made in economic analyses. This is a criticism leveled at all welfare economics, mitigated here by the fact that, because the rich person and the poor person are assumed to have the same utility function, comparison between utilities makes some sense. The second, more important criticism is that the behavioral hypothesis of decreasing marginal utility of wealth cannot be inferred from the traditional models of individual behavior in which risk is not present. In these models, if one utility function with decreasing marginal utility of wealth is consistent with the preferences of the consumer, any monotonic increasing transformation of this function is also consistent with them. But the monotonic transformations that transform the marginal utility of wealth from a diminishing into an increasing function always exist. Thus, the decreasing marginal utility of wealth cannot be inferred from these models.

Another justification for redistribution in general (for progressive taxation in particular) has been based on the assumption of general risk aversion: if everybody were risk averse (that is, the marginal utility of wealth diminished everywhere), redistribution from the rich to the poor could be justified. The problems with this reasoning are the same as those raised by the assumption that people are, in general, risk averse. If the hypothesis is accurate, people should neither gamble nor gamble and insure themselves at the same time. Although Friedman and Savage's (1948) suggestion that for some ranges of wealth the marginal utility of wealth is decreasing and for others increasing may shed light on the fact that people both gamble and insure themselves, the justification for redistribution is lost.

The differences between these explanations and the one proposed here are, therefore, that it is not assumed that people are altruistic, that there are social-welfare functions, or that a comparison can be made among people's utilities. Rather, the leapfrogging instinct becomes associated with crime, in both a narrow and a broad sense. Spending on private security, laws, and police can mitigate the effect. Taxes can substitute for such self-insurance payments and be more effective. All societies, at all times, have pursued a combination of these three strategies. People spend on locks, on alarm systems, on private security. They also spend on police and legal services. Also all societies have had progressive taxation of wealth – even if by another name (see Brenner 1983, 1985).

This argument points to an additional difference between this and other approaches: the one suggested here relies on a dynamic model, whereas the others are static. This difference also explains the contrast in the lines of investigation to be pursued to verify the accuracy of the various explanations. According to traditional ones, it is the shape of the utility function that should be discovered: whether concave or convex and at what ranges of wealth it changes shape. According to the one proposed here, one should carry out a historical examination, considering the origins and first growth of a tax, law, or institution and examine whether the innovation was introduced when deviations from customary behaviour were on the rise. This was the line of investigation carried out in my previous studies.[22] The arguments presented in this section have been used in Chapters 2 and 5, implicitly or explicitly.

After a while I began to understand the issues and realized, to my amazement, that arbitrators were not really concerned about who was right and who was wrong, what

was true and what false, but each was looking for twists and turns to justify his party
and to contradict the arguments of his opponent.

Isaac Bashevis Singer, In My Father's Court

Comparisons with Other Approaches

A comparison between the theory of risk-taking presented here and the traditional one in economics has already been made above and elsewhere.[23] There are additional theories that have not been mentioned yet or have only been touched on. I focus attention on these models now.

A great deal of the experimental research on risk-taking behavior carried out by psychologists is either hard to interpret or unclear as to what it implies about behavior in the real world.[24] Before examining some results, I emphasize that the model presented here does not offer an alternative approach for carrying out any laboratory research. The model makes clear-cut predictions about gambling, insurance, and reversal of decisions. But these reactions all stem from the fact that people are leapfrogged with significant amounts at stake. These situations cannot be replicated in laboratories. Answering a question in a laboratory about spending is not quite the same as pulling money out of your pocket.

Consider first several simple examples typical of laboratory experiments and the problems that arise when one tries to interpret them. Thaler (1980) found a behavioral regularity that he called the endowment effect. This effect stipulates that an individual will demand much more money to give something up than he or she would be willing to pay to acquire it. He observed this effect in cases that involve risks and in cases that do not. For example:

Suppose you won a ticket to a sold-out concert that you would love to attend, and the ticket is priced at $15. Before the concert you are offered $50 for the ticket. Do you sell? Alternatively, suppose you won $50 in a lottery. Then, a few weeks later, you are offered a chance to buy a ticket to the same concert for $45. Do you buy? Many people say they would not sell for $50 in the first case and would not buy for $45 in the second case. Such responses are logically inconsistent.[25]

But are they? Not necessarily.

When answering the first question, people may imagine a situation where the owner of the ticket hired a babysitter, bought new clothes for the occasion, and set a rendezvous with friends. So, although he or she is offered $50, the full price of forgoing the opportunity of using the ticket at the last minute may far exceed $50 (this price also taking into account the disappointment such a decision might cause one's friends). The second scenario implies that one has $50 more that may be spent as one wishes when no other complementary expenditures have been made. If such are the situations that one imagines when answering the researcher's question, there is no inconsistency in the answers. This touches on a fundamental problem with all such experiments. No matter what the questions are, what goes on in the mind of people who answer them, the associations they make, is impossible to discern.

Thaler gives another example of laboratory experiments that, according to him, relate to the value people place on their lives. People were asked to evaluate these strategies:

Risk Situation 1: While attending the movies last week you inadvertently exposed yourself to a rare, fatal disease. If you contract the disease, you will die a quick and painless death in one week. The chance that you will contract the disease is exactly 0.001 – that is, one chance in 1,000. Once you get the disease there is no cure, but you can take an inoculation now which will prevent you from getting the disease. Unfortunately there is only a limited supply of inoculation, and it will be sold to the highest bidders. What is the most you would be willing to pay for this inoculation? (If you wish, you may borrow the money to pay at a low rate of interest.)

Risk Situation 2: This is basically the same as situation 1 with the following modifications. The chance you will get this disease is now 0.004 – that is, four in 1,000. The inoculation is only 25 percent effective – that is, it would reduce the risk to 0.003. What is the most you would pay for the inoculation in this case? (Again, you may borrow the money to pay.)

Risk Situation 3: Some professors at a medical school are doing research on the disease described above. They are recruiting volunteers who would be required to expose themselves to a 0.001 (one chance in 1,000) risk of getting the disease. No inoculations would be available, so this would entail a 0.001 chance of death. The 20 volunteers from this audience who demand the least money will be taken. What is the least amount of money you would require to participate in this experiment?[26]

The typical median responses were that people would pay $800 in Situation 1 and $250 in Situation 2, and charge $100,000 in Situation 3. Thaler states that "economists would argue that the answers should all be about the same (they would allow for a small difference between situation 3 and the other two, but nothing like the magnitude observed)."[27]

It is unclear why one would expect a small difference between Situations 1 and 3. Problem 1 refers to a situation that can be described by the following inequality:

$$0.001\ U(\text{death}) + 0.999\ U(W) < U(W - h) \qquad (64)$$

(whatever the "utility of death" means), where h is the amount one is willing to pay for eliminating a risk that one is already subject to. In contrast,

Situation 3 is one where a new market is offered through which one can become rich. The formal description of Situation 3 is:

$$U(W) < 0.001\,U(\text{death}) + 0.999\;U(W + H). \tag{65}$$

In other words, Situation 1 provides people only with the opportunity to give up part of their wealth. Situation 3 provides them with the opportunity to become significantly richer.

Thus, there seems to be no inconsistency between the two replies. But even if in another experiment one found inconsistent answers to such questions, one could question how much weight to give such laboratory results. Twenty-year-old students' answers to this type of question may not tell us much about how they, or older people, might behave if they really found themselves in the circumstances described by these questions. Would a young Stanford MBA student really accept $100,000 for a 0.001 chance of dying within a week? Once translated to everyday language, the experiments seem rather silly.

Consider now another set of experimental problems. Kahneman and Tversky (1986a, b) gave the following:

Problem 1: Choose between:

   A. 25% chance to win $240 and
       75% chance to lose $760.
   B. 25% chance to win $250 and
       75% chance to lose $750.

It is easy to see that B dominates A, and all respondents chose accordingly. Formally, what this choice implies is that:

$$0.25U(W_0 + 240) + 0.75U(W_0 - 760)$$
$$< 0.25U(W_0 + 250) + 0.75U(W_0 - 750). \tag{66}$$

Then, Kahneman and Tversky set this:

Problem 2, decision (1): Choose between:

   C. a sure gain of $240
   D. 25% chance to gain $1,000 and
       75% chance to gain nothing.

Eighty-four percent chose C, which implies that for them:

$$U(W_0 + 240) > 0.25U(W_0 + 1,000) + 0.75U(W_0). \tag{67}$$

Decision 2 in this same problem was:

E. a sure loss of $750
F. 75% chance to lose $1,000 and
    25% chance to lose nothing.

Eighty-seven percent chose F, which implies that for them:

$$0.75U(W_0 - 1,000) + 0.25U(W_0) > U(W_0 - 750). \qquad (68)$$

Kahneman and Tversky found that 73 percent of respondents chose C and F, and only 3 percent chose D and E; they suggest that this choice is inconsistent with the choice in Problem 1. For, they argue, if one adds the sure gain of $240 (C) to F, that yields a 25 percent chance to win $240 and a 75 percent chance to lose $760. This is A in Problem 1. Similarly, they add the sure loss of $750 (E) to D, which yields a 25 percent chance to win $250 and a 75 percent chance to lose $750. This is B in Problem 1. They suggest that this is a "violation of invariance, [and] the findings also support the general point that failures of invariance are likely to produce violations of stochastic dominance and vice versa."[28]

It is unclear why this example violates either principle. The invariance principle states that different representations of the same choice problem should yield the same preferences. But if people interpret the two problems as shown in the translation to Conditions (66)–(68), there is no way one would be able to compare Condition (66) on one side and Conditions (67)–(68) on the other. Adding C and F and comparing the result to the result of adding D and E was not a choice given to respondents. Thus, Problem 2 is not a different representation of Problem 1: it is a different problem.

Neither does it seem related to the dominance principle, which states that if one option is better than another in one state and at least as good in all other states, the dominant option should be chosen. It is unclear how the aforementioned experiment violates this principle.

There are other experiments, however, that pose more serious problems of interpretation and that at first sight seem to violate the invariance principle. The next example comes from a study of preferences between medical treatments. Respondents were given statistical information about the outcomes of two treatments for lung cancer. The same statistics were presented to some respondents in terms of mortality rates and to others in terms of survival rates. The respondents then indicated their preferred treatment. The information was presented as follows.

Problem 1 (Survival frame)

Surgery: Of 100 people having surgery 90 live through the postoperative period, 68 are alive at the end of the first year and 34 are alive at the end of five years.

Radiation Therapy: Of 100 people having radiation therapy all live through the treatment, 77 are alive at the end of one year and 22 are alive at the end of five years.

Problem 2 (Mortality frame)

Surgery: Of 100 people having surgery 10 die during surgery or the post-operative period, 32 die by the end of the first year and 66 die by the end of five years.

Radiation Therapy: Of 100 people having radiation therapy, none die during treatment, 23 die by the end of one year and 78 die by the end of five years.[29]

The outcome of the experiment was that the overall percentage of respondents who favored radiation therapy rose from 18 percent in the survival frame to 44 percent in the mortality frame, and the framing effect was not lower for experienced physicians or for business students with sophisticated statistical knowledge.

Kahneman and Tversky give the experiment as an example of the failures of invariance, arguing that the "inconsequential difference in formulation produced a marked difference." But is the difference in formulation really inconsequential? Not at all.

When I read the "mortality frame," the problem seemed abstract and easy to translate into a mathematical condition. The association the wording of the problem brought to mind was narrow: death and nothing else. In contrast, when I read the "survival frame," the association brought to my mind was completely different. The word "live" immediately brought up the question of what type of life such treatment enables. Life at the hospital? In a room shared by four or eight other people, depending on one's insurance? With yellowed skin and loss of hair? Weakened and sitting in a wheelchair at the mercy of overworked nurses? In other words, whereas the mortality frame brings to mind an abstract problem with just one variable – death – the survival frame is linked with a much more complicated problem associated with the phrase "live through treatment," which made radiation seem a less attractive option than in the second formulation.

In other words, if somebody were to ask me what I should have predicted as the reaction to the two formulations, the answer would have been that radiation would be perceived as the less attractive option within the survival frame (as it happened to be). One can argue, of course, that the people who answered the questions could have made that translation. But why would one expect them to make the effort? Their lives were not at stake. For them, choosing between the options was just an abstract exercise. This is not an issue of framing at all, but one in which words bring different associations to people's mind. They can never be precise enough to lead to the type of conclusions that Kahneman and Tversky reach. Actions matter. Words in laboratory experiments mean little, if anything.

Of course, if monetary rewards are given out in laboratories, then the conclusions may be relevant for behavior outside the laboratory as well – for the monetary ranges that happened during the experiment. But to extrapolate from losing or gaining $100 in a laboratory to ways in which people behave when millions are at stake makes no sense. People are ready to hire a babysitter and go out for a night on the town and spend some $500. The restaurant may turn out to be bad, and the show too. So they "lost" $500. Does such an experiment in having fun imply anything about how these people may allocate a portfolio with hundreds of thousands or millions at stake? As the evidence in this book shows, the answer is a simple no.

The fact that words are important and that using different words may change a problem by bringing different associations to mind, even if, according to some, they describe the same events, has been emphasized many times in a variety of contexts.[30] Guido Calabresi, for example, starts his book *Ideals, Beliefs, Attitudes and the Law* with the following example:

Suppose ... a deity were to appear to you, as president of this country or as controller of our legal system, and offer a gift ... which would make life more pleasant, more enjoyable than it is today ... The ... deity suggests that he can deliver this gift in exchange for one thing ... the lives of one thousand young men and women ... who will each year die horrible deaths.[31]

When he asked the students "Would you accept?" they almost uniformly answered no.

Obviously, however, as Calabresi immediately points out to the students, they and society have accepted such gifts; one of them is known as the private automobile, one of the greatest devices for mass destruction ever invented (fifty thousand lives are sacrificed each year in the United States, rather than the one thousand of the example, for the privilege of using it).

Would people react differently if I rephrased Calabresi's problem in the following less poetic terms:

Owing to people's creativity, their divine inspiration over centuries, our generation is offered "the car." Needless to say, it makes life more pleasant and more enjoyable, and it raises standards of living. Without it we would be poorer, and poorer also means less healthy, which, in turn, implies that we may die younger. However, accepting this gift from our ancestors means that 1,000 young people will die, on average, every year.

One can speculate that when presented with this version of the problem, the students would uniformly have answered yes to the question of accepting the car.

What this example shows is not that the invariance principle fails, but rather that the phrasing of some problems matters. Whereas Calabresi's formulation suggests, at first sight, an abstract example (the word "deity" today immediately brings philosophical rather than concrete issues to mind), to which the students responded correspondingly (i.e., viewing it as unlinked with a concrete problem), the "modern" translation brings up a clear-cut problem. If one really wants to test whether the invariance principle fails, one must be very careful to check whether it is indeed the same choice that is described by the different representations. Thus, the issue is not, as Kahneman and Tversky state, a matter of framing the same question differently. When one changes the words, it is not just the frame that is changed but the meaning of the question itself.

Let us now return to one of Allais's (1953) well-known examples and reexamine its possible interpretations. He argued that there is no doubt that if people were offered the choice between getting 100 million francs for sure and getting 500 million with a probability of 98 percent and nothing with a probability of 2 percent, they would prefer the 100 million in their pockets. Translated to mathematical language, this response implies that:

$$U(W_0 + 100) > 0.98U(W_0 + 500) + 0.02U(W_0). \tag{69}$$

Next Allais defined three possible outcomes:

$$P_1 \begin{cases} 0.98 & 500 \text{ million} \\ 0.02 & 0 \end{cases}$$

$$P_2 \begin{cases} \text{certitude of} \\ 100 \text{ million} \end{cases} \tag{70}$$

$$P_3 \begin{cases} \text{certitude of} \\ 1 \text{ franc} \end{cases}$$

and defined the following new games:

$$P_1' \equiv \frac{1}{100}(P_1) + \frac{99}{100}(P_3)$$

$$\equiv \begin{cases} \dfrac{0.98}{100} & 500 \text{ million,} \\ \dfrac{99}{100} & 1 \text{ franc} \\ \dfrac{0.02}{100} & 0 \end{cases} \cong \begin{cases} \dfrac{0.98}{100} & 500 \text{ million,} \\ \dfrac{99.02}{100} & 0 \end{cases} \qquad (71)$$

and

$$P_2' \equiv \frac{1}{100}(P_2) + \frac{99}{100}(P_3) \cong \begin{cases} \dfrac{1}{100} & 100 \\ \dfrac{99}{100} & 0 \end{cases}, \qquad (72)$$

where ($\cong$ denotes the approximation that the $1 =$ franc outcome is put together with the one where nothing can be won. Allais interprets the fact that people prefer P_1' to P_2' as implying that:

$$\frac{0.98}{100} U(W_0 + 500) + 0.9902 U(W_0)$$

$$> \frac{1}{100} U(W_0 + 100) + 0.99 U(W_0), \qquad (73)$$

which when rearranged implies that:

$$\frac{1}{100} U(W_0 + 100) < \frac{0.98}{100} U(W_0 + 500) + \frac{0.02}{100} U(W_0), \qquad (74)$$

which contradicts Condition (69). He attributes the contradiction to the fact that certainty and probabilities close to rare are evaluated differently from other ranges of probabilities.[32] This, according to him, leads to a violation of one of the postulates of rational behavior.

This conclusion may be unnecessarily drastic. The question is: do people in a laboratory bother to make the translation to Condition (73), or do they just make the approximation that 0.98/100 is 1 percent? If they do the latter approximation – and why wouldn't they? – there is no contradiction between their choice between P_2' and P_2' and Condition (69). The main issue here, as in the previous discussion, is that people may not necessarily examine questions in laboratories the way they would if they faced similar problems in real life. In fact, there is nothing in Allais's example that people can relate to a real-world situation. Nobody was ever offered 100 million francs just like that, and no lottery ever offered a 1 percent chance of winning a large prize (the chance is closer to 1 in 14 million in the Canadian 6/49 game, for example). Thus, the answer to the question concerning the choice between P_1' and P_2' may, at best, only suggest that people render 0.98 as approximately 1 percent (why not? what was at stake?), an approximation they may not necessarily make if faced with a real-world situation, as the case study summarized next suggests.[33]

Bob Moore, who was once an IBM financial executive, worked on the planning of the System 360, which revolutionized the computer industry in the 1960s. A senior engineer in charge of the team responsible for designing the integrated circuits around which the computers would be built worked with Moore to put together the estimated cost schedule for their development.

Months later, seeking to cut costs, Moore asked the engineer what would happen if his budget was reduced by $2 million. "Nothing," said the engineer. "I mean, what will it cost the project in terms of time or quality of the product?" asked Moore. "It will simply increase the probability of failure beyond its current level," answered the engineer. Moore gave an additional $1 million to the engineer.

Would Bob Moore's answers in a laboratory experiment reveal that he might make such a decision? It is doubtful. What this case study illustrates is that whereas in a laboratory people may make approximations (like neglecting a 0.02 percent change in probability) – thus answering abstract questions by making additional abstractions – they may not do so when they have to make decisions when their wealth and reputation are at stake. The paradoxes, violations, and inconsistencies obtained in laboratory experiments do not necessarily imply that people are irrational, but that one must be skeptical of the way people respond in artificial environments when their money and reputation are not at stake. The fact that regularities are obtained in such laboratory experiments is not surprising. The consistency only implies that in that artificial environment people make the same approximations.

Although the next experimental results seem consistent with the model presented here, my reservations about experimental studies should be kept in mind. I mention these studies to give a more rounded picture of the types of results that have been obtained in such experiments, rather than to provide strong evidence to support the model. The strong evidence can only come from examining people's behavior outside the laboratory, from the types of examination made here and in my previous work.[34]

Standard risk-aversion theory, combined with the frequent assumption of either a quadratic utility function or normality in the distribution of the random variables, implies that the covariance with market returns of returns on an investment should be considered as an investment criterion in addition to the mean or expected return (an implication discussed in Fisher 1906, Allais 1953, and Markowitz 1959, among others). But does higher variance necessarily diminish the attractiveness of a venture?

As shown in the preceding sections, the answer to this question within the model presented here is negative. People may avoid ventures with small variance but bet on others with large ones. The intuition is simple: increased risk means greater spread. So, although people may become poor through a venture, it is such a venture that provides them with the opportunity to become significantly rich too, an opportunity that ventures with small variances do not provide.

Slovic emphasizes that in experiments people choose according to decision rules such as "Minimize possible loss" or "Maximize possible gain" rather than basing their preference on variance per se. "Variance appears to have correlated with the preferences only because it also correlated with these other strategies," and he remarks that "this result is in accord with comments made by Lorie (1966) who complained that it was absurd to call a stock risky because it went up much faster that the market in some years and only as fast in other years, while a security that never rises in price is not risky at all, if variance is used to define risk."[35]

Finally, let us return to various points in Kahneman and Tversky's approach to which the leapfrogging model presented bears a number of similarities. They set up their model so that gains and losses were defined by the amount of money that was obtained or paid when a prospect was played, the reference point taken being the status quo or one's current assets. They also note that whereas such a situation may characterize some problems of choice, there are others in which gains and losses are coded relative to an expectation or aspiration level that differs from the status quo.

They give this example: "An entrepreneur who is weathering a slump with greater success than his competitors may interpret a small loss or gain [as] relative to the larger loss he had reason to expect."[36] This statement, however, implies comparisons with *others* (an assumption that Kahneman and Tversky do not discuss any further), not just with one's aspirations. It is precisely on this point that the approach presented here differs significantly from theirs, and this point also implies the use of different methodology for trying to falsify it.

For one cannot re-create in a laboratory the reference group relative to which one shapes one's behavior. With the minuscule terms at stake in laboratory experiments, nobody can outdo his or her fellows or be outdone by them, and nor does the group participating in the experiment represent the individual's reference group.

But for this significant difference, the other assumptions are similar.[37] Kahneman and Tversky note that a discrepancy between the reference point and the current asset position may also arise because of changes in wealth to which one has not yet adapted, and that such changes alter the preference order of prospects. This assumption also implies in their model that "a person who has not made peace with his losses is likely to accept gambles that would be unacceptable to him otherwise."[38] Thus, they emphasize that the location of the reference point emerges as a critical factor in the analysis of decisions.

The difference between their approach and the one presented here is that to prove their point, Kahneman and Tversky have to assume that the utility function is S-shaped (being steepest at the reference point), that there is a weighting function, and so on. In contrast, in the approach presented here, none of these assumptions seem necessary. The utility function may be linear in both W and $\alpha(\cdot)$: the results concerning attitudes toward gambling, insurance, and entrepreneurial ventures are obtained because of the typical shape of the social pyramid and the unexpected fluctuations among the ranks defined within this pyramid (for the moment, there seems to be no reason to make more complicated assumptions on nonlinearity).

Conclusion

There are numerous additional aspects of the model presented here that have been explored in the work of R. Brenner (1983, 1985, 1987). The points that have been emphasized here are only those judged pertinent to the subjects discussed in this book: gambling, betting on new ideas, risk-taking, regressive and progressive taxation, insurance, and decision making when leapfrogged. As noted, the model also suggests that one should investigate the origins of institutions, laws, and opinions, a line of investigation carried out in Chapters 3 and 4 – a line that, by the way, was strongly recommended by Coase (1937) but has rarely been pursued.

How could I examine the vast variety of human experience across countries and time from the unified, simple departure point summarized here? The answer is that I make a conceptual separation between the static initial conditions that represent the complicated state of the world, defined by the perplexingly complex customs, traditions, institutions and simple universal laws of movement that determine people's deviation from it – creativity, which is a deviation – among others.

Some might think that if the rules are simple, then the resultant behavior must also be simple, and my approach, simplistic. Those perplexingly complex customs and traditions must be the consequence of complex rules, right? Wrong. What I found was that despite the simplicity of the rules, with people betting on a variety of ideas, the consequences were far from simple. The consequences depended on institutions that shaped the directions toward which creativity was channeled. In turn, these institutions themselves started during crises, when people bet on some new ideas and brought these institutions into existence. These insights into human nature show how such simple rules of deviation – and chance, a matter of timing and place – bring about both complexities and eventual, occasional simplifications. These views are all implicit behind the analyses in this and my earlier books.

Human Nature and the Civilizing Process

Reuven Brenner

Which briefly compares various views of human nature.

The model's simplicity may remind readers of Ockham's suggestion that the unnecessary multiplication of assumptions should be avoided and to look for the simplest model that sheds light on the widest range of evidence. That is what I tried to do.

Bets on Ideas

The terms "gamble" and "probability" are used in two different contexts throughout the book and Appendix 1. When speaking about lotteries and insurance, the word "probability" has been used to represent the notion of a probability distribution – the assignment of probabilities to a set of related events, events that could be repeated many times. These probability distributions were assumed to be the same for everyone.

But the term "probability" has also been used in a totally different context: to represent the degree of belief an individual has attached to the success or the failure of implementing a new idea, a deviation from customary behavior. These are ideas that cross our minds, but that we bring to life in some circumstances and not others.

How this probability got into our minds, I do not know. In Appendix 1, this probability is somehow "there." To use a medical vocabulary: perhaps a "radical" before it becomes free. But one acts upon the probability only when leapfrogged. Our ancestors might have called bringing such ideas to life divine inspiration. The words I have used *seem* clearer: risk-taking, creativity, or entrepreneurship. However, these are just words that we are accustomed to; they neither are more precise than the ones used by our ancestors nor more revealing about traits of human nature that predispose some to such acts.

Thus, one could raise the question, if I did not define what probability is, how could I build theories of creativity without such a definition? The question is legitimate and my answer pragmatic.

In discussions about creativity and crime, probability is a degree of belief that stayed the same in the two situations that have been compared. Only one's leapfrogging, or being leapfrogged, leads to action. The reversal of the inequality defines a change of mind in the sense that outsiders observe people doing something significantly different from before. That the idea crosses someone's mind is not observable and irrelevant. If I wanted to be more precise I should have probably said that the mind (i.e., the idea) was there (i.e., in the back of one's mind); it was merely latent. Or, that the "radicals" are there, but they are not "free."

Psychologists and neurobiologists have examined how the human mind works. For a long time psychologists have followed the approach of not asking what goes on in people's minds, arguing that it is impossible to check whether the answers are accurate. The question they raised was the following: how do people react to various changes in circumstances? This question is similar to the questions raised in the leapfrogging model in Appendix 1.

The approach can also deal with many elements that psychologists have left out of their analysis, and by using ordinary, everyday language (avoiding words like "cognition," "conation," "affect," and using instead "thinking," and "wanting," and words such as "envy," "ambition," and "fear"). The opinions of some psychologists should be noted: Taylor (1979) attributes to Theodore Schneirla of the American Museum of Natural History the view that all behavior can be traced to two responses: approach and withdrawal. According to Schneirla, one constantly weighs possibilities and considers losses and gains. The model reflects such behavior and suggests when the trade-offs are solved. Recall de Mandeville's view, briefly quoted in Appendix 1, that I discuss at length in Brenner (1985; 1994, Chapter 3).

Neuroscientists and chemists have also expressed their views on the human mind. If my views are correct, then the neuroscientists who stated that brain research favors determinism are wrong (for a summary of their views, see Taylor 1979). Chance (in the sense of probability) and necessity (consequence of leapfrogging) mold into one in the human brain, and no logical distinction can be drawn between them – not in the model presented in Appendix 1 anyway.

Several neuroscientists and chemists have expressed this view. "The enormous complexity . . . of the interactions possible . . . suggests that . . . output may not be predictable on the basis of unit properties alone"; "[thought is] 'active uncertainty.' It is a casting about among alternatives and an assigning of probabilities to different outcomes which is the constitutive feature of thought."[1]

Some implications of the model seem consistent with the views of biologists less than a century ago, Hans Driesch among them. He believed that life and living processes can never be explained by the laws of physics and chemistry. Driesch postulated a "vital force" to explain the ability of the living to form and repair themselves.[2] The elusive probability may be compatible with this view.

It also follows that the argument of brain chemists that some substances regulate and create emotion may be interpreted in the following way. If one finds that a level of chemical substance in the body is associated with depression or addiction, and then administers a drug to change that level, one may not be able to answer why this happens but may restore the chemical balance (with unpredictable side effects).

Creativity, Uncertainty, and Risk-Taking

According to the views presented here, people bet on new ideas, deviating from customs and traditions, when they are leapfrogged. In what direction the creativity is channeled depends on the institutions of society and access to sources of capital, discussed in this book too but in detail in Brenner (2002).

Many writers from ancient to modern times have implicitly associated thinking and creativity with suffering, loss of status, and some disorder – though not leapfrogging.[3]

Adam Smith, in a lesser-known essay titled "The History of Astronomy," wrote explicitly that men "have seldom had the curiosity to inquire by what process of intermediate events [a] change is brought about. Because the passage of the thought from the one object to the other is by custom become quite smooth and easy," and that "it is well known that custom deadens the vivacity of both pain and pleasure, abates the grief we should feel for the one, and weakens the joy we should derive from the other. The pain is supported without agony, and the pleasure enjoyed without rapture; because custom and the frequent repetition of any object comes at last to form and bend the mind or organ to that habitual mood and disposition which fits them to receive its impression, without undergoing any violent change."[4]

Similar statements have been made by poets and writers, not just philosophers. Anatole France, in his *The Revolt of the Angels*, notes sarcastically, "In Ialdabaoth army, happily for us, the officers obtain their post by seniority. This being the case, there is little likelihood of the command falling into the hands of a military genius, for men are not made leaders by prolonged habits of obedience, and close attention to minutiae is not a good apprenticeship for the evolution of vast plans of campaign."[5] These people do not make history. Risk-takers do.

Other aspects of the view of human nature discussed in Appendix 1 are implicit in other writings. Wordsworth wrote that "Wisdom is offtimes nearer when we stoop; than when we soar"; Jean-Paul Sartre stated, "Genius is not a gift, but rather the way out one invents in desperate situations"; and Marcel Proust, in *Remembrance of Things Past*, wrote, "Everything great in the world comes from neurotics. They have composed our masterpieces. We enjoy lovely music, beautiful paintings, a thousand delicacies, but we have no idea of their cost, to those who invented them, in sleepless nights, spasmodic laughter, rashes, asthmas, epilepsies." In the chapter "The Past Recaptured," he notes, "Happiness is beneficial for the body, but it is grief that develops the powers of the mind." The leapfrogging model translates this statement, which is a broader implication of Milton Friedman's adage, "There is no such thing as a free lunch." Creativity is no exception to this observation, and led to the title of the concluding chapter in my 1983 book: "Happy People Do Not Have a History," "happy" there meaning passively content (not actively joyful). One must be young and naive to choose that title, but there it is.

One can find similar opinions expressed in Samuel Johnson's statement, "The mind is seldom guided to very rigorous operations but by pain or the dread of pain." John Dewey (1930) argued long ago in *Human Nature and Conduct* that thinking was an adaptive behavior triggered by unfulfilled expectations, while William Faulkner said more than once that he created characters in violent circumstances in an effort to get at the truth of the human heart.

One can also find this viewpoint, expressed differently, in the writings of Isaiah Berlin. In his essays on Moses Hess, Karl Marx, and Benjamin Disraeli, he suggests that only when one belongs to a community can one manage a full life undistorted by neurotic self-questioning about one's true identity and be free from feelings of inferiority, real or imaginary. Those who do not belong, however, "hit upon various more or less conscious solutions to their problems of self identity." These lead eventually to original insights, "a neurotic distortion of the facts," as Berlin puts it. In fact, Berlin thinks that many of Marx's and Disraeli's ideas evolved in the first place not as tools of analysis, but as comforting myths to rally oppressed spirits, perhaps those of the authors themselves.[6]

In the more technical language of the management literature some similar views have been expressed by Herbert Simon (though he admits in his 1957 work that his intention was to build a new vocabulary rather than a theory):

1. Where performance falls short of the level of aspiration, search behavior (particularly search for new alternatives of action) is induced.
2. At the same time, the level of aspiration begins to adjust itself downward until goals reach levels that are practically attainable.
3. If the two mechanisms just listed operate too slowly to adapt aspirations to performance, emotional behavior – apathy or aggression, for example – will replace rational adaptive behavior.[7]

Simon's first proposition reflects one facet of my model. His second proposition, while plausible, will not always hold true. Some people (call them entrepreneurs) may turn out to be determined enough and may bet on new ideas until they achieve their expectations. But Simon is right, in part, in his third proposition, when he states that when aspirations are not achieved one may bet on criminal acts and that the lack of achievement takes its emotional toll. However, he is misleading in calling the alternative rational adaptive behavior. If somebody becomes suddenly poor, why is it rational for that person to adapt to the new situation by just staying poor, rather than starting to bet on new ideas? It should be emphasized that if one defines search behavior (described in Simon's first proposition) as rational, one must also define the aggressive one as such, as both types stem from the same trait, a trait precisely defined by the leapfrogging instinct. But Simon's implicit view of human nature bears some resemblance to mine (though his vocabulary is different). In his book with James G. March, he writes:

We may conclude that high satisfaction, per se, is not a particularly good predictor of high production nor does it facilitate production in a causal sense. Motivation to produce stems from a present or anticipated state of discontent and a perception of a direct connection between individual production and a new state of satisfaction.[8]

Finally, Shils's observation on the linguistics associated with this subject should be noted: "'Originality' in its first usage in the English language did not describe the working of man's innate genius. It referred, rather, to the greatest of all burdens of the past, 'original sin' . . . : the 'fall' of man from his state of grace and his consequent expulsion from the Garden of Eden."[9]

"Originality," which now generally has a positive connotation (though some fight to preserve tradition and custom and return to an imagined past), thus initially and unsurprisingly had a rather ambiguous one. After all, tasting from the tree of knowledge and opening Pandora's box led to criminal acts too. Shils also notices that a "genius" originally was a demon who possessed a human being and made him or her perform acts beyond the power of ordinary human beings. Plato noted that during the creative act people are out of their minds: this statement received a literal interpretation with mathematical symbols in Appendix 1.

Briefly, the model presented in this book and in my previous ones suggests a simple departure point for examining many aspects of human behavior. It captures many ideas that have been offered throughout the ages, adding twists, articulating them differently, and exploring different directions with simplifying implications.

Because people do not behave according to categories, there are no categories in the model. The terms "economic," "sociological," and "psychological" represent mere inventions of new vocabularies and draw on academic traditions. The words I use are simple, as they are kept in check by the leapfrogging model. Whereas economists often talk about uncertainty, creativity, and innovation, there is no correspondence whatsoever between their words and their models.

Unclear language is a sign of unclear thinking. So, I have tried first to define a few words with precision and then to use *only* these words throughout the analysis. Heer has pointed out that "all intellectual discussions in our time are struggles for language," and he furiously attacked fashions of playing with and inventing words rather than trying to define a few with precision.[10] There are no new words in this book – only very old ones: "fear," "envy," "ambition," "trust," "network," "customs," "rich," and "poor." The novelty may be only in the use of the term "leapfrogging" to capture all these terms and bring them together.

APPENDIX THREE

A Statistical Profile of Gamblers

Reuven Brenner, Gabrielle A. Brenner, and Claude Montmarquette

Which shows statistical ways to test some of the views in the book, in attempts to falsify them.

Quebec Data

To test the views presented in the text, we estimated the following relationship (by a multiple regression model and a log-linear function):

$$\text{TOT}_i = \beta_0 + \beta_1 \text{SCHOL}_i + \beta_2 \text{AGE}_i + \beta_3 \text{WEALTH}_i + \beta_4 \text{CHIL}_i + \beta_5 \text{INC}_i$$
$$+ \beta_6 \text{PER}_i + \beta_7 \text{FAM}_i + \varepsilon_i,$$

where we define the variables used as follows:

TOT_i = annual total spending on lottery tickets of respondent i as percentage of total family income

SCHOL_i = number of years of schooling of respondent i

AGE_i = age of respondent i

WEALTH_i = an index giving the actual family wealth position of respondent i relative to what it was when he or she was young. If it did not change, the index was equal to 1; if it worsened, the index was less than 1; and if his or her position improved, the index was greater than 1

CHIL_i = number of children of respondent i

INC_i = personal income of respondent i

PER_i = personal income of respondent i as percentage of family income

FAM_i = family income of respondent i

ε_i = an error term

The reasons for including these variables are the following. The views presented in the text and Appendix 1 about risk-taking make predictions about the relationship between leapfrogging and expenditures on lottery tickets. The sample does not allow for a straightforward testing of such relationships, because information on wealth is not available. Also, as noted, the motivation for buying lottery tickets stems from two different sources: (1) people who are relatively poor plan to spend a greater fraction of their wealth on tickets than do rich people, and (2) people who have suddenly been leapfrogged may decide to buy such tickets. But this last group can be found in any wealth bracket: misfortune and being leapfrogged by the Joneses can happen to anyone. If the data collected do not separate between the two groups, we may not necessarily observe that the average income of the lottery-ticket-buying public is significantly lower than that of the public at large. Only if the fraction of poor people who plan to buy lottery tickets constitutes a large fraction of buyers can we expect such an outcome.

Second, the data available refer to monetary income and not to wealth. But monetary income is a misleading indicator of wealth. We would expect that, holding monetary income constant, older people and people with more dependents are disproportionately represented among ticket buyers. A twenty-year old with $50,000 may be rich, whereas a sixty-year-old with $50,000 may be poor. What are the latter's chances of ever "making it" and having a good life? Another variable that may complement the information on relative wealth is the level of education. One may expect that, ceteris paribus, the lower is one's level of education, the lower are one's expectations for future increases in income and thus the lower is one's wealth. If so, people with less education will plan to spend a greater fraction of their wealth on lottery tickets.

In addition to the prediction about the relationship between planning to buy lottery tickets and wealth, the other prediction that we can test concerns people who would buy spontaneously when leapfrogged. According to the model's predictions, such people will tend to spend more on lotteries than before. If we take one's wealth relative to the wealth of one's family during childhood (assuming that family wealth shapes one's aspirations), we would expect that people who bettered their own position will buy fewer lottery tickets than before and that those whose position worsened will buy more.

Thus, we expect β_1, β_3, β_5, and β_7 to be negative and β_2 and β_4 to be positive. We expect β_6 to be positive, as the greater is one person's contribution to the total family income, the family's relative wealth will be perceived as less secure (as its income depends more on this one person's income).

Table 1 provides the results of the estimation in Column 1. β_2, β_5, and β_6 are of the expected sign and are significant; β_3 is of the expected sign but insignificant. The coefficients of schooling, β_1, number of children, β_4, and family income, β_7, did not have the expected sign. β_4 is also statistically insignificant. After having ascertained by an F test that β_4 is insignificant,

Table 1. *Regression results: Quebec survey (log-linear form) (N = 851)*

Coefficient (hypothesis)	Dependent variable	(1)	(2)
	CONSTANT	-5.2^*	-5.1^*
		(-3.3)	(-3.3)
$\beta_1\ (-)$	SCHOL	0.4^{**}	0.4^{**}
		(2.3)	(2.4)
$\beta_2\ (+)$	AGE	0.5	0.45
		(2.0)	(1.97)
$\beta_3\ (-)$	WEALTH	-0.58	-0.57
		(-1.1)	(-1.08)
$\beta_4\ (+)$	CHIL	-0.07	$-$
		(-0.5)	$-$
$\beta_5\ (-)$	INC	-5.6^*	-5.6^*
		(-9.0)	(-9.0)
$\beta_6\ (+)$	PER	7.4^*	7.4^*
		(4.1)	(4.1)
$\beta_7\ (-)$	FAM	4.2^*	4.2^*
		(5.8)	(5.8)
F statistics		77	90
R^2		0.38	0.38

Note: Signs in parentheses are the expected signs in the Coefficient column. In Columns 1 and 2, t-statistics are in parentheses.

* Statistically significant at the 1% level.

** Statistically significant at the 5% level.

we reran the regression without number of children. Column 2 in Table 1 presents the results. There are no major changes in the other coefficients.

The results in Table 1 do not refute the prediction of the model: the higher is one's income, the less one spends on lottery tickets; the older one is, the more lottery tickets one buys. It also seems that the more upwardly mobile one is, the less one buys lottery tickets.

A result that seems to contradict a prediction is that of the influence of schooling and family income. Because several previous studies that rely on other data sets (summarized in the text) have found that there is an inverse relationship between years of schooling completed and expenditures on lotteries, we did some further testing with this data set, but the results did not improve. The only explanation we can think of is the following. The model predicts gambling behavior for two groups of people (the relatively poor who plan to buy tickets and those who buy spontaneously). The latter group may belong to any class and have any level of schooling (which may explain why the coefficient for number of children does not come out as expected). Only if the data set included only people from the first group would one expect to obtain a positive relationship between low levels of schooling and relative expenditures on gambling. For the other group, one would not expect such a relationship and could argue that the opposite is true.

Suppose that somebody with little schooling loses his or her job. Transfer payments and other benefits significantly diminish fluctuations in that person's wealth, and he or she may not start gambling or may not spend more on it. However, for those with more schooling, such compensations are far from reaching the expected level of wealth and the status it defined. Thus, he or she may start gambling. This explanation is reinforced by the result we obtained in the following test. We split the data set in two: one set included people with less than ten years of schooling, and the other included people with ten or more years of schooling. We then reran the regression on each subset. For the sample with ten or more years of schooling, the relationship between years of schooling and relative expenditures on gambling is negative, whereas it is positive for the sample with less than ten years of schooling. This same explanation may hold true for the positive relationship between relative expenditures on gambling and family wealth.

Canadian Data

In spite of the strong reservation mentioned in the text, we tested our views on the data set provided by Statistics Canada's *Family Expenditures in Canada* of 1982 and estimated the following relationship:

$$
\text{TOT}_i = \gamma_0 + \sum_{j=1}^{3} \gamma_1^j \text{NAC}_i^j + \sum_{j=1}^{5} \gamma_2^j \text{AGE}_i^j + \sum_{j=1}^{4} \gamma_3^j \text{REG}_i
$$

$$
+ \sum_{j=1}^{2} \gamma_4^j \text{STAT}_i^j + \sum_{j=1}^{4} \gamma_5^j \text{ED}_i^j + \sum_{j=1}^{2} \gamma_6^j \text{LANG}_i^j \tag{1}
$$

$$
+ \sum_{j=1}^{3} \gamma_7^j \text{ENF}_i^j + \gamma_8 \text{INC}_i + \sum_{j=1}^{2} \gamma_9^j \text{IM}_i^j + \eta_i,
$$

where the variables used are defined as follows:

TOT_i = annual spending on lotteries of the family unit i as a percentage of its total after-tax income

AGE_i^j = dummy variables that characterize the age of the head of the family unit, where
$\text{AGE}^1 = 1$ if the head is between thirty and thirty-nine years old;
0 otherwise

$\text{AGE}^2 = 1$ if the head is between forty and forty-nine years old; 0 otherwise

$\text{AGE}^3 = 1$ if the head is between fifty and fifty-nine years old; 0 otherwise

$\text{AGE}^4 = 1$ if the head is between sixty and sixty-nine years old; 0 otherwise

$\text{AGE}^5 = 1$ if the head is seventy years old or older

The omitted age category is twenty to twenty-nine. Thus, all the coefficients are relative to this category.

REG_i^j = dummy variables to indicate the province or region where the family unit lives, where

$\text{REG}^1 = 1$ if the family lives in the Atlantic Provinces; 0 otherwise

$\text{REG}^2 = 1$ if the family lives in Quebec; 0 otherwise

$\text{REG}^3 = 1$ if the family lives in the Western Provinces except British Columbia; 0 otherwise

$\text{REG}^4 = 1$ if the family lives in British Columbia; 0 otherwise

The omitted category is Ontario.

STAT_i^j = dummy variables to indicate the marital status of the head of the family unit, where

$\text{STAT}^1 = 1$ if the head of the family unit was never married; 0 otherwise

$\text{STAT}^2 = 1$ if the head of the family unit was neither married nor ever married; 0 otherwise

The omitted category is a married head.

ED_i^j = dummy variables to indicate the level of education of the head of the family, where

$\text{ED}^1 = 1$ if the head of the family either has some secondary education or has completed secondary education; 0 otherwise

$\text{ED}^2 = 1$ if the head has some postsecondary education; 0 otherwise

$\text{ED}^3 = 1$ if the head has a college degree or certificate of postsecondary education; 0 otherwise

$\text{ED}^4 = 1$ if the head has a university degree; 0 otherwise

The omitted category is less than nine years of primary education.

LANG_i^j = dummy variables to indicate the mother tongue of the head of the family, where

$\text{LANG}^1 = 1$ if the mother tongue is French; 0 otherwise

$\text{LANG}^2 = 1$ if the mother tongue is neither English nor French; 0 otherwise

The omitted category is English as mother tongue.

NAC_i^j = dummy variables to indicate whether members of a family receive unemployment insurance, where

$\text{NAC}^1 = 1$ if one member of the family receives unemployment insurance; 0 otherwise

$\text{NAC}^2 = 1$ if two members of the family receive unemployment insurance; 0 otherwise

$\text{NAC}^3 = 1$ if three or more members of the family receive unemployment insurance; 0 otherwise

ENF_i^j = dummy variables indicating the number of children in the family. We defined three such variables, depending on whether there were one, two, or three or more children in the family. The category omitted is no children.

INC_i = income of the family unit

IM_i^j = dummy variables indicating the immigration status of the family unit, when

$\text{IM}^1 = 1$ if the head of the family unit immigrated before 1960; 0 otherwise

$\text{IM}^2 = 1$ if the head of the family unit immigrated between 1961 and 1970; 0 otherwise

$\text{IM}^3 = 1$ if the head of the family unit immigrated after 1971; 0 otherwise

The omitted category is a native-born head.

We expect both γ_1^j and γ_2^j (corresponding to the receipt of unemployment insurance and the age variable, respectively) to be positive. The coefficients γ_3^j may be of either sign, depending on regional differences that are not captured in other variables. As noted in the preceding section, evidence exists for greater participation in the traditionally poorer regions of Canada, Quebec and the Maritimes; this would mean a positive coefficient for both γ_3^1 and γ_3^2.

We also expect that the coefficients γ_5^j will be negative, as the reference category for education is the one indicating the least education (fewer than nine years of primary education). The coefficients of the number of family members, γ_7^j, should be positive, and γ_8, the coefficient of income, should be negative.

The signs of γ_7^j, the number of children living with the family, γ_6^j, the language spoken in the family, and γ_9^j, the immigration status of the family unit, are not determinate. Nevertheless, the following arguments may give some idea of the expected signs of γ_6^j and γ_9^j. Several studies have mentioned that

Catholics are more likely to gamble than Protestants.[1] As there are relatively more Catholics among French-speaking Canadians than among English-speaking ones, we expected that γ_6^1, the coefficient of Francophone families, would be positive. This argument is reinforced by the fact that, as noted in the text, French Canadians generally earn less than their English-speaking counterparts. As for immigration status, as immigrants are uprooted from their traditional way of life and have possibly not settled into their new country, we expect that new immigrants play lotteries relatively more than native-born Canadians. We would also expect immigrants of longer standing to play more than native-born Canadians, ceteris paribus.

As noted in the text, a significant percentage of families answered that they did not buy lottery tickets. We are thus in the presence of a dependent variable equal to zero in a significant number of observations. The correct way to estimate Equation (1) is thus through probit analysis.[2] The results of this analysis are given in Table 2.

Surprisingly, the results in Table 2 mostly fail to disprove our predictions. All age categories except the last (seventy and older) gamble more than the younger group, pointing to a positive relationship between lottery spending and age. Why didn't we get the same result for the seventy-and-older group?

First, elderly people may be in poor health and thus less able to buy lottery tickets. Second, they may have more trouble than a younger person in recalling how much they spent on tickets during the year. But note that if we compare these results with those in Table 3, where we used a least-squares method to estimate the relationships for only those families that answered that they bought lottery tickets (thus eliminating all families that said that they did not buy lottery tickets), we see that families whose heads were seventy or older bought more tickets than the younger groups, though fewer than the age categories from fifty to sixty-nine. Perhaps for many in this age group, even if they won, they could not enjoy "the good life" because they might not have been in good health. Clotfelter and Cook also found that the oldest age group (seventy and older) played less.[3]

The coefficients of the number of people receiving unemployment benefits are also positive (i.e., family units where one or more members receive unemployment benefits buy proportionally more lottery tickets than do units with no unemployed member. But note that in Table 3 this result is inverted for families with three or more members who receive unemployment benefits.). On a geographical level, residents of Western Canada buy fewer lottery tickets than Ontarians, and the result is statistically significant. The result of the comparisons between Ontarians and residents of

Table 2. *Analysis of Statistics Canada's data set (N = 10,938; F = 33)*

Coefficient	Hypothesis	Independent variable	Estimate	t-Statistics
γ_1^1	(+)	NAC^1	0.08*	6.7
γ_1^2	(+)	NAC^2	0.07*	2.9
γ_1^3	(+)	NAC^3	0.10	1.4
γ_2^1	(+)	AGE^1	0.04*	3.2
γ_2^2	(+)	AGE^2	0.05*	3.1
γ_2^3	(+)	AGE^3	0.08*	5.0
γ_2^4	(+)	AGE^4	0.06*	3.4
γ_2^5	(+)	AGE^5	-0.04^{**}	-2.2
γ_3^1	(+)	REG^1	-0.11^*	-5.9
γ_3^2	(+)	REG^2	0.01	0.6
γ_3^3	(?)	REG^3	-0.11^*	-10.6
γ_3^4	(?)	REG^4	-0.12^*	-7.9
γ_4^1	(?)	STAT^1	-0.11^*	-7.4
γ_4^2	(?)	STAT^2	-0.11^*	-8.4
γ_5^1	(−)	ED^1	0.03*	2.8
γ_5^2	(−)	ED^2	0.06	0.2
γ_5^3	(−)	ED^3	-0.05^*	-3.2
γ_5^4	(−)	ED^4	-0.21^*	-10.3
γ_6^1	(+)	LANG^1	0.03**	2.0
γ_6^2	(?)	LANG^2	0.01	0.8
γ_7^1	(+)	ENF^1	-0.006	-0.4
γ_7^2	(+)	ENF^2	-0.008^*	-2.5
γ_7^3	(+)	ENF^3	-0.07	0.9
γ_8	(−)	INC	0.03*	9.4
γ_9^1	(+)	IM^1	-0.02	-0.1
γ_9^2	(+)	IM^2	-0.003	-0.1
γ_9^3	(+)	IM^3	0.004	0.1

Note: Signs in parentheses are the expected signs.
 * Statistically significant at the 1% level.
** Statistically significant at the 5% level.

the Atlantic Provinces and Quebec is not as clear cut. The result in Table 2 suggests that residents of the Atlantic Provinces play less than Ontarians (and the result is again statistically significant). But the result in Table 3, based on families who did buy lottery tickets, is not statistically significant. The difference may be due to the difference in acknowledged participation rates in buying tickets in the two regions. As noted in the text, 40 percent of families in the Atlantic Provinces and only 29 percent in Ontario said they did not buy lottery tickets. As for Quebecers, the numbers in Table 2 suggest that they play more than Ontarians, though the result is not statistically significant; the numbers in Table 3 suggest that among the families that did play the

Table 3. *Analysis of Statistics Canada's data set: Families that admitted to buying lottery tickets* $(N = 7,083; F = 17.2; R^2 = 0.24)$

Coefficient	Hypothesis	Independent Variable	Estimate	t-Statistics
γ_1^1	(+)	NAC^1	10.3	1.7
γ_1^2	(+)	NAC^2	32.9*	2.7
γ_1^3	(+)	NAC^3	−36.7	−1.1
γ_2^1	(+)	AGE^1	17.1**	2.2
γ_2^2	(+)	AGE^2	27.6*	3.2
γ_2^3	(+)	AGE^3	59.4*	6.7
γ_2^4	(+)	AGE^4	51.1*	5.3
γ_2^5	(+)	AGE^5	33.2*	2.9
γ_3^1	(+)	REG^1	−18.1	−1.8
γ_3^2	(+)	REG^2	−10.2	−1.1
γ_3^3	(?)	REG^3	−48.9*	−6.5
γ_3^4	(?)	REG^4	−44.6*	−5.4
γ_4^1	(?)	STAT^1	1.9	0.2
γ_4^2	(?)	STAT^2	−17.4*	−2.4
γ_5^1	(−)	ED^1	7.3	1.1
γ_5^2	(−)	ED^2	−16.3	−1.7
γ_5^3	(−)	ED^3	−25.2*	−2.7
γ_5^4	(−)	ED^4	−60.5*	−5.6
γ_6^1	(+)	LANG^1	32.7*	3.5
γ_6^2	(?)	LANG^2	26.8*	3.0
γ_7^1	(+)	ENF^1	−25.1*	−3.4
γ_7^2	(+)	ENF^2	−39.2**	−2.0
γ_7^3	(+)	ENF^3	7.7	0.1
γ_8	(−)	INC	0.002*	10.2
γ_9^1	(+)	IM^1	−4.7	−0.5
γ_9^2	(+)	IM^2	32.8**	2.5
γ_9^3	(+)	IM^3	52.9*	3.8

Note: Signs in parentheses are the expected signs.
   * Statistically significant at the 1% level.
  ** Statistically significant at the 5% level.

lottery, Quebecers played less than Ontarians, though again the result is not statistically significant. Thus, we cannot conclude that Quebecers buy more (or fewer) lottery tickets than Ontarians, contrary to our previous findings. In contrast, contrary to our previous findings, the Maritime Provinces do not play less than Ontario. But we have more confidence in the earlier data.

As we predicted, there seems to exist a negative relationship between level of education and lottery participation. People with a college or university degree buy relatively fewer lottery tickets than do people who did not complete secondary education. This result is statistically significant. However,

Table 4. *Definition of additional variables and symbols*

Age	Age of the head of the family
NCHD	Number of children in the family under age sixteen
NUB	Number of members of the family receiving unemployment insurance benefits
INC	After-tax family income

people who completed secondary education played more. People who had some postsecondary education played more, as much as, or less than people who did not complete primary education (the coefficient being statistically insignificant in all three regressions). As for mother tongue, people whose mother tongue is English buy relatively fewer lottery tickets than do people whose mother tongue is not. Families whose head is married participated more in the lottery than units whose head had any other marital status. Although, among the families who bought tickets, families whose head was never married may have bought relatively more tickets (but the result is not statistically significant). The only results that are contrary to the predictions are those for families with children versus families without children, and for income. Families with children play relatively less than do families without children, and families with higher incomes play relatively more than do families with lower incomes. Possibly we can relate this last result to the significant (40 percent) underreporting on lotteries we found. The results are improved when we assume that poor people underdeclare their expenditures more than do rich people. The more sophisticated statistical analysis concerning this point is presented next.

How to Correct for Underdeclared Lottery Expenditures

Let Equation (2) define the determinants of the exact annual spending on lotteries of the Jth family as a percentage of its total after-tax income:

$$\ln(E^*/\text{INC})_i = \gamma_0 + \gamma_1 \text{INC}_i + \gamma_2 \text{INC}_i^2$$

$$+ \sum_{k=3}^{p} \gamma_k x_{ik} + \zeta_i, \tag{2}$$

where E_i^* = the unobserved exact lottery expenditures by the family unit

INC$_i$ = the after-tax income of family i; x_{ik}, $k = 3, \ldots p$ = the other variables of the model, defined in Table 4;

ζ_i = an error term with the usual properties.

Consider that

$$E_i^* = (1 + B_i)E_i, \qquad (3)$$

where E_i is the reported expenditure and B_i is an adjustment coefficient that equals the difference between the family's unobserved exact lottery expenditures and the reported expenditures divided by the reported survey expenditures.

According to the arguments presented in Chapter 3, the poor and the leapfrogged have greater incentives to gamble (but either society condemns their spending or they receive the small prizes disproportionately and do not declare them); thus, let us assume that the adjustment coefficient varies among families according to the following relationship:[4]

$$B_i = B_0 + \beta_1 \text{INC}_i + \beta_2 \text{INC}_i^2. \qquad (4)$$

This relationship implies that the adjustment coefficient depends nonlinearly on the income of the family unit i. Depending on the signs and sizes of the coefficients β_1 and β_2, this equation may examine the assumption that families with lower incomes significantly underdeclare their expenditures on lotteries.

With reported lottery expenditures in the survey, Equation (2) becomes:

$$\ln(E/\text{INC})_i = \gamma_0 + \gamma_1 \text{INC}_i + \gamma_2 \text{INC}_i^2$$
$$+ \sum_{k=3}^{p} \gamma_k x_{ik} - \ln(1 + B_i) + \zeta_i. \qquad (5)$$

Assume that the underdeclaration of lottery expenditures does not exceed 100 percent and that the overdeclaration is always less than 100 percent – that is, $-1 < B_i \leq 1$. With Equation (4) and a series expansion of $\ln(1 + B)$ up to the second term, we obtain, after some manipulation, the following relationship:

$$\ln(E/\text{INC})_i = \left(\gamma_0 + \frac{1}{2}\beta_0^2 - \beta_0\right) + (\gamma_1 - \beta_1 + \beta_0\beta_1)\text{INC}_i$$
$$+ (-\beta_2 + \beta_0\beta_2 + \beta_1^2/2)\text{INC}_i^2 + \beta_1\beta_2\text{INC}_i^3$$
$$+ \left(\beta_2^2/2\right)\text{INC}_i^4 + \sum_{k=3}^{p} \gamma_k x_{ik} + \zeta_i \qquad (6)$$
$$= \theta_0 + \theta_1\text{INC}_i + \theta_2\text{INC}_i^2 + \theta_3\text{INC}_i^3 + \theta_4\text{INC}_i^4$$
$$+ \sum_{k=3}^{p} \gamma_k x_{ik} + \zeta_i.$$

The coefficients of the model are identified except for β_0.

It is at this point that we integrate the accurate information on lottery revenues (which we would not need if the information on expenditures were not biased). By using the sum of declared expenditures, E, and the observed revenues of lottery enterprises, E^*, we can obtain an aggregate adjustment coefficient B from the following equation:

$$E^* = (1 + B)E. \tag{7}$$

From Equations (3) and (4) we obtain:

$$E_i^* = (1 + B_i)E_i$$
$$= E_i + \beta_0 E_i + \beta_1 \text{INC}_i E_i + \beta_2 \text{INC}_i^2 E_i. \tag{8}$$

Summing up all the family units, assuming $\sum E_i^* = E^*$ and using Equation (7) (recalling that the value of B is known), we obtain:

$$\beta_0 = B - \beta_1 \sum_i \text{INC}_i E_i / E - \beta_2 \sum \text{INC}_i^2 E_i / E. \tag{9}$$

Results

The data set we use is the same as in the preceding section. The initial sample size is 10,938, but because it is weighted according to the ten provinces to represent the Canadian population, the adjusted sample size for each regression may vary accordingly.[5] Table 4 defines the variables and symbols that have not been defined yet.

Thirty-five percent of respondents in the sample declared that they did not spend on lotteries. Thus, one has to deal with this specification bias issue to explain lottery expenditures.[6] To obtain consistent estimates for the regression coefficients of Equation (6), we used the two-stage estimators proposed by Heckman (1979). The results of the probit analysis of the probability of spending on lotteries reject the assumption of randomly missing observations,[7] but the inverse of the Mills' ratio introduced to correct for the sample selection bias proved statistically insignificant.

Table 5 presents the regression results both without correction for the underdeclared lottery expenditures and with correction. Most coefficient estimates are statistically significant, and the $\bar{R}^2$ are reasonable, given the large number of observations in the sample ($N = 7,083$). As expected, there are important differences between the two results for the income variables. But for most of the other variables the differences are minor. One exception is the EDUC variable; its coefficient is negative and statistically significant in

Table 5. *The determinants of lottery expenditures (N = 7,083)*

Variable	With correction for underdeclarations	Without correction for underdeclarations
REG[1]	0.0200	−5.610
	(0.19)	(−0.59)
REG[2]	−0.0087	0.0021
	(−0.15)	(0.03)
REG[3]	−0.2750	−0.4077
	(−1.82)	(−3.04)
REG[4]	−0.1960	−0.2897
	(−1.68)	(−2.76)
STAT[1]	0.0150	−0.0627
	(0.14)	(−0.66)
STAT[2]	−0.1179	−0.1831
	(−1.28)	(−2.22)
LANG[1]	0.2332	0.2598
	(3.620)	(4.12)
LANG[2]	0.1043	0.1180
	(1.83)	(2.09)
IM[1]	0.0024	−0.0224
	(0.04)	(−0.36)
IM[2]	0.1276	0.1162
	(1.57)	(1.44)
IM[3]	0.2921	0.2986
	(3.36)	(3.44)
AGE	0.0435	0.0574
	(2.63)	(3.87)
$(\text{AGE})^2$	−0.0003	−0.0005
	(−2.00)	(−3.17)
NCHD	−0.0841	−0.1050
	(−2.94)	(−3.97)
NUB	−0.0099	−0.0323
	(−0.18)	(0.64)
ED[1]	−0.0089	0.0023
	(−2.01)	(0.05)
ED[2]	−0.1599	−0.1714
	(−2.69)	(−2.89)
ED[3]	−0.2425	−0.3084
	(−2.65)	(−3.61)
ED[4]	−0.4597	−0.6496
	(−2.08)	(−3.31)
INC	−0.5078	−0.2999
	(−3.59)	(−4.63)

(Continued)

Table 5. *(continued)*

Variable	With correction for underdeclarations	Without correction for underdeclarations
$(\text{INC})^2$	0.1405	0.0050
	(2.58)	(0.40)
$(\text{INC})^3$	−0.0200	–
	(−2.62)	
$(\text{INC})^4$	0.0010	–
	(2.71)	
CONSTANT	−0.589	−6.62
	(−9.45)	(−12.06)
$(\text{Mills' ratio})^{-1}$	−0.2593	0.1244
	(−0.62)	(0.34)
$\bar{R}^2$	0.1409	0.1403

Note: All t-statistics are in parentheses.

the corrected regression, a change that is in the direction of supporting the predictions of the model.

Focusing on the corrected version, we see that many results are in accord with predictions made by the model. The French-speaking Canadians (LANG^1) spend more on lotteries than do English-speaking families, and it is well known that French Canadians earn less than English-speaking Canadians. (This may not be the only reason for the French Canadians' greater propensity to gamble; Catholics everywhere gamble more than Protestants, and French Canadians are mostly Catholic, but we did not have data on religious background.) Table 5 shows that recent immigrants (IM^3) spend more than both less-recent immigrants (IM^1, IM^2) and native-born Canadians (the omitted category). Also, as expected, up to the age of seventy-two and a half, people gamble more with age. Strong results supporting the model occur in the education variables. The more educated spend much less on lotteries. However, the results for the number of children living with the family and the number of members in the family receiving unemployment benefits do not support the model.

Before considering the results for the income variable, let us discuss the adjustment coefficients for the underdeclared lottery expenditures.

Recall that for 1982 the relationship between declared expenditures and the respective provincial lottery revenues, E/E^*, equaled 0.70 (taking into account that approximately 10 percent of the revenues come from foreigners). Thus, from Equation (7) we obtain a conservative value of 0.43 for B, the aggregate adjustment coefficient. Using B and the coefficient estimates

Table 6. *Adjustment coefficients and income elasticities*

Income (in 10^4)	Adjustment equation[a]	Income elasticities[b]	
		With correction	Without correction
0.5	1.05	−0.23	−0.15
1.0	0.86	−0.53	−0.29
2.5	0.43	−1.86	−0.69
3.0	0.33	−2.45	−0.81
6.0	0.19	−7.47	−1.44

[a] Adjustment equation: $B_1 = 1.271 - 0.4474\text{INC}_i + 0.0447\text{INC}_i^2$.

[b] Income elasticities $\frac{\delta(E/\text{INC})\text{INC}}{\delta\text{INC}(E/\text{INC})}$ with correction: -0.3870INC_i. -0.1432INC_i^2; without correction: $-0.2999\text{INC}_i + 0.01\text{INC}_i^2$.

obtained from the regression analysis (defined in Equation (6)), we can find β_0 (in Equation (9)) and the coefficient estimates for the adjustment equation defined in Equation (4). Table 6 presents the corresponding adjustment coefficients for different levels of family income.[8]

These results show the importance of correcting for the underdeclared lottery expenditures: for a low-income family, the underdeclaration reaches 100 percent.[9] Table 6 also shows the income elasticities of money spent on lotteries relative to the family income. There are considerable downward biases in the income elasticities when underdeclared expenditures are not corrected for. As family income rises, the uncorrected income elasticities represent between 65 percent and a mere 19 percent of the corrected income elasticities. The corrected negative income elasticities seem to strongly support the model presented here.[10]

Conclusion

The preceding statistical analyses are useful not only because they enable the testing of the hypotheses advanced here, but also because they show a way to deal with problems of under- and overdeclarations of consumption patterns in surveys – if one has a model suggesting why people make such incorrect declarations. As mentioned, underdeclarations are typical when alcohol, tobacco, and gambling consumption are questioned. (Overdeclaration – bragging, that is – seems to be a problem when a person's sexual prowess is questioned.) But by using the relatively accurate data on the revenue side of these three industries, one can obtain better elasticity estimates.

The study also points to a more general problem concerning demand curves. We found few studies (an exception being Houthakker and Taylor 1970) that made attempts to contrast estimated total expenditures from survey data with the revenues of the respective sectors to check the reliability of the results. For many sectors, the lack of this step may not pose a major problem, as there is no reason to believe that people systematically under- or overdeclare spending on, say, bread or clothing. Still, if people significantly underdeclare expenditures on gambling, alcohol, and tobacco (not to mention expenditures on drugs, prostitutes, and offshore investments), they may consciously either declare more than they spend on legal items with a positive connotation or underdeclare income. Because expenditures on all items with a negative association, illegal or legal, are well into the tens of billions of dollars, there may be significant overdeclaration on ordinary items for which, a priori, one would have thought that only random errors existed. Thus, the problems dealt with in the last section may have broader implications for both future econometric analysis and the confidence one gives to elasticity estimates derived from aggregate sectorial data for unbiased items.

Notes

Chapter 1: From Religion to Risk Management

1. On usury, see the discussion in Brenner 1983, and also in later chapters herein. On opposition to financial markets, see Brenner 2002 and Chapters 4 and 5 of this book. The biblical condemnation refers to restrictions in a tight, close family in a relatively small society – where it makes sense. See the discussion in Brenner 1983, Chapters 2 and 3.
2. See Ezell 1960, p. 2; *Encyclopedia Judaica* 1971, "Lots," pp. 510–12; Bolen 1976, pp. 7–9.
3. Although nobody today knows exactly what the Urim and Thummim were, one interpretation is that they were two dice, one used for a positive answer and the other for a negative one. Huizinga (1955, pp. 7–9) mentions that the word "Urim" has affinities with a root that means "casting lots" and "shooting" as well as "justice, or law": *yore* means "shoot" and *thorah* refers to "law."
4. Even in our days, the selection of soldiers for the Vietnam War was made with the help of a government lottery (Blakey 1977, p. 656). By this means, superiors could avoid feeling responsible for the death of a soldier.
5. Drawing lots remained a decision-making tool for Jews in the first century, as can be seen from two cases reported by Flavius Josephus in *Jewish Wars*. When Josephus, a general of the rebellion against Rome, was defeated, he took refuge in the city of Jotapata, besieged then by Vespasian. Against Josephus's advice, the defenders considered mass suicide instead of capture. He convinced them to draw lots to kill one another instead because suicide is abhorrent to God (pp. 202–3). Josephus also reports the mass suicide of the defenders of Masada on the Dead Sea, the last remaining bastion of the rebellion against Rome. The defenders decided to kill themselves instead of falling into the hands of the enemies. After killing their families, they drew lots among themselves to choose ten who would kill the others. The ten then drew lots to choose one who would kill the others (Ch. 23). See *Encyclopaedia Judaica* 1971, pp. 510–12.
6. See Hasofer 1967. The quarrelsome nature of the priesthood reminds us of many petty quarrels in academia today.
7. Sumner and Keller 1927, vol. 3, pp. 2069–70; Caillois 1958, p. 231; Pryor 1977. Some writers (e.g., Lea, Tarpy, and Webley 1987) interpret this evidence as implying that

people played games of chance. Others have perceived the casting of dice and use of cards as instruments of religion and magic, yet they have still written that these acts were perceived as games of chance. See, for example, Martinez 1983, p. 14; Feinman, Blashek, and McCabe 1986, p. 3. Devereux (1980, App. A, pp. 1016–21) presents an argument similar to ours. He then writes that "to appeal a matter to chance, is to appeal directly to God, for he decides the outcome of chance events" (p. 1021). This argument is inappropriate because the notion of chance had no place in these systems of beliefs (see *Encyclopaedia Judaica* 1971, pp. 501–512). But the Mesopotamian idea is that gods and people are subjects to the fall of the lots (ibid.).

8. See Rosenthal 1975, p. 33.

9. See Rouse 1957, p. 16.

10. There is disagreement about what the biblical and Greek stories tell us. See the discussion on Cain and Abel in the concluding chapter. Vico, in his "New Science" (1982), argues that the stories are all metaphors and use a language that we no longer understand. See also Berlin 1976. R. Brenner (1983, 1985) discusses a number of examples.

11. Huizinga 1955, p. 94; supra note 2.

12. Cohen (1964, p. 199) notes that Tyche "was represented with a rudder to guide the ship of life, or with a ball and a wheel, or with Amalthea's horn of plenty," and she was often blindfolded, as was the goddess of justice, to suggest impartiality.

13. Rubner 1966, p. 15. Note that the word "luck" is only a rough equivalent of the Greek word *tyche. Tyche* does not necessarily refer to random or uncaused events, but what happens to a person as opposed to what he or she does or makes. See extensive discussions on this point in Nussbaum 1986, Ch. 11.

14. Suetonius (1961) mentions that Augustus created categories of magistrates who were chosen by lots. Moreover, the vestal virgins were chosen by lots among patrician girls.

15. Huizinga 1955, p. 57.

16. Wesley 1958–9, vol. 8, p. 451; Thomas 1971, p. 119. Some view the substitution of astrology for religious beliefs as a sign of cultural decline rather than mere substitution of one form of decision making for another. They argue that "man had previously understood in terms of what the poets, historians and philosophers had made him – a being not exempt from weakness and villainy, but yet versatile, adventurous, resourceful, enterprising, adaptable, aspiring and in great measure his own master. Now he had shrunk to being the puppet of the stars, whose relation to the powers that rule his destiny could be presented in a mathematical diagram" (Cohen 1964, p. 189). This complaint should sound familiar. The problems are not in using geometry or other branches of mathematics to check the consistency of arguments, but in using the mathematics of movements of planets, falling bodies, and chromosomes to describe people's behavior. Cohen (p. 173) notes that astrology has left its mark on the language: the word "consider" initially meant "contrasting the influence of the various stars" (*sidera*) on the "contemplated" decision, where "contemplation" means the construction of a diagram of the sky in quarters (*templum*). In Britain, 20 million people are estimated to read the daily horoscopes, and in France *Elle* claims to have the best such column (Cohen 1964, pp. 172–4). Also, Nancy Reagan's use of astrology became a cause célèbre during her husband's presidency.

17. See Cohen 1964, ch. 10, especially pp. 186–9. For discussion of chance and fate in Greek religion, see Murray 1955. For a brief discussion in a different context, see Brenner 1985, appendix to Ch. 1.

18. Quoted in Cohen 1964, p. 188.

19. Perkins 1958, p. 8, quoting W. Fowler. Cohen (1964, p. 199) remarks that of all the Roman deities, Fortuna seems to have been the most popular. Every marketplace had an altar in her honor, and in the Forum a splendid temple was dedicated to her. It was apparently the favored spot for women seeking to maintain their husband's attention.

20. Starkey 1964, p. 35.

21. See Thomas 1971; Cohen (1964, pp. 150–1) gives as an illustration the poem "Fortuna Imperatrix Mundi" ("Luck Rules the World"), written during the twelfth century (best known from Carl Orff's use of it in the cantata *Carmina Burana*). He also notes that in the sixteenth century when Montaigne, traveling in Italy, reached Rome, his books were returned with the warning "not to be too lavish of the word Fortuna where Providence would be more in place (p. 151, quoting *The Diary of Montaigne's Journey to Italy*).

22. See Franklin 2001 for evidence on how people tried to deal with risk before they came up with probability theory in the seventeenth century.

23. Mackay 1841, pp. 281–303; Eade 1984; Tester 1987, pp. 176–201.

24. See Brenner 1983 on sacred languages.

25. Mackay 1841, pp. 281–90; Eade 1984.

26. See Brenner's "Making Sense out of Nonsense," pp. 11–48, in Colander and Brenner 1992.

27. See the detailed discussion and reference in R. Brenner 1985 and 1994, Hutt 1979.

28. Followers of Thomas Kuhn cherish this view. See the discussion about this view, and a comparison of Kuhn's views with those of Karl Popper, in Brenner's "Making Sense out of Nonsense" in Colander and Brenner 1992.

29. See Brenner's "Making Sense out of Nonsense" in Colander and Brenner 1992, and Brenner 2002, Chapters 6 and 7.

30. Decisions cannot be independent if financial power is not dispersed.

31. We emphasize the word "independent" for a simple reason: if most funds flow through governments, which then redistribute them, opinions will not be independent, even if such countries put on the veil of democracy. Without democratized capital markets, democracy is a sham. See Brenner 2002 and Chapter 8 in this book for discussion and wide-ranging evidence.

32. See Lowenstein 2000 on LTCM.

33. Stone 1965; Stone 1972, p. 110; Goldstone 1986.

34. Plumb 1967, p. 5.

35. See Stone 1965, 1972; Plumb 1967; R. Brenner 1985, Ch. 3; Goldstone 1986.

36. Cochrane and Kirshner 1986, pp. 368–9. See also Thomas 1971, pp. 78–85. According to Thomas, Calvin pointed out that the perils of daily existence would have made life intolerable for people who believed that everything happened by chance and that they were subject to every caprice of fortune (p. 81).

37. Thomas 1971, p. 78.

38. Dunkley 1985, p. 86.

39. Ibid., p. 84.

40. According to Malcomson (1981, pp. 14–16), typical comments of social analysts during this period emphasized that social order was not a human construct, but divinely ordained: God, not humans, had created social inequality. "There is nothing more . . . certain, than that God Almighty hath ordained and appointed degrees of Authority and Subjection; allowing Authority to the Master, and commanding obedience from servants unto him," said one text in 1681. Inequality "is not by chance," reported another published in 1693. Texts written between 1708 and 1746 repeated the same ideas. The clergy and the relatively well-to-do wrote these texts, and as Thomas points out (1971, pp. 127–8, 198–206), they do not reflect poorer people's attitudes.
41. See also Malcolmson 1981, Ch. 4; Walvin 1978, p. 48.
42. That being their only way to access capital (except, perhaps, crime).
43. It is precisely this idea that some groups reject. Max Weber noted that religion has met a general need: "The fortunate is seldom satisfied with the fact of being fortunate. Beyond this, he needs to know that he has a *right* to his good fortune. He wants to be convinced that he 'deserves' it, and above all that he deserves it in comparison with others" (1946, p. 271; italics in original). Schoeck (1969) gives an alternative explanation about envy and the institutions invented to mitigate it. He concludes that the ability to provide hope and happiness for believers, either rich or poor, may be no more than the provision of ideas that free both the envious person from envy and the person envied from his sense of guilt and fear of the envious. See R. Brenner (1983, 1985) on these points, and R. Brenner (2002) on how democratizing financial markets solves many of these problems.
44. Rosenthal 1975, p. 159.
45. Such successes strengthen people's beliefs that the model of society they have bet on must be the "right" one. See McNeill 1963, pp. 461–6. For implications of how people learn what might be good models of society, see Brenner 2002, 2006.

Chapter 2: Anything Wrong with Gambling as a Pastime?

1. Some ideas might be valid. The problem is that they survive long after the circumstances in which they arose disappeared. See R. Brenner 1983, 1985, and 2002 for examples.
2. The Greeks believed that Palamedes invented dice and played with his fellow soldiers to relieve boredom during the ten-year siege of Troy. Gambling remained popular entertainment in ancient Greece and in ancient Rome too: at the Circus, the emperors threw down numbered pieces of parchment, and winning numbers represented a claim on prizes. Heavy betting also took place at the chariot races.
3. Blakey 1977, pp. 4–5. Dunkley (1985) mentions an even earlier statute of Charles V of France, dated March 15, 1369, which advocates archery but prohibits dice and gambling (p. 37).
4. Ibid., pp. 5–7; Sasuly 1982, Ch. 1.
5. Malcolmson 1973, p. 5; Blakey 1977, p. 6; Sasuly 1982, p. 37.
6. See R. Brenner 1987, especici/ally Ch. 7.
7. Blakey 1977, ch. 2. Blakey also remarks that the origin of some opposition may have been economic envy: "During their struggle for spiritual reform in England, the Puritans developed a deep scorn for the lifestyles of those who opposed them.

Economic envy was probably intertwined with the contempt, for the Puritans were originally drawn from the lower and middle classes" (p. 43). See Appendix 1 on envy and R. Brenner (1983, 1985) on the type of acts this sentiment leads to, and how words are invented to disguise the sentiment.

8. The Quran too repeatedly states: "They ask thee concerning liquor and gambling [*maysir*]. Tell them: There is great harm in both and also some profit for people, but their harm is greater than their profit" (2:220). "O, ye who believe, liquor and gambling [*maysir*], idols and divining arrows are but abominations and satanic devices. So turn wholly away from each of them that you may prosper. Satan desires only to create enmity and hatred between you by means of liquor and gambling and to keep you back from remembrance of Allah and from Prayer" (5:91–3).

9. Ch. 17, Massachusetts Province Laws 1736–7, as quoted in Blakey 1977, p. 48.

10. Miers and Dixon 1979, p. 377.

11. In China gambling was often banned or severely restricted for the same reason. Lam (2005) reports that Chinese emperors believed that gambling could create serious social problems.

12. On crime rates when customs break down, and on social instability in general and during the Industrial Revolution, see R. Brenner 1985, Ch. 3. On gambling and leisure in this context, see also Bloch 1951. He remarks that gamblers are condemned for their failure to perform the normal productive functions ordinarily expected of them, and that leisure may be respectably enjoyed only when work is put first (p. 215).

13. As during Purim, in Jewish tradition, when drinking, dressing up, and gambling are allowed.

14. See Malcolmson 1973, 1981; Bailey 1978; Walvin 1978; and Cunningham 1980, who give detailed accounts of popular recreations during the eighteenth and nineteenth centuries and contrast them with recreations of earlier times. On rites related to gambling in other societies, see Geertz's (1973) chapter on Balinese cockfights, pp. 412–15.

15. Dunkley (1985) reports a decision of a French court in 1708 that condemned peasants who, attracted by gambling gains, lost considerable sums when they could not pay their taxes (p. 27).

16. See Hacking 1990.

17. Quoted in Read 1979, pp. 107–8. See also Walvin 1978, p. 6; Cunningham 1980, pp. 58–62.

18. Josiah Tucker, *Six Sermons on Important Subjects* (1772), quoted in Malcolmson 1973, pp. 92–3.

19. See Walvin 1978 and Elias 1986 on the changing attitudes.

20. Quoted in Cunningham 1980, p. 46. See also Walvin 1978, Ch. 1.

21. Cunningham 1980, p. 17. See also Harrison 1964. Harrison quotes W. Howitt's claim in 1838 that the decline in brutal sports represented a "mighty revolution" in popular pastimes and summarizes the process underlying the decline. Urbanization deprived working people of space, and mechanization deprived them of physical exercise during working hours. The substitutes, by codifying sporting rules and regulating games of uncertain duration, saved time. See also Harrison 1971, pp. 330–1.

22. Cunningham 1980, p. 19.

23. Statistics in general were a great obsession of the times in France, England, and Germany, though there was a difference in how the countries used statistics. Germany

used them for the state to get a better handle on people, whereas in the other two countries their purpose was to define what was normal, for example by providing details on deviant behavior, suicide, and various illnesses.

24. See the next chapter and Appendix 1 on "leapfrogging."
25. The information on drinking draws on the work of Harrison 1971 and Walvin 1978.
26. Some who like boxing today would probably consider cockfighting cruel.
27. A selection of these articles is reprinted in Razzell and Wainwright 1973.
28. Ibid, pp. 9–10.
29. Malcolmson 1973, p. 104. See also Harrison 1971, pp. 321–6.
30. Harrison 1971, p. 50.
31. See discussion in Malcolmson 1973, Ch. 5, especially p. 87.
32. Malcolmson 1973; Lee 1976; Bailey 1978; Walvin 1978; Read 1979; Cunningham 1980.
33. Harrison (1971, p. 300) notes that railways promoters, coffeehouse keepers, dancing halls, promoters of new sporting events, and promoters of tea and soft drinks (e.g., the Schweppes) offered some of the slowly emerging alternatives.
34. Cunningham 1980, p. 180. After 1885 church attendance as a proportion of the population was still declining (Read 1979, p. 265).
35. See Malcolmson 1973, ch. 6; Cunningham 1980. The attacks, as noted, always had their class undertones. Harrison remarks that "eyes accustomed to the very different class relations of the mid-twentieth century may see in organizations like the temperance movements' mere attempts to impose middle-class manners on the working class" (1971, p. 24). But he shows that this is not accurate. Elite working men helped the temperance movement, and the movement was a source of reliable men for key factory posts (p. 96). Harrison also notes: "In the early Victorian period, the teetotalers and prohibitionists directed attention away from the other-worldly paradise toward an earthly utopia" (p. 31). The temperance movement tried to change people's attitude toward diet and viewed poverty as a result of mistaken ways of spending. McKibbin remarks that "the whole edifice of working-class thrift was, in fact, built up on burial insurance . . . , a . . . saving that consumed up to 10 percent of a household budget" (1979, p. 161). Part of that amount was spent on drinking during rituals of death, a custom the temperance movement attacked too (Harrison 1971, p. 93).
36. Quoted in Malcolmson 1973, p. 97. It is more likely that such views reflected extrapolations of the nobility, who, as Barnhart (1983, p. 25) points out, were in the grasp of "gambling mania that captured England after the Restoration of Charles II in 1660." He notes that the mania "reached its peak in 1745." One reason was that during the nobility's exile in France they saw the profligate gambling at King Louis XIV's court, a major entertainment there, though of little consequence because the courtiers were playing among themselves, assured of their position at the court.
37. Harrison too concludes that "most drunkenness in nineteenth century England resulted from a social situation; teetotalers, by treating it as though it were compulsive or addictive, were usually on the wrong track" (1971, p. 355). Whereas legislation concerning drinking was, in part, based on inaccurate information about people's social requirements (as Harrison notes on p. 380), so were other laws. Housing laws, for example, arose not only from bad housing, but also from a desire to prevent

sexual promiscuity. Public supervision of the water supply sprang largely from the desire to curb drunkenness (Harrison 1971, p. 207). Read too asks, "Did drinking cause poverty, or was poverty a cause of drinking?" and concludes, "many middle-class commentators, too readily accepted that drunkenness was the main, even the sole, cause of poverty" (1979, p. 112). Booth's London survey found that only 13 percent of the poor and 14 percent of the very poor owed their misfortune directly to drink. Illness, unemployment, and family size were the main causes of working-class poverty (p. 112).

38. In principle, people can lose money quickly in gambling, but this happened to a tiny minority. See discussion in Chapters 3 and 5.

39. Dixon 1980a, pp. 111–12.

40. Quoted in Dixon 1980a, p. 112.

41. Walvin 1978, Ch. 5; Read 1979, pp. 228–32. The slump in the 1880s was not linked to the significant fall in birthrate in the 1860s; see Read 1979, p. 383, on the demographic changes.

42. Read 1979, pp. 228–32, 300–2; Dixon 1980a, pp. 111–17; Dixon 1991, pp. 53–63.

43. Read 1979, p. 300.

44. See Read 1979, pp. 228–32, on the appearance of the term "technical education."

45. Dixon 1980a, pp. 112–13.

46. Quoted in ibid., p. 112.

47. They did pay attention to the tariffs imposed in other countries. See Read 1979, pp. 228–35.

48. Dixon remarks that "anti-gambling writers came to regard their attack on working class betting as a crusade to save England from economic and social disaster, to maintain political stability, to preserve the Empire, even to halt the degeneration of the English race and so to defend civilization" (1980a, p. 117).

49. But gambling and drinking were linked in people's minds. "In the view of some commentators, gambling was not only as bad or worse than drink: it was 'one of the forcing-beds of intemperance itself' (Chamberlain 1890, p. 20) . . . It was also a worse evil: drunkenness 'destroys the individual and his family' by slow degrees, but gambling may wreck the whole family " (Hawke 1894, p. 711).

50. See Dixon 1981a, p. 29, and Harrison 1971, who remarks that "the drink interest in the 1820s was allied with the powerful agricultural interests: this helps to explain the temperance reformer's political impotence in the 1830s; and the regional variations in the support for this movement" (p. 57). Read (1979, p. 111) notes that the 1871 licensing bill provoked opposition from the drink interest and was withdrawn, and another was defeated in 1872. On the events surrounding the lack of success in prohibiting horse racing, see Blakey 1977; Dixon 1981a, 1991, Ch. 3.

51. See Ogle 2006.

52. Wheeler developed what is referred to as pressure politics, which today is called Wheelerism. See http://en.wikipedia.org/wiki/Wayne˙Wheeler.

53. Dixon 1980a; 1981a,b; 1991. On the Labor Party's reaction in Australia, see O'Hara, 1987.

54. Robert Slaney, as quoted in Cunningham 1980, p. 184.

55. Cunningham 1980, p. 184.

56. Dixon (1980a) concludes that "in political terms, the 1906 Act can be seen as a restatement of who (and whose values) ruled the country" (p. 109). "Gambling and

socialism are linked in Seton Churchill's influential *Betting and Gambling*, 1894" (p. 110).

57. See discussion and sources in R. Brenner 1985.

58. At this point, one may raise the following question: why prohibit gambling rather than regulate it? According to Dixon, the British were unfamiliar with administrative law. An influential writer on the topic was A. V. Dicey, who wrote: "'In many continental countries, and notably in France, there exists a scheme of administrative law . . . which rests on ideas foreign to the fundamental assumptions of our English common law, and especially to . . . the rule of law' . . . Dicey was . . . out of date, but his work was . . . influential and blighted legal thought about State administration for decades . . . The lack of discussion of administrative methods of control meant that regulation of betting by the use of licensing and registration was not regarded as a viable option by a tradition-bound Home Office, despite the inevitable comparison to the growing administrative regulation of drink. Their tool was criminal law" (1981a, p. 27).

59. See Rubner 1966, pp. 14–17.

60. Dixon 1981a, pp. 61–2. On additional legal angles, see Street 1937.

61. Quoted in Dixon 1980a, p. 124.

62. Ch. 17, Massachusetts Province Law 1736–7, as quoted in Blakey 1977, p. 48.

63. Quoted in Devereux 1980, p. 175. For other Depression-era opinions, see Deveneux 1980, pp. 170–212.

64. Blakey 1977, pp. 111–27.

65. See Stendhal 1970.

66. Ibid. Barbaja was the entrepreneur who installed gaming tables first in La Scala, then at opera houses in Naples and Palermo.

67. David (2006, p. 580) points out, "The opera house provided the only form of public entertainment available to wealthy and educated Italians. Since the end of the eighteenth century, even meetings in private houses required police permission if more than a dozen people were involved." This rendered opera houses suspect to the police, and they were always under police surveillance.

68. See Schwartz 2006, pp. 483–484, for a description of the changes in Las Vegas in entertainment.

69. See Calder 2001, Brenner 2002. The argument here is similar to arguments made about properly structured leveraged buyouts for companies.

Chapter 3: Are You Rich?

1. The formal translation of these arguments is in Appendix 1 and implications about human nature in Appendix 2. The broader implications of this view are examined in R. Brenner 1983, 1985, 1987, and 2002.

2. This instinct, combined with Adam Smith's instinct for trading and bartering, explains the wealth of nations when combined with access to capital markets. All societies, even those that remain poor, traded and bartered. But only those developing institutions to allow for financial markets prospered. See R. Brenner 1983 and 2002.

3. See R. Brenner 1983, 1985, 1994 and 2002.

4. Although the approach does not fit into economists' orthodox, standard framework based on risk aversion (see the detailed discussion in Appendix 1).

5. See Friedman and Savage 1948; Markowitz 1952; Alchian 1953; Arrow 1970; Schoemaker 1982. The late Milton Friedman admitted that whereas in his 1948 article with Savage they used the existence of multiple prizes to rationalize the upper concave section of the utility function, they subsequently came to the conclusion that it was not a valid rationalization. Most recent articles about risk-taking either make slight mathematical variations on the traditional approach or carry out laboratory experiments. See the collection of articles in Kahneman, Slovic, and Tversky 1982; Arkes and Hammond 1986; and Hogarth and Reder 1986. The value of laboratory experiments in explaining behavior in circumstances with large sums at stake is questionable in light of the model and evidence presented in this chapter and Appendix 1. See also Cohen 1964, p. 61, on this point. Zeckhauser (1986, p. 260) also notes that economists have not succeeded in shedding light on gambling.
6. Freud 1929.
7. For a summary of psychological interpretations that still rely on Freud's initial insight, see Kusyszyn 1984; Lea, Tarpy, and Webley 1987. On compulsive gamblers, see Bergler 1957; Herman 1967ab; Lea et al. 1987; for a different view, see Dixon 1980b.
8. Friedman and Savage (1948), however, suggest that the poor may have greater incentives to gamble, but they do not translate their argument to the mathematics of their model.
9. On nonconventional avenues of social mobility, see Devereux 1980; Tec 1964. See also R. Brenner 1983, Chs. 1 and 2. Frey notes what Downes et al. (1976) remarked, namely, "the absence of any hypotheses, much less any interrelated propositions about gambling behavior that could be designated a theory. Thus, several quasi-theories or propositions about anomie, alienation, working-class culture, functionalism, decision-making, risk-taking, work-centered leisure, and home centeredness were tested by Downes and his associates" (1984, p. 118). For various approaches, see also Newman 1972; Lester 1979.
10. See Appendix 1.
11. See R. Brenner 1983, 1985, and 1987.
12. See references in R. Brenner 1985, Ch. 2.
13. The statistical appendix was done with Claude Montmarquette.
14. Weinstein and Deitch 1974, p. 36. See also Desperts 1982, emphasizing that in France it was always the large draw that provided the attraction.
15. Sullivan 1972, p. 111. See also Cohen 1964, p. 48, on the preference for fewer but larger prizes.
16. Commission on the Review of the National Policy toward Gambling 1976, p. 157; Landau 1968, p. 34. Such findings are also reported in Kallick et al. 1979. Koeves also notes that "the real love of the South American masses remains the lottery. In Mexico, special drawings reward the winner with $250,000 and Argentina's Christmas Special dishes out the grand total of $1,500,000. One of the most familiar sights in the streets of South America are the street vendors offering tickets . . . consisting of old men in rags, barefoot kids, or cripples. Some of the vendors make the rounds and shout out their numbers at the crack of dawn, hoping that a particular purchaser has dreamed about that particular number" (1952, pp. 57–8).
17. Rubner 1966, pp. 17, 45. He notes that the pronounced preference of the public for big prizes can best be studied by comparing investments in football fixed-odds and treble-chance pools; the former, with relatively small prizes, is more akin to betting,

whereas the latter is but a modified lottery with high prizes. More than four out of five investors in 1965–6 preferred the treble chance, and the football-pool promoters were so convinced of the relative attractiveness of the large prizes that they enhanced them at the expense of the lower dividends (pp. 45–6).

18. Of respondents, 58 percent in Cameroon and 54 percent in Senegal reported that they would play more if the prize were bigger. See Brenner, Lipeb and Servet 1996.

19. Already in the seventeenth and eighteenth centuries, observers noted the attraction of big prizes. Murphy (2005) remarked that the prospect of riches was the powerful incentive for those centuries' players. See also Gigerenzer et al. 1989.

20. Sprowls 1954, p. 354.

21. Commission on the Review of National Policy 1976, p. 163. Native American tribes have introduced bingo games with very high stakes. These games are different from traditional ones and are similar to lotteries.

22. Sprowls 1970, p. 82. Garrett and Sobel (2004) found that the size of the top prize and the chance of winning it offers incentives to buy, whereas small prizes do not.

23. See Appendix 1 on leapfrogging, and Appendix 2.

24. See also Lea et al. 1987.

25. A similar picture emerges from Spiro's study (1974).

26. Newman 1972, p. 85. Newman takes into account the varying retention rates in different gambling activities. From the £1.497 million ($3.548 million) turnover in 1964, he arrives at net expenditures of £269 million ($637 million), with the average annual net expenditure for each Briton a mere £4,85 ($11.50), less than the cost of a packet of cigarettes a week. Kinsey (1963) draws a similar picture. He estimates that in 1950 even those who played at least once a week spent an annual total of $140 on dog-race wagers, $14 on football pools, and $28 on off-track betting on horse races. The percentages of adults who gambled frequently on the three games were, respectively, 1, 28, and 11.

27. This reversal should be expected. Unlike a lottery, a casino takes up the gambler's time. Unsurprisingly, Newman also found that betting shops are concentrated in districts inhabited mostly by people belonging to the lower manual-labor classes (1972, p. 99). On alternatives to time spent gambling, Grussi mentions that in ancient regime France, jealous husbands encouraged their wives' gambling to prevent dalliance (1985, p. 115).

28. Sturz 1988.

29. Rubner notes that frequently one hears that lotteries and sweepstakes are wicked because they depend on chance, whereas sports betting ought to be permitted because it depends, to some extent, on knowledge (1966, pp. 3–5). These arguments are misguided, as Rubner pointed out. During a cold spell at the beginning of 1963, football matches could not be played for several consecutive weeks. But national football was played in playacting sessions on televisions, with prominent figures guessing what the results would have been had the matches been played. He concludes that "national football as an instrument permitting gambling to take place during ice and snow is commendable, but it also exposes the hollowness of the claim that filling out a football coupon calls for substantially more skill than picking a lottery ticket out of a hat" (p. 4). See also Cohen and Hansel 1956, p. 142.

30. Walker 2007.

31. Tec 1964.

32. Sources can be found in R. Brenner 1983. It should have been noted that for the sample to be unbiased, the number of tickets bought should have been taken into account. We did not have that information.

33. This enables us to reject the possibility that the winners are an unbiased sample of the general population (at the 2 percent level).

34. Kaplan et al. (1979) undertook this survey for Loto-Canada.

35. The hypothesis that, but for statistical error, the proportions among the younger and older are the same may be rejected at the 5 percent and 10 percent significance level, respectively. This test is based on a comparison of the percentage of the people among the winner's sample and in the general population. A draw of a young winner in the general population is a random variable with binomial distribution. As the sample is large for statistical purposes (more than forty), we assume that this variable has a normal distribution and test the hypothesis that the two proportions are the same.

36. The sample included winners of C$1 million and more in Ontario, C$100,000 and more in Quebec, and C$50,000 or more in the other provinces. Thus, it is not exactly a random sample of lottery winners or of the lottery-ticket-buying population. However, if there is bias, its direction is not clear. We assume that the sample is random.

37. In a 1984 survey of lottery winners in the United States, including 576 winners in twelve states, Kaplan found that "prior to winning, [the] respondents' incomes were clustered in the *lower* range with 69 percent of the winners and 75 percent of their spouses earning less than $20,000 a year" (1985a, p. 10). In a later study of this same data set, he also found that the average age of winners was slightly greater than fifty-four (1985b). A 1984 Loto-Québec survey also found that people in the age group of thirty-five to sixty-four were much more likely to be regular lottery-ticket buyers.

38. The falling behind may also be due to a legal rule that forbids one from seizing the existing opportunities. Dunkley (1985) quotes the French historian Lavise, who attributed the prevalence of gambling among nobility in France at the time of Louis XIV to the fact that the resources of many aristocrats were too limited to finance the standard of living that their social status demanded. Since the fifteenth century, French nobility were forbidden to engage in trade or business. So the only way they could not fall behind was to gamble (pp. 20–1). If they lost, they went to Louis's court.

39. Robert Sylvestre Marketing 1977, Vol. 4, Tables 1–5, Series 9.

40. R. Brenner 1985, Table 2.5, p. 62.

41. Devereux 1980, p. 807.

42. In an article in the *Wall Street Journal*, Ronald Alsop (1983) gives examples of unemployed workers who, in the midst of a recession, saw the lottery as their last hope. One of them said of his weekly bet: "The way things are now, I've got to try something." Li and Smith also found, in their 1976 study of a 1971 Gallup survey of attitudes toward gambling, a statistical link between frustrated expectations and propensity to gamble.

43. Campbell and Converse 1972, pp. 172–3.

44. See Royal Commission on Bilingualism and Biculturalism 1967, Vol. 3, p. 21; Kuch and Haessel 1979; Vaillancourt 1979; Lacroix and Vaillancourt 1981.

45. See Tec 1964, p. 93.

46. Dunstan (1997) summarizes research on gamblers and concludes that Catholics were more likely to gamble than Protestants and other religious groups and less likely to disapprove of gambling than other religious groups.

47. Tomes (1983, p. 129) found that male Catholics earn 7 percent less and Protestants 6 percent more than the mean income of his sample.

48. These numbers are from the 1976 Canadian census.

49. These estimates were calculated using the weights given by Statistics Canada, which reflect the different rates of response among regions, family unit interviewed, and so forth.

50. In 1985 the revenues of the various lotteries in Canada exceeded US$2 billion dollars, and it has been estimated that Americans spend $200 million annually on Canadian lotteries. See *Wall Street Journal* 1986.

51. Although this explanation may be plausible for some countries, it might not be for others where lottery winnings are not taxed (e.g., Canada). Underdeclarations of lottery expenditures seem to be a universal phenomenon (see Rubner 1966, p. 123). In fact, another notable property of the data set comes to the fore when we look at the answers to the question of whether people spent any money on lotteries. In 1982 40 percent in the Atlantic Provinces and 26.5 percent in western Canada said they never bought lottery tickets. But penetration studies of Loto-Québec found that in 1984, 84 percent of Quebecers bought such tickets and 92 percent admitted to having bought them at least once in their life. (These numbers were given to the authors privately by Loto-Québec.) In the end, people answered the Statistics Canada survey misleadingly either on purpose or inadvertently. Considering that a large proportion of the population in the Atlantic Provinces receives welfare and other benefits, the reluctance to acknowledge spending on lotteries is not surprising.

52. Another explanation may be that a person may not reveal to his or her partner that he or she spends a few dollars a week on lotteries.

53. McKibbin 1979.

54. Ibid.

55. Rubner 1966, p. 123; for comments on studies based on surveys, see Glock 1967, p. 249, and Moser and Kalton 1972, pp. 379, 389–90, neither of which suggests solutions to correct the error.

56. Dixon notes that "the lack of officially collected information on gambling seriously hampered constructive discussions about gambling in Britain down to the Rothschild Commission which concluded, in 1978, that 'there is a serious shortage of reliable and accessible information about participation in the various forms of gambling, how the gambling industry works. How much is staked and spent, and how much excessive gambling there is, is markedly lacking'" (1981a, p. 26).

57. See Brenner and Brenner 1990, section 3 in the appendix.

58. Commission on the Review of the National Policy, p. 68.

59. Gallup 1972; Cornish 1978, p. 39.

60. Smith and Razzel 1975; Downes et al. 1976.

61. Devereux 1980, p. 827.

62. Downes et al. 1976.

63. Newman 1975, p. 543; see also Newman 1972.

64. Newman, like Tec (1964), found that "a possible change in life situation was conceived only in terms of higher income ... A noticeably more aspiring attitude seemed to prevail amongst 'the gamblers,' expressed in greater preoccupation with pay issues, with acquisition of consumer goods and ... budget awareness, a determination to make optimal use of one's financial resources" (1972, p. 223). Herman (1967b) is also struck by the evidence of careful deliberations and disciplined composure on the part of racecourse attendees.

65. Tec 1964.

66. See summary of Kusyszyn's work in Skolnick 1982.

67. Weinstein and Deitsch 1974. See Lea et al. 1987 for a summary of similar evidence.

68. Royal Commission on Betting, Lotteries, and Gaming 1951, pp. 40, 49–50, 53.

69. Ibid., p. 52. The report also adds that, though the authors do not doubt some connection between dishonesty and excessive gambling among people of a generally dissolute character, they cannot regard this as evidence that gambling, in itself, causes crime. The authors also could not find evidence to support the view that gambling causes juvenile delinquency. For parts of the report referring to these issues, see Marx 1952, pp. 195–207.

70. Rowntree 1901, p. 144, quoted in Dixon 1981a, p. 10.

71. See U.S. Department of Treasury 1999.

72. Allen 1952; Tec 1964.

73. Cornish 1978, p. 68.

74. See Promus Companies Incorporated 1994.

75. Campbell (1976) quotes Schragg's conclusion here. Newman also concludes that "gambling constitutes for the overwhelming majority of participants, a pastime rather than an addiction. Both frequency of participation, as well as volume of expenditure appears to be moderate, and subject to personal self-direction and control. For no more than a small and numerically insignificant minority can gambling ... be regarded as unmanageable and obsessive" (1972, p. 226). But Perkins wrote: "[gambling] is the easy, but mistaken reaction to risk, and is retrogressive rather than progressive in its effects ... Gambling is the stay-at-home, squalid, imaginary, mechanical, anaemic, and unlovely adventure of those who have never been able to encounter or create the real, necessary, and salutary adventure of life" (1950, pp. 34–5). This may be true, but not everyone is an adventurer. Some prefer to daydream for $1 a week.

76. Note, though, that financial institutions often charge large fees for principal-protected notes, and only the after-fee capital is protected.

77. See Kaplan, 1978 and 1985a.

78. Kaplan, 1985a, pp. 6, 8, 16–17.

79. According to Kaplan (1978), among the winners of relatively big prizes (more than $250,000) the quarterly, average expenditure on lottery tickets before winning was $67. After winning, this amount increased to $100. This increase implies a decrease in the percentage of the wealth dedicated to the purchase of lottery tickets, when $\frac{67}{W} \geq \frac{100}{W+250,000}$, where W is the individual's initial wealth. For this condition to be fulfilled, the initial wealth had to be less than $500,000. The characteristics of the winners fulfill this condition.

80. Lindh and Ohlsson (1996) do not include age of players in their statistical examination. Nor do they raise the question of whether the turn to self-employment is

a fiscal gimmick to save on taxes by incorporating. They find that receiving a lottery prize increases the probability of self-employment from 0.074 to 0.114, whereas receiving inheritance increases the probability to 0.094 (see p. 1518). Their objective was to determine whether liquidity constraints prevent entrepreneurship rather than anything related to gambling or risk-taking.

81. Rubner 1966, p. 25.
82. Devereux 1980, p. 785.
83. Guttman (1986) remarks that Andrew Carnegie was in favor of taxing inheritance: he believed that a parent who leaves enormous wealth to children generally deadens their talents and energies and tempts them to lead less useful lives than they otherwise would.
84. A similar conclusion is reached in Lea et al. 1987.
85. There also are the James Bond movies, where Bond displays his mental alertness and moral superiority either in a casino (*Casino Royale*) or in a card game (*Goldfinger*). True, these movies are fantasies and are about risk-takers with generous bank accounts, whereas the other movies mentioned in the text are about ordinary people trying to manage their lives.
86. See Nabokov 1981. Bolen (1976, p. 10) quotes P. C. Squires's study "Fyodor Dostoyevsky: A Psychological Sketch" (*Psychoanalysis Review*, 24 [1935]), which made a similar point. Squires also concluded that Dostoyevsky's intemperate gambling was an artistic necessity and that it was during the period after he lost everything that the creative spirit moved him with renewed force.
87. See *Diagnostic and Statistical Manual* (DSM–III).
88. There may be a few who commit suicide, but the numbers seem negligible – painful as each such case is for all concerned. Reckless living may also lead to reckless driving, and likely death, even if this is not classified as suicide.
89. Excluding suicide, as mentioned in note 88.
90. In developing countries, state lottery officials admit that they consciously appeal to the poorer strata of the population. In Mexico a state lottery in which the top prize is US$2 million has existed for 203 years, and when a wealthy person wins – a rare occurrence – lottery players and officials alike are dismayed. Foster notes that in traditional peasant societies "modern lotteries are ... functional equivalents of buried treasure tales ... One elderly informant, when asked why no one has found buried treasures in recent years, remarked that this was indeed true but 'Today we Mexicans have lotteries instead' ... The man who goes without lunch, and fails to buy shoes for his children in order to buy a weekly ticket, is not a ne'er-do-well; he is the Horatio Alger of his society who is doing what he feels is most likely to advance his position ... The odds are against him, but it is the *only* way he knows in which to work toward success" (1967, p. 318; italics in original). In December 1984, a humble home for the elderly and a Spanish emigrant to Australia received the big prizes in Spain's Christmas lottery. Lottery officials were quoted as saying that the big prize ("El Gordo," or "the Fat One") breeds a spirit of generosity and that Spaniards are happiest when the piece is shared or goes to the poor. The same month, Claude Carpentier, a forty-eight-year-old electrician who had been unemployed for four years, won C$4 million in the Lotto 6/49 draw (*Montreal Gazette*, Dec. 23, 1984). A retired truck driver who died of cancer six months later won Canada's largest lottery prize, C$13.9 million, in January 1984.

Chapter 4: Betting on Futures and Creating Prices

1. There has been fraud in financial markets, as in all others. And there have been many innovative financial instruments used either by incompetent people or within organizations where there was no accountability. Think about Barings Bank, which collapsed in 1995 after it was unable to meet its cash requirements following unauthorized speculative trading in derivatives at its Singapore office by Nick Leeson. The issue was not financial instruments, but lack of accountability and bad organization within Barings.
2. See extensive discussions and references on these points in Brenner 1983, Chs. 2 and 3, and Thomas 1971, especially pp. 662–80.
3. State usury laws are enforceable through civil suits filed by debtors who claim excessive interest charges. Commercial credit in most states is exempt from usury statutes; agricultural credit is unregulated but not exempt from state interest rate controls.
4. See Brenner 2002 For the types of problems solved there, five sources of capital were used, because one category was separated in two distinct ones.
5. See Brenner 2002, for an exploration of implications of this starting point.
6. See Brenner 1994, Ch. 3.
7. See Brenner 1994 and 2002.
8. Jacoby 1952, p. 19; Perkins, 1950, p. 56; Sasuly 1982, p. 41.
9. See Favier 1987 and 1998.
10. See Favier 1991; See Briys and Varenne 2000 for a discussion of this Genoese case in another context.
11. See Daston 1987, p. 247. Such reluctance led to mispricing. The implicit distinction is between risk and uncertainty. See Brenner 1983 for a discussion of Frank Knight's views and a sharp distinction between the two notions. Appendix 1 also discusses these two notions briefly.
12. See Noonan 1957 and Brenner 1983, Ch. 3 on usury, the origins of the word "interest," and changing attitudes toward lending money. Ayres pointed out that forbidding banking and the medieval principle of the just prize froze "the orders of society in proportions they assumed in the Middle Ages. What was interdicted was neither commerce, nor wealth but the increase of commerce at the expense of feudal powers" (1944, p. 28).
13. Daston 1987, p. 256n9.
14. Ibid.
15. See Zelizer 1979, pp. 45–6, 73.
16. See also Bernstein 1996, Ch. 5, on the development of insurance companies.
17. See Brenner 1983, Chs. 1, 2, and 4, on discussion and evidence.
18. Thomas 1971, p. 659.
19. See Garber 1989 and 2000; Day 2004a, 2004b, and 2006.
20. See also Brenner 1983, on why people would take more risks in general under such circumstances. See also Garber 2000.
21. See Garber 2000; Day 2004a, 2004b, and 2006.
22. See Brenner 1994, Ch. 3.
23. Daston 1987, p. 249.
24. See Hacking 1990, p. 49.
25. Daston 1987, p. 248.

26. Ibid. 1987, p. 253. The point made in this paragraph is linked with Coase 1937. He argued that the basic issue concerning firms that is worth investigating is their origin. As argued in Appendix 1, one implication of the model was that testing should be linked with an investigation of the origins of some institutions. Another point worth repeating is one made in R. Brenner 1983, 1985, and 1987, namely, one cannot separate economic issues from others. The fact that insurance companies were a substitute for roles played by witches and beliefs in magic makes this point clear.

27. Daston 1987, p. 253.

28. Boyle 1921, pp. 182–96.

29. Blakey 1977, p. 98; Labys and Granger 1970, pp. 2–6. MacDougall (1936), himself confused, quotes a large number of confused legal decisions. See also Street 1937, for discussions of legal problems in the United Kingdom.

30. Blakey 1977, pp. 342–3.

31. Quoted in ibid, pp. 393–4.

32. See Teweles, Harlow, and Stone 1969, pp. 6–7.

33. Quoted in ibid., p. 6.

34. Quoted in ibid., p. 7.

35. Note that cases arriving before the courts were brought up by people who did not want to pay their debts.

36. John T. Flynn, *Security Speculation*, as quoted in MacDougall 1936, p. 69.

37. *Albers v. Lamson*, 42 N.E. 2d 627, 639 (Ill. 1942), as quoted in Kreitner 2000, p. 22.

38. Hieronymus 1971, p. 286. He also remarks that the seasonal variation in onion prices during the period of active futures trading was approximately equal to the cost of storing onions from harvest to spring, and that "from these things it follows that the more the risks that are assumed and financed by speculators, the lower will be the cost associated with the commodity processes" (p. 287). See also Teweles et al. 1969.

39. Boyle (1921) found similar evidence when he compared fluctuations in the price of wheat before futures trading was started with fluctuations afterward (though other factors must be allowed in this case). In the 1890s farmers passed a resolution condemning futures trading in wheat on the grounds that it lowered the price of wheat. Three weeks later, five hundred members of the National Association of American Millers passed a resolution condemning futures trading on the grounds that it raised the price of wheat. The correlation between the accusations and the groups' interests are evident.

40. Betting associated with polities have a long history. Seventeenth-century English wagers on the progress of conflict during wartime were used to hedge risks of overseas trade. See Scott 1910, p. 383, and Murphy 2005.

41. See Fisher 1924, p. 348

42. See Mackay 1841, p. 1.

43. See exploration of this view in R. Brenner 1983, 1985, and 2002. This view underlies the analyses in this book, as the discussions on sources of capital in the various chapters show.

44. See Whitaker, Clifton, and Foote 1987, p. 29.

45. *Wall Street Journal*, "Notable and Quotable," October 20, 1988.

46. See Mulherin, Netter, and Overdahl 1991, p. 606.

47. See Hochfelder 2001 and 2006.
48. Hochfelder 2006. This decade saw deflation of roughly 20 percent, as measured by the wholesale price index.
49. See Hochfelder 2006.
50. Western Union, for instance, paid the New York Stock Exchange and the Chicago Board of Trade from $50,000 to $100,000 for the right to send their quotations.
51. The bucket shops subsequently lost a string of cases concerning quotations on other exchanges after the 1905 decision. See Mulherin, Netter, and Overdahl 1991, pp. 623–4.
52. Perkins (1999) claims that this figure is too high. In a private communication with the authors, Hochfelder said he based his numbers on the work of Warshow (1924), though other estimates differ. Berle and Means (1968, p. 334, Appendix K) estimate that in 1927 there were between 4 million and 6 million individual shareholders, even though the total number of book shareholders was on the order of 14 million. The duplication happens because a shareholder might own stock in a number of companies and show up on the books in separate entries.
53. See Murphy 2005, p. 242.
54. See Ashton 1898, p. 275.
55. See R. Brenner 1983 and 1985, and Appendix 1 on leapfrogging.
56. Friedman 1969, p. 286.
57. Fisher 1924, p. 347; see also Teweles et al., 1969, p. 406.
58. Miers and Dixon (1979) note: "respectability had to be acquired by a commercial world too closely associated with the problems of gambling. In the eighteenth century it was not only that stockholders sold lottery tickets along with shares; their whole business was regarded as a type of gambling. Scandals line the South Sea Bubble, and Acts penalising stock-jobbing and declaring public companies common nuisances were only the clearest signs that both institutionally and in public opinion, legitimate insurance and share dealings were little different from gambling. In much the same way as the Gaming Act of 1845 reinforced the integrity of the law of contract to protect genuine capital transactions, so the abandonment of the lotteries brought legitimation and respectability to genuine capital investment" (p. 379).

Chapter 5: Gambling as Banking

1. See Ewen 1932, p. 24; Blanche 1950; Rubner 1966, p. 14. In Flanders in 1579, for example, Antoine Fererist was given the right to sell lotteries where the prizes were pieces of furniture.
2. Quoted in Ezell 1960, p. 13.
3. That is also how insured people spend in the unfortunate event of death or fire. A difference between winning a lottery or receiving insurance money is that, in the first case, the couple may enjoy the winnings together, whereas only surviving parties enjoy insurance money after someone's death.
4. Retailers may object to gambling. But there does not seem to be any reason to prefer fashion to gambling. The fact that fashion is what makes wearing clothes fun, and motivates some to work harder to afford being fashionable, does not make it different from gambling.

5. If we consider governments sitting at the gambling table, and assume that they are accountable to voters for the way they tax, borrow, and spend, we must assume that, as winners, they would spend the money responsibly too. (If they do not, the issue is not gambling but lack of accountability because of inappropriate political institutions, a point the next chapter examines).

6. The Federal Reserve stuck rigidly to its statutory obligations to maintain the purchasing power of the dollar, but never ventured to change the narrow asset classes for which it would lend money. It only extended credit to a bank's holdings of government securities, excluding other bonds, real estate, and, of course, equity. The Fed's real bills doctrine stated, in Timberlake's (2007) words, "that an independent resurgence of production in the real sector of the economy was the only proper basis for growth in money and credit. They expected such growth to manifest itself in applications for new business loans, but they were first determined to see the monetary system purged of 'speculative' and long-term 'credit'" (p. 215).

7. For example when rent controls bring about arson, nobody outlaws building real estate. Instead, the demand comes for stricter and harsher law enforcement. Thus, although the sequence of events linking rent control and arson is well established, rent control regulations are still on the books in many parts of the world.

8. Tacitus's *Germania* reports of the ancient Germans that they "are so reckless in their anxiety to win, however often they lose, that when everything else is gone they will stake their personal liberty on a last decisive throw. A loser willingly discharges his debt by becoming a slave" (1970, p. 121).

9. The information in this paragraph is based on the work of Blakey 1977, pp. 13–15.

10. See Stone 1965 and 1972. But in France, Grussi notes, Louis XIV encouraged excessive gambling among nobility at court to ruin them and thus diminish their ability to revolt (1985, p. 61).

11. Quoted in Cochrane and Kirshner 1986, p. 368–9.

12. Quoted in Thomas 1971, p. 84. For Cooper, see Chapter 1 in this book.

13. Thorner 1955, pp. 161–2.

14. See discussion in Thomas 1971, p. 122.

15. See Stone 1972.

16. See Stone 1965 and 1972, p. 110; Goldstone 1986.

17. While these changes were taking place, one-third to one-half of the population was at the bottom. Their life expectancy was short. Even among nobility, life expectancy at birth for boys born in the third quarter of the seventeenth century was about thirty years. Bubonic plague was endemic until the last quarter of the seventeenth century – we saw in the previous chapter briefly a link between the plague and the last few years of the so-called tulipmania. In 1563 twenty thousand Londoners died; in 1593, fifteen thousand; in 1625, forty-one thousand; and in 1666, some sixty-eight thousand. Along with disease, fire was the greatest single threat to security and wealth. See Thomas 1971, pp. 4–5. See also G. Brenner 1985, on the link between changing life expectancy and changing inheritance laws.

18. Plumb 1967, p. 5.

19. According to Malcomson (1981, pp. 14–16), typical comments during this period emphasized that social order was not a human construct but divinely ordained: God, not man, had created social inequality. Accepting these views, the teachings

went, was a condition for achieving happiness. The clergy and the relatively well-to-do wrote these teachings and, as Thomas points out (1971, pp. 127–8, 198–206), do not reflect poor people's attitudes. This was also the period when the new entrepreneurial class, linked to industry, expanded and established itself. Of course, before the 1760s industrialists could be found in Europe. But as Bergier points out, "some of them . . . merely organized commercially the output of a host of wage-earning artisans, without ever attempting to modify . . . the methods and techniques involved" (1971, p. 408).

20. See Stone 1965 and 1972; Plumb 1967; R. Brenner 1985, Ch. 3; Goldstone 1986; Malcomson 1981, Ch. 4; Walvin 1978, p. 48.

21. It is precisely this idea that some groups may reject. Max Weber noted that religion has met a latent demand: "The fortunate is seldom satisfied with the fact of being fortunate . . . he needs to know that he has a *right* to his good fortune. He wants to be convinced that he 'deserves' it, and above all that he deserves it in comparison with others . . . Good fortune thus wants to be legitimate fortune" (1946, p. 271; italics in original). Schoeck (1969) gives an alternative explanation that bears similarities to the view of human nature, underlying this book, about envy and the institutions invented throughout history to mitigate it, as explained in Appendix 1. He concludes that the ability to provide hope and happiness for believers, be they rich or poor, may mean no more than providing ideas that free both the envious person from envy and the person envied from his sense of guilt and his fear of the envious. See also Geertz 1973, pp. 433–47, and Olmstead 1967, Ch. 4, on how religion and games of chance may achieve similar objectives.

22. These English attitudes are not unique. In the New World perceptions of games of chance and of sports and their value depended on who was playing them. Historians, such as Fabian (1982) and Findlay (1986), noted that planters of Virginia, concerned with establishing their status, did not initially welcome traditional cockfights to the colony, as rich and poor intermingled when placing their bets. But by the mid-eighteenth century, as the Virginia gentry felt secure in their position, they not only welcomed the entertainment, but also presided over both cockfights and horse races and dominated in the betting that accompanied all sporting events.

23. Tom Brown, *Amusements Serious and Comical*, ed. A. L. Hayward (New York: Dodd, Mead, 1927; first published in 1700 as *London Amusements*), pp. 52–3, as quoted in Devereux 1980, p. 243. See also Malcomson 1973, Ch. 1.

24. As quoted in Blakey 1977, p. 33.

25. Andrew Steinmetz, *The Gambling Table: Its Votaries and Victims* (London: Tinsley, 1870), as quoted in Devereux 1980, p. 242; and see descriptions of such resentments in Devereux's book when he discusses horse racing. Miers and Dixon (1979, p. 380) remark that it was the mixing of the classes in the surviving traditional recreations that so provoked the indignation of middle-class moralists. See also Sasuly (1982, pp. 44–5), who remarks that by the 1840s English society was one with shifts in class lines, and "adventurers, sharpers, and even highwaymen" had access even to private clubs where the nobility gambled. See also Fabian 1982, pp. 52 and 315.

26. Blakey 1977, p. 30. He quotes R. and J. Dodsley's work *A Modest Defense of Gaming*, published in 1754. In this book it is argued that, in contrast to the viewpoint expressed in earlier centuries, gaming developed the nation's officer corps. Officers who had seen their fortunes change were viewed as more suited for command than

nongamblers: "Men in easy circumstances are not the fittest to go upon desperate Adventures . . . Those who have charged through a Troop of Creditors, are most likely to have the same success when they face the enemy" (quoted in Blakey 1977, p. 30).

27. Having people get rich by having fun seemed inconsistent with this view – even if in games like poker, skill plays a role, or in black jack, an unusual photographic memory ensures that the player can come out ahead. Black Jack is the only card game where the odds are in favor of players endowed with such a "natural resource."

28. See Matthieu Marais 1720, *Journal et mémoires sur la régence et le règne de Louis XV*, quoted in Gleeson 2000, p. 157.

29. See Garber 1989, pp. 535–60.

30. Mackay 1841, pp. 89–97. See also Schama 1988, Ch. 5, especially Sec. 3.

31. See Brenner 1983, Ch. 3.

32. See Brenner 1994, Ch. 3, on Amsterdam and the Dutch Republic. The migration contradicts Weber's facile Protestant ethics. Jews, Catholics (who wanted to get into trade and banking), and immigrants turned Amsterdam into the miracle of the seventeenth century, just as such migration turned Hamburg, Hong Kong, Singapore, Taiwan – and of course the United States and Canada – into the miracles they became. Of course, migration combined with religious tolerance and institutions ensuring the dispersion of powers. See Brenner 1994, 2002.

33. See Bridbury 1992.

34. See Garber 1989.

35. See Walker 1999, pp. 29, 31, and 52.

36. See Bellhouse 1991.

37. Lien-Sheng 1950.

38. See Walker 1999 and Dunkley 1985. In 1670 a commentator noted that in gambling large sums of money are often lost, but "usually paid back punctually, since if anyone failed to do so, he would lose credit, and would be excluded from society" (Walker 1999, p. 40). Venetian nobles rarely informed on one another. Because gambling debts were illegal, if a noble occasionally did not fulfill his oral commitment, the recovery sometimes, though rarely, involved violence. See end of the chapter for similar arrangements that emerged in the United States during the 1970s.

39. See Walker 1999, p. 67.

40. See Ore 1956, Walker 1999. Cardano wrote in his biography that he hoped to play with people of higher rank, because that is the only way to develop a network among the rich, who could one day be a source of capital. On Cardano and gambling during the Renaissance and later, see also Bernstein 1996, Chs. 3 and 4.

41. See Knight 1921, Brenner 1983, and Appendix 1.

42. See Breen 1980.

43. See Weiman 1991. He also shows that this lottery system created in fact a secondary market in land and effectively was a privatization of government lands in situations with scarce financial capital.

44. R. Brenner (1982, 1985, 2004) explores the relationship among trust, contracts, and demographic variables in broader contexts.

45. The sources are indirect. See Brown 2006.

46. See Gilbert 1958 and Brown 2005.

47. See this theme explored broadly in Brenner (2002 and 2004), concerning mobile and immobile societies.

48. See Dary 1995.
49. It would be hard to make a more precise statement because there were almost no hard money banks lending in the West during the initial exploration and development periods. Once discoveries were made and railroads built, eastern hard money banks began to lend much larger sums than the soft money banks could.
50. Ore 1956, pp. 185–6. Today some social scientists refer to safety valves when they make such arguments. Sasuly also remarked: "It was scarcely an accident that a disproportionate number of the new race courses were established in the northern counties of England [historians have made reference to the desperate poverty of the Catholic gentry of the seventeenth and eighteenth centuries.] And it seems highly probable that some of the genuinely great sums staked on Thoroughbred races represented a last hope of paying off debts and preserving a landhold ... And ... rather similar was seen in Detroit Race Course in 1980, when recently unemployed automobile workers went to the races in larger numbers than ever before" (1982, p. 11).
51. Switzerland was one of the poorest places in Europe: it took imagination to transform rocks into tourist attractions and to decide on secret banking. Antigua and Costa Rica gambled on both tourism and online gambling and the Cayman Islands on offshore banking.
52. See Brenner 1984 and 2002.
53. Of course, once some of these places stumble on significant natural resources, they "freeze." See discussion and evidence in Brenner 2002, Ch. 1.
54. See Murphy 1997.
55. Brenner (2002) refers to five sources, because he separates savings and inheritance. Here, for convenience, the two are classified under one category: family.
56. Venkatesh (2006) describes similar arrangements today in the ghettos of U.S. cities. He describes how residents get around bad credit by borrowing money from the community. They then do not repay the debt with money. Small businesses give the homeless a place to sleep and the homeless substitute for night watchmen; a prostitute and a grocer barter for food.
57. See Friedman and Schwartz 1963, p. 417 – 178: Timberlake 2007.
58. See Bordo, Choudri, and Schwartz 2002, pp. 9–11, 24.
59. See Bernanke 1993, p. 261, and discussion in Timberlake 2007.

Chapter 6: Lottery Is a Taxation, and Heav'n Be Prais'd, It Is Easily Rais'd

1. See Schwartz 2005.
2. See Brenner (1994, 2002) on the tools of direct democracy. At present, Switzerland is the only western country to make political decisions in this systematic way. The United States and Canada were moving in this direction when the Great Depression struck. See Brenner 2002, and Chapter 7 in this book.
3. As explained in Brenner (1994, 2002), these are the equivalent of properly functioning stock markets in the political sphere. Whereas stock markets prevent mispricing from lasting too long, properly functioning direct democracy could do the same with mistaken regulatory and fiscal policies.
4. See Ewen 1932, p. 31.
5. See Ewen 1932, p. 28.

6. Yet, except Switzerland, none of the other western democracies practice the institutions of "direct democracy" to decide on spending, taxing and role of government systematically. See Brenner 1994 and 2002.

7. These issues are the subject of Brenner (1994, 2002).

8. Confirming analyses in Chapter 3.

9. Of course, whenever gambling was outlawed, criminal elements managed the business. Margolis (1997), reviewing both the literature and the data available, found little evidence to support the view that the presence of casinos has a meaningful impact on crime rates. Once gambling was legalized, the criminals stayed involved, as they were the only ones who knew the business. But that does not imply that they were still committing crimes. Under communism, all trade was prohibited and everyone who traded was a "criminal." Once communism fell, it is not surprising that these "criminals" became businesspeople and entrepreneurs. See more detailed discussion on impacts of prohibitions in the next chapter.

10. Riley 1999.

11. The Italian government tried to structure the deal in a way that the €3 billion would not be added to government borrowing. Initially it was not. But in 2002, the European Union's statistical office ruled that it must be included. The fact that Italian statistics have often been a magic trick is well known. See Brenner 1994, Ch. 1. On Italian lotteries, see Varma 2003.

12. Whether the higher ratings will translate into lower yields is yet to be seen.

13. In 1466 Madame Jan van Eyck, widow of the Flemish painter, organized a lottery to raise money for the poor of Bruges (Fleming 1978, p. 57).

14. Kinsey 1959, p. 13; Labrosse 1985, Ch. 1, pp. 12–16.

15. Handelsman 1933, pp. 45–7.

16. Blanche 1950; Ezell 1960, p. 2; Rubner 1966, p. 14.

17. Coste 1933, p. 83; Desperts 1982. People were already familiar with lotteries there. Betting on the outcome of elections was already known. It occurred in 1520 during elections for the Great Council of Genoa. The form this betting took is the source of the modern number games: five senatorial candidates were chosen at random from a predetermined list of aspirants. People bet on who would be selected. From this developed the game of lotto, where numbers from one to ninety were substituted for the names. This is still the standard lotto system (Smith 1952; Labrosse 1985, p. 15).

18. Coste 1933, p. 21; Leonnet 1963, p. 13.

19. Leonnet 1963, p. 15. The revenues also provided funds for a hospital. The restoration of more than half of the Parisian churches between 1714 and 1729 was financed by revenues from lotteries.

20. Cohen 1964, p. 44.

21. See Labrosse 1985, for a review of French lotteries. Coste (1933, p. 23) gives a list of the public projects that were financed by lotteries in France: the Parisian general hospital in 1660, fire pumps in Paris in 1701, the relief of Lyon's poor in 1699, a hospital in Amiens, and a school in Angers.

22. The lottery of the Roman states began in 1732. The pope's involvement with the lottery may have convinced the Catholic Louis XVI that lotteries were a legitimate means of raising money (Leonnet 1963, pp. 17–18).

23. Coste quotes Pierre Gaspard Chaumette, the public prosecutor for the department of Seine, who called the state lottery "a scourge invented by despotism to quiet the

people by giving them a false hope" (1933, p. 28). During the debate at the National Assembly, Comte de Mirabeau sent an open letter to his fellow members accusing those in favor of a lottery of supporting a "tax whose proceeds stem from folly or despair" (Leonnet 1963, p. 37).

24. The argument presented at the Council of the Five Hundred (as the parliament was then called) sounds almost modern: "Of all kind of contribution, no other has fewer detractors and more supporters than the lottery...All other taxes must be paid whether one wants them or not. One is free not to contribute to the lottery" (Handelsman 1933, p. 18). The partisans of its continued suppression also used modern arguments: "Ask the desolated mother whose children die of hunger; she will tell you: My husband was addicted to the lottery and we are left without resources. Ask this firm why it is bankrupt; the lottery is the cause" (quoted in Leonnet 1963, p. 42).

25. Leonnet 1963, pp. 49ff.

26. Henriquet 1921, p. 23.

27. Ezell 1960, p. 4.

28. Woodhall 1964; Ashton 1893, pp. 20ff.

29. Ezell 1960, p. 9.

30. Ashton 1893, p. 40.

31. Ezell 1960, p. 9.

32. Murphy 2005, p. 230.

33. For the details of this lottery, see Woodhall 1964.

34. See Murphy 2005.

35. See Murphy 2005, Ewen 1932.

36. To give an idea of how widely lotteries were used, Ashton (1898, p. 229) states that in a randomly picked issue of *The Tatler* of 1710, no fewer than six lotteries were mentioned, some with money prizes and some with merchandise prizes.

37. See Glaisyer 2006, p. 6.

38. See Brenner 1994, Ch. 3.

39. See Cohen 1953; Ewen 1932. Cohen notes that the lottery component was added during the eighteenth and nineteenth centuries as a sweetener because, otherwise, the government could not raise funds without charging higher interest.

40. Ezell 1960, p. 9.

41. See Raven 1991.

42. Murphy 2005, p. 244.

43. Ashton 1898, p. 230.

44. See Ewen 1932; Raven 1991. See also Browning 1971, for the various features and sweeteners of lotteries between 1750 and 1760. See Cohen 1953 for a summary of terms of debt lotteries between 1694 and 1784.

45. Government borrowing was often different in the eighteenth century from what it is today. There could be no new loans without simultaneous new taxes (rather than backing spending and loans by taxing future incomes but without "funding" them explicitly). See Browning 1971. He notes that the financing of the Seven Years' War, for example, did not bring about inflation because the government did not issue unbacked currency.

46. Quoted in Murphy 2005, p. 244.

47. See Raven 1991, p. 376.

48. The 1823 declaration authorizing the final Lottery Act came as an aside during the debate on the candle tax, with the government "taunting the opposition that unless the tax was renewed he would be unable to pursue his new intention of abandoning lotteries" (Raven 1991, p. 385). This observation reinforces the previous points about why it is preferable to have political institutions that allow voters to decide on issues separately rather than vote on a mishmash.
49. Ashton 1898, pp. 239–40.
50. See Raven 1991, p. 382.
51. Ewen 1932, p. 369.
52. Similar characteristics can be detected in the history of lotteries in Poland. Introduced by an Italian around 1748, the lotto game soon attracted the attention of the Polish diet, which in 1768 established a system of state concessions to the private lotteries' promoters to increase the state's revenues. As in other European countries, calls were heard during the nineteenth century to abolish the main lottery on the grounds that it exploited the poor. This opinion led to its abolition in 1840. But the class lottery, with tickets too expensive for the poor, continued undeterred until 1915, when war ended it. At the end of the war, the new Polish Republic resurrected the state lottery. See Handelsman 1933.
53. See Raven 1991, p. 388, quoting from a 477-page study of the select committee.
54. Details of the history of lotteries in early America can be found in Smith (1952), Ezell (1960), Devereux (1980), and the other sources referred to herein.
55. Ezell 1960, p. 28.
56. See Lee and Passel 1979, p. 20, on incomes during that time.
57. A. Spofford, "Lotteries in American History," *American Historical Association Annual Report*, 1892, as quoted in Blakey 1977, p. 75.
58. Dasgupta (2005, p. 13) shows that the Yale lottery raised less than expected.
59. Ezell 1960, p. 49.
60. Suits 1979.
61. Blanche 1950, p. 78.
62. Blakey 1977, p. 167. He gives a detailed description of events surrounding gambling in New York. He remarks that "during the 1830's and 40's, New York was gripped by the evangelical Christian reform movement experienced in different forms in many parts of the country... Liquor, slavery, the lack of institutions for the poor, and women's status as second-class citizens all came under attack" (p. 152) in addition to gambling. At the same time, as in England, horse racing was viewed differently: "In *Van Valkengurgh vs. Torrey* [1828], the court relied on a literal reading of the word 'racing' and declared that trotting was not affected by the law" (p. 175).
63. Gribbin and Bean (2005) note that "stronger centralized government had greater ability to collect tax revenues (McGowan, 1994, p. 12). The federal government's expenditures were being financed primarily by tariffs, excise taxes on alcoholic beverages (from the 1860s onward), and proceeds from the sale of land (Niebert 2000, p. 27). State governments started to collect taxes and property taxes were becoming the major source of revenue for both state and local governments" (p. 354).
64. The spur under which the Massachusetts legislature acted was the suicide of a thirty-five-year-old bookkeeper and treasurer of a large Boston mercantile house who had gambled away all his property and had embezzled $18,000 of his employer's money (Ezell 1960, p. 211).

65. Details of the history of Canadian lotteries are taken from Labrosse (1985).
66. Ibid., pp. 55ff.
67. Ibid., p. 69.
68. Ibid., p. 64.
69. Ibid., pp. 76–9.
70. The church first had an amendment passed that permitted raffles of unsold objects with a value of no more than $50. But with the passage of the British North America Act in 1867, Quebec obtained its own assembly, which passed the new law (ibid., p. 83).
71. Kinsey 1959, p. 20.
72. For the story of the Spanish lottery, see Altabella 1962.
73. Labrosse 1985, p. 63.
74. Landau 1968, p. 3.
75. Handelsman 1933, pp. 22ff.
76. Kinsey 1959, p. 28.
77. Rubner 1966, p. 38.
78. Landau 1968, p. 19.
79. Blakey 1977, pp. 111–27.
80. Rubner (1966, p. 99) also remarked that the socially prominent Harriman deliberately violated postal regulations in connection with a drawing sponsored by her group to be brought into court, and so arouse public interest. See also Devereux 1980, pp. 165–212, on the debates surrounding games of chance during the Great Depression.
81. Devereux 1980, pp. 170–212. In 1931 Nevada legalized gambling statewide (Sasuly 1982, p. 233).
82. Devereux 1980, p. 204.
83. Ibid., pp. 209–10.
84. See quotations from various judgments on the legality of contests in Blakey 1977, Ch. 6. Bender remarks that "25 million Americans ... try at least two contests a year. Over 12 millions are definitely contest conscious and try as many as they have time and ideas for" (1938, p. 3).
85. Ibid., pp. 121–2.
86. See Devereux (1980, p. 181).
87. Bender 1938, p. 3. It may not be surprising that these groups were against the legislation of gambling. See Blakey 1977, p. 104.
88. Numerous industries may dislike the new ways of selling – advertising-dependent media being prominent among them. Although lotteries would have to be advertised, the revenues from advertising would have dropped, because instead of $10 million having been spent on ads, perhaps only $6 million would have been spent. One must beware of negative editorials of the contests at the time, which may disguise self-interest and have nothing to do with sincere moral stands.
89. Perkins 1950, p. 30.
90. Ibid., p. 37. Miers and Dixon note that "for the 1932 Royal Commission, the objections of principle, that they entailed socially harmful consequences, itself resolved into two lines of argument, which have been standard weapons of the objectors' armoury. The first is that lotteries, involving no element of skill, foster a belief in the value of chance, which conflicts with the general dictates of the protestant

work ethic, which places value on thrift and industry as the route to material (and spiritual) reward ... Although a common argument, that lotteries foster a belief in luck, it is one which is double-edged, for the capitalist system itself which relies upon acceptance of the work ethic, is to a degree a risk-based enterprise" (1979, p. 394).

91. Leonard 1952; Newman 1972, p. 28. It is not accidental that it was on July 31, 1933, that for the first time in its history, China introduced a formal state lottery. Whang (1933) notes, however, that Hwo-Wei, a form of lottery. was popular among the lower classes of Shanghai though publicly prohibited.

92. *New Statesman and Nation,* June 6, 1931, quoted in Devereux 1980, pp. 779–80.

93. In 1964 New Hampshire became the first state to introduce a state lottery as an explicit substitute for either a sales tax or an income tax. The lottery was an instant success – with 90 percent of the lottery tickets purchased by out-of-state residents. All northeastern states followed suit within ten years, and to prevent the outflow of funds, New York legalized lotteries in 1966.

94. However, the greatest growth of state lotteries occurred between 1980 and 1990. By 1985, 58 percent of the U.S. population lived in states with some form of lottery. By 2001 only two states (Utah and Hawaii) did not have some form of legalized gaming. See Briggs 2003.

95. I am grateful to Christian Christiansen for personal exchange on the data. The data draws on Christiansen Capital Advisors' Newsletter Insight: The Journal of the North American Gaming Industry, vol. 4, no. 7.

96. As quoted in Dixon 1991, p. 341.

97. See Dixon 1991, p. 341.

98. As quoted in Dixon 1991.

Chapter 7: Politics and Prohibitions

1. See Blum and Kalven 1953.

2. For an exercise in proving that lotteries are regressive, see Walker 1998.

3. See Brenner 1994 and 2002, on direct democracy.

4. See Appendix 1 and discussion in R. Brenner 1983 and 1985. That view of human nature suggests why the rich would spend more on insurance in various forms e.g., self-insurance, spending on law enforcement and police, or redistributzion of part of their wealth to prevent crime against property. How the taxes and policies are rationalized, and by what jargon, is another story. However, the arguments do not specify how progressive taxes should be: high and complex taxes bring about evasion, and a misallocation of talent as more people enter law, accounting, and finance.

5. As noted in Ch. 6, this can lead to misspending and future liabilities, as when issuing bonds backed by future revenues from lotteries.

6. See R. Brenner 1983, 1985 and 1990, and Appendix 1.

7. See Brenner's three chapters in Colander and Brenner 1992.

8. Eichenwald 1987.

9. Blakey 1979, p. 76.

10. See Walsh 2007 on the many conflicting numbers concerning New Jersey's pension fund.

11. Kaplan 1985; Livernois 1985; Mikesell and Zorn 1986. Livernois erroneously infers redistributive effects by looking at what net revenues from state lotteries are spent on. Kaplan (p. 99) notes that politicians consider earmarked lottery revenues – for example, for education, the most commonly earmarked category – as an exchange item in their budgets. Monies realized from a lottery are allocated to education, but total education funds may not increase because a like amount may be withheld from other sources.

12. It is ironic that today lotteries are attacked because of their alleged regressivity, whereas in the past gambling was attacked because it allowed the richer to lose money at the tables or become venture capitalists.

13. It is not clear what critics, relying on regressity arguments against lotteries from the spending angle, contemplate as alternatives. See arguments drawing on regressivity in Clotfelter and Cook 1989; Daniels 1992; Hansen 2004 and 2007.

14. See Hansen 2007; D'Ascoli 2006; Fink and Rork 2003; McGowan 2001.

15. See Schwartz 2005, p. 31.

16. See McKibbin 1979, p. 172.

17. Bolen (1976, p. 29) mentions these points and makes reference to Meriwether's book. Gerald Williams, a poor resident of Harlem, said when buying a lottery ticket with a chance of winning a big prize: "the big difference between Lotto and life is that in this game everyone has the same chance" (quoted in *Newsweek* 1985). O'Hara remarks that in Australia "for the less wealthy gamblers, gaming and betting provided one of the few opportunities to change their station in life. This was particularly relevant in a society where even a relatively small windfall could place the successful gambler on the path to success" (1987, p. 4).

18. See Haller 1970, p. 620. Koeves 1952, p. 58.

19. See Schwartz 2005, pp. 142–5.

20. Arthur Andersen (1997) tries to evaluate the economic impact of casinos on three communities. Its conclusion is that they created thousand of jobs and diminished welfare spending.

21. Strumpf (2003) quotes a report from the National Gambling Impact Study Commission that estimated "that individuals wager between $80 and $380 billion dollars with illegal bookmakers."

22. See Schwartz 2005, pp. 172–3.

23. See D'Ascoli 2006 and Hansen 2004 for summaries of such evidence.

24. See Hansen 2004, p. 35. The paper is published by the Tax Foundation. Hansen's e-mail is signed "staff writer and webmaster." I do not know how much time or how many resources she has to get deeply into this or other issues she covers.

25. Richard McGowan (1994) notes that the spread of lotteries in the 1980s was a consequence of the Cold War. With President Ronald Reagan's new federalism, spending on some social services became the responsibility of the states. Instead of raising taxes, they chose to legalize gambling.

26. See Brenner 1994, 1999, and 2002.

27. See Brenner 1994 and 2002, for a discussion of the Swiss system.

28. See Gribbin and Bean 2005.

29. See Schwartz 2005, p. 115.

30. See Barnhart 1983.

31. See Ch. 6, n.24.

32. Rubner 1966, p. 12
33. See discussions in Ch. 6; Miers and Dixon 1979, pp. 376–9. Rubner (1966, p. 19) remarks that the amount of money wagered on insurance was to have equaled the sales volume of the actual lottery tickets, and that there were on average two hundred insurance offices operating during this period. Ashton (1893, p. 298) notes that at their peak there were four hundred offices. See also Blakey 1977, p. 897.
34. On Sweden, see Allen 1952 and Tec 1964. On China, see Whang 1933.
35. W. Turner, *Gambler's Money* (1965), quoted in Blakey 1977, p. 432.
36. Blakey 1977, p. 465.
37. See Brenner 2002, Chs. 1 and 3.
38. Ibid., p. 466. This outcome is not unlike the situation in England, where the honesty of bookmakers is noteworthy.
39. See Brenner 1994.
40. See Dunstan 1997, p. 5.
41. Weinstein and Deitch 1974; Blakey 1977, pp. 208–9.
42. Blakey 1977, pp. 195–8. He remarks that the 1971 Joint Legislative Committee on Crime discovered that an arrested gambler faced only a 2 percent chance of going to jail, and even then his sentence would be light. In one heavy gambling district, of 1,225 arrested bookies, only 10 were fined more than $500, only 19 were imprisoned, and only 3 of the 19 received sentences in excess of ninety days. It was also estimated that each arrest cost the public forty times the fine recovered.
43. Ibid., pp. 197–8. In testimony before the legislature, it was revealed that the typical person involved in off-track betting earned $12,300 a year, was a high school graduate forty-two years of age on average, male, white, often of Italian or Irish extraction, very often Catholic, and a blue-collar worker who was not a compulsive gambler. Forty-three percent had prior experience with some form of illegal gambling. Ibid., pp. 211–12.
44. Clotfelter and Cook 1989, pp. 39.
45. See Blakey 1977, pp. 142–203; Devereux 1980, Part 3. It should be noted that even racetracks were of questionable legality, because they derived their revenues from gambling.
46. Blakey 1977, pp. 121–2; Reuter 1985, p. 15.
47. See O'Hara 1987 and 1988; Dixon 1987; and extensive evidence and sources quoted therein.
48. Blakey 1977, pp. 123–5.
49. Ibid., pp. 201–2. Judge Van, in his dissent, showed more common sense when he argued that "engaging in the business of public gambling by quoting and laying insidious odds to a multitude of people was the evil aimed at, not the making of record of the business which is comparatively innocent" (p. 202).
50. Blakey (1977, p. 384) remarks that Nebraska's agrarian interests dictated an absolute ban on gambling as soon as they gained control of the legislature.
51. Ibid., p. 350, italics in original quoting an unpublished paper by Haller, "Bootleggers and American Gambling 1920–1045: An Overview," and relying on Haller 1970.
52. Blakey 1977, p. 674. Drawings from the Louisiana lotteries took place daily in Boston, Cincinatti, Denver, and San Francisco. Legislators were bribed. New York, to protect the success of its own lotteries, passed a law in 1759 that imposed a fine on anyone

who sold foreign lotteries inside the state (ibid., p. 137). On Australia, see Rubner 1966, p. 148.

53. Blakey 1979, p. 73; 1977, pp. 682, 701–2. Blakey, quoting Senator Eastland, also remarks that the impact of the mail prohibition was that the lottery statutes in their present form did not cover many forms of betting "transported daily across State lines, for they do not meet the traditional definition of a lottery.... Even out-and-out lottery tickets may be shipped across state lines with impunity if they are printed in blank, shipped, and then locally overprinted with the paying numbers" (1977, p. 583). But it was already during the Great Depression in the 1930s that the Irish Sweepstakes experienced great success, which fact was used in arguments during the 1960s to justify the legalization of lotteries.

54. See Gruson 1987, from which one can infer that 50 percent of the buyers of the Maryland's small communities near the border come from Delaware. She notes that Delaware's problem is faced by many of the twenty-two states that were operating lotteries: "It is getting more difficult to attract people to play lottery games that offer anything less than million-dollar jackpots." Gruson also remarks that the attraction of big prizes "led eight states, including New York, to consider banding together to offer regular multi-state lottery drawings. Officials estimate that it could often produce jackpots of $80 million, nearly double the current record of $41 million, set two years ago in New York" (Blakey, 1979, p. 71). In Nevada, where by the 1960s gambling was the largest industry, similar aspects of the industry were not lost on politicians, who realized that the state depended heavily on outsiders for its tax dollars (Blakey 1977, p. 467). According to Blair (1986) sixteen of the twenty-two states with lotteries and the District of Columbia discussed banding together to offer a regular multistate lottery drawing that officials said would increase state revenues and produce jackpots of more than $50 million.

55. Hood 1976, p. 170.

56. Ibid. Hood notes that this does not imply that the law was ineffective. It prevented the development of large-scale bookmaking businesses.

57. Dixon 1984, p. 2, quoting the assistant commissioner of the Metropolitan Police in 1923.

58. Dixon 1984, p. 35. According to Dixon, the evidence from England, based on autobiographies and memories of men who had contact with bookmakers after the passage of the 1906 law, is unequivocal. Payoffs to the police were an inevitable part of the street bookmaker's expenses, taking the form of either a bribe or "betting with the bookmaker on the simple system of receiving on winners but not paying on losers" (p. 66), and he concludes that whereas "before the war, the police had greeted the Street Betting Act as an addition to their power, they now began to perceive it as a threat to their authority" (p. 67).

59. See Dixon 1991, p. 321.

60. As quoted in Dixon 1991, p. 322.

61. Dixon 1991, p. 329.

62. See Schwartz 2005, p. 133.

63. As quoted in Dixon 1991, p. 334.

64. As quoted in Dixon 1991, pp. 335–6.

65. See Dixon 1991, p. 340. The association with gangs and violence is not surprising, as noted in earlier chapters. When an outlawed activity is pursued, the enforcement of

contracts involves violence, whether in drugs, prostitution, or, under communism or countries in transition from regimes outlawing all business, in potentially every trade.

66. Lerner (2007) makes a similar observation as we made about the gambling laws in the United Kingdom. He notes that New York's immigrants found out that the main objective of the "dry lobby" was to keep an eye on the habits of the poor, the foreign born, and the working class.

67. According to Lerner (2007), arrests for intoxication in New York increased during Prohibition, as did alcohol-related hospitalization.

68. Inadvertently, Prohibition had effects similar to those discussed in Ch. 5; namely, that groups that previously never met now intermingled. Lerner (2007) notes that New Yorkers also ventured into clubs in parts of the city, such as Harlem, where they never went before.

69. See discussion in Schwartz 2005, pp. 134–40.

70. See Schwartz 2005, p. 201.

71. In 1995 the British shifted from soccer pools to lotteries. Pool operators' revenues fell by 25 percent, and wagers at the 9,300 betting shops were down by 4 percent. See Parker-Pope 1995.

72. Aaron Brown is the author of this section.

73. The Wire Act of 1961 says: "Whoever being engaged in the business of betting or wagering knowingly uses a wire communication facility for the transmission in interstate or foreign commerce of bets or wagers of information assisting in the placing of bets or wagers on any sporting event or contest, or for the transmission of a wire communication which entitles the recipient to receive money or credit as a result of bets or wagers, shall be fined not more than $10,000 or imprisoned not more than two years, or both." 18 U.S.C. para. 1084.

74. See Vallerius and Balestra 2006.

75. Much of the legal activity surrounding Internet gambling has focused on the federal Wire Act. The act was adopted in the early 1960s to address telephone bookmaking and strictly prohibited gambling over the wires. See Schwartz 2005. The Department of Justice in both the Clinton and the Bush administrations has expressed the view that the Wire Act prohibits all forms of Internet gambling. However, the U.S. Court of Appeals for the Fifth Circuit ruled in re MasterCard Int'l Inc. (313 F.3d 257, 263 [5th Cir. 2002]), that the statute's language reaches only sports betting. The Wire Act refers to "bets or wagers or information assisting in the placing of bets or wagers on any sporting event or contest." But, as we note, there are exceptions in various states. See Stewart 2006.

76. Similar arguments hold for the drug business. The war against it is ongoing, the use of drugs has not diminished, and the cost of the war, as measured in the United States, far underestimates its impact because its destabilizing effects on Latin American and Asian countries is not being taken into account. However, the drug industry should be subject to regulations of a different nature from alcoholic beverages, gambling, or cigarettes.

77. The fact that some charities are among the vocal opponents of gambling and lotteries is not surprising. They compete for small change. The fact that Indian reservations oppose the competition is not surprising either. Indian gaming is an issue only because there is prohibition in the rest of the United States or various monopolies

and tax arrangements. State support for gambling on Indian reservations started with a 1988 suit by Native Americans in California which resulted in the passage of the Indian Gaming Regulatory Act. The legislation allowed Native Americans the right to achieve sovereign-nation status. Such recognition means that they cannot be taxed and they can do whatever is legal in the state. Not surprisingly, their tax-free status causes problems.

78. Already the online gambling business is a good example that when an activity is lightly taxed (or untaxed) it grows quickly.

Chapter 8: How Gamblers and Risk-Takers Correct the Future

1. See United Nations 2002.
2. See Brenner 1983, Ch. 2.
3. There has been blurring of lines, such as in behavioral finance, economic anthropology, law and economics, and economic history. But most topics covered by these fields have been relatively narrow, and none has tried to deal with bigger events and put together a picture. This book is one in a series of my attempts to do so.
4. See Brenner 2002.
5. See Brenner 1983, Ch. 2.
6. See Brenner 2002, Ch. 1.
7. See Brown 2006.
8. See Brenner 1983; Franklin 2001.
9. In Islam, the concept of "institutions" is missing, notes Franklin (2001, p. 354) in a summary of the literature.
10. See Berman 2003, p. 6.
11. See North and Weingast 1989; Pipes 1999, p. 150.
12. See Brenner 2002 and 2004.
13. See Brenner 2002; Chua 2003.
14. Some commented that our 1990 book was antireligious. Not so. The book says nothing about genuine beliefs in divinity. Life on earth is unique; the Big Bang is unique. And uniqueness defies scientific explanation. Through one point, one can draw endless lines.
15. See Tocqueville 1835, p. 19.
16. See implications about today's universities in particular in Brenner 2002.
17. See Landes 1998.
18. See Boorstin 1983, p. 60–61.
19. Boorstin 1983, pp. 498 ff.
20. This, however, does not imply that it would be good for the Chinese to float their currency. That is a different story. See Brenner 2006.
21. North 2005.
22. See R. Brenner 2002.
23. See R. Brenner 1992a and 1994.
24. See R. Brenner 1985, 1994, and 2002.
25. Norway appears to be on its way to becoming another example of how natural riches may be a problem for a country. Before the oil boom, Norway survived by hard work and self-reliance. Now, after three decades of oil money and a generous social net funded by it, apparently Norwegians have let their work habits slip. On any given

day, 25 percent of Norwegians are absent from their work, with the rate higher among government employees, who constitute half of the workforce. The conventional statistical measures do not reveal decline because the rents for oil riches keep Norway rich. But one should not be surprised that after one generation of less discipline, Norway may wake up as a bigger version of Nauru, once oil is exhausted or its price goes down significantly. See Alvarez (2004).

26. See *Jerusalem Post* 1999, pp. 26–33. Also Kallick et al. (1979), in their survey, found that Catholics and Jews display high rates of gambling, while those belonging to the so-called "Bible-oriented" sects show low figures. Wasserman (1982) says also that there was a "relatively high incidence of compulsive gambling amongst Jews."

27. See Brenner 1983, Chs. 4 and 5.

28. In countries too well endowed with natural riches, governments can maintain their monopolistic financial intermediary status sustaining large military and bureaucracies and preventing capital markets from developing. See R. Brenner 2002.

29. See Brenner 2002 on the movement of the vital few.

30. Such societies create illegal options on use of military force that go by different names.

31. Schoeck 1969, p. 238.

Appendix 1: Gambling and Risk-Taking

1. Stigler 1965, p. 14.

2. The deeper philosophical implications of these assumptions are explored in the work of R. Brenner (1983, 1985).

3. Comparisons with their views can be found in R. Brenner (1983, 1985), though later in this appendix I discuss some facets of their models.

4. Friedman and Savage (1948), for example, argued that the utility function is sometimes convex and sometimes concave. But if one does not know where exactly, the model will not be falsified. In private correspondence with the author (letter dated June 22, 1987), Friedman said he was wrong when he used the existence of multiple prizes to rationalize the upper concave section of the utility curve.

5. March (1988) attributes risk-taking behavior to a difference between realized wealth and the wealth the individual aspired to. However, he does not present a formal model of risk-taking.

6. The evidence presented in R. Brenner (1983, 1985) suggests that such a distinction should be made.

7. It may be useful to note that whereas people may buy fractional tickets by buying in groups, such pooling is not costless. Somebody who is unemployed may find it difficult to pool resources with others, or people may sometimes forget to pay, in which case, if the group happens to win, frictions arise and reach the courts. People may even disagree about what to do with the small prizes. One of my colleagues who commented on this book revealed that he stopped pooling with his father-in-law because he did not want to spend the small winnings on lotteries, whereas his father-in-law did. Of course, most people probably discuss such issues and may even enter contractual agreements before pooling.

8. See R. Brenner 1983 and 1985. This problem was brought to my attention by Milton Friedman.

9. It does not take much time to buy tickets; one can even reserve them by phone.

10. If fairness is defined as $(1 - p)h = p(H - h)$, then the same condition is obtained as for lotteries. See R. Brenner 1983, pp. 52–3.

11. The conditions examined next may remind one of the arguments in Rothschild and Stiglitz (1970). But there is a significant difference, as in their model the utility function depends on wealth only, whereas here two variables have to be taken into account.

12. This result contrasts with that of Rothschild and Stiglitz (1970). The reason is that here an increased variability has both benefits and costs in term of changing one's rank, something that an investment with a smaller spread does not have.

13. Mackay 1841 (1980), pp. 98–9.

14. Hey 1979, p. 232.

15. Ibid., pp. 232–3.

16. R. Brenner 1983, Ch. 2; 1985, Ch. 2.

17. These issues are discussed in detail in R. Brenner (1983, 1985, 1987). Cancian (1979, Ch. 2) has a somewhat similar discussion. It may be interesting to note that Frank Knight's opinion that human consciousness itself would disappear in the absence of uncertainty (discussed in Arrow 1970, Ch. 1) receives a literal interpretation in this model. Also, Knight's intuition that if all risks were measurable, then risk aversion would not give rise to any profit, receives a clear interpretation in this model. Only when innovations take place and demands must be discovered (a process linked with the notion of uncertainty) will profits exist. Arrow notes that Knight's proposition, "if true, would appear to be of the greatest importance; yet, surprisingly enough, not a single writer, as far as I know, with the exception of Hicks ... has mentioned it, and he denies its validity" (1970, p. 30). The statement is accurate within this model.

18. Or, as pointed out in R. Brenner (1983, p. 56), a person may be called a terrorist by some and a freedom fighter by others.

19. For a summary of the evidence, see R. Brenner 1983, Chs. 1, 2; 1985, Ch. 2; 1987, Ch. 2.

20. Knight's words, as recalled by Gary S. Becker (1983).

21. R. Brenner 1983, 1985, and 1987.

22. See R. Brenner 1983, Ch. 1; 1985, Ch. 2, where a brief comparison with Freud's approach to gambling is made.

23. See the many studies in Kahneman, Slovic, and Tversky 1982; Arkes and Hammond 1986; Hogarth and Reder 1986; Zeckhauser 1986; Lea, Tarpy, and Webley 1987; March 1988. See also additional references and discussions in Schoemaker 1982 and Shefrin and Statman 1984; see also a discussion on survey methods in general in Glock 1967 and Moser and Kalton 1972.

24. Thaler 1986a, p. 164.

25. Ibid., p. 163.

26. Ibid.

27. Kahneman and Tversky 1986b, p. 72.

28. McNeil et al. 1982, quoted in Kahneman and Tversky 1986b, pp. 70–1.

29. Ibid., p. 71.

30. See Bloch 1953; Orwell 1957, p. 149; R. Brenner 1983, pp. 25–6, 80–2; 1985, pp. 30–1, 114–15. In the latter, additional references can be found on this point.
31. Calabresi 1985, p. 2
32. A point repeated in Vicusi 1989.
33. See Solman and Friedman 1982, pp. 114–15.
34. R. Brenner 1983, 1985, 1987; Brenner and Brenner 1987. But to study preference formation, reference should be made to studies based on direct questions about satisfaction, like Easterlin (1974), and in particular the numerous ones that Kapteyn has done in collaboration with coauthors (1978, 1982, 1985); Van de Stadt, Kapteyn, and van de Geer 1985 in particular.
35. Slovic 1986, p. 190. The model also gives a literal interpretation to the statement made by a player in the stock market who wrote: "If I hadn't made money some of the time, I would have acquired market wisdom quicker" (Lefèbvre, 1968, p. 30, quoted by Slovic 1986, p. 188).
36. Kahneman and Tversky 1979, p. 286.
37. They also bear resemblance to Simon 1959, p. 87, discussed in March 1988.
38. Kahneman and Tversky 1979, pp. 286–7.

Appendix 2: Human Nature and the Civilizing Process

1. F. O. Schmitt, as quoted in Taylor 1979, p. 65; John Dewey, as quoted in Taylor 1979, p. 273.
2. See Taylor 1979, p. 297.
3. See R. Brenner 1983 and 1985 for detailed discussion.
4. Smith 1980, pp. 44–45; ibid., p. 37.
5. France 1953, p. 206.
6. Berlin 1981.
7. Simon 1959, p. 87.
8. March and Simon 1958, p. 51.
9. Shils 1981, p. 152.
10. Heer 1966, p. 474.

Appendix 3: A Statistical Profile of Gamblers

Sections 1 and 2 were coauthored by Gabrielle A. Brenner. Sections 3, 4, and 5 were done in collaboration with Claude Montmarquette and Gabrielle A. Brenner.
1. See Tec 1964, p. 93.
2. See Theil 1971, pp. 628ff.
3. Maryland, Clotfelter, and Cook 1989, p. 97.
4. Other specifications were tried but were not supported by the data. Note that a more general and complex specification will add an error term to Equation (4).
5. The sample size may even exceed 10,938, as some observations are repeated to respect the weights corresponding to the provinces.
6. Thirty-five percent may be an overestimation, as some people may have reported not buying lottery tickets at all, even though they did buy them. But it is difficult to assess the importance of this problem.

7. The probability of χ^2_{p-1} exceeding the calculated χ^2 is less than 0.01. Thus, we reject the model, subject to the constraint that all regression coefficients (except the error term) are 0 at a confidence level of 99 percent.

8. There are actually two sets of solutions corresponding to the adjustment equation, as $\theta_4 = \frac{1}{2}B_2^2 \Rightarrow B_2 = \pm0.0447$. We use $B_2 = 0.0447$, because with this solution all people in the survey underestimate their lottery expenditures. With $B_2 = -0.0447$, we find that families earning less than \$12,000 overestimate their lottery expenditures and that higher-income families greatly underestimate their lottery expenditures. But these results contradict our evidence from other sources. See R. Brenner 1983, Ch. 1; 1985, Ch. 2.

9. As shown in Table 6, the underdeclaration reaches slightly more than 100 percent for very low-income families, suggesting some difficulties with the truncated series expansion at these levels of income.

10. For further details, see Brenner, Montmarquette, and Brenner 1987.

Bibliography

Alchian, A. A. (1953), "The Meaning of Utility Measurement," *American Economic Review* 42: 26–50.

Allais, M. (1953), "Le comportement de l'homme rationnel devant le risque: Critique des postulats et axiomes de l'École Américaine," *Econometrica* 21(4): 503–46.

Allen, David P. (1952), *The Nature of Gambling*. New York: Coward-McCann.

Alsop, Ronald (1983), "State Lottery Craze Is Spreading, but Some Fear It Hurts the Poor," *Wall Street Journal*, Feb. 24, p. 31.

Altabella, José (1962), *La lotería nacional de España (1763–1963)*. Madrid: Dirección General de Tributos Especiales.

Alvarez, Lizette (2004), "Norway Work Ethic Slips on Oil-coated Slope," *International Herald Tribune*, July 26.

American Psychiatric Organization (1980), *Diagnostic and Statistical Manual of Mental Disorders*. 3d ed. Arlington, VA: American Psychiatric Publishing.

Arkes, Hal R., and Kenneth R. Hammond, eds. (1986), *Judgment and Decision Making*. Cambridge: Cambridge University Press.

Arrow, K. J. (1970), *Essays in the Theory of Risk-Bearing*. Amsterdam: North-Holland.

Arthur Anderson (1997), *Economic Impacts of Casino Gaming in the United States*, Vol. 2, study prepared for the American Gaming Association.

Ashton, John (1893), *A History of English Lotteries*. Detroit: Singing Tree, 1969.

Ashton, John (1898), *The History of Gambling in England*. London: Duckworth.

Ayres, C. E. (1944), *The Theory of Economic Progress*. Chapel Hill: University of North Carolina Press.

Bailey, Peter (1978), *Leisure and Class in Victorian England*. London: Routledge and Kegan Paul.

Barnhart, Russell T. (1983), *Gamblers of Yesteryear*. Las Vegas, NV: GBC Press.

Becker, G. S. (1983), "The Fire of Truth: A Remembrance of Law and Economics at Chicago, 1932–70" (ed. E. W. Kitch), *Journal of Law and Economics* 24: 163–234.

Bellhouse, D. R. (1991), "The Genoese Lottery," *Statistical Science* 6(2, May): 141–8.

Bender, Eric (1938), *Tickets to Fortune*. New York: Modern Age Books.

Bergier, J. F. (1971), "The Industrial Bourgeoisie and the Rise of the Working Class," in *The Industrial Revolution*, pp. 397–451, ed. Carlo. M. Cipolla. Glasgow: Fontana/Collins, 1973.

Bergler, Edmund (1957), *The Psychology of Gambling*. New York: Hill and Wang.

Berle, Adolf A., and Gardiner C. Means (1968), *The Modern Corporation and Private Property*, rev. ed. New York: Harcourt Brace Jovanovich.

Berlin, Isaiah (1976), *Vico and Herder*. London: Hogarth.

Berlin, Isaiah (1978), *Karl Marx*, 4th ed. Oxford: Oxford University Press.

Berlin, Isaiah (1981), *Against the Current*. Oxford: Oxford University Press.

Berman, Harold J. (1983), *Law and Revolution*. Cambridge, MA: Harvard University Press.

Berman, Harold J. (2003), *Law and Revolution II*. Cambridge, MA: Harvard University Press.

Bernanke, Ben S. (1993), "The World on a Cross of Gold: A Review of 'Golden Fetters: The Gold Standard and the Great Depression, 1919–1939,'" *Journal of Monetary Economics* 31(2, April): 251–67.

Bernstein, Peter (1996), *Against the Gods*. New York: John Wiley & Sons.

Blair, William G. (1986), "16 States Consider Joint Lottery Game," *New York Times*, July 13.

Blakey, Robert G. (1977), *The Development of the Law of Gambling, 1776–1976*, Washington, DC: National Institute of Law Enforcement and Criminal Justice.

Blakey, Robert G. (1979), "State Conducted Lotteries: History, Problems and Promise," *Journal of Social Issues* 35(3): 62–87.

Blanche, Ernest E. (1950), "Lotteries Yesterday, Today and Tomorrow," *Gambling, Annals of the American Academy of Political and Social Science* 269: 71–6.

Bloch, Herbert A. (1951), "The Sociology of Gambling," *American Journal of Sociology* 57 (November): 215–21.

Bloch, Marc (1953), *The Historian Craft*. New York: Alfred A. Knopf.

Blum, W. J., and H. Kalven Jr. (1953), *The Uneasy Case for Progressive Taxation*. Chicago: University of Chicago Press, 1966.

Bolen, Darell W. (1976), "Gambling: Historical Highlights and Trends and Their Implications for Contemporary Society," in *Gambling and Society*, pp. 4–38, ed. William R. Eadington. Springfield, IL: Thomas.

Boorstin, Daniel J. (1983), *The Discoverers*. New York: Random House.

Bordo, Michael D., Ehsan Choudri, and Anna J. Schwarz (2002), "Was Expansionary Monetary Policy Feasible During the Great Contraction: An Examination of the Gold Standard Constraint," *Explorations in Economic History* 39(1): 1–28.

Bordo, Michael D., and Anna J. Schwarz (1995), "The Performance and Stability of Banking Systems under 'Self-Regulation': Theory and Evidence," *Cato Journal* 14(3): 453–79.

Borell, J. (1975), "Study of Gamblers and Drug-Takers in H. M. Prison, Pentonville," paper prepared for discussion at a consultation on compulsive gambling, May 22.

Boyle, James E. (1921), *Speculation and the Chicago Board of Trade*. New York: Macmillan.

Breen, T. H. (1980), *Puritans and Adventurers: Change and Persistence in Early America*. Oxford: Oxford University Press.

Brenner, Gabrielle A. (1985), "Why Did Inheritance Laws Change?" *International Review of Law and Economics* 5: 91–106.

Brenner, Gabrielle A., and Reuven Brenner (1987), "Why Do Lotteries Have Multiple Prizes?" working paper, Institut d'Économie Appliquée, HEC Montréal, Montreal.

Brenner, Gabrielle A., Martial Lipeb, and Jean-Michel Servet (1996), "Gambling in Cameroon and Senegal – A Response to Crisis?" in *Gambling Cultures*, pp. 167–78, ed. Jan McMillen. London: Routledge.

Brenner, Gabrielle A., Claude Montmarquette, and Reuven Brenner (1987), "Lottery Expenditures: What Do People Say and What Do They Do? An Econometric Analysis," working paper, Department of Economics, University of Montréal.

Brenner, Reuven (1983), *History: The Human Gamble*. Chicago: University of Chicago Press.

Brenner, Reuven (1985), *Betting on Ideas: Wars, Invention, Inflation*. Chicago: University of Chicago Press.

Brenner, Reuven (1987), *Rivalry: In Business, Science, among Nations*. Cambridge: Cambridge University Press.

Brenner, Reuven (1992a), "Macroeconomics: The Masks of Science and Myths of Good Policies," in *Educating Economists*, pp. 123–51, ed. David Colander and Reuven Brenner. Ann Arbor: University of Michigan Press.

Brenner, Reuven (1992b), "Making Sense Out of Nonsense," in *Educating Economists*, pp. 11–48, ed. David Colander and Reuven Brenner. Ann Arbor: University of Michigan Press.

Brenner, Reuven (1994), *Labyrinths of Prosperity: Economic Follies, Democratic Remedies*. Ann Arbor: University of Michigan Press.

Brenner, Reuven (1996), "Gambling, Speculation, and Insurance: Why They Continue to Be Confused and Condemned," *Journal of Applied Corporate Finance* 9(3, Fall): 118–28.

Brenner, Reuven (1999), "Capital Markets and Democracy," *Journal of Applied Corporate Finance* 11(4, Winter): 66–74.

Brenner, Reuven (2002), *Force of Finance: Triumph of Capital Markets*. New York: Thomson/Texere.

Brenner, Reuven (2004), "Unsettled Civilizations: How the US Can Handle Iraq," *Asia Times*, June 23, http://www.atimes.com/atimes/Front_Page/FF23Aa01.html.

Brenner, Reuven (2006), "US Dollar and Prosperity: Accidents Waiting to Happen," *Cato Journal* 26(2, Spring/Summer): 317–32.

Brenner, Reuven, and Gabrielle A. Brenner (1990), *Gambling and Speculation*, Cambridge: Cambridge University Press.

Bridbury, A. R. (1992), *The English Economy from Bede to the Reformation*. Woodbridge, UK: Boydell & Brewer Press.

Briggs, J. B. (2003), "Socialized Gambling," *Reason*, July (3).

Brinner, Roger E., and Charles T. Clotfelter (1975), "An Economic Appraisal of State Lotteries," *National Tax Journal* 28: 395–404.

Brys, Eric and François de Varenne (2000), *The Fisherman and the Rhinoceros: How International Finance Shapes Everyday Life*. Chichester, UK: John Wiley & Sons.

Brown, Aaron (2004), "Risk, The Ugly History," *Wilmott* 13(September/October): 18–20.

Brown, Aaron (2006a), "Let's Put the 'Fun' Back into Funded Debt," *Wilmott* 23(May/June): 20–2.

Brown, Aaron (2006b), *The Poker Face of Wall Street*. Hoboken, NJ: John Wiley.

Browning, Reed (1971), "The Duke of Newcastle and the Financing of the Seven Years' War," *Journal of Economic History* 31(2, June): 344–77.

Brunk, Gregory G. (1981), "A Test of the Friedman-Savage Gambling Model," *Quarterly Journal of Economics* 96: 341–8.

Caillois, Roger (1958), *Les jeux et les hommes*. Paris: Gallimard.

Calabresi, Guido (1985), *Ideals, Beliefs, Attitudes and the Law.* Syracuse, NY: Syracuse University Press.

Calder, Leondol G. (2001), *Financing the American Dream: A Cultural History of Consumer Credit.* Princeton, NJ: Princeton University Press.

Campbell, Angus, and Philip E. Converse (1972), *The Human Meaning of Social Change.* New York: Russell Sage Foundation.

Campbell, Felicia (1976), "Gambling: A Positive View," in *Gambling and Society,* ed. William R. Eadington. Springfield, IL: Thomas: 218–28.

Cancian, Frank (1979), *The Innovator's Situation.* Stanford, CA: Stanford University Press.

Chafetz, Henry (1960), *Play the Devil: A History of Gambling in the United States from 1492 to 1955.* New York: Potter.

Chamberlain, H. H. (1890), "Gambling and Betting," *Minutes of the Tract Committee, 1886–1893.* London: Archives and Library of the Society for Promoting Christian Knowledge.

Chua, Amy (2003, 2004): *World on Fire.* New York: Anchor Books.

Clotfelter, Charles T., and Philip J. Cook (1989), *Selling Hope: State Lotteries In America.* Cambridge, MA: Harvard University Press.

Coase, Ronald (1937), "The Nature of the Firm," *Economica* 4: 386–405.

Cochrane, Eric, and Julius Kirshner (1986), *The Renaissance. Vol. 5 of Reading in Western Civilization.* Chicago: University of Chicago Press.

Cohen, Jacob (1953), "The Element of Lottery in British Government Bonds, 1694–1919," *Economica,* n.s., 20(79, August): 237–46.

Cohen, John (1964), *Behaviour in Uncertainty.* New York: Basic.

Cohen, John, and Mark Hansel (1956), *Risk and Gambling.* New York: Philosophical Library.

Colander, David, and Reuven Brenner, eds. (1992), *Educating Economists.* Ann Arbor: University of Michigan Press.

Commission on the Review of the National Policy toward Gambling (1976), *Gambling in America.* Washington, DC: Government Printing Office.

Cornish, D. B. (1978), *Gambling: A Review of the Literature and Its Implication for Policy and Research.* London: HMSO.

Coste, Pierre (1933), *Les loteries d'état en Europe et la Loterie Nationale.* Paris: Payot.

Cunningham, Hugh (1980), *Leisure and the Industrial Revolution c. 1780–c. 1880.* New York: St. Martin's.

Daniels, Stephen (1992), "Is the Lottery a Tax?" Policy paper, Raleigh: North Carolina Family Policy Council.

Dary, David (1995), *Seeking Pleasure in the Old West.* New York: Knopf.

D'Ascoli, Joseph (2006), "The Lure of Gambling: What State Governments Can Gain from the Legalization and Expansion of Gambling," senior honor economics thesis, Boston College.

Dasgupta, Anisha S. (2005), "Public Finances and the Fortunes of the Early American Lotteries," Paper 9, Yale Law School Student Scholarship Series.

Daston, Lorraine J. (1987), "The Domestication of Risk: Mathematical Probability and Insurance, 1650–1830," in *The Probabilistic Revolution,* Vol. 1, pp. 237–60, ed. L. Krüger, L. J. Daston, and M. Heidelberger. Cambridge, MA: MIT Press.

David, John A. (2006), "Opera and Absolutism in Restoration Italy, 1815–1860," *Journal of Interdisciplinary History* 35(Spring): 569–94.

Day, Christian C. (2004a), "Chaos in the Markets: Moral, Legal and Economic Signals in Three Fantastic Bubbles," Working Paper, Social Science Research Network, http://papers.ssrn.com/sol3/papers.cfm?abstract_id=572123.

Day, Christian C. (2004b), "Is There a Tulip in Your Future? Ruminations on the Tulip Mania and Innovative Dutch Futures Markets," *Journal des Économistes et des Études Humaines* 14(2, December): 151–70.

Day, Christian C. (2006), "Chaos in the Markets: Moral, Legal and Economic Signals in Three Fantastic Bubbles," *Financial History* 24(85, Winter): 24–27, 38.

Desperts, Jean (1982), "Quand Louis XIV jouait à la loterie," *Histoire* 24: 86–90.

Devereux, Edward C. (1980), "Gambling and Social Structure," Ph.D. diss., Harvard University.

Dewey, John (1930), *Human Nature and Conduct*. New York: Modern Library.

Dixon, David (1980a), "Class Law: The Street Betting Act of 1906," *International Journal of the Sociology of Law* 8: 101–28.

Dixon, David (1980b), "The Discovery of the Compulsive Gambler," in *Essays in Law and Society*, pp. 157–79, ed. Zenon Bankowski and Geoff Mungham. London: Routledge and Kegan Paul.

Dixon, David (1981a), "The State and Gambling: Development in the Legal Control of Gambling in England, 1867–1923," paper presented at the Fifth National Conference on Gambling and Risk-Taking, Lake Tahoe, NV, October 22–25.

Dixon, David (1981b), "Discussion," in "Leisure and Social Control," pp. 21ff., ed. Alan Tomlinson, working papers, British Sociological Association/Leisure Studies Association Joint Study Group on Leisure and Recreation, University of Birmingham.

Dixon, David (1984), "Illegal Gambling and Histories of Policing in Britain," paper presented at the Sixth National Conference on Gambling and Risk-Taking, Atlantic City, NJ, December 9–12.

Dixon, David (1987), "Responses to Illegal Betting in Britain and Australia," paper presented at the Seventh International Conference on Gambling and Risk-Taking, Reno, NV, August 23–6.

Dixon, David (1991), *From Prohibition to Regulation: Bookmaking, Anti-Gambling, and the Law*. Oxford: Clarendon Press.

Downes, D. M., B. P. Davies, M. E. David, and P. Stone (1976), *Gambling, Work and Leisure: A Study across Three Areas*. London: Routledge and Kegan Paul.

Dunkley, John (1985), *Gambling: A Social and Moral Problem in France, 1685–1792*. Oxford: Voltaire Foundation at the Taylor Institution.

Dunstan, Roger (1997), *Gambling in California*. Sacramento: California Research Bureau.

Eade, J. C. (1984). *The Forgotten Sky*. Oxford: Clarendon Press.

Easterlin, Richard A. (1974), "Does Economic Growth Improve the Human Lot? Some Empirical Evidence," in *Nations and Households on Economic Growth*, pp. 89–125, ed. P. David and M. Reder. New York: Academic Press.

Eichenwald, Kurt (1987), "Are Lotteries Really the Ticket?" *New York Times*, supplement, January 4.

Elias, Norbert (1986), "An Essay on Sport and Violence," in *The Quest for Excitement: Sport and Leisure in the Civilizing Process*, pp. 150–74, Norbert Elias and Eric Dunning. Oxford: Blackwell Publishers.

Encyclopaedia Judaica (1971). Jerusalem: Keter.

Ewen, C. L'Estrange (1932), *Lotteries and Sweepstakes: An Historical, Legal, and Ethical Survey of Their Introduction, Suppression and Re-Establishment in the British Isles.* London: Heath Cranton Limited.

Ezell, John Samuel (1960), *Fortune's Merry Wheel: The Lottery in America.* Cambridge, MA: Harvard University Press.

Fabian, Ann Vincent (1982), "Rascal and Gentlemen: The Meaning of American Gambling, 1820–1890," Ph.D. diss., Yale University.

Favier, Jean (1998), *Gold and Spices: The Rise of Commerce in the Middle Ages,* trans. C. Higgitt. New York: Holmes & Meier Publishers. Originally published as *De l'or et des épices, naissance de l'homme d'affaires au Moyen Âge.* Paris: Fayard, 1987.

Favier, Jean (1991), *Les grandes découvertes.* Paris: Livre de Poche.

Feinman, Jeffery P., Robert D. Blashek, and Richard J. McCabe (1986), *Sweepstakes, Prize Promotions, Games and Contest.* Homewood, IL: Dow Jones–Irwin.

Findlay, John M. (1986), *People of Chance: Gambling in American Society from Jamestown to Las Vegas.* Oxford: Oxford University Press.

Fink, Stephen, and Jonathan Rork (2003), "The Importance of Self-Selection in Casino Cannibalization of State Lotteries," *Economics Bulletin* 8(10): 1–80.

Fisher, Irving (1906), *The Nature of Capital and Income.* New York: Macmillan.

Fisher, Irving (1924), "Useful and Harmful Speculation," in *Readings in Risk and Risk-Taking,* pp. 346–9, ed. Charles O. Hardy. Chicago: University of Chicago Press.

Fleming, Alice (1978), *Something for Nothing: A History of Gambling.* New York: Delacorte.

Foster, George M. (1967), "Peasant Societies and the Image of Limited Good," in *Peasant Societies: A Reader,* pp. 300–23, ed. J. M. Potter, M. N. Diaz, and G. M. Foster. Boston: Little, Brown.

France, Anatole (1953), *The Revolt of the Angels.* New York: Heritage Press.

Franklin, James (2001), *The Science of Conjecture: Evidence and Probability before Pascal.* Baltimore: Johns Hopkins University Press.

Freud, Sigmund (1929), "Letter to Theodor Reik, April 24," in *Thirty Years with Freud,* pp. 155–6, Theodor Reik. London: Hogarth, 1942.

Frey, James H. (1984), "Gambling: A Sociological Review," *Annals of the American Academy of Political and Social Science* 474(July): 107–21.

Friedman, M. (1961), "Real and Pseudo Gold Standards," *Journal of Law and Economics* 4(4): 66–79.

Friedman, M. (1969), "In Defence of Destabilizing Speculation," in *The Optimum Quantity of Money and Other Essays,* pp. 285–91, Chicago: Aldine.

Friedman, M. (1992), *Money Mischief: Episodes in Monetary History.* New York: Harcourt, Brace, Jovanovic.

Friedman, M., and L. J. Savage (1948), "The Utility Analysis of Choices Involving Risks," *Journal of Political Economy* 56: 279–304.

Friedman, M., and A. J. Schwartz (1963), *A Monetary History of the United States, 1867–1960.* Princeton, NJ: Princeton University Press and National Bureau of Economic Research.

Gallup Social Surveys (1972), *Gambling in Britain.* London: Gallup.

Garber, Peter M. (1989), "Tulipmania," *Journal of Political Economy* 97(3): 535–60.

Garber, Peter M. (2000), *Famous First Bubbles: The Fundamentals of Early Manias.* Boston: MIT Press.

Garrett, Thomas A. (2001), "The Leviathan Lottery? Testing the Revenue Maximization Objective of State Lotteries as Evidence of Leviathan," *Public Choice* 109: 101–17.

Garrett, Thomas A., and Russel S. Sobel (2004), "State Lottery and Revenues: The Importance of Game characteristics," *Public Finance Review* 32(3): 313–30.

Geertz, Clifford (1973), *The Interpretation of Cultures*. New York: Basic.

Gigerenzer, Gerd, Z. Swijtink, T. Porter, L. J. Daston, J. Beatty, and L. Krüger (1989), *The Empire of Chance: How Probability Changed Science and Everyday Life*. Cambridge: Cambridge University Press.

Gilbert, Kenneth (1958), *Alaskan Poker Stories*. Seattle, WA: R. D. Seal.

Glaisyer, Natasha (2006), "'Venturing Fortunes': Lotteries and the Financial Revolution, 1694–1756," paper presented at Money, Power, and Print: Interdisciplinary Studies of the Financial Revolution in the British Isles, 1688–1756, June 2006, Armagh, Northern Ireland.

Gleeson, Janet (2000), *Millionaire: The Philanderer, Gambler, and Duelist Who Invented Modern Finance*. New York: Simon & Schuster.

Glock, Charles Y., ed. (1967), *Survey Research in the Social Sciences*. New York: Russell Sage Foundation.

Goldstone, Jack H. (1986), "State Breakdown in the English Revolution: A New Synthesis" *American Journal of Sociology* 92(2, September): 257–322.

Gribbin, Donald W. and Jonathan J. Bean (2005), "Adoption of State Lotteries in the United States, with a Closer Look at Illinois," *Independent Review* 10(3): 351–64.

Gruson, Lindsey (1987), "Delaware Joins 3 States in Big Lottery," *New York Times*, April 19.

Grussi, Olivier (1985), *La vie quotidienne des joueurs sous l'ancien régime à Paris et à la cour*. Paris: Hachette.

Gubert, Romain (2006), "La guerre des Jeux a commencé," *Le Point*, 28 September: 102–4.

Guttman, George (1986), "Change the Rules on Death and Taxes," *Wall Street Journal*, October 21.

Hacking, Ian (1990), *The Taming of Chance*. Cambridge: Cambridge University Press.

Haller, Mark (1970), "Urban Crime and Criminal Justice: The Chicago Case," *Journal of American History* 57(2, December): 619–35.

Handelsman, Joseph Armand (1933), *Les loteries d'état en Pologne et dans les autres pays d'Europe: Les emprunts à lots*. Paris: Marcel Giard.

Hansen, Alicia (2004), "Lotteries and State Fiscal Policy," Background Paper No. 46, Washington, DC: Tax Foundation, October.

Hansen, Alicia (2007), "Gambling with Tax Policy: States' Growing Reliance on Lottery Tax Revenues," Background paper No. 54, Washington DC: Tax Foundation, July.

Harrison, Brian (1964), "Contributions to Discussion on Work and Leisure in Preindustrial Society, by Keith Thomas," *Past and Present* 29(December): 63–6.

Harrison, Brian (1971), *Drink and the Victorians*. London: Faber and Faber.

Hasofer, A. M. (1967), "Random Mechanisms in Talmudic Literature," *Biometrika* 54(1/2, June): 316–21.

Hawke, J. (1894), "Our Principles and Programme," *New Review* 10: 705–17.

Heavey, Jerome F. (1978), "The Incidence of State Lottery Taxes," *Public Finance Quarterly* 6 (October): 415–25.

Heckman, James J. (1979), "Sample Selection Bias as a Specification Error," *Econometrica* 47(January): 153–61.

Heer, Friedrich (1966), *The Intellectual History of Europe*, trans. J. Steinberg. New York: World Publishing Co.

Henriquet, Paul (1921), "Les loteries et les emprunts à lots," Ph.D. diss., Law Faculty, University of Paris.

Herman, Robert D. (1967a), *Gamblers and Gambling: Motives, Institutions and Controls.* Lexington, MA: Heath Lexington.

Herman, Robert D. (1967b), "Gambling as Work: A Sociological Study of the Race Track," in R. D. Herman (ed.), *Gambling.* New York: Harper and Row, pp. 87–104.

Hey, John D. (1979), *Uncertainty in Microeconomics.* New York: New York University Press.

Hieronymus, Thomas A. (1971), *Economics of Future Trading: For Commercial and Personal Profit.* New York: Commodity Research Bureau.

Hochfelder, David (2001), "Partners in Crime: The Telegraph Industry, Finance Capitalism, and Organized Gambling, 1870–1920," paper, Institute of Electrical and Electronics Engineers History Center, http://www.ieee.org/portal/cms_docs_iportals/iportals/ aboutus/history_center/hochfelder.pdf).

Hochfelder, David (2006), "'Where the Common People Could Speculate': The Ticker, Bucket Shops, and the Origin of Popular Participation in Financial Markets, 1880–1920," *Journal of American History* 93(2, September): 335–58.

Hogarth, R. M., and M. W. Reder, eds. (1986), *Rational Choice.* Chicago: University of Chicago Press.

Hood, Christopher C. (1976), *The Limits of Administration.* London: Wiley.

Houthakker, H. S., and Lester D. Taylor (1970), *Consumer Demand in the United States: Analyses and Projection*, 2d ed. Cambridge, MA: Harvard University Press.

Huizinga, Johan (1944), *Homo Ludens: A Study of the Play Element in Culture.* Boston: Beacon, 1955.

Hutt, W. H. (1979), *The Keynesian Episode.* Indianapolis, IN: Liberty Fund.

Jacoby, Oswald (1952), "The Forms of Gambling," in *Gambling in America*, pp. 19–25, ed. Herbert L. Marx Jr. New York: Wilson. Originally published in *Annals of the American Academy of Political and Social Science* 269(May), 1950, 39–45.

Jerusalem Post (1999), "What Makes the Jews Gamble?" August 16, pp. 26–33.

Josephus, Flavius (1959), *The Jewish Wars*, trans. G. A. Williamson. Harmondsworth: Penguin.

Kahneman, Daniel, Paul Slovic, and Amos Tversky, eds. (1982), *Judgment under Uncertainty: Heuristics and Biases.* Cambridge: Cambridge University Press.

Kahneman, D., and A. Tversky (1979), "Prospect Theory: An Analysis of Decisions Under Risk," *Econometrica* 47(March): 263–91.

Kahneman, D., and A. Tversky (1986a), "Choices, Values and Frames," in *Judgment and Decision Making*, pp. 194–210, ed. H. R. Arkes and K. R. Hammond. Cambridge: Cambridge University Press.

Kahneman, D., and A. Tversky (1986b), "Rational Choice and the Framing of Decisions," in *Rational Choice*, pp. 67–95, ed. R. M. Hogarth and M. W. Reder. Chicago: University of Chicago Press.

Kallick, Maureen, Daniel Suits, Ted Dielman, and Judith Hybels (1979), *A Survey of American Gambling Attitudes and Behavior.* Ann Arbor: Institute of Social Research, University of Michigan.

Kaplan, H. Roy (1978), *Lottery Winners: How They Won and How Winning Changed Their Lives.* New York: Harper and Row.

Kaplan, H. Roy (1984), "The Social and Economic Impact of State Lotteries," *Annals of the American Academy of Political and Social Sciences* 474(July): 91–106.

Kaplan, H. Roy (1985a), "Lottery Winners and Work Commitment: A Behavioral Test of the American Work Ethic," working paper, Florida Institute of Technology.

Kaplan, H. Roy (1985b), "Lottery Winners in the United States," working paper, Florida Institute of Technology.

Kaplan, H. Roy, and Carlos J. Kruytbosch (1975), "A Behavioral Test of Job Recruitment," mimeograph.

Kaplan, H. Roy, Victor Tremblay, Daniel Koenig, and Marjolaine Martin (1979), *Survey of Lottery Winners: Final Report*. Ottawa: Loto Canada.

Kapteyn, A., B. M. S. van Praag, and F. G. van Herwaarden (1978), "Individual Welfare Functions and Social Reference Spaces," *Economic Letters* 1: 173–8.

Kapteyn, A., and T. Wansbeek (1982), "Empirical Evidence on Preference Formation," *Journal of Economic Psychology* 2: 137–54.

Kapteyn, A., and T. Wansbeek (1985), "The Individual Welfare Function: A Rejoinder," *Journal of Economic Psychology* 6: 375–81.

Keynes, J. M. (1921), *Treatise on Probability*. London: Macmillan.

Keynes, J. M. (1936), *The General Theory of Employment, Interest and Money*. London: Macmillan, 1970.

Kinsey, Robert K. (1959), "The Role of Lotteries in Public Finance," Ph.D. diss., Columbia University.

Kinsey, Robert K. (1963), "The Role of Lotteries in Public Finance," *National Tax Journal* 16(1): 11–19.

Knight, F. (1921), *Risk, Uncertainty and Profits*. Chicago: University of Chicago Press, 1971.

Koeves, Tibor (1952), "You Can Lose Your Shirt Anywhere in the World," in *Gambling in America*, pp. 55–60, ed. Herbert L. Marx, Jr. New York: Wilson. Originally published in *United Nations World* 2(March 1948): 19–21.

Kreitner, Roy (2000), "Speculation of Contract, or How Contract Law Stopped Worrying and Learned to Love Risk," *Columbia Law Review* 100(4, May): 1096–1138.

Kuch, Peter, and Walter Haessel (1979), *Une analyse des gains au Canada*. Ottawa: Ministère de l'Industrie et du Commerce.

Kusyszyn, Igor (1984), "The Psychology of Gambling," *Annals of the American Academy of Political and Social Sciences* 474(July): 133–45.

Labrosse, Michel (1985), *Les loteries ... de Jacques Cartier à nos jours*. Montreal: Stanké.

Labys, Walter C., and C. W. J. Granger (1970), *Speculation, Hedging and Commodity Price Forecasts*. Lexington, MA: Heath, Lexington Books.

Lacroix, Robert, and François Vaillancourt (1981), *Les revenus de la langue au Québec*. Montreal: Conseil de la Langue Française.

Lam, Desmond (2005), "The Brief Chinese History of Gambling," mimeograph, University of Macau.

Landau, Michael (1968), *A Manual on Lotteries*. Ramat Gan, Israel: Massada.

Landes, David (1998), *The Wealth and Poverty of Nations*. New York: Norton.

Layton, Allan, and Andrew Worthington (1999), "The Impact of Socio-Economic Factors on Gambling Expenditures," *International Journal of Social Economics* 26(1/2/3): 430–40.

Lea, E. G., M. R. Tarpy, and P. Webley (1987), *The Individual in the Economy*. Cambridge: Cambridge University Press.

Lee, Alan J. (1976), *The Origins of the Popular Press in England, 1855–1914*. London: Croom Helms.

Lee, Susan Previant, and Peter Passel (1979), *A New Economic View of American History*. New York: Norton.

Lefèbvre, E. (1968), *Reminiscence of a Stock Operator*. New York: Pocket Books.

Lemelin, Clément (1977), "Les effets redistributifs des loteries québécoises," *L'Actualité Économique* 53: 468–75.

Leonard, John D. (1952), "How Britain Gambles on Sports," in *Gambling in America*, pp. 109–12, ed., Herbert J. Marx Jr. New York: Wilson. Originally published as "The Big 'Flutter,'" *New York Times Magazine*, October 22, 1950.

Leonnet, Jean (1963), *Les loteries d'état en France aux XVIIIé et XIXe siècles*. Paris: Imprimerie Nationale.

Lerner, Michael A. (2007), *Dry Manhattan: Prohibition in New York*. Cambridge, MA: Harvard University Press.

Lester, David, ed. (1979), *Gambling Today*. Springfield, IL: Thomas.

Li, Wen Lang, and Martin H. Smith (1976), "The Propensity to Gamble: Some Structural Determinants," in *Gambling and Society*, pp. 189–206, ed. William E. Eadington. Springfield, IL: Thomas.

Lien-Sheng, Yang (1950), "Buddhist Monasteries and Four Money Raising Institutions in Chinese History," *Harvard Journal of Asiatic Studies* 13(1/2, June): 174–91.

Lindh, Thomas, and Henry Ohlsson (1996), "Self Employment and Windfall Gains: Evidence from the Swedish Lottery," *Economic Journal* 106 (439, November): 1515–26.

Livernois, John R. (1985), "The Redistribution Effects of Lotteries: Evidence from Canada," *Public Finance Quarterly* 15(3): 339–51.

Lorie, J. H. (1966), "Some Comments on Recent Quantitative and Formal Research on the Stock Market," *Journal of Business* 39: 107–10.

Lowenstein, Roger (2000), *When Genius Failed: The Rise and Fall of Long-Term Capital Management*. New York: Random House.

MacDougall, Ernest D. (1936), *Speculation and Gambling*. Boston: Stratford.

Mackay, Charles (1841), *Extraordinary Popular Delusions and the Madness of Crowds*. New York: Harmony, 1980.

Malcolmson, Robert W. (1973), *Popular Recreations in English Society 1700–1850*. Cambridge: Cambridge University Press.

Malcolmson, Robert W. (1981), *Life and Labour in England, 1700–1780*. New York: St. Martin's.

Mandeville, Bernard de (1714), *The Fable of the Bees; or, Private Vices, Public Benefits*. New York: Capricorn Books, 1962.

March, James G. (1988), "Variable Risk Preferences and Adaptive Aspirations," *Journal of Economic Behavior and Organization* 9: 5–24.

March, James G., and Herbert A. Simon (1958), *Organizations*. New York: John Wiley.

Margolis, Jeremy (1997), "Casino and Crime: An Analysis of the Evidence," report prepared by Altheimer & Grey for the American Gaming Association (December).

Markowitz, M. (1952), "The Utility of Wealth," *Journal of Political Economy* 80: 151–8.

Markowitz, M. (1959), *Portfolio Selection: Efficient Diversification of Investments*. New York: Wiley.

Marx, Herbert L., Jr., ed. (1952), *Gambling in America.* New York: Wilson.

McConnell, John J., and Eduardo S. Schwarz (1993), "The Origins of Lyons: A Case Study in Financial Innovation," in *The New Corporate Finance,* pp. 298–305, ed. Don Chew. New York: McGraw-Hill.

McGowan, Richard (1994), *State Lotteries and Legalized Gambling: Painless Revenue or Painful Mirage?* Westport, CT: Quorum.

McGowan, Richard (2001), *Government and the Transformation of the Gaming Industry.* Cheltenham, UK: Edward Elgar.

McKibbin, Ross (1979), "Working-Class Gambling in Britain, 1880–1939," *Past and Present* 82 (February): 147–78.

McLoughlin, Kevin (1979), "The Lotteries Tax," *Canadian Taxation* 1(January): 16–19.

McNeil, B. J., S. G. Parker, H. C. Sox, Jr., and A. Tversky (1982), "On the Elicitation of Preferences for Alternative Therapies," *New England Journal of Medecine* 306: 1259–62.

McNeill, William H. (1963), *The Rise of the West.* Chicago: University of Chicago Press.

McNeill, William H. (1974), *Venice: the Hinge of Europe 1081–1797.* Chicago: University of Chicago Press.

Meriwether, Louise (1970), *Daddy Was a Number Runner.* Englewood Cliffs, NJ: Prentice-Hall.

Miers, David, and David Dixon (1979), "National Bet: The Re-emergence of Public Lotteries," *Public Law,* 372–403.

Mikesell, John L., and C. Kurt Zorn (1986), "State Lotteries as Fiscal Savior or Fiscal Fraud: A Look at the Evidence," *Public Administration Review* 46 (July/August): 311–20.

Miller, A. C. (1935), "Responsibility for Federal Reserve Policies, 1927–29," *American Economic Review* 26(3, September): 442–56.

Moser, C. A., and G. Kalton (1972), *Survey Methods in Social Investigation,* 2d ed. New York: Basic.

Mulherin, J. Harold, Jeffry M. Netter, and James A. Overdahl (1991), "Prices Are Property: The Organization of Financial Exchanges from a Transaction Cost Perspective," *Journal of Law and Economics* 34(October): 591–644.

Murphy, Anne L. (2005), "Lotteries in the 1690s: Investment or Gamble?" *Financial History Review* 12(October): 227–46.

Murphy, Antoine E. (1997), *John Law: Economic Theorist and Policy-Maker.* Oxford: Oxford University Press.

Murray, Gilbert (1955), *Five Stages of Greek Religion.* Garden City, NY: Doubleday.

Nabokov, Vladimir (1981), *Lectures on Russian Literature.* New York: Harcourt Brace Jovanovich.

Needham, Joseph, with Wang Ling, eds. (1954–84), *Science and Civilization in China,* 6 vols. Cambridge: Cambridge University Press.

Neibert, David (2000), *Hitting the Lottery Jackpot: Government and the Taxing of Dreams.* New York: Monthly Review Press.

Newman, Otto (1972), *Gambling: Hazard and Reward.* London: Athlone.

Newman, Otto (1975), "The Ideology of Social Problems: A Gambling Case Study," *Canadian Review of Sociology and Anthropology* 12(4): 541–50.

Newsweek (1985), "The Lottery Craze," September 2.

Noonan, John T., Jr. (1957), *The Scholastic Analysis of Usury.* Cambridge, MA: Harvard University Press.

North, Douglass C. (2005), "Institutions and the Process of Institutional Change," *International Management* 9(3): 9–18.

North, Douglass C., and Barry R. Weingast (1989), "Constitutions and Commitment: The Evolution of Institutions Governing Public Choice in Seventeenth-century England," *Journal of Economic History* 49(4, December): 803–32.

Nussbaum, Martha C. (1986), *The Fragility of Goodness: Luck and Ethics in Greek Tragedy and Philosophy.* Cambridge: Cambridge University Press.

Ogle, Maureen (2006), *Ambitious Brew: The Story of American Beer.* New York: Harcourt.

O'Hara, John T. (1987), "Class and Attitude to Gambling in Australia: A Historical Perspective," paper presented at the Seventh International Conference on Gambling and Risk-Taking, Reno, NV, August 23–6.

O'Hara, John T. (1988), *A Mug's Game: A History of Gaming and Betting in Australia.* Sydney: University of New South Wales Press.

Olmstead, Charlotte (1967), "Analyzing a Pack of Cards," in *Gambling,* pp. 136–52, ed. Robert D. Herman. New York: Harper and Row.

Ore, O. (1956), *Cardano: The Gambling Scholar.* Princeton, NJ: Princeton University Press.

Orwell, G. (1953), "The Road to Wigan Pier," in *England, Your England and Other Essays.* London: Secker & Warburg.

Orwell, G. (1957), "Politics and the English Language," in *Inside the Whale and Other Essays.* New York: Penguin. First published in *Horizon* 76 (1946): 252–65.

Parker-Pope, Tara (1995), "Britons Bypass Soccer Pools to Play Lottery," *Wall Street Journal,* January 8.

Perkins, Benson E. (1950), *Gambling in English Life.* London: Epsworth, 1958.

Perkins, Edwin J. (1999), *Wall Street to Main Street: Charles Merrill and Middle-Class Investors.* Cambridge: Cambridge University Press.

Pipes, Richard (1999), *Property and Freedom.* New York: Knopf.

Plumb, J. H. (1967), *The Growth of Political Stability in England.* London: Macmillan.

Promus Companies Incorporated (1994), "Response to Robert Goodman's 'Legalized Gambling as a Strategy for Economic Development.'" Memphis: Promus.

Pryor, Frederic (1977), *The Origins of the Economy.* New York: Academic Press.

Raven, James (1991), "The Abolition of the English State Lotteries," *Historical Journal* 34(2): 371–89.

Razzell, P. E., and R. W. Wainwright, eds. (1973), *The Victorian Working Class: Selections from Letters to the Morning Chronicle.* London: Cass.

Read, Donald (1979), *England 1868–1914.* London: Longman.

Reuter, Peter (1985), *Disorganized Crime.* Cambridge, MA: MIT Press.

Riley, Jason L. (1999), "Will Uncle Sam Trump Internet Gamblers?" *Wall Street Journal,* May 14.

Robert Sylvestre Marketing Ltd. (1977), "Le marché québécois des lotteries," survey commissioned by Loto-Québec, vol. 4.

Rosen, Sam, and Desmond Norton (1966), "The Lottery as a Source of Public Revenues," *Taxes* 44: 617–25.

Rosenthal, Franz (1975), *Gambling in Islam.* Leiden: Brill.

Rothschild, M., and J. E. Stiglitz (1970), "Increasing Risk I: A Definition," *Journal of Economic Theory* 2: 225–43.

Rouse, W. H. D. (1957), *Gods, Heroes and Men of Ancient Greece*. New York: New American Library.

Royal Commission on Betting, Lotteries, and Gaming (1951), *Report*. London: H.M.S.O.

Royal Commission on Bilingualism and Biculturalism (1967), *Report*. Ottawa: Ministry of Supply and Services.

Rubner, Alex (1966), *The Economics of Gambling*. London: Macmillan.

Sasuly, Richard (1982), *Bookies and Bettors: Two Hundred Years of Gambling*. New York: Holt, Rinehart and Winston.

Schama, Simon (1988), *The Embarrassment of Riches*. Berkeley: University of California Press.

Schoeck, Helmuth (1969), *Envy*. New York: Harcourt, Brace and World.

Schoemaker, Paul J. H. (1982), "The Expected Utility Model: Its Variants, Purposes, Evidence and Limitations," *Journal of Economic Literature* 20 (June): 529–63.

Schwartz, David G. (2005), *Cutting the Wire*. Reno: University of Nevada Press.

Schwartz, David G. (2006), *Roll the Bones: The History of Gambling*. New York: Gotham Books.

Scodel, A. (1964), "Inspirational Group Therapy: A Study of Gamblers' Anonymous," *American Journal of Psychotherapy* 18: 115–25.

Scott, W. R. (1910), *The Constitution and Finance of English, Scottish and Irish-Joint-Stock Companies to 1720*, Vol. 1. Cambridge: Cambridge University Press.

Seligman, Daniel (2000), "At Odds with Odds," *Wall Street Journal*, November 11.

Sewell, R. (1972), "Survey of Gambling Habits of a Short-Term Recidivist Prison Population," in *The Facts about the "Money Factories,"* ed. G. E. Moody. London: Churches' Council on Gambling.

Shefrin, H. M., and M. Statman (1984), "Explaining Investor Preference for Cash Dividends," *Journal of Financial Economics* 13: 293–302.

Shils, Edward (1981), *Tradition*. Chicago: University of Chicago Press.

Simon, Herbert A. (1957), *Administrative Behavior*. New York: Macmillan.

Simon, Herbert A. (1959), "Theories of Decision-Making in Economics and Behavioral Science," in *Microeconomics Selected Readings*, pp. 85-98, ed. E. Mansfield. New York: Norton, 1971.

Skolnick, Jerome H. (1982), "The Social Risks of Casino Gambling," in *Casino Gambling in America*, pp. 22–7, ed. William R. Eadington. Reno, NV: Bureau of Business and Economic Research. First published in *Psychology Today*, July 1979: 52–64.

Slovic, Paul (1986), "Psychological Study of Human Judgement: Implications for Investment Decision Making," in *Judgment and Decision Making: An Interdisciplinary Reader*, pp. 173–93, ed. Hal R. Arkes and Kenneth R. Hammond. Cambridge: Cambridge University Press.

Smith, Adam (1776), *The Wealth of Nations*. Chicago: University of Chicago Press, 1976.

Smith, Adam (1980), "The History of Astronomy," in *Essays on Philosophical Subjects*. Indianapolis, IN: Liberty Books.

Smith, Stanley S. (1952), "Lotteries," in *Gambling in America*, pp. 61–6, ed. Herbert L. Marx, Jr. New York: Wilson. Originally published in *Journal of Criminal Law and Criminology* 38 (Jan.–Feb. 1948): 547–56.

Smith, S., and P. Razzell (1975), *The Pool Winners*. London: Caliban Books.

Solman, P., and T. Friedman (1982), *Life and Death on the Corporate Battlefield*. New York: Simon and Schuster.

Spiro, Michael H. (1974), "On the Tax Incidence of the Pennsylvania Lottery," *National Tax Journal* 27(2): 57–61.

Sprowls, Clay R. (1954), "A Historical Analysis of Lottery Terms," *Canadian Journal of Economics and Political Science* 20(3): 347–56.

Sprowls, Clay R. (1970), "On the Terms of the New York State Lottery," *National Tax Journal* 23(1): 74–82.

Starkey, Lycurgus Monroe, Jr. (1964), *Money, Mania and Morals: The Churches and Gambling*. New York: Abingdon.

Statistics Canada (1982), *Family Expenditures in Canada*, Cat. 62–555, Ottawa: Statistics Canada.

Stendhal (1823), *Life of Rossini*, trans. and annotated by Richard N. Coe. New York: Orion Press, 1970.

Stewart, David O. (2006), *An Analysis of Internet Gambling and Its Policy Implications*. Washington, DC: American Gaming Association.

Stigler, George (1965), *Essays in the History of Economics*. Chicago: University of Chicago Press.

Stigler, Stephen (2003), "Casanova's Lottery," *University of Chicago Record* 37(4): 2–5.

Stone, Lawrence (1965), *The Crisis of the Aristocracy, 1558–1641*. Oxford: Oxford University Press.

Stone, Lawrence (1972), *The Causes of the English Revolution, 1529–1642*. New York: Harper and Row.

Street, Howard A. (1937), *The Law of Gaming*. London: Sweet and Maxwell.

Strong, B. (1983), *Interpretations of Federal Reserve Policy in the Speeches and Writings of Benjamin Strong*. ed. W. Randolph Burgess. New York: Garland.

Strumpf, Koleman (2003), "Illegal Sports Bookmakers," working paper, Department of Economics, University of North Carolina at Chapel Hill.

Sturz, H. (1988), "A Sure Thing in the Casino: What Older People Spend Best Is Time," *New York Times*, editorial, April 3.

Suetonius, Caius Silentius Tranquillus (1961), *Vie des douze Césars*. Paris: Livre de Poche.

Suits, Daniel B. (1979), "Economic Background for Gambling Policy," *Social Issues* 35(3): 43–61.

Sullivan, George (1972), *By Chance a Winner: The History of Lotteries*. New York: Dodd, Mead.

Sumner, William Graham, and A. G. Keller (1927), *The Science of Society*, 3 vols. New Haven, CT: Yale University Press.

Tacitus, Cornelius (1970), *Germania*, trans. H. Mattingly. Harmondsworth, UK: Penguin.

Taylor, Gordon R. (1979), *The Natural History of the Mind*. New York: Penguin Books, 1981.

Tec, Nechama (1964), *Gambling in Sweden*. Totowa, NJ: Bedminster.

Tester, Jim (1987), *A History of Western Astrology*. Suffolk, UK: Boydell.

Teweles, R. J., Charles V. Harlow, and H. L. Stone (1969), *The Commodity Futures Trading Guide*. New York: McGraw-Hill.

Thaler, R. H. (1980), "Toward a Positive Theory of Consumer Choice," *Journal of Economic Behavior and Organization* 1:39–60.

Thaler, R. H. (1986a), "Illusions and Mirages in Public Policy," in *Judgment and Decision Making*, pp. 161–73, ed. H. R. Arkes and K. R. Hammond. Cambridge: Cambridge University Press.

Thaler, R. H. (1986b), "The Psychology and Economics Conference Handbook: Comments on Simon, on Einhorn, and on Tversky and Kahneman," in *Rational Choice*, pp. 95–100, ed. R. M. Hogarth and M. W. Reder. Chicago: University of Chicgo Press.

Theil, Henry (1971), *Principles of Econometrics*. New York: Wiley.

Thomas, Keith (1971), *Religion and the Decline of Magic*. New York: Scribner.

Thorner, Isidor (1955), "Ascetic Protestantism, Gambling and the One-Price System," *American Journal of Economics and Sociology* 15(1):161–72.

Timberlake, Richard H. (2007), "Gold Standard and the Real Bills Doctrine in U.S. Monetary Policy," *Independent Review* 11(3, Winter): 325–54.

Tocqueville, Alexis de (1835), *Democracy in America*, ed. Richard D. Heffner. New York: New American Library, 1956.

Tomes, Nigel (1983), "Religion and the Rate of Return on Human Capital: Evidence from Canada," *Canadian Journal of Economics* 16(February): 122–38.

Tsai, Kellee S. (2002), *Back-Alley Banking: Private Entrepreneurs in China*. Ithaca, NY: Cornell University Press.

United Nations (2002), *Arab Human Development Report*. New York: United Nations Publications.

U.S. Department of the Treasury (1999), *A Study of the Interaction of Gambling and Bankruptcy*. Washington DC: Government Printing Office.

Vaillancourt, François (1979), "La situation démographique et socio-économique des francophones du Québec: Une revue," *Analyse de Politique* 4(5): 542–52.

Vallerius, Bradley, and Mark Balestra (2006), *IPO: I-Gaming Public Offerings*. St. Charles, MO: River City Group.

Van de Stadt, H., A. Kapteyn, and S. van de Geer (1985), "The Relativity of Utility: Evidence from Panel Data," *Review of Economics and Statistics* 2: 179–87.

Varma, Jayanth (2003), "Putting 'Private Finance' Back into the Private Finance Initiative," in *India Infrastructure Report 2003: Governance Issues for Commercialization*, pp. 174–200, ed. Sebastian Morris. New Delhi: Oxford University Press.

Venkatesh, Sudhir A. (2006), *Off the Books: The Underground Economy of the Urban Poor*. Cambridge, MA: Harvard University Press.

Vico, Giambattista (1982), *Selected Writings*, ed. and trans. Leon Pompa. Cambridge: Cambridge University Press.

Vicusi, K. W. (1989), "Prospective Reference Theory: Toward an Explanation of the Paradoxes," *Journal of Risk and Uncertainty* 2(September): 235–63.

Walker, Ian (1998), "The Economic Analysis of Lotteries," *Economic Policy* 13(27): 357–402.

Walker, Jonathan (1999), "Gambling and the Venetian Noblemen c. 1500–1700," *Past and Present* 162: 28–69.

Walker, Sam (2007), "The Man Who Shook Up Vegas," *Wall Street Journal*, January 5, pp. W1, W10.

Wall Street Journal (1986), "Canada Lotteries Attract U.S. Dollars, As Well As a Lot of American Complaints," April 8.

Walsh, May Williams (2007), "New Jersey Diverts Billions and Endangers Pension Fund," *New York Times*, April 4.

Walvin, James (1978), *Leisure and Society, 1830–1950*. London: Longman.

Warshow, H. T. (1924), "The Distribution of Corporate Ownership in the United States," *The Quarterly Journal of Economics* 39(1, November): 15–38.

Wasserman, Martin (1982), "Alcohol, No! Gambling, Yes: A Matter of Survival in Aztec Society," *Addiction* 77(3): 283–86.

Weber, Max (1946), *From Max Weber: Essays in Sociology*, ed. and trans. H. H. Gerth and C. Wright Mills. New York: Oxford University Press.

Weiman, David F. (1991), "Peopling the Land by Lottery? The Market in Public Lands and the Regional Differentiation of Territory on the Georgia Frontier," *Journal of Economic History* 51(4, December): 835–60.

Weinstein, David, and Lilian Deitch (1974), *The Impact of Legalized Gambling: The Socioeconomic Consequences of Lotteries and Off-track Betting*. New York: Praeger.

Wesley, John (1958–9), *The Works of John Wesley*, 14 vols. Grand Rapids, MI: Zondervan.

Whang, Paul K. (1933), "The National State Lottery," *China Weekly Review*, August 19, p. 498.

Whitaker, Mark, Tony Clifton, and Donna Foote (1987), "Thatcher's Two Britains," *Newsweek*, June 22.

Woodhall, Robert (1964), "The British State Lotteries," *History Today* (July): pp. 497–504.

Zeckhauser, Richard (1986), "Comments: Behavioral versus Rational Economics: What You See Is What You Conquer," in *Rational Choice*, ed. R. M. Hogarth and M. W. Reder. Chicago: University of Chicago Press.

Zelizer, Viviana A. Rotman (1979), *Morals and Markets: The Development of Life Insurance in the United States*. New York: Columbia University Press.

Name Index

Subject Index

addiction, 62–5, 93, 101. *See also* compulsion, compulsive, gambler, gambling

adventurers, 111–12, 134, 139; and planters, 111–2

alcohol, 24–5, 29–30, 54, 148, 178–9, 235; taxation of, 1. *See also* drink, leisure, prohibition

ambition, 214–20. *See also* envy, leapfrogging

"animal spirits," 8–9, 205–6; *See also* decision-making, leapfrogging, human nature, macroeconomics

astrology, 7, 9, 10, 110. *See also* decision-making, risk, macroeconomics, uncertainty

"bank nights," 145–6

banks, banking,10–1, 90, 96–8, 115–21, 127, 139, 140, 205; and gambling, 90, 115–6, 127; in Scotland, 69. *See also* central banks, financial institutions, investment banks, lotteries, "soft money," banks, poker, public finance

betting: on ideas, 198–200, 251–3; on elections, 109–110; on models of societies, 205–6; on sports 38, 46–7, 148, 162, 168, 179–86, 235. *See also* gambling, futures, wagering

Bible, 3, 72, 195–7, 211. *See also* civilization, decision-making, language

bingo, 34, 35, 40, 45, 144, 163. *See also* entertainment, gambling, leisure, pastimes

bookmaking, and bookmakers, 31, 33, 47, 172, 173, 179, 180–1, 191–2. *See also* betting, gambling, horse racing

bootlegging, 162. *See also* prohibition

bucket shops, 78, 79, 84–6, 89, 107; as financial intermediaries 84. *See also* futures, property rights, telecommunication

bureaucracy, 8, 18, 94, 127, 154, 207

capital, markets, 68–9, 72, 86, 99, 197, 202–6, 208, 210; and crime, 69; and family, 69; and government, 69, 121, 202, 205, 208; and dispersion of power, 68–9, 83, 197, 203, 232–3; sources of, 69–70, 115, 117, 202, 205–6, 208. *See also* banking, financial institutions, financial markets, soft-money banks, poker banks, venture capital, wealth

casinos, 17, 40–1, 46, 84, 89, 92, 94, 127, 151, 160–1, 180. *See also* entertainment, gambling, leisure, pastimes

central banks 8, 113, 122. *See also* banks, gold standard, venture capital, Federal Reserve